# OBJECTIONS TO PHYSICALISM

# OBJECTIONS TO PHYSICALISM

*edited by*

HOWARD ROBINSON

CLARENDON PRESS · OXFORD
1993

Oxford University Press, Walton Street, Oxford OX2 6DP
Oxford New York Toronto
Delhi Bombay Calcutta Madras Karachi
Petaling Jaya Singapore Hong Kong Tokyo
Nairobi Dar es Salaam Cape Town
Melbourne Auckland
and associated companies in
Berlin Ibadan

Oxford is a trade mark of Oxford University Press

Published in the United States
by Oxford University Press, New York

British Library Cataloguing in Publication Data
Data available

Library of Congress Cataloging in Publication Data
Objections to physicalism / edited by Howard Robinson.
Includes bibliographical references and index.
1. Materialism. I. Robinson, Howard.
B825.025 1993 146'.3—dc20 92-28443
ISBN 0-19-824256-5

Typeset by Graphicraft Typesetters Ltd, Hong Kong
Printed in Great Britain by
Biddles Ltd., Guildford and King's Lynn

# CONTENTS

vi                    *Contents*

# Introduction

i

In recent philosophy the term 'physicalism' has been used both in broader and in more restricted senses. According to the broadest current sense it designates any form of materialism: the upshot of this is that it is the name for *any form of materialism that is nowadays fashionable.* In its restricted sense it is a particular species of materialism, and does not include all the current theories.

The restricted sense can be approached in the following way. Materialism is the theory that all the *substances* that exist are physical substances. Materialism allows for the possibility that physical substances may possess, at a basic level, certain odd, non-physical *properties*, in addition to their physical properties. The 'dual aspect' or 'attribute' theory of mind is a theory of this sort. It might also allow that there can be immaterial *abstract* objects, because these are not substances in the relevant sense, and are not part of, and do not interact with, the spatio-temporal system. On this view, numbers, universals, or propositions might be held to exist and to be non-physical, consistently with materialism. Physicalism, in the restricted sense, is narrower and more ambitious and says that, at the basic level of characterization, all things and all properties are physical. Even here, there are weaker and stronger versions of the theory. At its most reductive, physicalism claims that things possess only the properties invoked by *physics* proper. This was the sense originally given to the word by the logical positivists, who hoped to reduce everything to a unified science based on physics.[1] This can be weakened to the claim that the properties referred to in any physical science will do. Perhaps weakening it further, those properties which common sense regards as physical can also be included. These latter, however, can safely be taken as including only the traditional primary qualities—which are, of course, the properties invoked by the

[1] See e.g. Otto Neurath, 'Physicalism', in R. Cohen and M. Neurath, eds., *Philosophical Papers, 1913–45* (Dordrecht, 1972), 52–7.

physics of the seventeenth century—and not secondary qualities. In general, although common sense treats secondary qualities as physical properties in their own right, the physicalist follows the philosophers of the seventeenth century in thinking them physically suspect, unless they can be identified with or reduced to primary qualities.

The above remarks relate to materialism and physicalism as global theories, but they need not be treated as theories about everything. One could, for example, have a materialist or physicalist theory of man and hence of the human mind, whilst believing in the existence of non-human immaterial spirits. And though, as I say above, one could not be a physicalist *tout court* and accept the existence of abstract objects, one could be a physicalist *about everything else* and do so. In fact the dispute is usually about the nature of mind, which is treated as if it were the test case for the plausibility of any kind of materialism. But if a theory cannot cope with abstract objects, this should be food for thought, for two reasons. First, and rather loosely, because the intelligibility of the world depends (if they exist) on universals, numbers, and propositions, and there is something odd about an ontology that cannot accommodate the grounds of its own intelligibility. Second, because of the connection between thought and at least such abstract objects as propositions and concepts it looks as if an ontology which cannot accommodate these abstract objects will not be able to cope with thought itself, and, hence, not with mind. Discussion of physicalism in any of its forms is, therefore, relevant to its plausibility as a theory of mind.

As I said initially, this relatively straightforward distinction between physicalism and materialism does not quite correspond to current usage. There is a tendency for all the currently fashionable forms of materialism to be called, by proponents and opponents alike, 'physicalism', even though some of them look more like what would once have been classified as a dual aspect theory. This is particularly true of those theories that make use of the idea that the mental *supervenes* on the physical, whilst not being *reducible* to it. I think that the thought is that supervenience makes the mental more tightly dependent on the physical than does a traditional dual attribute theory and hence merits the name of 'physicalist'. How successful this is as a physicalist strategy is examined by David Smith in Chapter 10 below.

My attempts to characterize physicalism might have given the impression that the alternative to it is some less reductive form of materialism. This was not, of course, my intention; there are many theories more dualist than dual attribute materialism, and my silence on other theories is only due to my attempt to give a working definition of physicalism by explaining its relation to materialism in general. Nor is it the aim of most of the essays in this book to present alternative accounts of mind; the common feature of these essays is that they reject certain fashionable theories which are usually labelled 'physicalist', but not all of which are physicalist in the restricted sense. This book is written in opposition to a fashion and a trend. It therefore shares in the indefiniteness of the phenomenon which it is attacking, but the physicalist syndrome will, nevertheless, be recognized by anyone active in contemporary philosophy of mind.

ii

There are two features of the mind which have most generally been thought to constitute problems for materialism: these are its capacity for thought and its possession of consciousness. The first seven essays in this volume are principally concerned with the former and the next six with the latter.

In classical and medieval philosophy, opposition to materialism rested principally on the difficulty of providing a materialist understanding of thought. Plato believed the intellect immaterial because the Forms are immaterial and intellect has an affinity with the Forms it apprehends.[2] Aristotle did not believe in Platonic universals, but he propounded a more tightly argued case than Plato's for the immateriality of thought.[3] He held that the intellect was immaterial because if it were material it could not receive all forms. Just as the eye, because of its particular physical nature, is sensitive to light but not to sound, and the ear to sound and not to light, so, if the intellect were in a physical organ it could be sensitive only to a restricted range of physical things; but this is not the case, for we can think about any kind of material object. This remained the crucial philosophical objection to materialism throughout the Middle Ages.

[2] *Phaedo*, the so-called 'affinity argument', 77e–80b.  [3] *De anima*, 3. 4.

It is common for modern Aristotelians, who otherwise have a high view of Aristotle's relevance to modern philosophy, to treat this argument as being of purely historical interest, and not essential to Aristotle's system as a whole.[4] Consequently, they put it, and its conclusion, aside and claim that philosophers before the seventeenth century were, in essence, not moved by the sort of objections to physicalism that preoccupy moderns. The Aristotelian tradition is treated as being morally, if not actually, an ally of physicalism.

It is true that, from Descartes, the philosophically crucial features of mind are the various facets of consciousness—sensation, self-awareness, and introspection—not intellect as such, and it is materialism's difficulty in coping with consciousness that has preoccupied modern philosophy. Nevertheless Aristotle's views on intellect are paralleled by certain contemporary worries about the physicalization of our intellectual capacities. In general terms, Aristotle's worry was that a material organ could not have the range and flexibility that we ascribe to human thought. His worries concerned the cramping effect that matter would have on the range of *objects* that intellect could accommodate; modern concerns centre on the restriction which matter would impose on the range of rational *processes* that we could exhibit. Gödel, for example, believed that his famous theorem showed that there are demonstrably rational forms of mathematical thought of which humans are capable which could not be exhibited by a mechanical or formal system of the sort one might think that a physical mind would have to be. Recently, a distinguished physicist has argued that Turing's halting problem has similar consequences.[5]

In fact, the sheer physicality of a system seems to impose two interconnected restrictions on its ability to think. First, there is rigidity of performance. Second is the difficulty a physicalist framework has in accommodating semantics, intentionality, and meaning. The first problem is exemplified in Gödel's and Turing's

[4] e.g. K. V. Wilkes, *Physicalism* (London, 1978), 115–16. An alternative interpretation of Aristotle is presented by Howard Robinson in 'Aristotelian Dualism', *Oxford Studies in Ancient Philosophy*, 1 (1983), 1–25.

[5] For the philosophical interpretation of Gödel, see J. R. Lucas, 'Minds, Machines and Gödel', *Philosophy*, 36 (1961), 112–27. For Turing, see Roger Penrose, *The Emperor's New Mind* (Oxford, 1990).

worries about formal systems; a more accessible version of it is well set out by Daniel Dennett. He cites the case of the wasp *sphex*.[6] It performs a fixed ritual when bringing food back to its nest. It first leaves the food outside the nest and enters to check on its eggs, then returns outside to bring in the food. This appears to be intelligent behaviour, but if the food is moved slightly while the wasp is in the nest it will replace the food in its original position and recheck the eggs. If the food is moved again the whole process will be repeated, and so on. By interrupting the ritual constantly, one could lock the wasp in a circle of incompleted rituals, which it would perform until it dropped of exhaustion. *Sphex* does not have the *nous* to see that it need not recheck the eggs. The trouble with *sphex* is that the ritual in question is 'hard wired' into its system, giving it no flexibility. Such unresponsiveness to the environment is incompatible with intelligence, and a physical organism could be much more environmentally sensitive than *sphex*. But if we are just thinking machines, then some degree of sphexishness must infect our behaviour, though, no doubt, at a much more sophisticated level; the restriction is endemic to the implementation of a procedure by a system constrained by physical causation. Only a creature whose operation was ultimately teleological would not be at the mercy of the rigidities implicit in any mechanical realization of a design. Dennett plays down this residual sphexishness, arguing that an organism as sophisticated as a human being approximates as near as one could desire to genuine rationality.[7] How this response misses the point is shown by the second restriction physicality imposes on thought, namely the difficulty it creates for semantics, intentionality, and meaning. This difficulty is the source of sphexishness.

As Dennett says, an intelligent physical system can only be a syntactic engine, not a semantic one. By this he means that, for a physicalist, any causal powers that a sign possesses must be entirely due to such properties as its size, shape, and mass, and *not* to its meaning. The semantic content of a state does not, as such, have any causal role. This is the explanation of why we are 'a little bit sphexish'.[8] But Dennett is not worried by this because it is no shock to find that we are ever so slightly imperfectly rational.

---

[6] See e.g. 'Skinner Skinned', *Brainstorms* (Hassocks, 1978), 65.
[7] *Elbow Room* (Oxford, 1984), 31 ff.    [8] Ibid.

This, however, misses the point. What a sophisticated syntactic engine ever so slightly fails to do is *mimic* perfectly a semantic engine.[9] It does not just fail to be a perfect semantic engine, it fails to be semantic at all, as is shown by its revealing, though well disguised, trivial failures of performance. If you believe that human rationality is, in some real way, semantically driven, depending on what our psychological states *mean*, not just on their physical contours, then a physicalist model of thought will not be possible. If *sphex* understood what it was trying to do, and if understanding is not a mere epiphenomenon, then there would always be the possibility of a rational modification of behaviour.

Dennett tries to rescue the semantic dimension by adopting what he used to be prepared to call his 'instrumentalism': the human brain is a machine some of whose processes we can *see as* possessing a meaning that they do not actually possess.[10] We interpret each other as having genuinely meaningful states, but, strictly speaking, as physical, we cannot possess such states. The problem with this theory is that *seeing something as* having a meaning can only be done by something that really can appreciate meaning: but, if physicalism is true, the interpreters are no more genuine semantic engines than the things that are interpreted as if they were, and, hence, are not capable of genuine acts of *interpretation* at all.

It is, of course, a principal upshot of Searle's famous 'Chinese Room' argument that we cannot avoid intrinsic intentionality.[11] Paul and Patricia Churchland in reply reject intrinsic intentionality, but agree that mental states have 'independent intentionality', which they call 'translational content'.[12] Of this they say:

Translational content is not environmentally determined, nor is it observer-relative, but it is most certainly a *relational* matter, a matter of the state's inferential/computational relations within a system of other such states. Accordingly, it is entirely possible for translational content to be

[9] 'Three Types of Intentional Psychology', in *The Intentional Stance* (Cambridge, Mass., 1987), 61.

[10] For Dennett's original views, see the introduction to *Brainstorms*, modified in *The Intentional Stance*, 69 ff.

[11] John Searle, 'Minds, Brains and Programs', *Behavioral and Brain Sciences*, 3 (1980), 417–58.

[12] Paul and Patricia Churchland, 'Functionalism, Qualia and Intentionality', in P. M. Churchland, *A Neurocomputational Perspective* (Cambridge, Mass., 1989), 23–46.

possessed by the states of a machine—as the realization of a purely formal program. (pp. 43–4)

Here the Churchlands seem simply to be asserting that the sort of syntactic operations that Searle is performing in his 'Chinese room' are sufficient for content and that, therefore, he does—or could—understand Chinese in performing those operations. This seems not only obviously wrong, but to be contrary to what all other supporters of the syntactic theory of mind affirm, namely that semantics is superadded by causal relations to the external world.[13]

Dennett, in his more recent work, distances himself from the description 'instrumentalist' and claims that his theory could equally well be characterized as 'mild realism'.[14] What he is realistic about, however, are the behavioural patterns on the basis of which we ascribe mentality. He does nothing—and could do nothing, consistently with his principles—to suggest that any *internal* cognitive state (as opposed to overt behaviour) really possesses intentionality.

Dennett's problem is only one version of a general difficulty for the physicalist. Because, given the standard physicalist interpretation of matter, nothing physical can ever possess semantic properties intrinsically, the physicalist is always pressed towards an externalist account of content, with meaning permanently deferred from conscious contemplation.[15] A sign means something only because of its association with or difference from some other sign, or its causal relation to some external object. These relations are not something that the mind can grasp, for *apprehension* of the connection—or web of connections—*as such* would itself be something more than the occurrence of a merely 'syntactic' sign. The associationism of the empiricists, Dennett's instrumentalism, and the computational 'syntactic' theory of the mind all fall into the same dilemma: they deny that meaningfulness is present

[13] Searle has convincingly developed his original argument in 'Is the Brain a Digital Computer?', *American Philosophical Association Proceedings*, 64 (1991), 21–37. He argues that, from a computational perspective, syntax is no more intrinsic than semantics, depending equally on the purposes of an interpreter.

[14] See e.g. 'Real Patterns', *Journal of Philosophy*, 88 (1991), 27–51.

[15] A strict analytical reductionism would allow physical objects to possess semantic properties, though in the form of behavioural dispositions, not internal states. I argue against such reductionism in Chapter 7.

at the bedrock level, and want it to be constructed at a certain level of complexity. But they cannot allow that level of complexity to be *experienced* as bearing meaning without bringing it in again as a primitive; and if they deny that it is experienced, then the major reason for bringing it in at all—namely to accommodate the phenomenology of thought—is lost.[16]

George Myro, in the first paper in this volume, offers a bold criticism of physicalism from the opposite and Cartesian perspective. He reverts to the plain phenomenology of the situation: whatever the problems with certain difficult features of thought, there is a certain aspect of thinking which is perfectly clear to the one doing the thinking, roughly, it is perfectly clear to one that one is thinking the things, whatever they are, that one is consciously thinking. Myro argues that this perfectly clear access to at least this aspect of our thinking is incompatible with physicalism: he argues that no physical aspect of anything can be perfectly clear in this way. The appeal to this perfect clarity of thinking fits in well with my remarks above against Dennett and other externalists. There *must* be a primitive givenness of thought, because no reductive treatment could ever grant us any real grasp on our thinking; and because it is a primitive givenness, then our only grasp on it can be by its simply being perfectly clear to us what it is.

I said earlier that the Aristotelian tradition was concerned with the restriction that physicalism would impose on the possible objects of thought, whereas modern worries concern the machinery of thought. But it now seems that these are not so different. Rigidity in the machinery of thought stems from an inability to allow that a direct intuitive grasp on semantic content may be (part of) what drives our thinking, and semantics concerns the *content* of our thoughts—that is, the objects of our intellectual activity. Aristotle's only sin was his moderation. He was too generous when he allowed that a physical organ could receive some forms and not others. If by 'form' one means 'concept' and if a concept is something with real semantic content, then nothing that was physical —nothing that was a purely syntactic engine—could receive any forms at all.

---

[16] I develop this point at slightly greater length in 'The Flight from Mind', in R. Tallis and H. Robinson, eds., *The Pursuit of Mind* (Manchester, 1991), 9–25: this ref., 13–16.

iii

The idea that content must be intrinsic to thoughts seems to be closely connected with the idea that concepts are something like universals and, hence, are abstract objects. Physicalists, on the whole, do not like such objects. This is particularly difficult when coping with numbers, which seem resolutely object-like, and abstract. Perhaps abstract objects would be tolerable for the physicalist if they remained in their abstract realm, but it is difficult to see how they could fail to become involved with those mental states in which we do arithmetic. Many materialists in the past have tried to save the situation by being nominalists about numbers. There seems to be a general feeling now that this will not work, and Hartry Field suggested instead that, though the rationale of arithmetic is Platonist, there are in fact no numbers: arithmetic is fictional and it is as if there were numbers, which there aren't. This view has come in for severe criticism, mainly on the grounds that it is impossible to understand why arithmetic should work if it is a fiction. This has encouraged Penelope Maddy to develop a materialist form of Platonism, and in Chapter 2 Bob Hale shows that this materialist strategy also fails. Maddy combines Platonic realism with materialism by treating sets as spatio-temporal objects that we can perceive: they are located just where their members are located. Theoretical generalizations about sets cannot be treated as spatio-temporal: these she compares to theories in physics, which, though not themselves spatio-temporal, *are made true by* their role in explaining the basic perceivable data. Hale shows that this attempt to have the best of both worlds does not work because the analogy between set theory and physical theory does not hold. The basic laws in physics are empirical generalizations based on the behaviour of perceivable objects, but Maddy agrees that it is implausible to regard the basic laws of set theory as empirically generalized from the perceptible nature of sets. Instead she makes them *a priori* truths about sets, which are justified by the fact that they sustain higher-order laws. Hale argues that this is viciously circular, because he higher-order laws are justified by their relation to basic laws. Physicalistic Platonism has no principled way of relating the laws—basic or higher—of set theory to the ontology which is supposed to underpin them.

The semantically driven nature of thought and our consequent actions concerns both Ralph Walker and Grant Gillett. Walker argues, in effect, that we cannot be syntactically driven engines like *sphex*. The very fact that we are prepared to affirm that some of our beliefs are sound commits us to the existence of certain principles of reason as fundamental constituents of the universe, and to our being genuinely sensitive to these principles. The principles of reason must be objective or we would have no reason to believe that the conclusions they led to were true, as opposed to being things we are prone to think; and they are metaphysically ultimate because they are prescriptive, which no mere physical (or mental) fact could be.

Walker argues that the only plausible alternative to taking the principles of reason to be prescriptive is to take them to consist in the mere fact that they tend to lead from true premises to true conclusions and to locate their action-guiding force in our desire to achieve the truth. He has a variety of objections to this, but the principle one is that we could never be in a position to assert that they had the *general* property of preserving truth. I think the thought behind Walker's resistance to a more traditional Platonism is similar to Kripke's reservations about grasping the generality of a rule, as against its particular instances, given that we can never survey all the instances.[17] If there is a response to this it is that such a nominalist confinement of our apprehension to the particular misses the point: that it is able to apprehend the generality, as such, in things, is the defining property of intellect; generality ultimately cannot be constructed. I do not believe that this disagreement affects the outcome of the argument, however, for there are no plausible materialist accounts of necessity in the Platonic—as opposed to prescriptive—sense. Conventionalist solutions are open to the objections Walker makes to subjectivist accounts; and identifying necessity with facts about possible worlds achieves nothing if our knowledge of possible worlds rests entirely on *a priori* intuitions about modality.

No less important than the irreducibility of the principles of reason is the reality of our contact with them. If physicalism were correct we would be like *sphex*, with our behaviour approximating to the dictates of reason but actually following other laws blindly. Walker argues that this cannot count as actually following

---

[17] Saul Kripke, *Wittgenstein and Rule-Following* (Oxford, 1976).

reason and so contradicts the minimally anti-sceptical assumption that we are sometimes moved by reason as such.

Walker is concerned, in a Kantian way, with the irreducibility of certain principles of theoretical reason. Grant Gillett follows a similarly Kantian route to show that physicalism cannot cope with practical rationality. Using Kant's account of action and freedom, he brings out in detail the difference between, on the one hand, explaining actions by citing reasons and, on the other, causal explanation. Gillett argues that the incommensurability of these two kinds of explanation creates a serious problem for physicalism, because the explanation of action must, for a physicalist, be causal. As actions are explained by reasons, the incompatibility of the two kinds of explanation is embarrassing. Some materialists—for example, D. M. Armstrong—have argued that reasons can be *analysed as* a species of cause, but Gillett's use of Kant shows how different the two modes of explanation are and, therefore, how implausible such a reduction is.[18] Only Davidson, with his anomalous monism, tries to reconcile them without reduction. Gillett, however, provides convincing reasons for rejecting anomalous monism. The materialist is, therefore, without any way of reconciling the logic of the explanation of actions by reasons, and the logic of explaining them causally to which he is committed by his materialism.

There are two ways out of this problem which Gillett does not consider, but both are desperate and are covered by other anti-physicalist strategies. Both, too, involve denying that explanations by reasons are ever full-bloodedly true, the truth being provided by the causal explanation. First, one might follow paleo-Dennett and treat rationalization as a useful way of interpreting behaviour which is instrumentally useful but not realistically true. We have already seen that this will not do. Second, one could take the eliminativist path and say that rationalization should be dropped in favour of causal explanation. The inadequacies of eliminativism are discussed in section v below.

Perhaps the most general challenge to the physicalist's ability to cope with semantics and intentionality comes from George Bealer. Bealer distinguishes between *natural* properties and relations and

---

[18] D. M. Armstrong, *A Materialist Theory of the Mind* (London, 1968), 200–4.

'Cambridge' properties and relations. These latter are, like *grue*, complex and artificial. Using this distinction, Bealer proposes a general analysis of intentionality based on some ideas of Brentano. Central to this analysis is the requirement that intentional relations be *natural* in the indicated sense. He then argues that any satisfactory general analysis of intentionality must, on pain of counter-examples, incorporate this requirement. Bealer's main point is that even if there are plausible physicalist (presumably functionalist) analyses for *particular* types of mental state, such as belief and desire, no satisfactory *general* analysis of intentionality is possible within the physicalist framework, for an additional layer of natural relations cannot be countenanced *within that framework*. That is, a satisfactory general analysis will involve judging things as similar in respect of the intentional relations they share when they are not naturally similar from a physicalist perspective; intentionality is a Cambridge property from that perspective. But it is obvious that similarities in intentional states are genuine, not grue-like, so physicalism is not ontologically complete.

It might be objected that this sets an unreasonably high standard for physicalism. It is more or less equivalent to demanding that only type identity will do, that only those things are real which are natural kinds on the physical level. Long ago Ryle conceded that certain psychological states were 'many track' dispositions—that is, possessed no natural physical unity. Is it not allowable to cut up the world in different ways for different purposes? But Bealer is surely correct. Certainly intentional phenomena have something in common, namely, their intentionality. So if, as Bealer argues, a satisfactory general analysis of intentionality requires positing an additional layer of natural relations not countenanced within the physicalist framework, the physicalist cannot consistently say what it is that intentional phenomena have in common in virtue of which they are intentional. Moreover, *why* should it be natural or necessary to cut the world up in ways that, physicalistically, have no natural rationale, if physicalism is correct? If these frameworks served a legitimate purpose within a physicalist ontology, then why they do so should be susceptible to a physicalist (or topic neutral) account. References to specifically human purposes to explain the point of these frameworks would be self-refuting unless the notion of purpose or goal can itself be made respectable within the physicalist ontology.

iv

What the foregoing arguments seem to show is that the physicalist cannot accommodate our intellectual powers. The most daring take this as showing that these powers are not part of ultimate reality; that is, that the whole realm of thought, meaning, semantics, and intentionality can be eliminated, for it is only part of a pre-scientific view of the world. This 'eliminative materialism' is backed up by a pragmatist methodology: we believe only in those things that it is theoretically convenient to believe in, and a physicalistic naturalism is said to be the simplest, and, hence most convenient, theory. But is it correct that this is the most convenient theory? That we are thinking and that we are conscious may seem to be facts that we can know with a very high degree of certainty: Warner and Myro argue this for sensation and thought correspondingly. Can it really be convenient—in a legitimate sense—to omit these obvious facts? The pragmatic approach seeks to avoid this objection by denying that anything is 'given' with a degree of certainty that can trump theoretical convenience. Nevertheless, some account must be taken of the difficulty we have in seeing how to do without 'folk psychology'. Quine is a pragmatist who argues that, on the one hand, we cannot avoid postulating intentional states, but that, on the other, they are not part of ultimate reality. The burden of Steven Wagner's paper is that a pragmatist cannot consistently relegate psychological states to this secondary status; Quine's system represents an unsuccessful compromise between pragmatism and our realist intuitions. According to Quine, 'folk psychology' is a 'grade B' theory, in contrast to one that figures in an ultimate characterization of reality. But what is the rationale for ranking in this way theories that are all *empirically* unavoidable? Wagner argues that, for a consistent empiricist, as Quine claims to be, this discrimination would only be justified if it served some empirical purpose. He canvasses various respects in which it might be deemed useful, and shows that the advantage is illusory. The conclusion is that only a dogmatic realist, and not a consistent empiricist, could employ the distinction. A pragmatist who allows any sort of status, other than straightforward falsehood, to our ordinary psychology, has no legitimate reason for eliminating or in any way demoting it.

V

Paul Churchland is one philosopher who seems to deny that there
is any serious pragmatic need to retain our current intentional
notions. Belief, and the rest of propositional psychology, could
actually be replaced by some new set of cognitive notions. The
would-be knock-down argument against his denial of the existence of belief is that one would then seem to be putting oneself in
the pragmatically self-contradictory position of *believing* that there
are no beliefs. Churchland says that this argument is no better
than the following one which operates to prove the existence of a
substance called 'vital spirit': there must be vital spirit because
anyone in the position to claim that vital spirit does not exist must
be alive and, hence, possess vital spirit: if the claim that vital spirit
does not exist were correct, the speaker would be dead and so his
words would be empty sounds.[19]

The situation is not as straightforward as either the knock-
down objection to elimination, or the knock-down reply, suggest.
But the objection is nearer the truth. The 'vital spirit' obscurantist
is being unreasonable because other mechanisms can be suggested
which do the same job as vital spirit was supposed to perform.
The question is to find a characterization of 'same job' which does
not make it analytic that the 'job' is performed in a certain way.
The job in this case is to sustain life. The 'spiritist' seems to be
defining 'life' as what you have if you possess vital spirit, but we
can in fact grasp the notion of life independently of this account
in terms of what living things can do, and we can see that other
processes might facilitate that. What is the relatively neutral account of the job that folk psychology and any candidate replacement
must do? The crudest answer would be that they explain certain
types of behaviour. This very reductive answer is not enough, for
it is agreed that something internal which merits the term 'cognition' must come into the process.

It is not clear to me how far elimination is meant to go in
purging the internal cognitive component of the features of folk
psychology. The eliminitivist might try either of two paths. He
might agree that there are theories (such as eliminitivism) and

---

[19] Paul M. Churchland, 'Eliminative Materialism and the Propositional Attitudes', in *A Neurocomputational Perspective*, 1–22: this ref., 22.

propositions (such as that there are no beliefs), identifying these with meaningful sentences. Then he has to provide an account of our relationship to these sentences which is not in terms of believing, etc. Obviously, nothing is done by a mere alteration of jargon and talking of 'holding' or 'assenting to': at best, this would provide an account—possibly reductive—of what believing is. The problem is that it is difficult to see what sort of relationship to a meaningful sentence would do the same job as belief without being virtually equivalent to it or an analysis of it. Churchland seems to be adopting a theory that accepts meaningful sentences but rejects *believing* them when he argues that an account of meaning can be provided that does not invoke belief.[20] On the other hand, he sometimes seems to be adopting the other, more radical, path. He says that a more advanced cognitive theory would not require the concept of truth, and this suggests that (indicative) sentences would not figure in such a theory: so both belief and its traditional objects would disappear.[21] Now it is difficult to see how an account that lacked truth-bearers could do the same job as folk psychology. If that job were merely to produce a causal account of behaviour, then it might be possible, but it is impossible to imagine what else could do, *from a subjective point of view*, the job done by such things as my believing that there is an external world, that I am now writing, that I like certain pieces of music, etc. Without having these things, or virtual equivalents, it is impossible to imagine *experiencing* the life of an intelligent being. The fundamental point is that unless internal cognitive states possess an intentionality which makes them *about* the external world, and other things, then we would have no explicit and articulate internal life, and all would be darkness within: but if they do possess such intentionality they do not seem to differ in any philosophically fundamental way from beliefs.

Physicalists of most kinds—not just eliminativists—are in desperate need of sanitized notions of cognition and representation

---

[20] Paul M. Churchland, *Matter and Consciousness* (Cambridge, Mass., 1984), 48. Churchland talks as if avoiding a Gricean theory of meaning is sufficient for giving an account that makes no reference to belief. This is not so. Davidson's truth conditions theory of meaning is the only available alternative to Grice's, but according to that account, we can only select the correct theory of meaning for a language if we choose the theory which, charitably, attributes to speakers the maximum number of true *beliefs*.

[21] A *Neurocomputational Perspective*, 19.

in which intentionality is somehow rendered safe. In general, Churchland creates the impression that so long as the mode of representation employed is non-verbal, the traditional problems of intentionality and physicalism do not arise. But this cannot be the heart of the matter, for 'aboutness' is the problem and that is a property of anything that can be called a 'representation', whether or not it is linguistic. The magic notion which is supposed to bridge the gap between the mental and the physical is *information*. Information is held to be naturally present in the physical world, *passim*, and to possess intentionality because it is *about* something. At first sight this might seem to be more like panpsychism than like physicalism, but the fact that information theory is a branch of mathematics and is used to describe what are agreed to be purely physical systems creates a confidence that the notion must be respectable. The most important attempt to develop this respectable notion is found in Fred Dretske's *Knowledge and the Flow of Information*[22]—although the connection between his notion and the mathematical one is acknowledged to be dubious.

The obvious problem with any attempt to treat information physicalistically is that a signal is only information *to* someone, rather in the way that the marks that constitute the writing in a book would have no sense and convey nothing *in themselves*, if there were no readers. So the power of mind, in the form of the interpreter, remains primitive, and the problem is not essentially different from Dennett's. Dretske tries to get round this by defining information in terms of probability (which, in practice, means causal dependence), as follows.

A signal *r* carries the information that *s* is *F* = The conditional probability of *s*'s being *F*, given *r* (and *k*), is 1 (but, given *k* alone, is less than 1). (p. 65)

The parenthetical *k* 'is meant to stand for what the receiver already knows (if anything) about the possibilities that exist at the source' (p. 65). If some notion of information is to be used to illuminate or reform our understanding of propositional attitudes then a concept such as knowledge (which presupposes belief) should not figure in the account of information. Dretske's gloss on the meaning of *k* implies that, in the limiting case, there need be no

[22] Oxford, 1981.

knowledge *of the source* present, and this might seem to eliminate the circularity. But the circularity is deeper than this. If the notion of information is more primitive than propositional attitude notions and information is present in the physical world quite independently of the presence of minds, then there ought to be no need to ascribe to the 'receiver' any capacity for propositional attitudes, whatever their object. The assumption that the 'receiver' is the sort of thing that can know already contains the assumption that information is information only *for* a mind.

One might, in order to avoid this difficulty, simply eliminate reference to *k* from the definition, to signify that, in the foundational cases, nothing is presupposed about the receiver except its ability to be affected by the signal. The conditional probability of *s*'s being *F*, given *r*, the signal, will be 1 only if that signal could not have occurred if *s* had not been *F*—which means, roughly, that there is a law of nature connecting *s*'s being *F*, and the occurrence of *r*. But then in what sense is there information here, *except for someone who knows that there is some such law*, for only such a receiver would be informed of anything by the occurrence of *r*. The bare occurrence of events with unit probability cannot, as such, *constitute*, knowledge (or belief, or other forms of propositional content), which would have to be the case, at some level of complexity, if information, so defined, was to provide the wherewithal for rendering intentionality innocuous.[23]

## vi

The problems posed by consciousness centre on the subjectivity of experience. One common way of setting up the problem is as follows. Imagine someone who, from birth, lacks a basic sensory capacity; for example, he is deaf. Then imagine that he becomes the world's greatest authority on the physics and neurology of hearing, which, we assume, has reached complete development.

---

[23] Dretske's attempt to develop a sanitized notion of information is expounded and criticized in the article and peer review 'Precis of Knowledge and the Flow of Information', *Behavioral and Brain Sciences*, 6 (1983), 55–90. Searle attacks this use of 'information' in 'Is the Brain a Digital Computer?' For a debunking of attempts to treat these notions physicalistically, see Raymond Tallis, *The Explicit Animal* (London, 1991), 88–101.

However complete the physical science he knows, he will still be ignorant of what it is like to hear. As he knows all the relevant physical facts, what it is like to hear—the nature of the experience—must be a non-physical state of affairs. My own chapter is an attempt to defend this argument against various physicalist replies. Some physicalists—David Lewis, for example—face the problem head on and deny that the deaf scientist lacks any knowledge except a form of knowledge *how*—that is, he essentially lacks only the ability to respond directly to sounds. This is a behaviouristic view. Others try to accommodate the idea that he lacks more than this. I argue that this accommodation cannot be made, and then develop an argument against behaviouristic theories of perception. This argument is designed to give a rigorous expression to the intuition that behaviouristic theories are essentially third-personal and cannot be applied to oneself. They cannot, therefore, be applied to subjects at all.

Once it is established that the physicalist account of the world misses out something that we can label 'subjective', there is the task of finding further ways of characterizing these states of consciousness. One way in which mental states have often been supposed to be special is that they are known by their owner in a supremely authoritative—even incorrigible—way: indeed, incorrigibility has often been taken to be the mark of the mental. The doctrine of the incorrigibility of our knowledge of our mental states has been fiercely attacked by physicalists, for it is impossible, on their theory, that knowledge of any physical state should be incorrigible: for them, knowing is a causal relation, and any causal relation can go wrong. Richard Warner argues that a suitably reformed, but equally non-physicalist development of incorrigibility does indeed hold of our knowledge of our mental states. The traditional version of the doctrine won't work because recognizing something involves recognizing it as being of a certain kind, and this involves recognizing it as being like certain other things, and there is no infallibility about such judgements of similarity. Warner shows that revisions of the traditional doctrine which incorporate the requirement that our recognitional capacities are working properly save it from the usual objections and preserve the intuitions that lie behind it. We can always misidentify physical states for reasons unconnected with any fault in our capacities, but this is not possible for such sensations as pain: this represents a fundamental difference, of a traditional Cartesian sort, between mental and physical states.

Reductive theories of consciousness appear to be quite hopeless: we are stuck with what is, roughly at least, the traditional dualistic conception of consciousness. But perhaps that does not prevent us from opting for a form of weak materialism—something like what used to be called a 'dual aspect' or 'dual attribute' theory. The rationale for such an approach is that the only substantial *things* are physical, but that some of those things, most obviously living human bodies, possess special properties or states that are quite unlike anything physical. They are subjective states of the sort that the 'knowledge argument' shows reductive physicalism cannot accommodate.

The difficulty then is to distinguish weak physicalism from weak dualism. A weak dualist would argue that, even though the mind is not a substance, but only a Humean bundle of states, it cannot be said to belong to a body in any sense stronger than being causally dependent on it. In particular, mental states cannot be said to be non-physical states *of* the body. The problem is to find some relation between the mental and physcial which is stronger than causal dependence but does not require reduction. This problem is rendered more difficult because the metaphysics of the nature of substance and of substances' relations to properties is obscure and controversial.

Nicholas Nathan claims, however, that it is a sufficient condition for a property's *not* belonging to substance that it could exist without it: if the mental could exist without the physical it would not, therefore, be an aspect of the physical and weak materialism would be refuted. Nathan begins from two premises. The first is that, according to weak materialism, volitions are causally dependent on the brain. The second is that causal relations are contingent, as Hume claimed. The Humean doctrine of separate existences implies the possibility of an object's existing without any of its causes. This means that a volition could exist without the coming into existence of (and, hence, without the existence of) its associated body. Hence it is not just an aspect of its body.

Nathan is, in effect, setting against each other the contingency of causal relations and the closeness of the dependence that the weak materialist needs to affirm between mind and brain. The materialist might try to avoid this clash by denying that the relation between mind and brain is causal. The problem would be how to do this without falling into reduction and strong materialism. Davidson tries to combine the identity theory with weak materialism, but we have seen, in Gillett's chapter, that that does not work. Alternatively, one might argue that although the relation is causal, the mental supervenes on the physical in some stronger relation as well. Nathan's response is that causality is incompatible with non-contingency and hence rules out a mysterious stronger supervenience. Nathan considers the suggestion that there must be something stronger because volition requires an agent and that could only be the body. He then argues that volitions do not require agents, rather that, in roughly Humean fashion, agents are constructed from them.

The magic notion of supervenience is so pervasive nowadays that there are bound to be many who will not be convinced by this way of dealing with it: perhaps some will think Nathan's dependence on a Humean theory of causation gives them a way out. David Smith shows that invocation of supervenience is futile.

Just to make it plain that they are not reductionists, some defenders of supervenience claim that it is not a necessary relation, so that there are possible worlds in which dualism is correct and the supervenience of mental on physical does not hold. David Smith shows that this cannot be the case: if the mental supervenes on the physical in the actual world then it does in all worlds, and the relation is hardly weaker than token identity. The main difficulty is to provide a rationale for supervenience: why, given a non-reductive account of consciousness, should it not be possible for mental states to vary independently of any particular physical base: we can certainly imagine that they do so. Smith admits that conceivability, in the sense of imaginability, is not proof of possibility, but by developing a clear conception of physicality he is able to show just how arbitrary it is to deny the possibility of the independent variation of the mental and physical. The answer physicalists provide, he claims, is that mental properties are emergent in the sort of way that liquidity is emergent in water: no single molecule of $H_2O$ is liquid, but in a mass, liquidity emerges. This is the sort of model Searle, for example, uses to suggest that emergence can be real without menacing materialism. Smith shows that *qualia* cannot be treated in this way, because the physicalistically harmless cases of emergence bear a much closer relation to the topic neutral analysis of mental states than to a non-reductive theory.

Nevertheless, one might wonder whether anything of real metaphysical importance hangs on the difference between weak dualism and weak materialism; isn't it mainly an argument about labels? The answer is 'yes and no'. It may not make much difference whether the mind is a bundle of events which are, in the actual world, causally dependent on the body; or whether it is a bundle which is more strongly supervenient on the body in all possible worlds. In both cases, the mind is, in actual fact, non-substantial and wholly dependent on the body, whilst not being strictly physical itself. But in the background is a real metaphysical issue. Once reductive materialism has been abandoned, one faces the question of how the non-physical states fit into the machinary of the world. There is a dilemma. Do these states affect the operation of the physical world? If they do, then the unity of physical science is breached and the supposed problem of mind–body interactionism is reinstated. If mental states do not affect the world, then epiphenomenalism is correct, and your feeling of pain has no role in your crying out in pain. This theory is a last resort. One might reasonably say that one of the criteria for a theory's counting as weak *materialism* is that it find a way out of this dilemma. One way of expressing epiphenomenalism is to say that *if the mental states had been missing, but the physical situation just the same* then the same consequences would have followed. If the supervenience of the mental meant that this condition could not be met in any possible world then the sting might seem to be drawn from epiphenomenalism.[24] Similarly, the attempt to assimilate the emergence of the mental to the uncontroversial cases of emergence is also designed to steer the ship of materialism between the Scylla of epiphenomenalism and the Charybdis of dualist interaction. Searle claims that one can talk of interaction between different *physical* levels, thereby showing that it does not affect the unity of science. Smith's demonstration that these weak materialist strategies are unsuccessful leaves the materialist without any way of coping with his dilemma.

As has become clear, the difficulty for anyone trying to develop

---

[24] Ways in which physicalists try to defend the impossibility of this counter-factual whilst avoiding reductionism, and why such tactics fail, are discussed in my *Matter and Sense* (Cambridge, 1982), 20–5.

a theory in the region between full physicalism and traditional dualism is to devise a metaphysical framework within which we can articulate the relation between the body and mental states. This Peter Forrest sets out to do. He develops a theory which locates itself in the same region as weak materialism and weak dualism, and which he believes solves the problems facing the theories in their strong forms. He calls his theory 'one category dualism', though it is in some ways similar to weak materialism; for example, the *qualia* of mental states are non-physical qualities *of* properties of the brain. The essential anti-physicalist thrust of Forrest's system comes from taking seriously the manifest image of the world, regarding both physical and mental states. Physicalism is dismissive of the qualitative nature of things, either reducing qualities or eliminating them. Forrest regards them as real and explanatory. The *qualia* of pain, for example, though they are something over and above functional properties of the body are nevertheless appropriate to them: so just by having the *qualia* it is possible to understand why the behaviour is as it is. Forrest is modest about the impact of his theory on the problem of interactionism and epiphenomenalism. The rationale that experience of our mental states and the world provides for our actions is entirely in harmony with the causal upshot of the system *qua* physical. This leaves one with something more like parallelism than epiphenomenalism; but Forrest does not regard this as a complete solution to the problem.

Forrest's theory involves the (roughly) naïve realist assumption that physical objects possess sensible qualities, including secondary qualities, intrinsically rather than dispositionally. Many philosophers have doubted whether this is plausible. They would agree with Russell that sense-perception and science tell us about no more than the causal *structure* of the world. Michael Lockwood inverts J. J. C. Smart's famous doctrine of the topic neutrality of our knowledge of the mental, arguing instead that it is science that gives us no more than topic neutral knowledge of the world. He agrees with Russell that through perception and science we discover only causal structure; only in sensation do we grasp the intrinsic nature of anything. Russell concluded—and Lockwood agrees— that the *qualia* of our sensations are in fact the intrinsic nature of the matter that constitutes our brains. Lockwood is the only contributor to this volume who describes himself as a materialist, but his neutral monism is a far cry from any current form of physicalism. Although apparently bizarre, this is the nearest to a plausible form of materialism there is. Lockwood's paper is principally concerned with what he takes to be one of the main difficulties with such a theory, which he calls 'the grain problem'. The problem is that the texture and structure of experience do not seem to match the texture and structure of the brain. Lockwood believes that what is needed here is to invoke certain concepts from quantum-mechanics. Just as, in relativity, each observer is to be thought of as imposing a certain co-ordinate system on the space–time continuum, thereby breaking it down into the familiar space and time of common sense, so—Lockwood suggests—the conscious subject, introspecting his own brain state, is to be thought of as imposing a certain co-ordinate system on the (quantum-mechanical) *state space* of the relevant brain subsystem (a state space being an abstract space, points or vectors of which correspond to different possible states). For any physical system, quantum-mechanically regarded, there is a potential infinity of such co-ordinate systems, or *bases* as they are generally known, which correspond one-to-one with sets of *compatible observables*: sets of questions one can ask about the system, the answers to which admit of being known simultaneously. Lockwood's suggestion is that the differences in texture and structure between brain states, as revealed to the neurophysiologist, and the corresponding phenomenal states, as known to the conscious subject in introspection, are a consequence of the subject's self-awareness taking place under a radically different *basis* (or set of observables) from that which is implicitly being applied by the neurophysiologist. (Compare the way, in relativity, that two observers, in different states of motion, will construe the same set of events as standing in very different spatial and temporal relations, and will disagree about the shapes and masses of objects around them.) In quantum-mechanics, Lockwood stresses, no basis is *a priori* privileged with respect to any other; and relative to different bases, the same physical system may appear so different that it is far from obvious that the underlying reality is the same. For example, largely because they work from different bases, it took some time for scientists to realize that Heisenberg's 'matrix mechanics' and Schroedinger's 'wave mechanics' are essentially the same theory. Lockwood's theory is extremely speculative and exciting, but he is under no illusion that, even if correct, it would solve all the problems of materialism. There remain at least three major problems. First, though *qualia* are seen as the essence of matter, *awareness* of *qualia* remains an emergent phenomenon. (This must, Lockwood agrees, be something additional, because, if *qualia* constitute the essence of matter, all material objects contain them. But neutral monism is emphatically not meant to be a form of panpsychism, so awareness is something extra, possessed only by certain things.) Indeed, if we are to avoid both panpsychism and an emergence which involves 'nomological danglers', one of the constraints on an adequate physics must be that its laws explain and integrate not merely the phenomenal contents of experience, but also awareness of those contents. I do not see how physics could hope to do this. Second, Lockwood agrees with many other contributors to this volume that there is a problem about 'intrinsic meaning'. And, third, he does not see how to reconcile the 'static' conception of four-dimensional space–time that relativity requires with our experience of the flow of time.[25] Nevertheless, developments along Lockwood's lines seem to me to be the only ones open to the materialist.

Some philosophers have claimed that 'physicalism' is difficult to define; but, whatever else it might involve, a belief in the existence of mind-independent physical objects is certainly fundamental. John Foster attacks this cornerstone of any possible materialism. Because of the falsehood of naïve realism, Foster agrees with Russell and Lockwood that the most that science could tell us about a mind-independent world would be structural and causal facts: in its intrinsic nature it transcends our experience. The physical world would have to possess some intrinsic nature beyond the structural, which we could only conceive by analogy with the qualitative contents of our sense-fields. Foster's claim is that any such empirically transcendent world would not be the physical world, essentially because its space would not be physical space. He imagines cases in which nomological deviance in the behaviour of the objects in the transcendent world leads to a bad fit between the geometries of that world and the empirical world. He argues that physical space must follow the geometry of the empirical

---

[25] These remaining problems are discussed in Lockwood's *Mind, Brain and Quantum: The Compound 'I'* (Oxford, 1989), 7–14.

world and so physical space cannot be identical with the space of any experience-transcendent reality, as a sophisticated physical realism requires.

Objections to physicalism can take a defensive or an aggressive form: one can point out the present inadequacies of those theories currently on offer, or one can attempt to show that the overall project is radically misconceived. For the most part, the essays in this volume follow the former path, but the two strategies are not unconnected, for a patient uncovering of the way materialist theories persistently fall at the same simple hurdles can lead to a growing conviction that the programme is misconceived. A metaphysic that cannot accommodate the fact that we think and are conscious—and (though this has not been the topic of these essays) usually has little to say about the preconditions of the intelligibility of the world—misses out on the most salient features of existence.

# 1

# Thinking[1]

*George Myro*

i

The phenomenon of thinking has given rise to a great amount of philosophical puzzlement and controversy. Yet this itself seems paradoxical, since a classical philosophical view, extremely plausible to some and supported, I think, by certain of our ordinary, unreflective convictions, would seem to imply that thinking is among those matters which are clearest of all to us and least subject to puzzlement and serious controversy. So that, from a certain point of view, one may feel that the real philosophical puzzle about thinking is how there *can* be philosophical puzzles about it. How can a matter which is so clear to us be so unclear? Or does the fact of puzzlement and controversy all by itself refute one of the parties in the controversy: the one which maintains that thinking is among the matters which are clearest of all to us and least subject to puzzlement and serious controversy? It seems to me that even *this* is not clear!

A vague and one-sided diagnosis of the situation at this point might be along the following lines. Thinking *is* among those matters which are clearest of all to us. But it is not for that reason unpuzzling or not subject to serious controversy. For thinking is related in multifarious ways to a great many other matters, many of which, both *relata* and relationships, are far from clear. This is by itself a source of puzzlement and controversy which touches on thinking. But it may also happen that by experiencing a conviction

[1] This paper is the text of a lecture that George Myro (1935–87) delivered to the Philosophy Department at the University of Southern California *circa* 1980. Except for a few minor modifications, the exact text of the original manuscript is printed here. This manuscript, which is in the archive of Professor Myro's unpublished writings in Berkeley, did, however, contain various lengthy notes that have not been included.

concerning one of these unclearly related and/or unclear matters—a conviction which, from the standpoint of the present *parti pris* diagnosis, is bound to be mistaken—one may come to *seem* to see that thinking is not such a clear matter after all, and even be moved to theorize about it in ways which are in conflict with the clearness of it. It is not that one loses thereby the clearness about thinking. Rather, one experiences a sort of intellectual schizophrenia, wherein one feels incompatible convictions, one or the other of which might be more or less successfully pushed into the penumbra of attention. But the philosophical enterprise is to examine and re-examine the matters in question until, one may hope, clearness spreads and incompatibilities of conviction vanish.

Some such hypothesis might at least forestall the ruling out of one of the parties in the controversy about thinking—namely, the party advocating clarity—merely on the grounds that there is such a controversy.

One rather minor unclarity about matters related to thinking is: *What* thinking are we considering, or, if you prefer, what is meant by the word 'thinking' in the present context? Since the difficulty *is* rather minor, I will spare you most of the distinctions and clarification that might be made. I will content myself with indicating to you the kind of thinking I have primarily in mind by example. Seattle is farther north than Portland. Now I take it that as soon as I said what I just said you all came to be thinking for a short while that Seattle is, indeed, farther north than Portland. You probably did no such thinking about Seattle, Portland, and northwardness previously in the day, though of course you have thought—in the sense of: believed—that Seattle is farther north than Portland for quite a long time. So the kind of thinking that I am primarily interested in is the kind you *did not* do just before I said, 'Seattle is farther north than Portland' and *did* do as soon as I said it. I think it is this kind of thinking that used to be called in philosophical literature 'judging'. There are other relevantly related kinds of thinking and still other relevantly related mental goings-on about which one might want to say, *mutatis mutandis*, similar things to those which one might want to say about the kind of thinking I have indicated by example.

Occasionally my discussion may wander onto these other kinds of thinking, I hope without too much unclarity, confusion, or error. Perhaps I should illustrate just one more kind of thinking which is relevantly related to the previous. Seattle is farther west than Portland. Now again, I think, you did something as soon as I said what I just said that you did not do just before I said it. But this time—and I am expecting here suitable geographical ignorance—it would not be correct to say that you came to be thinking that Seattle is, indeed, farther west than Portland. In jargon: you did not *judge* it. And yet—and it is very hard to put it colloquially—what you would have judged if you had believed that Seattle is farther west than Portland did come to mind. A thought did occur. And it may or might have led to others—perhaps wondering whether it is so; perhaps thinking (judging): if so, then such-and-such; perhaps feeling: what a banal thing to use as a philosophical example. Anyway, what happened in you as soon as I said 'Seattle is farther west than Portland' seems to me to be a kind of thinking, and I think it is this kind which used to be called in philosophical literature 'entertaining'. Thus, it would be said that you *entertained* the proposition that Seattle is farther west than Portland.

Now, as you know, there is a classical philosophical view, associated, for better or for worse, in the first instance with Descartes, to the effect that such kinds of thinking as the two I illustrated and relevantly related ones and some other relevantly related goings-on in the mind are among the matters which are clearest of all to us. We, each one of us, know *perfectly* when such things go on or fail to go on in us, and we know *perfectly* what it is that goes on in us when one of these things does go on in us. If so, there is no room for puzzlement there, no room for theorizing, no room for serious controversy. To be sure, there might be room for unclarity or doubt about *what words* to use to talk about these things and room for using inappropriate or misleading words, but that is just a matter of difficulty in conveying what we know perfectly or understanding someone who is trying to convey to us what he knows perfectly.

Suppose we grant all this for the moment. Even so unclarity is beginning to creep upon us. For the above, apparently trivial concession, about what words to use to talk about the thinking we are supposedly so perfectly cognizant of, is not without its puzzles. For what exactly is the relationship between this kind of thinking and the words used to talk about it—indeed, between *any*

phenomenon and our talk about it? Is it not the case that reflection
on talk, and how it is related to what is talked about, pressure us
to adopt certain views about thinking? We are now considering the
relationship between talk and what it is talk about—the relationship
illustrated by my saying 'I was just thinking that Seattle is not
farther west than Portland' and my having just thought that Seattle,
indeed, is not farther west than Portland—words, one might say,
used to describe thinking. But what about the relationship when
talk is used to give expression to thinking—illustrated by my saying
'Seattle is not farther west than Portland' and my thinking that
Seattle, indeed, is not? Can it not be that a certain use of words
at least influences our thinking, or is it perhaps the case that
thinking involves, or even is, a certain use of words—either the
relatively straightforward ones of colloquial and technical speech
and writing or, perhaps, the more recondite ones of a possible
"language of thought"—in such a way that choice of words determines or constitutes what we think? If so, then the thesis of our
perfect knowledge of thinking is in potential collision with the
concession about possible trouble with talk about thinking. And
what of knowledge itself? Knowing, like believing, is not supposed
to be the kind of thinking about which we are supposed to enjoy
such perfect clarity. So must it be perfectly clear that we have
perfect knowledge about thinking?

I have tried to suggest that the thesis of perfect clarity of thinking—even if taken for granted for the moment—does not preclude
various kinds of unclarity which touch on thinking. This is intended,
on the one hand, to persuade the upholder of the thesis to be
prepared for puzzlement and controversy which touch on thinking
and, on the other hand, to reassure him, with the aid of the
diagnostic hypothesis earlier outlined, that the existence of puzzlement and controversy which touch on thinking does not by itself
refute the thesis of perfect clarity of thinking. He may continue to
hope that reaching clarity on the various related issues and on the
relationships may, after all, vindicate his thesis.

But this is no easy matter. And on very little reflection the thesis
of the perfect clarity of thinking itself turns out to be not very
clear and so not clearly true. Now how damaging is this to the
thesis? Must one maintain that if thinking is perfectly clear to us
then it must also be perfectly clear to us that it is? If so, then the
thesis is once more in danger of instant refutation. But perhaps it

can be saved from this fate by essentially the same manœuvre as before. What one could use here is some doctrine of local clarity on particular matters and global clarity about related matters and their various relationships. As long as global clarity is absent one should be able to maintain consistently both that there is local clarity on a particular matter and yet summational unclarity about it because of the absence of global clarity. The proof of the pudding would be the—perhaps unattainable—global clarity in which one could see without any summational unclarity at all that there had been local clarity on the particular matter, after all.

I feel acutely that what I have said so far has been lacking in both global and local clarity. But I felt it desirable to raise, in however inept a manner, the issue of whether one of the major participants in the controversy about thinking is refuted by the mere existence of such controversy.

## ii

I now want to turn to some components in the (I hope, merely summational) unclarity in the thesis of perfect clarity of thinking.

One might think: how can one have perfect clarity or perfect knowledge of anything, short of the whole? After all, anything has a multitude of properties, characteristics, features, aspects, and relations to all the other things. If perfect knowledge or perfect clarity concerning anything involves knowledge of or clarity about all aspects—as I shall call them for short—of it, then one has to agree with Spinoza and Tennyson that perfect knowledge or perfect clarity concerning anything is *eo ipso* perfect knowledge or perfect clarity about everything. And if we are modest enough not to lay claim to the latter, we must either abandon or reinterpret the thesis of the perfect clarity of thinking.

The thesis might be plausibly interpreted along the following lines. When I am thinking that Seattle is not farther west than Portland, I know as well as I could know (it is as clear to me as it could be clear) what it is I am doing—namely, thinking, specifically, *judging*—and what it is I am doing this with respect to— namely, Seattle's not being farther west than Portland. A certain regrettable artificiality and awkwardness is creeping into my terminology. But perhaps we may nevertheless proceed so that we may put through its paces the thesis that, though there may be trouble about how to talk about what is going on, it is perfectly clear what is going on. Let us even indulge whatever slight temptation we may feel that there are at least three "things" involved:

1. My thinking (judging) at the moment that Seattle is not farther west than Portland—presumably, an *event*.
2. Thinking (judging)—which is what I am doing in the course of this event—presumably, a *relation*.
3. Seattle's not being farther west than Portland—which is what I stand to in this relation in the course of this event—presumably, a *state* of affairs or a proposition.

I realize how all too quick this is. But notice that, in recompense, I am modestly leaving myself out of the catalogue of "things" involved. Seriously, though, is it not absurd to suppose that there are these three "things" involved? Is it correct? How does one tell? Surely, *this* matter does not become perfectly clear just as soon as one thinks that Seattle is not farther west than Portland! And yet does it not become *somehow* perfectly clear what it is one is doing then? Apparently, there is at least the temptation to use different combinations of words to "describe" ("report") what is going on then. And a lesser temptation to use different combinations of words to "describe" ("report") what it is that is perfectly clear to one then. Do these different options of combinations of words correspond to differences in what one might *think* about the matter? Well, we do have the option of saying "yes and no". Absolutely, there are differences in what one might think about the matter corresponding to the different combinations of words we might be tempted to use. But some of these "amount to others", are *different ways* of thinking *the same thing*. There are reasonably worked out theories of "thinkables" which, for example, allow two of them to be not "intensionally isomorphic" and so "different enough" but "logically equivalent" and so "same enough". So one might seek comfort in maintaining that when I am thinking that Seattle is not farther west than Portland, a number of "logically equivalent" but not "intensionally isomorphic" "thinkables" obtain, and that *one* of them—presumably, the one corresponding to the words 'I am now thinking that Seattle is not farther west than Portland'—is perfectly clear to me as obtaining, while the others are not. The others may become clear to me as obtaining if I come to "see" somehow that they are "logically equivalent" to the first. But this takes more than merely having that thought concerning Seattle, Portland, westwardness, and something's not being thus-and-so. This does not preclude the possibility of sentient creatures to whom, either because of difference in the language to which they are accustomed or some other difference in nature or training, one of the other "logically equivalent" "thinkables" is perfectly clear as obtaining while the one perfectly clear *to us* as obtaining requires discernment of "logical equivalence".

This seems to leave room for what I regard as the *philosophical* investigation of thinking: the search for "logically equivalent" though not "intensionally isomorphic" "thinkables" concerning thinking. Thus, suppose one could come to see that what one thinks when one is rightly tempted to "give expression" to it by saying 'I am thinking that Seattle is not farther west than Portland' is "logically equivalent" to what one thinks when one is rightly tempted to "give expression" to it by saying what I said in listing the three things which might be involved in my having the thought about Seattle. Then one would come to see that those three things *are* involved in my having that thought about Seattle.

But it must be admitted that these happy thoughts are rather undermined by prevalent doubts about "thinkables", "logical equivalence", and the like.

Anyway, the proposal I made to you a little while ago, that there are at least three things involved in my thinking that Seattle is not farther west than Portland and that it might be perfectly clear to me that they are so involved, is not past saving. What I want to focus on now is that, while it may be somehow perfectly clear to me that these three things are involved in what I am doing at the moment, I might be totally ignorant of—and even oblivious to—most of their properties, characteristics, features, aspects, and relations to other things. The event of my thinking (judging) that Seattle is not farther west than Portland might be one that gives Steve Schiffer great joy, the relation of thinking (judging) might be one which Gilbert Ryle refused to recognize, and the state of affairs or proposition, Seattle's not being farther west than Portland, might be one Paul Grice is particularly authoritative on. And yet

I might be completely ignorant and even oblivious of these features of the three "things" even though it should be perfectly clear
to me that these three "things" are involved in what I am doing
now. The point of the preceding is that once one allows that one's
thinking something and the things which might be involved in it
have a multitude of properties, characteristics, features, aspects,
and relations to other things and that one is generally ignorant
and even oblivious of most of these matters one must concede that
one can have clarity, perfect or not, of at most a very few of the
multifarious aspects of one's thinking and the things which might
be involved in it. So the thesis of the perfect clarity of thinking
pares down to: certain—rather few—aspects of thinking and things
which are involved in it are—perfectly(?!)—clear to us.[2]

I find this conclusion refreshing. For it seems to make clear
how—without abandoning a clarified, by being pared down, thesis
of perfect (?!) clarity of thinking—one can see room not only for
a *philosophical* investigation of thinking—in the way I suggested
above—but for an "empirical", "scientific" investigation of it and
the "things" which are or might be involved in it: efforts to discover
aspects and laws governing aspects which are perfectly (?!) clear
when one is simply engaged in thinking.

At the same time, I feel that refreshment should not be carried
too far. I feel sufficiently attracted to a pared-down thesis of the
perfect (?!) clarity of thinking to feel inclined to resist the idea that
"empirical", "scientific" investigations and discoveries—and even
*philosophical* investigations and discoveries—can show to be
illusory what appears, especially upon reflection which is known
to have already taken place, to be to us perfectly (?!) clear about
thinking.

[2] In the subsequent part of the script I have inserted after every occurrence of
'perfect' in connection with either "knowing" or "clearness" a parenthesis enclosing
a question-mark, followed by an exclamation-mark. This has to do with the following worry of mine which I cannot quite resolve. Suppose I am acquainted with
one certain aspect of a thing without being acquainted with various other aspects
of that thing. On my view, this rather casts doubt on an unrestrained view that I
know the thing in question perfectly. Should I then say that I know perfectly that
one aspect of the thing? It seems not; for there is a multitude of aspects of that one
aspect with which I am not acquainted.

A possible solution is that, for things which are or could be aspects of things,
being acquainted with them is perfect knowledge of them even if one is not acquainted with a lot of their aspects. One might, however, require that one should
be acquainted with their "principal aspect".

iii

I might now be expected to turn to what it is that is (supposed to be) perfectly (?!) clear about thinking when we are thinking. But that would be foolish of me, for if the thesis is right, it is already perfectly (?!) clear to all of you, and if you, nevertheless, experience some unclarity on the matter, it would, on my view, have to be summational unclarity and to be dispelled by discussing *other* issues and their bearing on thinking.

And there are plenty of other, but related, issues to discuss. For example, one might attempt to determine what other "thinkables" are "logically equivalent" to, though not "intensionally isomorphic" with, what is perfectly (?!) clear to us about thinking. Usually, such investigation is conducted under the aegis of determining the "logical form" and/or the "semantics" of "propositional-attitude" statements, and, as you know, the issues here are far from settled, chiefly, I think, because of unclarity about "logical form", "semantics", the nature of investigation into them, and the relationship of these to what is to us perfectly (?!) clear about thinking. Just as a biographical fact, I find most plausible the view that thinking is—is "logically equivalent" to—standing in a certain special consciousness-relation to something like a state of affairs or a proposition. But I do not for a moment regard this as perfectly clear.

What I do want to discuss for a little bit is the apparent bearing of the pared-down thesis of perfect (?!) clarity of thinking on what else might be reasonably said or discovered about thinking. You will recall that the pared-down thesis was that when someone is thinking, he is perfectly (?!) clear about at least one aspect of what he is doing. Let $A$ be this aspect or one of these aspects. I shall now put an interpretation on what this perfect clarity about $A$ consists in (is "logically equivalent" to). This interpretation is, I think, essentially a version of a classical position associated with the Cartesian thesis of the perfect clarity of thinking. The interpretation is this. When a man is thinking, he is so completely justified in thinking (not necessarily in that "form") that what he is doing has aspect $A$ that no possible evidence he might have or lack while doing the thinking in question could render him *not* justified in thinking that what he is doing has aspect $A$. Now I think that perfect (?!) clarity in this interpretation imposes a restriction on what *A* could be—be "logically equivalent" to. And this restriction explains the perennial proposal, perennially disputed, that thinking is "non-physical" or "non-material". But, first, leaving aside such metaphysical categories, let us see what the restriction is.

To try to make it clear, I shall try to insinuate a number of notions.

First, I shall try to insinuate the notion of a "logically clear-headed person". A logically clear-headed person is one who is justified in accepting *all* "logical equivalences" (a tall order?!) and does not make logical mistakes. This is intended to be interpreted in such a way that if *A* is "logically equivalent" to *B*, then a logically clear-headed person is justified in accepting *A* if and only if he is justified in accepting *B*, and is justified in accepting non-*A* if and only if he is justified in accepting non-*B*.

Second, I shall try to insinuate the notion of evidence based on "external senses". I hope that this will ring bells.

Third, I shall try to insinuate the notion of an "external" aspect. An *external* aspect is one such that there is a possible body of evidence based on external senses such that any logically clear-headed person who has that body of evidence based on external senses is justified in thinking that something has that aspect, and there is a possible body of evidence based on external senses such that any logically clear-headed person who has *this* body of evidence based on external senses is justified in thinking that something does *not* have this aspect.

And, fourth, I shall try to insinuate the notion that thinking something (remember, this may be merely a case of "entertaining" something!) is compatible with both being a logically clear-headed person and having any given possible body of evidence based on external senses which a logically clear-headed person could have.

I believe that it follows from these four notions and the interpreted pared-down thesis of the perfect (?!) clarity of thinking that aspect *A* is not—"logically equivalent" to—any *external* aspect. You will recall that aspect *A* is supposed to be the one or one of those that one is perfectly clear about as being an aspect of one's thinking when one thinks.

Now, if one should think it right to hold that all "physical" or "material" aspects are "external"—in the sense insinuated—then one would have to take the result I have just enunciated as amounting to the thesis that at least one aspect of one's thinking with respect to which one is perfectly (?!) clear is "non-material" and "non-physical". But I think it would take a lot of examining of other issues to tell whether it is right to hold that all "physical" or "material" aspects are "external"—in the sense insinuated.

But let me return for a moment to the insinuated notion of *externality*. For I surmise that the result I have enunciated may have consequences, perhaps, with the aid of certain further premises, with respect to certain issues which may be of interest to you. I have in mind the idea that when one is thinking, one is standing in a relation to *a bit of language*, either of an outwardly spoken or written, colloquial or technical, sort, or of a more recondite sort to be called "language of thought". I will here resort to the idea of various aspects of thinking which I introduced earlier. So I shall suppose that thinking has an aspect—let us say, *A*—which is perfectly (?!) clear to us, and various aspects—let *B* be an arbitrary one of them—which are neither perfectly clear to us nor "logically equivalent" to any that are.

Now, I have *no* inclination to hold that none of these latter aspects, *B*, is—"logically equivalent" to—standing in a relation to a bit of language of whatever sort. For all I know, perhaps, no one ever thinks without using a bit of language, and, perhaps, it is nomologically impossible for anyone to do this. What I wish to hold is that none of these *former* aspects, A—those which we are perfectly (?!) clear about—is—"logically equivalent" to—standing in a relation to a linguistic entity of whatever sort. For I take it that a linguistic entity, of whatever sort, *could* have meant something other than what it, in fact, means. And—here various other premises might be needed—this implies that one needs evidence based on external senses to determine what it, in fact, means. And—here still further premises might be needed—this implies that a linguistic entity's meaning something is an *external* aspect of it.

Hence—and here *still* further premises might be needed—being related to a (linguistic) entity which means such-and-such is itself an *external* aspect.

But I take it that *no* aspect of being related to a linguistic entity is a plausible candidate for being "logically equivalent" to thinking that so-and-so, unless it is an aspect of being related to a linguistic entity which *means* so-and-so. So if we suppose that the last-mentioned aspect *is external*—according to the paragraph next to the last—and we do adhere to the consequences of the four insinuations I have attempted, together with the interpreted pared-down thesis of the perfect (?!) clarity of thinking, then we must hold that thinking that so-and-so is not—"logically equivalent" to—standing in a relation to a linguistic entity of whatever sort.

None of the above rules out *every* form of the so-called Identity Theory or *every* form of the thesis that thinking is some sort of using language. For just as a cube may very well be a purple thing, while yet the cube's being a cube is not the same as its being a purple thing, so thinking *might* very well be a (certain) physical process or using of language, even though—as I have tried to make somewhat clear—thinking's being thinking *cannot* be the same as being a (certain) physical process or being some sort of using language.

iv

This last conclusion, and others we may have drawn, are based on suppositions I asked you to make or others you were inclined to make yourselves—except, perhaps, for what you saw when I inveigled you into thinking this or that about Seattle and Portland.

# 2

# Physicalism and Mathematics

## Bob Hale

It is no straightforward matter to give a satisfactory detailed characterization of physicalism and it may well be that for some purposes it is best to distinguish different interpretations of the position—some, no doubt, more plausible than others—for separate critical evaluation. But on any understanding of it that does not break faith with the broad, if somewhat vague, conception that informs and motivates it, physicalism is usually taken to be,[1] at least in part, an ontological thesis: there are in reality no entities—objects, properties, relations, events, or states of affairs—but physical ones. Just what being physical amounts to is again far from straightforward, but we can safely take it, I think, that it requires at least locatability in space and time. And that is enough for it to be clear that the physicalist confronts a serious-looking problem over mathematics which, taking its syntax at face value, is replete with reference to and quantification over abstract entities—numbers of various sorts, sets, and functions. The natural philosophy of mathematics for the physicalist is, it would seem, some version of nominalism. Indeed, this may appear to be not just the *natural* but the *only* philosophy of mathematics congenial to the physicalist. Thus the suggestion that he might rather embrace a species of *Platonism* is bound to seem outrageous. On any obvious construal, 'physicalistic Platonism' is just a contradiction in terms. Penelope Maddy thinks otherwise. In a recent paper,[2] she undertakes to show that 'if physicalism is the inspiration for nominalism, then there is a naturalised form of platonism which should be just as acceptable as the best form of nominalism'. By 'acceptable'

---

[1] Quine's version of the position is an exception: see W. V. O. Quine, 'Facts of the Matter', in R. W. Shahan, ed., *American Philosophy from Edwards to Quine* (Norman, Okla., 1977), 176–96.

[2] Maddy, 'Physicalistic Platonism', in A. D. Irvine, ed., *Physicalism in Mathematics* (Dordrecht, 1990), 259.

she means, of course, acceptable to a physicalist. By the best form of nominalism she understands the kind of non-reductive nominalism defended, in several writings published during the last decade, by Hartry Field.[3]

## i. Field's Nominalism and Maddy's Platonism

Field's brand of nominalism contrasts sharply with more orthodox versions in two principal, and connected, respects. Traditional adherents of the position[4] are apt to regard any talk of abstract entities as simply unintelligible. And, in consequence of this, they are committed—at least if they are to avoid an implausible rejection of virtually the whole of standard pure mathematics as likewise unintelligible—to a programme of reductive paraphrase or reinterpretation of its sentences, as involving reference to or quantification over no more than nominalistically acceptable entities of some sort. Field has no less distaste for the abstract than the orthodox, but he finds no fault with standard mathematics—replete with reference to numbers, sets, and functions—in point of intelligibility. It all makes perfect sense, without benefit of reductive paraphrase or reinterpretation. No such manœuvres are needed,[5] on Field's view, since acceptance that mathematical statements are, taken at face value, perfectly intelligible is *one* thing, and acceptance that they are *true* is quite another. Further—and here Field seems to me to be indisputably right—no commitment to the existence of the abstract entities of which pure mathematics purports to speak is incurred, unless its statements are believed to be true. But—or so Field contends—there is no compelling reason why anyone should espouse that belief. It is, he argues, simply an

---

[3] H. Field, *Science without Numbers* (Oxford, 1980); id., 'Realism and Anti-Realism about Mathematics', *Philosophical Topics*, 13 (1982), 45–69; id., 'Is Mathematical Knowledge Just Logical Knowledge?', *Philosophical Review*, 93 (1984), 509–52; id., 'On Conservativeness and Completeness', *Journal of Philosophy*, 81 (1985), 239–60; and id., 'Realism, Mathematics and Modality', *Philosophical Topics*, 19 (1988) 57–107. The last four articles are reprinted, with additions, in id., *Realism, Mathematics and Modality* (Oxford, 1989), ch. 1 of which makes significant further contributions to the defence.

[4] The classic manifesto is of course N. Goodman and W. V. O. Quine, 'Steps towards a Constructive Nominalism', *Journal of Symbolic Logic*, 12 (1947), 105–22.

[5] Just as well, perhaps, in view of the conspicuous absence of successful nominalistic reconstructions of any significant portions of standard mathematics.

illusion that mathematics needs to be true to be good, or useful, or justifiably used. All that is required, to accommodate or account for its utility, is a belief in its *conservativeness*—where, in essence, a mathematical theory $S$ is conservative if its union with any nominalistically formulated (e.g. physical) theory $N$ has no nominalistically statable logical consequences which are not consequences of $N$ by itself.

I share Maddy's view that Field's is the most promising available version of nominalism as a philosophy of mathematics. But I do not think it is finally tenable. In particular, there is a serious difficulty over just how Field can and should understand the claim that a given mathematical theory is conservative. In brief[6] this is as follows. Since conservativeness is defined in terms of consequence, which can in turn be defined in terms of consistency, we may focus on how Field is to understand the last notion. Familiarly, taken one way—model-theoretically—a theory is consistent if its axioms have a model. Since models are sets of a certain sort, this construal is ruled out for obvious reasons. Taken another way—proof-theoretically—a theory is consistent if no contradiction is formally derivable, in the underlying logic, from its axioms. But this too is ruled out—as Field himself agrees[7]—because derivations in the required sense are likewise abstract entities (abstract sequences of abstract expression types). Field himself commends the adoption of a primitive notion of possibility as affording a way out of the difficulty. A theory is to be consistent if and only if its axioms, and so its theorems, are possibly (collectively) true. There is no need to insist that this natural way of taking the consistency claim has to be further explained, either model- or proof-theoretically. With this I am inclined to think we should agree. But trouble remains. Since a belief in the conservativeness of a theory requires a belief in its consistency,

---

[6] What follows summarizes a criticism of Field presented originally in B. Hale, *Abstract Objects* (Oxford, 1987), ch. 5. It has since been developed and strengthened by Crispin Wright in his 'Why Numbers Can Believably Be', *Revue internationale de philosophie*, 42 (1988), 425–73. Hale, 'Nominalism', in Irvine, ed., *Physicalism in Mathematics*, attempts to take the discussion further. Field has attempted to rebut the criticism in the introductory essay in his *Realism, Mathematics and Modality*. I do not believe his reply is satisfactory, but cannot pursue the matter here; it is pursued in Bob Hale and Crispin Wright, 'Nominalism and the Contingency of Abstract Objects', *Journal of Philosophy*, 89 (1992).

[7] Cf. Field, *Realism, Mathematics and Modality*, 127.

this—taken together with Field's denial, in the interests of his nominalism, that mathematics is true—requires him to hold that mathematics is in fact false but might have been true, i.e. that it is at worst *contingently false*. Mathematical statements are false, on Field's view, because there just are no numbers, sets, etc.; but they might have been true—hence there might have been such things. But on what is their existence, or non-existence, contingent? It seems that, on the one hand, Field owes an account, in nominalistic terms, of how things would have had to have been otherwise, for mathematical statements to be true; but that on the other, no such account can be forthcoming if—as Field believes, and as is surely the case—mathematics is conservative (and so has, by itself, no nominalistic consequences).

The principal attraction of Platonism is that it allows us to view classical mathematics—including its substantial and impressive infinitary portion—as straightforwardly true. 'Compared with truncated versions of the subject'—as Maddy nicely puts it[8]— 'Platonism has the considerable advantage of preserving the classics.' The main obstacle she discerns in the way of its acceptance—and of course this is a problem any would-be Platonist, whether of a physicalistic persuasion or no, must confront—is the difficulty of providing a credible, non-mystical, account of mathematical knowledge consonant with a Platonist construal of the truths known as concerning distinctively mathematical entities and their properties and relations. Field's nominalism—according to which mathematics is to be taken at face value, but is, so construed, false—bypasses this problem, or rather exchanges it for the problem of explaining how a pack of lies can be so useful. A key component in Maddy's defence of the foregoing quoted claim consists in developing a non-traditional, naturalized, version of Platonism that meets the epistemological challenge head on, in a physicalistically acceptable fashion, and so allows the physicalist to accept classical mathematics as true.

Now of course, no physicalist can accept (unreduced) classical mathematics as true, *if* that involves accepting the existence of mathematical entities as normally understood by the Platonist. To explain how physicalistic Platonism need not be an impossible option, Maddy distinguishes—though she does not herself put

---

[8] Maddy, 'Physicalistic Platonism', 259.

it this way—what might be termed[9] three grades of Platonic involvement. We have:

1. The view that 'mathematics is the science of something objective which its statements attempt correctly to describe'.
2. 1 + the further claim that this 'something objective' consists of peculiarly mathematical objects.
3. 2 + the further claim that these mathematical objects are abstract, non-spatio-temporal, and perhaps necessarily existent.

Maddy goes in for grade 2 Platonism—i.e. she holds mathematics to be objective and object-based, but not that it deals in abstract, non-spatio-temporal objects. Indeed it is, as we shall see, crucial to her attempt to meet the epistemological challenge to hold that sets—for her, the fundamental type of mathematical entity—are located in space and time. Treating the commitment to the existence of abstract entities as a dispensable feature of Platonism has, as she notes, a somewhat awkward consequence when it comes to saying what *nominalism* amounts to. If, as is usual, this is taken to consist in the repudiation of abstract entities, then nominalism is compatible with Platonism as Maddy construes it. She seeks to avoid this awkwardness by endorsing Field's own characterization of nominalism as 'the view that there are no mathematical entities'.[10] Over this, she claims, there is clear disagreement.

Disagreement there certainly is, but there is some reason to question whether its true nature is best revealed by Maddy's characterization, as concerning the existence of mathematical entities. When Field depicts nominalism as denying the existence of mathematical entities, he is, I am sure, assuming that were there to be such things as numbers and sets, they would be outside space and time. In view of this, Maddy is endorsing the letter only, not the spirit, of Field's formulation of the nominalist's distinctive thesis. Since, for her, the entities mathematics is about—sets, at least[11]—are to be regarded as spatio-temporally located, what her physicalistic Platonism asserts to exist is not what Field's nominalism repudiates. Whilst there is some danger, perhaps, of a merely

---

[9] To echo the title of a famous paper by a notable (grade 3?) Platonist. My formulation of the options is taken straight from Maddy, 'Physicalistic Platonism', 260.        [10] Field, *Science without Numbers*, p. x.

[11] Maddy in fact takes numbers to be properties (of sets) rather than objects. See Maddy, 'Sets and Numbers', *Nous*, 15 (1981), 495–511, at 502 ff.

terminological dispute here, it seems to me that her position could—
with as much, if not more, justice—be seen as a species of nominalism. But it would, of course, be nominalism of a very different
sort from Field's. The real issue concerns whether mathematical
statements can be taken to be (non-vacuously) true, compatibly
with physicalism. As against Field, Maddy's thesis is that they *can*
be so taken: since sets—or so she claims—are spatio-temporally
located (and thus physicalistically acceptable) entities, we can take
set theory to be descriptive of the properties of the radically impure
hierarchy containing every set whose transitive closure comprises
just physical objects. This proposal is firmly and recognizably in
the orthodox nominalist tradition, that is, of reinterpreting a region of discourse which ostensibly deals in abstract entities as
involving only reference to and quantification over nominalistically
acceptable ones. What is novel is the surprising proposal that sets
themselves can be *entia grata* for the nominalist, so that there is
no call to fall back on implausible attempts to interpret mathematics
as about inscriptions, or the like.


## ii. The Science–Mathematics Analogy

As we have remarked, Maddy takes her main task, in defending
grade 2 Platonism, to be that of meeting the epistemological challenge. She shares the conviction, voiced by Field[12] and others, that
the orthodox (grade 3) Platonist has little chance of providing any
credible account of mathematical knowledge, and agrees with him
that the problem here—the seeming inexplicability of our referential
and cognitive access to mathematical objects as he conceives them—
derives not from their presumed acausality as such, but from their
standing in no sort of physical (e.g. spatio-temporal) relations to
us, in virtue of which we might be capable of identifying thought

---

[12] Field, *Realism, Mathematics and Modality*, 20–30, 67–8, 230–9. The problem about reference goes back ultimately to P. Benacerraf, 'What Numbers Could
not Be', *Philosophical Review*, 74 (1965), 47–73, and has been more recently pressed
by H. Hodes, 'Logicism and the Ontological Commitments of Arithmetic', *Journal
of Philosophy*, 81 (1984), 123–49. The epistemological problem was first formulated—to the best of my knowledge—in P. Benacerraf, 'Mathematical Truth', *Journal
of Philosophy*, 70 (1973), 661–79. Both have been quite widely discussed—for
further references, and some attempts to meet the difficulties, see C. Wright, *Frege's
Conception of Numbers as Objects* (Aberdeen, 1983), chs. 2 and 3, and Hale,
*Abstract Objects*, chs. 4, 6, 7 and 8.

or knowledge concerning them.[13] It needs to be argued that grade 2 Platonism fares better.

To meet this challenge, Maddy proposes an epistemology for mathematics which runs closely parallel, in broad conception and structure, to that already suggested by Gödel.[14] As is well known, Gödel held that we do enjoy something analogous to ordinary sense-perception in respect of the objects of set theory. He calls this mathematical intuition. His view appears to have been that this gives us knowledge of, or at least warranted belief in, the simpler, more elementary axioms of set theory, and he took 'the fact that the axioms force themselves upon us as being true' as supporting his belief in this quasi-perceptual access to sets, which may involve, he suggested, 'another kind of relationship between ourselves and reality' from that involved in sense-perception.[15] Other, more exotic and non-elementary, propositions of set theory are to be seen rather as having a role and epistemological status analogous to that of higher-level theoretical statements of physical science. Roughly, we accept them, not on the basis of their intuitive evidence, but as forming integral components of what we take to be the best theoretical codification of lower-level mathematical propositions including, crucially, those for which we do have quasi-perceptual evidence. Thus, commenting with evident approval on Russell's analogy between mathematics and the natural sciences, Gödel says:

He compares the axioms of logic and mathematics with the laws of nature and logical evidence with sense perception, so that the axioms need not necessarily be evident in themselves, but rather their justification lies (exactly as in physics) in the fact that they make it possible for these 'sense perceptions' to be deduced . . . I think that (provided 'evidence' is understood in a sufficiently strict sense) this view has been largely justified by subsequent developments, and it is to be expected that it will be still more so in the future.[16]

---

[13] It is not clear that this is correct, or that the objection to full-blooded Platonism can be sustained, if the requirement of causal connectability is replaced by something weaker. Space does not permit discussion here; the matter is pursued a little further in Hale, 'Nominalism', 141, n. 13.

[14] Cf. K. Gödel's papers of 1944 and 1947, 'Russell's Mathematical Logic' and 'What is Cantor's Continuum Problem?', reprinted—P. Benacerraf and H. Putnam, eds., *Philosophy of Mathematics: Selected Readings*, 2nd edn. (Cambridge, 1983), 447–69 and 470–85.

[15] Ibid. 484.          [16] Ibid. 451.

Maddy takes over Gödel's science/mathematics analogy, with its
two-tier structure, but parts company with him in her account of
the character of our cognitive access at the base level. Although
Gödel says little enough about this, the little he does say strongly
suggests that he envisaged our grasp of elementary axioms as
mediated by some sort of non-physical contact—the objects of set
theory are 'remote from sense experience' and those of transfinite
set theory, at least, 'clearly do not belong to the physical world
and even their indirect connection with physical experience is very
loose'.[17] Pretty clearly this ought to stick in the physicalist gullet,
and Maddy understandably wishes to replace it with something
more digestible—and less mysterious—whilst retaining the rest of
Gödel's picture.

The replacement hinges[18] on the claim that we can and do
*literally perceive* sets—or at least small ones whose members are
concrete objects. The suggestion may well seem preposterous; and
surely is so, if sets are conceived, as they usually are, to be abstract
objects, outside space and time. Sense perception is a causal process
and that requires its objects to be around roughly when and where
the perceiver is. Maddy is, of course, well aware of this obvious
objection. Her response to it is simply to deny its presupposition.
Sets *are* spatially located: the set of eggs in a particular carton is
where its elements are—or where the physical aggregate composed
of them is—namely, in the carton.[19] Quite generally, a set is where
the elements of its transitive closure are. Thus {my hat, {my left
shoe, my right shoe}} is just where {my hat, my left shoe, my right
shoe} is, and so on up the hierarchy of sets.[20]

---

[17] Cf. K. Gödel's papers of 1944 and 1947, 483.

[18] Or so it at first appears—the appearance is arguably deceptive, however. See
below, sect. iii.

[19] Cf. P. Maddy, 'Perception and Mathematical Intuition', *Philosophical Review*, 89 (1980), 163–96, at 179. Note that there, Maddy is disposed to admit that
'many sets, the empty set or the set of real numbers, for example, cannot be said
to have spatial location', and maintains only that sets of physical objects are
located. But her more recently espoused physicalism requires that *all* sets are located.
There is, of course, a nice question about how, if they can be, sets are to be
distinguished from physical aggregates.

[20] The hierarchy cannot of course be the usual pure hierarchy, comprising all
those sets which exist irrespective of what assumption is made about what non-sets
there are, i.e. all those sets which are built up, ultimately, from ∅, since there clearly
cannot be, on this approach, any such entity as the empty set. For the same reason,
it cannot be what would usually be reckoned an impure hierarchy, built up from
certain non-sets by first forming all possible sets of them, then taking all possible

Once it is granted that sets are spatially located, there is no very great difficulty, Maddy contends, with the idea that we are sometimes in perceptual contact with them. On the general account of object perception she favours,[21] the essential conditions for me to perceive an object of a certain sort in a particular place are that I acquire some perceptual beliefs about that object (in particular, that there is an object of that sort there) and that the object is involved in an appropriate way in the production of my belief state. Where what is held to be perceived is a set, she takes the causal condition to be satisfied provided that an 'aspect' of the set (the nearside faces of temporal slices of its elements) plays a part in producing some of my beliefs. Obviously a question may be raised as to whether beliefs about sets are *perceptual* beliefs. Insisting that perceptual beliefs come in bundles, not singly, Maddy adopts what may strike one as an unduly generous view of what beliefs are to be accounted perceptual:

any belief acquired on a given occasion which influences and is influenced by perceptual beliefs acquired on that occasion is to be considered a perceptual belief.[22]

One might suspect that just about any belief could be slipped past as perceptual, on the ground that it was acquired on some occasion of sensory stimulation and is capable of interaction with other beliefs then acquired. Thus, following a written proof presumably involves acquiring some perceptual beliefs about what's on the page, which influence my beliefs about what the proof proves. Perhaps the trivialization that threatens can be blocked by Maddy's requirement that perceptual beliefs be non-inferential, though this is far from clear. I shall not pursue the issue here, however.[23] Instead, granting for argument's sake that this and other worries

---

sets of sets or non-sets available at the preceding stage, and so on. We have instead what Maddy calls a 'radically impure hierarchy'—roughly, what results from subtracting from some impure hierarchy $\emptyset$ along with all those sets of whose transitive closure $\emptyset$ is an element. Maddy herself suggests that $\emptyset$ might be retained as an 'ideal or fictional element', in the interests of simplifying theory. It would of course be crucial here that the complexity is the *only* cost incurred by abstention.

[21] For which see Maddy, 'Perception and Mathematical Intuition', sect. ii.
[22] Ibid., 172.
[23] This and some other objections are aired in Hale, *Abstract Objects*, 78–83. Some of them, though apt in relation to her 1980 position, do no apply to her more recent work, since she has in the interim waved goodbye to $\emptyset$ and therewith to all pure sets. Others, it seems to me, still want answering.

that may be felt about her account of set perception can be
satisfactorily answered, I want to canvass a quite distinct and
independent cause for concern about the epistemological analogy
between natural science and mathematics, as Maddy deploys it.

There is, in addition to but consequent upon the departure from
Gödel's (grade 3) Platonistic interpretation of the analogy just
noted, a further point of difference which Maddy herself remarks
upon, but without—or so I shall be contending—fully realizing its
implications. Whilst Gödel's view as to the character of mathematical intuition is obscure in crucial respects, there is one point
on which it is clear enough, and this is that its output is knowledge of—or at least quasi-perceptually warranted belief in—certain *axioms* of set theory. It does not much matter, for present
purposes, exactly how the range of set theoretic propositions whose
truth is supposed to be thus ascertainable is circumscribed. The
important thing here is that the axioms Gödel had in mind as
knowable in this fashion will have been *general* propositions—
propositions concerning the results of operations on sets in general, in contrast with propositions about particular sets of objects,
such as the set of coins in your pocket or word-tokens on this
page. Whether he thought we might in the same quasi-perceptual
fashion acquire knowledge concerning the relations among particular small finite sets of physical objects is of no consequence
here. He plainly did think—though the idea is enormously problematic—that mathematical intuition supplies us with knowledge
of a sufficient basis of general set theoretic truths. But this feature
of Gödel's account is hardly one that Maddy could plausibly seek
to preserve, when Gödelian quasi-perception is replaced by perception literally understood. If ordinary, non-Gödelian, perception
of sets is admitted at all, its field of operation has to be strictly
confined to *particular* sets. The acquisition of *general* beliefs about
sets—even if the scope of their quantifiers is restricted to small
finite sets of physical objects—has to be a further step.[24]

The obvious question now confronting us is: what is the character of this further step? Granting for the sake of argument that
we may acquire perceptual beliefs about particular sets (at least

[24] Maddy is clear about this: 'This perception of sets is not yet analogous to
Gödel's intuition because it gives us knowledge only of particulars, not of general
axioms' (Maddy, 'Physicalistic Platonism', 267).

provided that the sets in question are not too big, and perhaps also that they are of very low finite rank), but noting that set perception of itself cannot give rise to any general knowledge or beliefs about sets, how should we conceive the epistemological credentials of low-level general propositions of set theory?

Well, the obvious line for the physicalist to take here—given the envisaged analogy between set theoretic and natural scientific knowledge or belief—is to claim that analogy is actually *closer* than Gödel suggested. For Gödel, the quasi-perceptual data against which more interesting and momentous set theoretic propositions are to be tested comprises what are, in effect, low-level generalizations concerning sets. But if, contra Gödel, it is maintained that sets are quite literally objects of sense perception, should not the data, to which all general set theoretic propositions, of whatever level, are directly or indirectly answerable, comprise perceptually verified singular truths concerning particular sets of physical objects? So that just as, roughly speaking, we have in the natural scientific case singular truths about particular matters of physical fact established by observation or experiment, with low-level 'experimental' or 'empirical' generalizations directly confirmed or disconfirmed according as they fit or fail to fit the observed facts, and, on top of them, higher-level theoretical generalizations whose acceptance or rejection is largely determined by their capacity to systematize and explain accepted lower-level generalities, so in set theory we would have observationally established singular truths about particular sets, with low-level, more elementary, axioms and theorems of set theory directly answerable to them, and erected on top of that, a superstructure of higher-level theory. In sum, the natural physicalist account, developed in this way, would retain Gödel's idea that our adoption of higher-level axioms may be motivated by their capacity to provide the most elegant and economical systematization and 'explanation' of lower-level generalities about sets, but it would take the parallel with natural scientific theories a stage further, by seeing those lower-level generalities as subject to experiential confirmation and disconfirmation by perceptual data relating to particular spatially located sets.

This is, it seems to me, the direction in which the science/mathematics analogy is most naturally developed, if—in the interests of providing a physicalistically acceptable account of set theory—

Gödelian intuition is replaced by literal sense perception as a source of mathematical evidence. But it is not the direction which Maddy herself takes in response to the obvious question of two paragraphs back. She suggests a very different account of the origin and epistemological status of the general set-theoretic beliefs which are to be seen as occupying the lower level in the two-tier structure integral to the analogy. Since there is, in my view, compelling reason to think that the natural development issues in a position which cannot be sustained, it is important to determine whether Maddy has disclosed a viable alternative.

### iii. Intuitive Beliefs about Sets

Maddy's own proposal—in essence, and skipping over much of the amalgam of neurophysiological fact and speculation with which she supports it—is that the sort of neural developments which, according to some workers in the field, underlie and explain physical object perception can be extended to allow for perception of sets of such objects, and that these neural developments would give rise to very general beliefs about the sorts of entities which produce them. In a little more detail, the kind of theory Maddy favours has it that our capacity to perceive—acquire perceptual beliefs about—entities of a certain kind, e.g. triangles, or physical objects generally, or (in her view) sets, involves the development of a complex neural structure—a triangle-, or physical object-, or set-detector—stimulation of which mediates perception of objects of that kind. Further, she contends,

the acquisition of each concept is accompanied by the acquisition of some very general beliefs about things of that kind; indeed, the structure of the detector itself determines some very general beliefs about things of the kind it detects . . . [thus] three-sidedness is, in a sense, "built into" the triangle-detector in the form of mechanisms stimulating eye movement from one corner to another, just as three-angledness is built into the form of the detector's three distinct cell assemblies for the corners themselves.[25]

The general beliefs—'intuitive beliefs' as she calls them—allegedly thus acquired in the case of physical objects are such as that physical objects can look different from different points of view,

---

[25] Maddy, 'Perception and Mathematical Intuition', 185.

that they exist in space and time, and that they do not cease to exist when one ceases to see them; and in the case of sets, that sets have number properties, that sets other than singletons have many proper subsets, that any property determines a set of things having that property, and so on.[26] Intuitive beliefs are themselves typically prelinguistic on Maddy's view; she suggests that the phenomenon, stressed by Gödel, of certain axioms 'forcing themselves upon us as being true' is to be explained in terms of their being 'fairly successful formulations' of such prelinguistic intuitive beliefs. As regards the epistemological status of such intuitive beliefs, Maddy insists that they are fallible (cf. the allegedly intuitive belief in naïve comprehension). She further tells us, in an important footnote, that

(i) set theoretic truths are not analytic; they are true by virtue of facts about independently existing sets,

(ii) intuitive beliefs are *a priori* because once the concepts are in place, no further experience is needed to support them, and no further experience will count against them (though theoretical evidence might count against their linguistic expressions).[27]

There is much that might be questioned in all this. In particular, a more detailed assessment of these ideas would look more critically than I shall do here at Maddy's speculation about physical object- and set-detectors. There may, perhaps, be available good grounds for supposing that we and other animals develop distinctive structures of cell assemblies in connection with the perception of determinate kinds of object—bugs, bananas, and the like. But it is very much open to question, in view of the extreme generality and comprehensiveness of the notion, whether it makes sense to extend this idea to physical objects in general: physical objects hardly constitute a determinate natural kind, and it is quite unclear how the postulated object-detector could be appropriately structured or how very general beliefs about physical objects could be built into that structure. And similar doubts suggest themselves in relation to the notion of a set-detector (which in any case could probably not develop, on Maddy's view, until our object-detectors were up and running). For present purposes, however, the crucial contention is that intuitive beliefs about sets are *a priori*, in a sense

[26] Cf. ibid. 185–6.
[27] Maddy, 'Perception and Mathematical Intuition', 190 n. 52.

that involves their being insusceptible of any sort of empirical disconfirmation. And the crucial question is whether she can take this line, without breaking faith with the science/mathematics analogy that informs her approach.

It may well appear that we can make no progress with this question unless and until we have a clearer idea than Maddy furnishes of the precise range of intuitive beliefs whose acquisition supposedly accompanies the development of the neural mechanism which, on her account, mediates our perception of sets. The examples she offers of beliefs which are probably involved in that development are all, in effect, highly general existential beliefs such as that given any two objects, there is a set whose elements are just those two objects, or that any things can be collected into a set.[28] It is indeed quite unclear how there could possibly be experiential disconfirmation of beliefs such as these—we have, presumably, no idea what would constitute attempting to 'collect' two or more objects together to form a set, but finding that, our best efforts notwithstanding, we could not bring it off. Maddy herself speculates that the belief that sets have number properties might prove false, but admits that it is 'hard to imagine' how this could be so.[29]

There is, nevertheless, good reason, as I shall now try to make clear, to deny that intuitive beliefs about sets can be thought quite generally to enjoy the kind of *a priori* status Maddy wishes to claim for them. Here it is essential to bear in mind the role assigned to beliefs of this kind in the overall epistemological picture whose acceptance she wishes to commend. They are collectively to constitute the base level in the two-tier structure, the upper level of which is to be thought of as occupied by more theoretical and more powerful propositions of set theory which commend themselves to us, not as intuitively correct (they do not, in Gödel's phrase, 'force themselves upon us as being true'), but—in accord with the proposed parallel with physical science—as contributing to the best overall explanatory systematization of lower-level, more elementary, general laws about sets. Our epistemic warrant for accepting such higher-level propositions or axioms of set theory is, in other words, to be thought of as *flowing upwards*—from base to superstructure, as it were. But it makes sense to view our

[28] Maddy, 'Perception and Mathematical Intuition', 186.      [29] Ibid. 187.

acceptance of such higher-level axioms as warranted, in the fashion Maddy, following Gödel, envisages, by their explanatory fruitfulness—their capacity to provide a systematic and explanatory codification of lower-level general propositions about sets—only if the latter propositions are themselves subject to independent critical appraisal—independent, that is, of whatever deductive relations obtain between lower-level beliefs and higher-level axioms. The effect of claiming *a priori* status for elementary general propositions about sets—so that although set theory is conceived as descriptive of a universe of independently existing, spatially located sets, at least some of which are objects of our perception, perceptually engendered beliefs can have no role in the evaluation of generalizations about them—is precisely to rule out such independent appraisal.[30] This in turn gives rise to a striking disanalogy between the methodology of set theory, as Maddy conceives it, and that of the natural sciences, where the low-level generalizations which it is the business of theories to explain are, of course, subject to observational or experimental confirmation and disconfirmation. My contention is that this is no dispensable feature: if there were no independent experimental or observational check on which lower-level physical generalizations are to be accepted as true, and hence as calling for explanation by physical theory—if the only check on which such generalizations ought to be accepted is consistency with accepted theory—then it could be no merit in that theory that it 'explained' those which are accepted. The claim that the theory deserves acceptance in virtue of its capacity to explain them would be simply fraudulent. The proposed analogy between physical theory and set theory effectively collapses, if low-level set theoretic generalizations are viewed as formulating *a priori* intuitive beliefs.

It may be objected that the claim for which I have just argued must be wrong, on the grounds that the procedure I have stigmatized as involving only a bogus analogy with natural science is precisely that which we quite properly and naturally follow in logical theory, so far as that is viewed as a general theory of valid argumentation. Specifically, the counter claim will be that in theorizing about validity, we begin with intuitive judgements about

---

[30] Unless they are subject to independent check of some *other*, presumably non-empirical, kind—but what might that be like?

the validity or otherwise of informal, everyday, arguments and
proceed to frame general formal principles of valid argumentation,
usually collectively constituting a formal system which purports to
characterize the class of valid inferences essentially involving a
certain well-defined logical vocabulary. One criterion for the acceptability of such a system is the extent to which it succeeds in
capturing or reflecting—and in some sense, explaining—our intuitive judgements. But it is not required that our efforts at systematic
and general characterization should slavishly respect the intuitive
judgements which underlie its construction. We are prepared for
there to be some give and take between the two; in particular, we
are ready to revise some of our logical intuitions in the light of an
otherwise good and successful logical theory which conflicts with
them. And now—so the envisaged objection runs—is this not pretty
well exactly how things proceed, on the account just criticized, in
the set theoretic case? And is it not a perfectly acceptable methodological approach?

It is beyond the scope of this discussion fully to evaluate the
conception of the epistemology of logical theory just adumbrated.
Fortunately, it is unnecessary, for present purposes, to do so. For
it is, I think, possible—granting for the sake of argument its approximate correctness—to disclose respects in which the suggested
parallel is crucially flawed, provided a modicum of care is exercised over the none too clear and rather slippery notion of 'logical
intuition'. Talk of logical intuition may refer to pretheoretical
judgements—roughly, judgements unguided by explicit theory—
concerning the validity or otherwise of *particular* inferences; or it
may, quite differently, refer to pretheoretical judgements about the
validity of *general* patterns of inference. Provided we keep this
distinction clearly in mind, it is not difficult to see that appeals to
intuition in the construction of general and systematic charac-
terizations of logical validity, and the interplay between such
intuitions and theory, need involve no conflict with my claim that
if higher-level, more theoretical, propositions are to command
acceptance in virtue of providing an explanatory systematization
of lower-level generalizations—in the present case, generalizations
about which inferences are valid—then the latter have to be subject
to critical assessment independently of the higher reaches of
theory. If the suggested parallel between the epistemology of set
theory, as Maddy conceives it, and our procedure in logical theory,

on this account, is to yield a defence of the former against the criticism I have urged, then it will have to be the case that intuitive beliefs of the second sort, about the validity of *general* patterns of inference, are on all fours, in relevant epistemic respects, with general intuitive beliefs about sets, when these are taken, as Maddy construes them, to be *a priori* and subject only to theoretical revision from above. But this they plainly are not. General beliefs about what patterns of inference are valid—'intuitive beliefs' if you like—are, on the contrary, subject to critical appraisal from below in routine ways, and centrally by the production of actual or imagined counter-examples, that is, citation of particular inferences of the general form in question, in which truth is not transmitted from premisses to conclusion. Recognition of the cogency of such counter-examples involves, in effect, intuitive judgements of validity of the other type distinguished. Such judgements, which are, of course, exercises of semantic competence in the language in question, are to the effect that certain particular statements—those forming the premisses—are, or could be, true, whilst another particular statement—the conclusion—is, or could be, false. It is judgements of this kind that play, if any do, a role analogous to the observation statements against which natural scientific theories are ultimately tested. It is a further question whether the methodology of logical theory is, in essential respects, the same as that of the natural sciences. But if it is, there is no reason apparent for supposing that rational prosecution of logical theory conflicts with the central claim on the basis of which I have argued that treating elementary general beliefs about sets as *a priori* precipitates collapse of the desired analogy between mathematics and natural science.

## iv. Set-Theoretic Empiricism

If the argument just given is good, then Maddy's actual position, involving as it does viewing sets as spatially located and perceivable, whilst denying that perceptually acquired beliefs about them can have any role in the epistemology of set theory, is untenable. A physicalist defender of the science/mathematics analogy ought rather, it seems, to embrace the 'obvious' line of thought briefly

sketched in Section ii. This amounts to a quite radical species
of empiricism about set theory, and it is important to be clear
just how radical it is. It is not merely that this kind of physicalist holds, with Quine, that set-theoretic propositions are in
principle vulnerable to revision on empirical grounds. On the
globally empiricist picture of 'Two Dogmas', the propositions
of logic and mathematics, though subject, in principle, to revision
in response to recalcitrant experience, are very remote from the
periphery, and need not, in consequence, be thought of as subject
to the very direct kind of empirical disconfirmation to which
low-level generalizations like 'All swans are white' are vulnerable.
By contrast, a physicalist who follows the line presently under discussion must hold that lower-level general propositions about
sets are potentially disconfirmable by perceptually ascertained facts
about the properties of particular finite sets of physical objects.

An analogous view about elementary arithmetic would be that
simple identities such as $3 + 8 = 11$, $5 \times 4 = 20$, etc., are empirical
generalizations which receive direct experiential corroboration from
counting 'experiments', and that explicit number-theoretic generalizations—thought of as occupying higher levels in the overall
theoretical structure—such as $a \times (b + c) = (a \times b) + (a \times c)$, or
more interestingly, the Peano axioms, receive more indirect experiential support. They are to be accepted because they afford the
best theoretical systematization of the lower-level generalizations
which, on this account, singular arithmetic identities formulate.
On this view, statements of the latter sort ought to be vulnerable,
at least in principle, to direct empirical disconfirmation. We should
be in the market, at least, for the discovery that $5 \times 4 \neq 20$, the
discovery coming about through our repeatedly finding that when
we count a collection of physical objects arranged, as we have
empirically verified, in a 4 by 5 array, some result other than 20
is obtained. And the parallel would seem to require that low-level
set-theoretic generalities, such as $a \cap (b \cup c) = (a \cap b) \cup (a \cap c)$,
are likewise susceptible, in principle, of direct empirical disconfirmation in much the same way. That is, something like the
following should be at least possible. We go through a small finite
set, composed of pieces of fruit of various kinds, first putting a
distinctive mark, \$, on those which are red or green. We then
go through all the pieces of fruit so marked, putting another distinctive mark, %, on those which are apples. Now we reassemble

the original collection and go through it again, putting a third distinctive mark, *, on each red apple and on each green apple, but on no other pieces of fruit. Since the first part of our experiment consists in taking the intersection of the apples with the union of the red and green pieces of fruit, and the second part consist in taking the union of the intersection of the apples with the red pieces together with the intersection of the apples with the green pieces, each piece of fruit should bear all three of our marks, or none of them (i.e. if our generalization is correct). So we are a little surprised to find that some piece of fruit bears the marks $ and % but not the mark *. No doubt our initial reaction will be to suppose that we have bungled the experiment—have put a mark on some piece of fruit when we should not have done, or have failed to mark a piece which we should have marked. But if the species of empiricism we are concerned with is correct, it should be possible that we get this sort of result, no matter what precautions are taken to ensure that we make no mistakes in performing the ingredient operations of our experiment. That is, it should be conceivable that we have the best possible reason to suppose that we have performed the experiment perfectly, and yet obtained results that are inconsistent with the principle that intersection distributes over union.

It seems clear that whether or not this *is* a genuine possibility should not depend upon *how many* pieces of fruit compose the original collection. So let us suppose there to be just two—one red, one green, both apples. And let us suppose that those whose task it is to inscribe the marks are carefully watched by observers, whose brief is to make sure that the markers perform in accordance with their instructions, that no marks fade, that no new piece of fruit appears and that no piece disappears during the course of the experiment. Then if it is to seem to the observers that the first marker does his job properly, it must seem to them that he makes the mark $ on both pieces of fruit. Similarly, if it is to seem to the observers that the second marker does his job properly, it must seem to them that he makes the mark % on both pieces of fruit. And finally, if it is to seem to them that the third marker does his job properly, it must seem to them that he puts the mark * on both pieces of fruit. And it is to seem to them that no mark disappears, etc. But then how can it possibly seem to them that there is a piece of fruit which does not have all three marks upon it? I think we will have to agree that this just isn't possible.[31]

It is, as previously remarked, less than clear just what range of intuitive beliefs about sets Maddy would wish to see as occupying the lower level in her two-tier structure. Since she does not explicitly include low-level generalizations of the kind featured in the preceding argument, it may be felt that that argument is misdirected. There are at least two reasons why this complaint has little force. First, it really matters not at all whether $a \cap (b \cup c) = (a \cap b) \cup (a \cap c)$ and its kin actually figure among the intuitive beliefs about sets which, on her view, accompany acquisition of the capacity to perceive sets. All that is required for my argument is that the axioms adopted for set theory will have such elementary set-theoretic generalizations as *consequences*—consequences which should, according to the species of empiricism under discussion, be empirically testable via their instantiation with respect to small finite sets of physical objects. Second, as far as the examples she actually gives are concerned, the suggestion that they might be disconfirmed in the requisite manner has no plausibility whatever. Even granting that we can, as Maddy claims, perceive (some) sets, we can make nothing of the idea that perceptually acquired evidence concerning particular sets might conflict with the general beliefs that sets have number properties, or that sets other than singletons have many proper subsets. We can, to be sure, envisage ourselves being forced to revise some of the beliefs she cites in this connection, such as the belief that every property determines a set. But—crucially here—the consideration which enjoins revision in this case (i.e. the fact that it leads to Russell's contradiction) is not empirical, but clearly *a priori*.

To sum up: if the central line of argument of this paper is sound, Maddy's attempt to combine a physicalistically acceptable

---

[31] I claim, of course, no originality for this line of argument. Readers of Edward Craig, 'The Problem of Necessary Truth', in S. Blackburn, ed., *Meaning, Reference and Necessity* (Cambridge, 1975), 1–31 will, I hope, recognize it as an attempt—inevitably somewhat crude and sketchy, for reasons of space—to adapt to the case in hand an argument he there develops against the putative possibility that we should have the best possible perceptual evidence that a properly conducted counting experiment has yielded counter-arithmetic results, inconsistent with, say, the proposition that $7 + 5 = 12$. As against this putative possibility, Craig's argument seems to me wholly convincing; whether its conclusion carries the implications for conventionalism that he takes it to have is a further question which I need not consider here.

ontology for set theory—according to which each set is spatially located—with an epistemology based upon the science/mathematics analogy she borrows from Gödel is unsuccessful. Taking the analogy seriously involves, her own view to the contrary notwithstanding, holding lower-level set-theoretic propositions to be vulnerable to empirical disconfirmation in ways that they are not. There is thus good reason to doubt that physicalistic Platonism, developed along the lines Maddy proposes, constitutes a viable philosophy of mathematics. There may yet, for all that I have sought to argue here, be some way of successfully combining acceptance of standard mathematics as a body of truths with insistence that such truths make no ontological demands beyond the concrete: but if so, we have yet to see its colours.[32]

[32] I should like to thank Crispin Wright for helpful reactions to an earlier draft of this paper.

# 3

# Transcendental Arguments against Physicalism

*Ralph Walker*

Kant believed transcendental arguments cannot establish the immateriality of the soul. He may have been right. But at least transcendental arguments can help us establish certain things which are incompatible with a thoroughgoing materialism. One of these is that there are in the universe certain objective laws, which cannot themselves be material (in any plausible sense of that word) or reducible to anything material. Another is that there are persons, beings who are capable of following these laws or of failing to follow them. Such persons may be material entities in the sense that they are made of matter, but their behaviour in following laws cannot adequately be accounted for in materialistic terms.

Transcendental arguments are arguments against the sceptic.[1] To be effective, therefore, they must start from premisses that cannot sensibly be questioned, and the validity of the inferences they draw must be beyond sensible question as well. Clearly enough, anything whatever *can* be called in question, but to doubt whether anything exists, or whether a straightforward instance of *modus ponens* is acceptable, would just be silly. Kant's transcendental arguments start from the premiss that we have experience, or knowledge. How much he builds into these terms is not always clear, but most of the time all that is needed is the assumption that we are aware of the content of at least some thoughts and sense-experiences (which is not to say that we interpret them correctly, or are right in the ascription of them to a single unitary self). A sceptic who doubted whether this is true, or queried our

---

[1] Kant, *The Critique of Pure Reason*, A 769/B 797; and see further my 'Transcendental Arguments and Scepticism', in E. Schaper and W. Vossenkuhl, eds., *Reading Kant* (Oxford, 1989), 55–76.

right to believe it true, would not be of great interest, for he would be placing himself beyond the reach of serious argument.

Kant's transcendental arguments typically have a second premiss, to the effect that *p* is a condition of the possibility of experience. This is tantamount to a conditional of the form 'If there is experience, then *p*.' It must also be beyond sensible doubt, though it may not be immediately self-evident. I think, and have argued elsewhere, that Kant can claim this status for it because he regards the second premiss as analytic.[2] It amounts to a piece of conceptual analysis whose truth, and whose justification, rests on that of the elementary principles of logic. Those principles themselves are also involved in drawing the conclusion of the argument, by an application of *modus ponens*: we can conclude that we are justified in holding *p* to be true, since the premisses on which it rests are true and beyond sensible doubt.

Kant would not deny that it may be reasonable to doubt certain of the principles put forward by logicians as elementary logical laws, such as the law of the excluded middle. As he says at the start of his *Logic*, 'the exercise of our own powers takes place according to certain rules which we first follow without being conscious of them', and their precise formulation may be a matter of some difficulty.[3] Nevertheless, it is clear in a wide range of cases when the rules are being followed and when they are not, and if this were not so argument could never get going: we should have no way of distinguishing good argument from bad, and so could only confront one another with assertions and counter-assertions. The sceptic who calls in question our reliance on elementary logic, by doubting for example Kant's uses of the principle '*A* that is *B* is *A*' or of *modus ponens*, does not need to be taken seriously, for he makes himself immune to arguments against him by refusing to accept anything as an argument.

It is therefore a presupposition of any transcendental argument, and a presupposition of any argument at all, that the rules of elementary logic should be valid. To say this, however, is effectively to provide a transcendental argument for their validity, at least if

---

[2] See my *Kant* (London, 1978), ch. 2, sect. i. For a contrary view see P. Guyer, *Kant and the Claims of Knowledge* (Cambridge, 1987), 419 ff.

[3] Kant, *Logic*, Introduction, sect. i: trans. R. Hartman and W. Schwarz (Indianapolis, 1974), 13; Ak. 9. 11. Here and in what follows 'Ak.' refers to the Berlin Academy edn. of *Kant's gesammelte Schriften* (1902–).

we slightly strengthen the first premiss from Kant's minimal form, adding to the claim that we are aware of the content of certain thoughts and experiences the further claim that we are capable of arguing rationally—or at any rate of recognizing the force of rational argument. The effect of the strengthening is only to bring out what is already presupposed by the use of the argument itself. Kant reiterates that without these rules 'no use of the understanding would be possible at all'.[4]

Besides these logical ones there are other modes of inference on which we regularly rely and which we regularly take to be justified. We must be right in this, some of the time at least, if warranted conclusions are to be drawn from the sense-experiences we have. Some philosophers have held that a transcendental argument with Kant's minimal first premiss is adequate to show that certain of the conclusions we draw about the external world are indeed warranted; Kant himself thought he could show that every event must have a cause and that causes are to be sought by looking for constant conjunctions.[5] Indeed, he thought he could show more generally that the principles of induction and of what we might call inference to the best explanation are warranted likewise, which is not of course to say that the results we get by using them are true in every case.[6] Other philosophers would question whether Kant's minimal premiss is adequate to yield conclusions of this sort. But if one agrees with them one only has to make a further strengthening of the premiss, and a strengthening which again cannot be called into serious doubt. One can strengthen it by adding that we are sometimes warranted in our interpretation of sense-experience or in our inferences from it, which it would again seem rather pointless to deny, even if, this time, the professional sceptic can do so without having to abandon *all* forms of argument. From that one can derive the conclusion that there must be rules of non-logical inference which we are justified in using—however problematic it may be just which these rules are or how they should be formulated. (In what follows I shall assume that the principles warranting induction and inference to the best explanation are principles of this

---

[4] Ibid., trans. Hartman and Schwarz, 14; Ak. 9. 12.
[5] *Critique of Pure Reason*, Second Analogy and A 144/B 183 f.
[6] Ibid., A 669 ff./B 697 ff.; and see my 'Kant's Conception of Empirical Law', *Proceedings of the Aristotelian Society*, suppl. vol. 64 (1990).

kind, but I shall only be using them as examples and without any attempt to state them precisely.)

It may seem an unexciting claim that there must be some principles of inference, both logical and non-logical, on which we can justifiably rely. What makes it more significant is the further claim, which is also Kant's though he does not develop it very fully, that these principles of inference must be laws which are real and objective in their own right: laws of pure reason. He assigns to them very much the same status that he assigns to the moral law, though the moral law is a law of pure practical reason, which tells us what we ought to do, whereas these laws are laws of pure theoretical reason, which tell us what we ought to believe.[7] Here I think Kant is right. They have the same objective and irreducible character as the moral law, and like it they are metaphysically fundamental constituents of the universe. It is no part of my present purpose to consider the moral law, however, and I bring it in here only to help clarify how Kant thinks of the laws of pure theoretical reason. Whatever may be thought about the nature of morality, Kant's view of the laws of theoretical reason could still be right, and I think must be. And their reality is something that any account of the world in purely material terms is unable to allow for—however broadly we construe 'purely material terms'.

In this they differ, of course, from man-made laws. Man-made laws require legislators, and their reality is not independent of what people think or feel about them. The laws of pure reason require no lawgiver, and they do hold independently of what anyone thinks or feels about them: and this is what is meant by calling them *objective*. More generally, they are *metaphysically ultimate*, in the sense that the fact that they obtain is not logically dependent upon anything else. In this they differ, for example, from holes, which exist in virtue of the shapes of physical objects, and they differ also from the laws of England, the existence of which is logically dependent on what people believe and do. And there is a further contrast: the laws of pure reason, unlike the laws of England, are (in a technical sense) *prescriptive*: as Kant says, they

---

[7] Kant, *Critique of Practical Reason*, trans. T. K. Abbott, 6th edn. (London, 1909), 97 ff. and 118; Ak. 5. 12 f. and 30. Kant, *Logic*, trans. Hartman and Schwarz, 16; Ak. 9. 14. See further my 'The Rational Imperative: Kant against Hume', *Proceedings of the British Academy*, 74 (1988), 113–33.

tell us 'not how we think, but how we ought to think'.[8] They tell us which inferences we ought to draw and which we ought not to draw, and this 'ought' is a kind of imperative which we cannot just ignore. Anyone who is aware of them at all must be motivated by them in the inferences he draws or accepts, and in the inferences he refuses to draw. One may be very knowledgeable about English law without being disposed, even slightly, to obey any of it, either because one prefers crime or because one lives in Peru. One cannot be aware of the laws of pure reason without having some inclination to obey them, and it is in their nature that this should be so. That is not to say that one always does obey them. One may have contrary inclinations, which are stronger. But to be aware of these laws is to see them as providing us with motives in this way, and if one does not see them as providing motives (and motives for oneself) one does not see them as laws.

The motives in question are motives for making some inferences and rejecting others; they are not motives for performing the sort of acts that are commonly thought the result of free choice. But the cases are sufficiently analogous to warrant the use of the word 'motive'. Inference is something that we do, and sometimes do rationally. When we do it rationally, we are following rules, and the rules determine what the rational course is. And rationality is not something we can take or leave: we are swayed, quite strongly and often decisively, by the awareness that a certain conclusion is the rational one to draw. We can of course be mistaken in what we take to be rational, and so draw the wrong conclusion. We can also decide to be irrational—studies of self-deception and bad faith are largely concerned with how this occurs. If we do, there remains in us a pressure towards the rational conclusion, and there is an analogy with the conflict of motives in ordinary cases of agency.

The laws of pure theoretical reason must be prescriptive in this sense, or in something close to it. Someone who saw no such force in these principles of inference—who saw the rationality of a conclusion as no reason whatever for accepting it—would be in the position of the uninteresting sceptic, utterly impervious to any form of argument. I think many people would also be willing to admit that they are objective, but I shall return later to the

[8] Kant, *Logic*, loc. cit.

transcendental defence of the claim that they must be. What many would however strongly object to is the idea that they are meta-physically ultimate, that is, that their obtaining is not logically dependent on anything else. For they take them to be derivative from certain other facts about the world: in the case of the laws of logic, the fact that they always take us from truths to truths, and in the case of the principle of induction, the fact that given the truth of the premises, the truth of the conclusion is likely (or something of the sort). These facts are perfectly objective—inde-pendent of what we think or feel about them—but there is nothing prescriptive about them. What introduces the element of prescriptivity is a concern on our part to get at the truth, or to get at what is likely to be true. Given that we have that concern, we have a motive for following these principles, rather as we have a motive for going to Sainsbury's if we have an urge to go to the largest grocer in Oxford and if Sainsbury's is the largest grocer.

This picture of things is mistaken. It is not in fact obvious that we really do have a general concern to get at the truth, but even if we do, it could not provide us with a motivation to follow the rules of inference in the way suggested unless it were not just *the case* that these principles lead us from true premises to true con-clusions (always or for the most part), but *believed by us* to be the case. The desire to go to the largest grocer provides a motivation for going to Sainsbury's only if one thinks that Sainsbury's is itself the largest grocer (or that going to Sainsbury's is in some other way a means to getting to the largest grocer). The decisive objection to the suggestion we are considering is that we have no reason, independent of the laws of pure reason themselves, to believe the relevant facts. Another objection, possibly less decisive, is that there are no such facts.

In the case of the laws of logic the alleged fact in which we should have to believe is that these laws always give us true conclusions when we apply them to true premises. Even if 'always' here just means 'on every actual occasion on which we use them' it is still going to be quite impossible to find out that this is so, unless perhaps by arguing that the laws of logic are themselves compelling laws and therefore must be assumed to give the right results. And if one were to argue in that way one would be presupposing that these laws are binding, whereas the suggestion we were considering was that their bindingness, their prescriptivity, was derived from our desire to reach the truth together with our belief that they always give us true conclusions when we apply them to true premisses.

One can hardly just *see* that the laws of logic are truth-preserving in the required way. The claim that is being made for them is a universal claim, to the effect that they always give the right results on every occasion of use—past, present, or future. It might be suggested that this is something we know non-empirically, and for which we require no further justification. Now it may be that there are certain beliefs we can simply see to be true by direct observation; this is a vexed question which there is no need to go into here. But it is hardly a matter of direct observation that the laws of logic are truth-preserving. What could be meant by saying that a belief of that kind requires no further justification? Only that the claim is one we *ought* to accept: it offends against no canons of rationality, no canons of sound argument—in other words, it is sanctioned by those *laws* which determine what we ought to believe and how we ought to argue. What else could it mean? Someone might propose that by saying a belief requires no further justification we mean it belongs to a type, the members of which are (perhaps as a matter of necessity) *likely to be true*, but that is clearly inadequate: there are many such beliefs whose epistemological status is decidedly shaky. If it is true that every even number greater than 2 is the sum of two prime numbers, it belongs to a type of belief whose members are not only likely, but bound, to be true, but that does not mean we can dispense with trying to find a proof of it.

An alternative suggestion might be that our belief that these laws always give the right results is justified by its coherence with the rest of our beliefs, and by the continuing empirical success of the system as a whole. The difficulty here is one of circularity. A reliance on the laws of logic themselves is indispensable in determining coherence and in recognizing any consonance with empirical observation. Our reliance on the laws of logic cannot therefore be dependent on our already having the belief, since they are required to justify it.

A possible reply is that the belief might be unjustified: it might simply be one we happen to hold, without being justified in holding it. It does not matter if nothing grounds it—we can still explain the bindingness of the laws of logic by saying it is due to this belief of ours, coupled with our interest in the truth. But in that case the laws of logic would have their force only so long as we continued to hold an utterly blind and arbitrary belief; and that seems clearly wrong. It is not open to us to adopt an alternative, equally arbitrary, belief instead and so to absolve ourselves from any need to follow them.

So it will not do to hold that the laws of logic owe their force to our belief that they will give us the right results, coupled with our interest in the truth. Essentially the same considerations apply in the case of non-logical principles, like the principle of induction. The suggestion in their case is that they are not metaphysically ultimate, because they hold in virtue of the fact that arguments of a certain type yield conclusions which are *likely* if the premises are true, and are binding on us because of our interest in the truth. But, again, this fact—if it is a fact—could not account for the bindingness of such principles of inference unless it were at least believed by us. Again, purely irrational belief would hardly do; and the contention that the belief is pragmatically justified by its fitting the course of our experience depends upon the prior acceptance of principles of non-deductive inference, without which the course of experience could justify nothing. Perhaps even more clearly, the belief that inductive arguments (across the whole of time past, present, and future) yield conclusions that are *likely* to be true provided their premises are is not the sort of belief one can simply see to be true. Unless, of course, one just means by 'likely to be true', 'supported by inductive argument', which would render the claim trivial and incapable of providing a factual basis for accepting the principles of inductive argument. In this case, it looks less attractive, even at first sight, to say that the belief is self-justifying or requires no justification; it is more immediately obvious than it was in the case of the laws of logic that whatever justification it has must lie in our acceptance of the principle of induction itself, and of analogous principles of inference.

So it cannot be true of the non-logical principles of inference, any more than it is true of the laws of logic, that they owe their force to facts about the results they yield. The situation can perhaps be seen more clearly if we ask what these facts could be anyway. If the idea were that they are simply facts about all the *actual* uses of particular types of argument in the past, present, and future, the status of these laws would be just the same as that of a principle licensing all arguments which conclude 'Mrs Thatcher was Prime Minister of Great Britain in 1989', whatever their premisses may be: no argument of *that* type will ever take one from true premisses to a false conclusion. Normally when we think of our principles of inference as valid we are claiming more for them than this: we think they are *reliable* in getting us to the truth, which is quite different from simply knowing that on all or most of the finite number of occasions on which they are actually used they do yield the right results. But it is not clear that their being *reliable* is any sort of fact about the world at all. It might be equated with the conclusion's following from the premisses, or being supported by them, but that is just another way of saying that the laws of pure reason license the inference, and it adds nothing further.

Providing any further elucidation is notoriously difficult, but it would seem that a necessary condition of getting any further— very probably not a sufficient condition—is that we should extend our consideration from actual cases of true premisses and true conclusions, to include all sorts of possible cases as well. In the case of logical laws at least, we could then say that the relevant fact is that in all *possible* circumstances, or in all possible worlds, the conclusion is true if the premisses are. This would be enough to differentiate the laws of logic from principles of the artificial type just specified, for although in the actual world these have a true conclusion there are possible worlds in which Mrs Thatcher was not Prime Minister in 1989. A difficulty arises however when we ask what 'all possible worlds' is supposed to include. If it were to include self-contradictory worlds, for example, it would seem no argument would turn out valid, not even the argument from $p$ to $p$, since in a self-contradictory world the truth of $p$ as premiss would not exclude its being untrue as conclusion. But it is often said that self-contradictory worlds are not possible worlds, and can therefore be left aside. If by 'possible worlds' we mean 'logically possible worlds', we are allowing as possible just those worlds admitted as such by our rules of deductive inference, that is, by just those principles like *modus ponens* whose validity we were attempting to explicate. It will hardly do to say that the validity of *modus ponens* consists in the fact that it always takes one from true premisses to true conclusions in all those worlds in which it takes one from true premisses to true conclusions.

An alternative view, which is perhaps David Lewis's,[9] is that we do not have to define 'all possible worlds' in this way. It is simply a matter of fact what possible worlds there are, and a rule of deductive inference is valid just in case it always leads from true premisses to true conclusions in every one of them. I would concede that if this view were correct there might indeed be facts of the kind we are looking for. But the epistemological problem of how we could ever know about all these worlds would remain insurmountable. We could not conceivably know, or have any reason to believe, that the laws of logic hold in every one of these worlds (since this is no longer simply a matter of stipulation); and it may also be asked how we could know anything at all about these possible worlds, or what ground we could have for thinking they exist.

The problem is even greater with the principle of induction. Here the premisses do not guarantee the truth of the conclusion, but it will not do to say instead that *most* uses of the principle in conjunction with true premisses give true conclusions, because if we confine ourselves to actual uses we shall again fail to capture the sense in which the principle is held to be reliable. Indeed, it may well not be true that most actual uses of it do yield the right results: induction does sometimes let us down, and there is no reason why it might not turn out that over the whole range of actual uses of the principle, past, present, and future, it gave us the right results less often than it let us down. It could be held that if we considered not just the actual uses of the principle, but all the possible uses of it, the majority of them must yield the right results. But since there are infinitely many possible uses which yield the wrong results, and infinitely many which yield the right results, this does not seem to make very much sense. What we think, of course, is that the premisses make the conclusion *likely*, but in calling it likely we are just reflecting the fact that the principle of induction is in force as a law of pure reason. If we meant anything other than that, it would have to be that an objective relation of likelihood obtains between the propositions constituting the premisses and the proposition constituting the conclusion. Again it is difficult to see what this real relation between propositions could amount to, besides how it could be known.

---

[9] D. Lewis, *Counterfactuals* (Oxford, 1973), 84–91.

We have been considering the suggestion that the laws of pure theoretical reason are not metaphysically ultimate, because their force derives from facts about the way the world is, together with a desire that we commonly have to get at the truth. The suggestion has turned out to be unsatisfactory because we could not be justified in believing the relevant facts obtained, and because there is good reason to doubt whether the world is like that anyway. It may still be argued, however, that these laws are at any rate not objective, in the sense I have been claiming for them: independent of anything that people think or feel about them. (In which case, of course, they could not be metaphysically ultimate either.) This objection may be encouraged by the thought that they are prescriptive, and many philosophers have felt there is some serious difficulty in saying that a principle can be both objective *and* prescriptive.

This difficulty has usually been raised in the context of the moral law, and the most familiar expression of it is Mackie's 'argument from queerness', to the effect that such laws would have to be 'entities or qualities or relations of a very strange sort, utterly different from anything else in the universe'.[10] If this 'argument' had any force, it would apply just as much to the principles of logical and inductive inference, conceived as objective prescriptions, as to the moral law.

As it stands, to call it an argument at all is rather overdoing things, since it would seem perfectly possible just to accept that such laws *are* utterly different from anything else in the universe. One could add that it is not very surprising that the universe should contain entities of utterly different kinds. But many people do feel that Mackie is obscurely pointing to a more genuine difficulty, which I think must be this. To say that a law is prescriptive is to say that anyone who is aware of it will necessarily be motivated to follow it (even though the motivation may not always be strong enough to overcome countervailing motivations.) To say it is objective is to say it holds independently of what anyone may think or feel about it. But these two things are not obviously consistent. For if it is an essential feature of these laws that they motivate people, how can they be independent of what people

---

[10] J. L. Mackie, *Ethics* (Harmondsworth, 1977), 38; and on this see further my 'The Rational Imperative'.

think or feel about them? It would seem that there is a necessary relation between the law's holding, and the motives that people feel.

The answer is that the laws motivate only those who are aware of them. It may be that everyone actually is aware of them, but the laws would still be there even if no one was, and even if no one existed. They are there, because they are metaphysically ultimate constituents of the universe; they differ from certain other constituents of the universe, like physical things or persons, in that it is impossible to be aware of them without being motivated by them. But (one may still ask) how can this be? If they obtain in their own right, is it not up to me what attitude I take towards them, if indeed I take any? This may be true in the case of physical things and persons, but it is not true in the case of laws. It is of course true that it is up to me what I actually *do*—whether I actually follow them or not; for I may have countervailing motivations. But it is not up to me whether or not I am motivated by them.

Still, if the laws are objective, it must be possible for me to be mistaken about them. One of the marks of objectivity is that mistakes are possible, for there is always a logical gap between something objective and my judgement about it or my attitude towards it. Mistakes about the *content* of laws are familiar and not (in this context) problematic: mistakes about what the laws of logic are, or what the proper principles of scientific inference may be, are put right through systematic reflection and discussion with others, and it may be—though it is a large issue—that mistakes about the content of the moral laws can be put right in a somewhat similar way. But must it not be equally possible to be aware of these laws without being in any way motivated by them?

It is tempting to say that their prescriptive character is so central to them that one could not properly be said to be aware of *them* without being motivated. Just to say that would risk resting too much on what is essentially a verbal point, a point about whether one should be said to be 'aware of' a law if one were aware of it as a *possible* rule without being in any way motivated to follow it. What really matters is that one cannot be aware of these laws *as they themselves are* without being motivated by them, because their prescriptivity is an intrinsic feature that they themselves possess. It is because they are as they are, and not because we are as we are, that they are binding. Kant put it by saying they are binding 'not merely for men, but for all *rational beings as such*': that is just his way of stressing that their bindingness is not dependent on 'the contingent conditions of humanity'.[11]

Of course one thing is relevant about human nature. It is relevant that we are, in Kant's sense, rational beings, which means something like: beings capable of apprehending the laws of pure reason, and of following them (or, where there are countervailing motives, failing to follow them). The important thing is that if we apprehend them properly—if we apprehend them for what they are—it does not depend on us whether or not we are motivated by them. Any other rational being, however differently constituted, would be motivated by them too. In just the same way, to say that something's squareness or mass is an objective property is to say it is a property that it has independently of what anyone thinks or feels about it, which means that any rational being, however differently constituted from us, would apprehend it as square or as having mass, if he apprehended its nature accurately.

So much for the objection that a principle *cannot* be both objective and prescriptive. But the reply may serve to sharpen a doubt whether these principles actually *are* objective. After all, why should we think that whatever motivation *we* may feel to obey these laws would similarly be felt by any rational being? Short of finding Martians or other alien beings differently constituted from ourselves it would seem impossible to put it to the test. But the same difficulty faces the idea that we are aware of anything that is genuinely objective at all—shape, or mass, or anything else. And although we may be prepared to concede that colours are not objective in this sense, being not independent of sensory reactions which may be specifically human, we do normally think that we are also aware of things and properties that are fully objective and independently real.

Could we be wrong to think this? I have, after all, been referring to Kant a good deal, and Kant's own view of shape and mass, and even of space and time and the whole spatio-temporal world as we know it, is that it is *not* independent of cognitive capacities that may indeed be specifically human. The spatio-temporal world, as

---

[11] Kant, *Groundwork of the Metaphysics of Morals*, 2nd edn., pp. 28 f.; Ak. 4. 408 (H. J. Paton's translation, *The Moral Law*, 3rd edn. (London, 1953) gives these paginations in the margins).

we know it through the senses and through the discoveries of
physical science, is then objective only in a weaker sense: instead
of being independent of what anyone may think or feel about it,
it is common to all human beings and shared amongst them, and
so independent of what any particular one of us may think (which
is why any of us may from time to time get aspects of it wrong).
This is not the place to launch into a discussion of Kant's
metaphysics, but it is worth observing that he himself considered
no coherent account could be given of the world as we know it
without the admission that we must recognize at least *something*
as independently real and objective in the full sense. I think he was
right about this, and I have tried to argue it in another context.[12]
But if anybody thinks that perhaps there is *nothing* we can recognize as fully objective, as being thus or so independently of
what anyone thinks or feels about it, I cannot refute their position
here, and I cannot satisfy them that there are laws that have this
status. Theirs is not an unintelligible or an indefensible view; but
it is a strange one.

To get further we must again strengthen the premiss from which
our transcendental argument is to start. What we had before was
just that we are aware of the content of at least some thoughts and
sense-experiences, and are capable of recognizing the force of
argument. We must add that we are able to recognize some sort
of reality which is fully objective (whether or not it includes familiar properties like shape and mass). We must be able to recognize
it, in the sense that we must be capable of having some beliefs
about it which are rationally grounded. This is a more controversial claim, but it is one which I think most philosophers and most
ordinary people are prepared to grant—even, to regard as obvious. They think we can have a reasonable belief in such a reality,
even though the reasons available to support it may not be conclusive. If they are right, we must be aware of laws that are fully
objective. For what is needed to make our belief reasonable is a
recognition of just such laws.

Suppose we are aware of some objective state of affairs $Q$. $Q$
can be this desk's having a certain shape; or it can be the existence
of somebody else's mind; or it can be the existence of Kant's
things as they are in themselves. Now we might be aware of $Q$

---

[12] *The Coherence Theory of Truth* (London, 1989), ch. 4.

directly, as some people think we are directly aware of the sizes and shapes of things, or we might be aware of it indirectly, through receiving sensory information which we interpret as giving us evidence that this is the case. If we are aware of $Q$ indirectly, then our acceptance of $Q$ must be based on principles of inference which we accept as reliable guides to the truth—reliable guides to the way things objectively are. And even if we are aware of $Q$ directly, there is nothing in the immediate consciousness of $Q$, just by itself, which can assure us that $Q$ is an objective state of affairs; for that we have to rely on principles of inference as well. We may not do this consciously, but when we think about the matter it is clear that it is only by relying on principles of inference, accepted as reliable guides to the truth, that we can justify thinking that $Q$ is objectively the case, and not just a feature of our own immediate awareness. So either way our acceptance of $Q$ as an objective state of affairs depends on our acceptance of certain principles of inference; and these will have to include the basic laws of logical and non-logical inference.

If these laws are to do what is required of them—that is, to provide us with grounds for belief in the objectivity of $Q$, even if not conclusive grounds—it cannot be that their appeal as laws is due only to the psychological constitution of our particular species, for if that were so it would be a mistake to claim that they provide *grounds*: they would merely seem, to people appropriately constituted, to do that. There is only one way to avoid this conclusion, but it is one we have already found to be untenable. It could be suggested that our acceptance of these laws, our readiness to follow them, is indeed something peculiar to our species, or perhaps even to subgroups within it—but that they do nevertheless provide grounds for belief in the objectivity of $Q$, just because of the *fact* that they provide reliable guides to the truth. This suggestion we saw reason to reject, mainly because the belief in their reliability could have no rational basis unless it were derived from accepting the laws themselves, though partly too because it seemed very doubtful whether there was any such *fact* as the one just cited.

We must, then, accept such laws, as objective prescriptions, if we are to have grounds for believing in the objectivity of anything. This is not deeply surprising, for to say that one is justified in believing anything is to say that, in the circumstances, one *ought* to believe it, or that one is entitled to believe it—no one ought to dispute one's right to. It suggests a further question, though: how are these objective prescriptions themselves justified? If a reasonable belief must have grounds, surely the reasonable acceptance of a prescription—the acceptance of it as an *objective* prescription—must have grounds too; what can they be?

If what has just been said is correct, the only grounds there could be for accepting a law as objective would have to be provided through our acceptance of other laws, or perhaps that same law itself, as objective. For we have just seen that the acceptance of such laws is needed in order for us to have grounds for accepting the objectivity of anything. This means that although the attempt to provide a justification for, say, a specific logical law might avoid circularity, because it might show how that law was derived from others or supported by them, the *general* enterprise of providing grounds for these laws will be bound to be circular in the sense that it must presuppose their validity. But that does not mean that there is anything wrong with it. It is, of course, just the argument that I have been trying to give: a transcendental argument, to the effect that we must recognize laws that are objectively valid if we are to have justified objective beliefs. The argument is obviously circular in a sense, but circularity is by itself no defect in an argument. It is a defect in an argument only if the premisses are disputed, or the principles of inference on which the argument turns. In the present case, as with transcendental arguments generally, these are not likely to be disputed very seriously by most people, so that the accusation of circularity amounts to the observation that the conclusion just makes explicit what had already been (perhaps only implicitly) accepted. But to say that is to say that the argument is sound.

Beyond this no further justification of these laws, and their objective status, is either possible or necessary; except in one respect. We can seek to show that they are consistent with one another. I have not tried to do that here, for it would involve an investigation of just what the laws are, and that I have been trying to avoid. If they turned out, for example, to be inevitably inconsistent, their claim to objectivity would have to be given up—and so would any claim to have justified beliefs about an objective world. But beyond showing them to be consistent, there is nothing more that can be done in their defence, and nothing more that can intelligibly be asked for. Any further justification would inevitably presuppose these laws themselves.

This may seem to be unsatisfactory, but it is not really so. The apparent unsatisfactoriness is due to wishing we could find an argument that starts from no assumptions and takes nothing for granted at all. The method of transcendental argument derives from the recognition that this wish is empty. What one must start from are premises and principles of inference that will not seriously be disputed by the people one is interested in arguing with.

I have not claimed to refute those who, while allowing that we are aware of the content of at least some thoughts and sense-experiences, and are capable of recognizing the force of argument, nevertheless refuse to admit that we are aware of a reality that is objective in the sense of being fully independent of what anyone thinks or feels about it. This is not because I think that task impossible, but because the task is a large one, and has been largely discussed. I have tried to carry it through myself else-where.[13] On the other hand anyone who doubts even that we are sometimes aware of the content of our thoughts and sense-experiences does not need refutation, and is not open to it, since he will concede nothing that would allow an argument to get going. In the same way anyone who refuses to admit the force of argument can be convinced of nothing—but this is something that need not disturb us.

To refuse to admit we can ever be justified in any of our beliefs would be tantamount to refusing to admit the force of argument; for a justified belief is one that can be supported by argument. There are philosophers who take this line, thinking that our idea of justification is an illusion; but one must ask how much they are really claiming. If they are seeking to reject the idea of argument altogether, then nothing can constitute an argument for their position, nor will they ever admit anything as an argument against it; rightly, for no argument can be produced against it, without already presupposing by its use the possibility of argument. If, more moderately, their claim is that we commonly misconceive what justification and argument involve, and that the truth of the matter is just that we regularly approve of certain of those sets of statements that we call 'arguments', and disapprove of others,

---

[13] In *The Coherence Theory of Truth*.

then they need to be taken more seriously. They cannot of course claim that their position is justified, in the sense of 'justified' which they are rejecting, but they can claim that there are 'arguments' which lead to it and which are of the types that people approve of. But the question must then be, how much they are really denying. They accept that arguments are guided by principles, and that these principles constitute standards for their assessment. What they are denying is that these standards are objective: on their view, they are just standards we happen to approve of. In that case, though, it is worth noticing that if they tried to provide an argument for believing there are objective states of affairs (of any kind) the argument would have to be, by their own standards, a bad one. This may not disturb them—they may regard argument as inappropriate in such a context. But if they did provide an argument, it would have to be one of a kind we *dis*approve of. For it leads to a conclusion about how things objectively are, but does so by relying on principles of inference which are not reliable guides to the truth but merely principles we happen to like. An argument of this sort is clearly not one that we approve of.

The laws on which we rely must be objective as well as prescriptive. They must also be metaphysically ultimate. If they were not, then in view of their prescriptivity they would have to be dependent either on attitudes of our own (which could serve to motivate us) or else on matters of fact to which we have attitudes. The former possibility denies their objectivity, and we have just rejected it. The only version of the latter that has any plausibility is the suggestion discussed earlier on, that they hold in virtue of the fact that sticking to them provides results that are likely to be true, coupled with a concern on our part to get at the truth. This was also rejected, on the grounds that even if there are such facts we have no reason to believe there are; and a parallel argument could be employed against any other version of the proposal.

Since they are metaphysically ultimate, we must conclude that there is more in the universe than a thoroughgoing materialism could permit. A thoroughgoing materialism I take to be committed to the thesis that everything there is is material, including therefore matter itself (to which may by courtesy be added energy, and perhaps anti-matter and negative matter as well), material properties, and relations which may obtain between material entities with such properties (including no doubt spatio-temporal relations). It would be committed also to holding that there are no other entities of any kind, unless they can be shown to be reducible to, or perhaps in some weaker sense dependent on, these material entities, properties, and relations. Of course any adequate analysis of what this involves would require an examination of what makes a thing or property 'material'. But without carrying out such an analysis it is clear enough that objective laws cannot count as such. And objective laws which are metaphysically ultimate cannot be reducible to, nor in any appropriate sense dependent on, what is material.

If besides these laws there are beings capable of acting on them, then whether or not these beings can themselves be called material things there must be something in their behaviour which cannot be fully explained in material terms. For it has to be explained by reference to these objective laws. It might be appropriate to use the word 'persons' to describe beings capable of acting from objective laws—amongst which one might wish to include the moral law, though that is another story. There are then (at least) two types of entity in the universe not accounted for by the thoroughgoing materialist: laws, and persons capable of following them.

An objection might be made to this last conclusion. It might be held that there are no 'persons' in this sense, but that the arguments we use are still valid arguments, because (as Kant put it) we act *in accordance with* the laws but not *for the sake of* the laws. This could not rescue the materialist, for the objectivity of the laws would remain, but in any case the objection is of much the same kind as one we have just considered. It would allow the conclusions people draw to be supported by their arguments, and it would allow that their claims about objective states of affairs could be justified by the evidence adduced in support of them. Our beliefs could be justified; but we could never know that they were. For to know that they are is to know that there is an objectively valid inference that supports them.

One might reply to this by asking whether it really matters, if our beliefs are in fact justified: indeed, why not admit that we can know that they are, if we believe that they are, and our belief is both true and supported by arguments which are in fact valid? Nothing much hangs on the use of the word 'know', but if the reply were correct we should have no reason to believe that state of affairs obtained. We should only be proceeding mechanically, or in computer fashion, in accordance with the laws, and our doing so would be due not to a recognition of the laws themselves but to some other cause. So far as we ourselves were concerned, we should be arguing in accordance with principles we just happened to hold, and not on principles which we held because they were right. Arguments founded on principles we just happen to hold, or just happen to approve of, do not provide us with adequate standards of justification *by the standards* that they themselves set.

The reason that what I have just said may seem unconvincing is that we tend to assume that the principles by which we argue are not principles we just *happen* to hold; we assume that we hold them because they are likely to yield truth. But if it is the case that their truth-relatedness somehow explains our holding them, the explanation can take one of two forms. Either it must make reference to the objective laws themselves; and if the objective laws enter into the explanation, we have to take account of them in explaining our behaviour, in the way the thoroughgoing materialist was unwilling to do. Or else it is not the laws themselves which explain our holding them, but some matter of fact. If the matter of fact were that they had proved successful in the limited range of cases in which we had used them in the past, this would provide no reason for thinking them likely to yield truth in new instances (since the principle of induction itself, or something like it, is one of the principles in question), and our propensity to think them so would be no more than irrational habit. The suggestion must therefore be that the matter of fact is just that these principles are indeed likely, quite generally, to yield the truth. But we have found reason to think that there is no such matter of fact.

The argument of the last few paragraphs is intended to be somewhat tentative. The issues that it raises are too large to be fully dealt with at the end of a paper that has already grown too long. If it is successful, it shows, against the materialist, that the world includes persons, beings capable of acting from objective laws which they recognize as such, and whose behaviour therefore requires reference to these laws for its full explanation. But even if it is not successful, it remains true that there must *be* objective laws, entities for which there would be no place in a thoroughly materialist universe.

# 4

# Actions, Causes, and Mental Ascriptions

*Grant Gillett*

One of the pivotal axioms of a physicalist theory of mind is that actions are caused by physical events and explained by laws of causality. Indeed, if this were abandoned then physicalist theory could supply no explanation for human behaviour. Davidson has challenged physicalist theories of mind on this basis. However, he claims that mental events are, in some sense, supervenient upon the physical events denoted by mental ascriptions, and while arguing for the irreducibility of mental ascriptions, he also espouses a causal theory of action: 'the primary reason for an action is its cause.'[1] I will argue, by using Kant's analysis of action, that causality as normally understood has no place in mental explanation. This tends to undermine the (Humean) assumption that there are causally effective mental events and that actions are produced by causal impulses.

## i. Kant on Mental Explanation[2]

Both scientific and logical thought are rule-governed activities and obey norms of rationality. The same norms govern the mental ascriptions which explain actions. The rule-governed nature of thought is most evident in the concepts which give thoughts their content.

The use of a concept is grounded on a restricted range of connections between different experiences; one cannot, for instance,

---

[1] D. Davidson, *Essays on Actions and Events* (Oxford, 1980), 12. (Henceforth referred to as *EAE*.)

[2] Throughout I will use the form B 000 to refer to the relevant pages of *The Critique of Pure Reason*.

apply the concept ⟨square⟩³ to a range of items on the basis that they share the same colour, one must make judgements about their shapes. The rules governing thought also determine which inferences should be made on the basis of concept use; for instance, they disallow transitions in thought such as ⟨that is a tree⟩ → ⟨therefore that eats meat⟩ → ⟨that might even be made of ice⟩.⁴ Thus we could say that "oughts" both operate at a fundamental level, determining the conditions which warrant a judgement that things are thus and so (or that a certain concept is instanced), and also govern what it would be right to conclude from certain premises and, indeed, how one should act given certain desires and beliefs. Because a train of thought must obey these constraints it cannot follow any old disposition caused by the occurrent inputs to a subject's mind. This implies that, *qua* rational subject, the human thinker is not merely the locus of a set of dispositions obeying causal laws but is also subject to rational constraints.

Kant expresses this feature of "mental acts" as follows: '[Reason] . . . views its objects exclusively in the light of ideas' (B 575). He argues that thoughts are free from causal compulsion by antecedent physical events because reasoning should be and is guided by what compels 'in the light of ideas' through their rational force and not just by what the subject is disposed to do. Therefore he rejects the Humean reading of practical reason whereby actions result from the causal or motive force of passions. Wolff remarks,

on Kant's view, the paradigmatic case of rational action is a case in which; first, I form a concept of some event, object, or state of affairs which I choose to bring into being; and second, I do something which I believe will actualize that which my concept represents. In short, I act so as to realize my end. When I thus act I am moved by thoughts. But I am moved by my thoughts qua representations having cognitive significance, not by thoughts qua mental events having temporal location and, hence, phenomenal causes and effects.⁵

---

³ ⟨ ⟩ indicates an element in mental life which may or may not be expressed by or correspond to an expression in a natural language.

⁴ Of course one could work very hard to fit a plausible story around this skeleton, but it would take some work to meet the intuitive norms of coherence that we use to judge mental ascriptions.

⁵ R. P. Wolff, *The Autonomy of Reason* (York, 1973), 111. For the expression 'cognitive significance' it would be fair to read 'conceptual/inferential role', and thus exhibit the obvious link to rationality. Note that this does not carry all the connotations of Frege's "sense", although it is obviously connected to it.

Some commentators, while conceding that thoughts explain actions on the basis of content and that content is not easily reduced to physical specifications, still argue that a thought, as it affects behaviour, is the thought of a physical being at a given point of time and therefore that thoughts are, in principle, tied to spatio-temporal conditions. But this merely places the thought as an explanatory entity in the mind of a member of the kingdom of rational beings (who may not be spatio-temporally individuated[6]).

Kant claims that human beings are active in the world; on the basis of rational/mental determinations, they decide and intend that things are or should be thus and so. Their thoughts and actions draw on concepts, which are governed by rules both in their applications and their conceptual connections within the (rationally structured) realm of 'ideas'. Therefore thoughts are regulated by prescriptive norms or 'norms for persons to follow'.[7] These rules (to be followed and not merely conformed to) apply to judgements about the contents of experience—that this or that is red, square, moving, impenetrable, and so on. Such judgements structure all one's understanding of the world and, thus, the basis on which one formulates reasons for action. Therefore reasons embed prescriptive norms governing the concepts in which they are framed and do not merely result from causal effects of input to the mind giving rise to dispositions.

The claim that subjects of experience, *qua* rational beings, have thoughts which obey "oughts" and are not merely conditioned by causal input looks more secure when we consider the normative properties of mental contents.

*First*, a subject's knowledge of his own judgements, unlike his knowledge of physical events, is not derived from sensory impressions. It is a feature of intentional activity that one "knows what one is doing" non-observationally and non-inferentially. My

---

[6] We should always read Kant as arguing about the nature of an item as located in some context of description, and thus the propriety of speaking of it in certain ways is always relativized to a certain type of discourse. He discusses conditions of individuation and modes of explanation considered in the light of their conceptual foundations and resists the simplistic idea that any event is 'at bottom' of this or that metaphysical type. Therefore metaphysical properties, for Kant, are reflections of the structure of our knowledge about phenomena of a given type. An ontology, for Kant, is always a connected set of knowledge claims and not a realm of objects and properties existing independent of all discourse.

[7] C. Peacocke, *Thoughts: An Essay on Content* (Oxford, 1986), 51–2.

descriptions of my own thought and action are immune to certain
types of error to which empirical knowledge is prone. My thoughts
about empirically known facts may be mistaken because my senses
are defective, because I apply the wrong concepts, or because I
apply concepts to a situation in a way different from any other
right-thinking rational subject.[8] But it is nonsensical to suggest
that I do not—in general and essentially—know which concepts I
am using when I think this or that (or when I intend to act thus
or so). If I were in doubt about which concepts I was using, then
I could not make any judgements at all. Thus one's knowledge of
oneself as judging that '*a* is *F*' is prior to and a universal presupposition of one's knowledge that '*a* is/is not *F*', just as one's
knowledge of oneself as intending to $\alpha$ is prior to and a universal
presupposition both of acts of $\alpha$-ing or any subsequent judgements
about them (e.g. as to whether they are prudent or in accord with
duty).

This is relevant to action because it implies that the agent knows
what he is doing (as he knows of his other mental acts) in a special
way. An action, we could say, is a bodily movement intended to
realize some conception. The conception makes it an action rather
than just a bodily movement or automatism (which may be sufficiently complex to resemble an action, even though unconscious[9]).
Thus what the subject conceives of himself as doing is part of any
adequate action explanation. And he has knowledge of this (it is,
after all, *his* conception which constitutes it as an action) in a way
quite unlike his knowing about any causal or physical event that
happens to or in him.

Thus there is an epistemological reason to doubt that the mental
ascriptions explaining actions denote causes which are independent
of the effects they produce and known about empirically like other
identifiable events.

*Second*, Kant claims that the *subject* "synthesizes" the contents
of experience by using concepts which unify different representations in accordance with rules for judgement. In applying a concept,

---

[8] Kant mentions this intersubjective condition for knowledge at B 848, but, as
far as I know, never develops it.

[9] e.g. a patient suffering temporal lobe epilepsy may perform an automatism
which only an experienced observer would distinguish from an action until it
emerged that the subject had no conception of doing anything at the time of the
activity, and indeed when tested may well be insensitive.

one judges that some aspect of this experience is the same (in ways determined by that concept) as an aspect of some other experience.[10] On this reading (Strawson's), acts of synthesis "subsume" experience under concepts. But one can also read "synthesis" as the selection or collation of just the information relevant to a given perceptual judgement. This is a pervasive feature of thoughts because a subject must selectively attend to those features of experience that warrant the application of a given concept in order to use that concept correctly.[11] "Synthesis" in the latter sense (assembly of the elements of present experience so as to discern the conditions which warrant the use of a concept) is a skill. It may be automatic but becomes a conscious, reason-governed exercise at times (e.g. 'Is that really a dog?'). These times make evident the underlying prescriptive features governing our judgements ('Am I right to judge this as being so?').

*Third*, Kant believed that a human subject as *agent*, could, in principle, act on the basis of reason alone, and thus that action differed from the causal production of events.

For a will is sensuous in so far as it is 'pathologically affected' i.e. by sensuous motives; it is animal . . . if it can be pathologically necessitated. The human will is certainly an *arbitrium sensitivum* not however *brutum* but *liberum*. For sensibility does not necessitate its action. There is in man a power of self-determination, independently of any coercion through sensuous impulses. (B 562)

This embodies an important claim about thought and action, least contentious in relation to thought. We have noted that one can go right or wrong in applying a concept, and that therefore a subject must judge whether the use of a concept in a given situation is appropriate rather than merely emitting a response on the basis of his disposition. One can respond to a situation as being thus and so but can also, in principle, ask 'Is this how it really is?'. For Kant, such judgements about experience are governed by rules (of the understanding) and are not merely reactions of or effects on the sensuous mind.

[10] This is Strawson's reading of 'synthesis' as subsumption of a particular under a general concept (P. F. Strawson, *Bounds of Sense* (London, 1976), 31–2).
[11] On this see my 'The Generality Constraint and Conscious Thought', *Analysis*, 47 (1987), 20–4; 'Learning to Perceive', *Philosophy and Phenomenological Research*, 48 (1988), 601–18; or *Representation, Meaning and Thought* (Oxford, 1992).

Actions are also subject (in principle) to rational scrutiny. One can always ask of oneself, 'But is this what I really want to do?' or 'Is this what reason tells me to do in this circumstance?'.[12] Thus there are, in a human being as rational agent, powers of self-censure, self-correction, and therefore self-determination which characterize mental content and the intentional activity it informs.

This feature of intentional behaviour means that an action can be understood only if one asks 'What was the reasoning behind this action?'. Kant remarks 'in our judgements in regard to the causality of free actions, we can get as far as the intelligible cause, but not beyond it' (B 585). Even when we discern antecedents other than the rational determinants of human action, we recognize that it is the reasons or conception behind the action that individuate it as being the action that it is. And a subject's reasons are formed 'in the light of ideas', not merely as a result of that subject being causally acted upon. Thus Kant also claims that practical reason is, in principle, subject to a *moral* "ought". One ought to act thus rather than so because it is in one's nature to obey rules and among the rules that we obey, there are moral rules which, for Kant, derive from the supreme (purely rational) imperative.

*Fourth*, whereas thoughts essentially have a rule-governed structure, causal transactions are essentially tied to spatio-temporal conditions. If $Y$ is asked to add $5 + 7$ and he gets 12, the spatio-temporal context of these elements plays no part in the mental operation performed. $Y$ should derive the answer, 12, regardless of empirical facts about the presentation of the problem in experience. Even when a thinker applies an empirical concept like ⟨dog⟩ to present experience, he does not do so purely for extensionally specifiable reasons. The bit of the world which counts as a dog is fixed by the fact that the application of the concept is warranted in a restricted range of conditions. In fact, as Kant recognizes, the entire structure of experience is rule-governed.

If $B$ perceives a chestnut shattered by a hammer then, for Kant, the structure and content of that event and the possibility of its

---

[12] I think this is close to what H. Frankfurt discusses in 'Freedom of the Will and the Concept of a Person', *Journal of Philosophy*, 68 (1971), 5–20, as an essential feature of persons.

representation as an event essentially depend on the way that *B* synthesizes it in space and time according to the laws of causality. The shattering of the chestnut as a perceived event is therefore determined by (rational) laws governing synthesis in space and time and cannot be understood apart from them. Those laws, even though they relate to spatio-temporal conditions, are part of the understanding and, according to Kant, not themselves a causally produced set of phenomena.

With mental phenomena, the analysis is more complex. Rufus discovers a piece of cheese and feels hungry. Now, his state is essentially time-related to food and eating but is also conceptualized. Without the constitutive temporal and causal relations it would not be hunger (hunger could not, for instance, be produced by imagining that one hears a wolf howling on a dark night); but one cannot fit the concept ⟨hunger⟩ to the experience without obeying rules which warrant that judgement. Thus the inner state is essentially causally and temporally conditioned, but is known as being the state it is on quite other grounds.

The thrust of Kant's argument is that the human agent has a stream of thoughts and attitudes which concern spatio-temporal events but, *qua* subject of experience, she applies to these acts and events concepts which obey the dictates solely of "ideas". Indeed, she structures her experience by 'acts and inner determinations which cannot be regarded as impressions of the senses' or mere causal effects of environmental conditions. The distinction between such inner determinations and physical events is evident in the subject's non-empirical knowledge of her mental contents and propositional attitudes, the fact that mental acts embed prescriptive norms, the fact that one has a normative attitude to one's own thoughts, and the fact that spatio-temporal antecedents do not fix mental contents.

There are two final points worth noting in Kant's approach to physical events, causality, and the mind.

A material object or event is individuated by spatio-temporal properties. But the essential properties of thoughts are inferential and representational. Thus thoughts are metaphysically different from properties or states of material objects which obey causal laws. As objects in an objective and causally ordered world, agents conform to causal laws, but thoughts do not obey these laws and thus, *qua* mental subjects, neither do agents.[13]

For Kant, causality 'makes a strict demand that something, *A*, should be such that something else *B* follows from it necessarily and in accordance with an absolutely universal rule' (B 124). Causes therefore determine or 'necessitate' their effects according to empirically discoverable laws of nature. He contrasts this *nomological causality* (which he shares with Davidson) with the 'causality of freedom' by which a series of events is initiated by a mental act or rational determination. Free actions are explained by intelligible causes or mental acts and are 'spontaneous' because they cannot adequately be explained by antecedent causes and the laws governing them.[14] The spontaneity resides in the subject's obeying "oughts" (whether epistemic or moral) in his intentional activity (thus it is not Hume's 'liberty of spontaneity' but is closer to the 'liberty of indifference'). It is best seen as the liberty of rational will to act in accord with rational principles to which it owes essential allegiance. Kant argued that to invoke causal principles in the explanation of free and rational action was to undermine both the validity of reason and the force of the moral "ought" (B 576). Thus a physical condition or affection of a human subject could not *necessitate* an action so as to ground a causal explanation.

Kant's argument against physicalist reductions of mental acts is similar in some respects to Davidson's. Both argue that rationality is an essential property of the mental and that it is irreducible to material/physical terms, but, Davidson, unlike Kant, endorses a causal theory of action.

## ii. Anomalous Monism

Davidson argues that *mental discourse embeds a norm of rationality* and therefore that mental explanation does not conform to

[13] Although Kant regarded it as an objective fact that we were rational subjects of thought, he did not think that the conditions which made that possible could be given by a purely conceptual analysis.

[14] It is of some interest that both Mackie and Von Wright give the causal efficacy of human agency a key place in the epistemology of causal connections. If they are correct then 'the causality of freedom' would be epistemically prior to our apprehension of the nature of all causal relations. But this is not a line that Kant pursues.

physical or functional laws, even though reasons are causes of actions.

Two ideas are built into the concept of acting on a reason (and hence, the concept of behaviour generally): the idea of cause and the idea of rationality. A reason is a rational cause. One way rationality is built in is transparent: the cause must be a belief and a desire in the light of which the action is reasonable. But rationality also enters more subtly, since the way desire and belief work to cause the action must meet further, and unspecified, conditions. The advantage of this mode of explanation is clear: we can explain behaviour without having to know too much about how it was caused. And the cost is appropriate: we cannot turn this mode of explanation into something more like science.[15]

Davidson's theory is as follows.

1. Mental events are picked out by mental terms.[16]

2. Mental explanations and descriptions are holistic in that propositional attitudes (PAs) have constitutive inferential connections to other ascriptions.[17]

3. PAs conform to certain principles of rationality.[18]

4. These principles constrain what counts as an adequate mental explanation.[19]

5. An adequate mental explanation identifies the causes of an action.[20]

6. Where there is a causal connection between two events there is some law which covers the events in question (the nomological character of causality).[21]

7. There are no deterministic causal laws which predict and explain mental events, *qua* mental events.[22]

8. Mental explanation is anomalous and thus irreducible to descriptions within the purview of physical sciences.

9. Mental events interact causally with physical events.

10. The causal connections between mental events hold in virtue of their token identical physical counterparts.

For Davidson, all PAs can be reasons (including beliefs, desires, and intentions). If we express PAs in the notation 'he wants that *X*', 'he believes that *X*', 'he intends that *X*', and so on, then the quasi-logical syllogisms that result assimilate mental explanations to transitions in truth-functional systems. An example might be:

---

[15] *EAE* 233.    [16] *EAE* 211.    [17] *EAE* 221.    [18] *EAE* 231.
[19] *EAE* 9.    [20] *EAE* 4.    [21] *EAE* 208.    [22] *EAE* 216.

(*a*) Tom believes that *A*-ing will get him food;
(*b*) Tom desires that he gets food;
(*c*) Tom does an action he believes to be *A*-ing.

The conclusion of such a practical syllogism (whether it be an action or an intention) may not however, be formally derivable from the premisses without rules such as 'To desire *X* and believe that *A*-ing will give you *X* details that you do something which counts as *A*-ing.' The problem is that such rules are either false or too weak to secure inferential closure in practical syllogisms. Therefore, as Davidson remarks, deductive inferences and lawlike generalizations about behaviour are not to be had,[23] and it seems as if mental explanations appeal to our informal understanding of what it is rational or 'makes sense' for a person to do. He argues that this is because mental ascriptions answer to 'considerations of overall cogency' in which the 'ideal of rationality partly controls each phase of what must be an evolving theory'.[24] Thus mental terms are irreducible to physical terms because they answer different norms and there is no reason to believe (indeed, a positive reason to doubt) that they can be related in lawlike ways.

The intuition that the norms governing mental and physical discourse preclude reduction seems, however, insufficient to deter committed physicalists. One could argue that the messy and anomalous nature of mental laws proves that they are a flawed attempt to explain behaviour. A better account would attend to the underlying physical states and events which mental terms denote. If we understood the relations (which Davidson concedes to be lawlike) between the states denoted by mental terms, then we could discard the misleading and inadequate mental scheme with which we currently work.

Davidson concludes that no clear specification of the causality operative in rational action is possible: 'we cannot hope to define or analyse freedom to act in terms of concepts that fully identify the causal conditions of intentional action',[25] but goes on to claim that 'there is no obstacle to the view that freedom to act is a causal power of the agent' (where a 'causal power' is a property which, under some description, falls under a nomological generalization). However, if mental explanations and the generalizations that they sustain are not lawlike, and the informal knowledge

[23] *EAE* 79.      [24] *EAE* 223.      [25] *EAE* 81.

about people, their wants, beliefs, and actions which we use to make sense of their behaviour draws on a very broad experience including many interactions with and observations of real people, we should be suspicious of the claim that mental terms (replete with all the 'messy' riches and nuances they show) have mechanistic, causal, or impersonal referents.

Davidson, having claimed that mental terms denote the states and events which cause bodily movements, also maintains that causal explanations rest on laws. 'If one event causes another, there is a strict law which those events instantiate when properly described. But it is possible (and typical) to know of the singular causal relation without knowing the law or the relevant descriptions.'[26] The lack of closed/deterministic mental laws implies that the covering laws (in virtue of which mental explanations *are* causal) must be at another level. Therefore mental explanations are causal in virtue of the laws which connect their physical referents. We do not know these laws and they do not bear any systematic relation to the mental explanations with which we are familiar. Thus, there are token–token identities between mental states and events and their physical counterparts, but not the type–type identities required for reductive (psycho-physical) laws to hold. This entails that even though the entities denoted by mental terms are physical events and states of the brain, the mental is not reducible to the physical.

Davidson regards actions as physical events which are picked out by mental descriptions. He supports his token-physicalism and his causal construal of mental explanation by arguing that it yields an account of the operativeness of certain reasons in the explanation of a given action. A mental explanation gives the correct account of the agent's reasons for an action when it picks out the states and events that, on this occasion, causally produce that action. Davidson is therefore open to the criticism that his account of causality (which is nomological) entails that mental explanations are not causal at all. The causal laws which ground the explanatory role of mental ascriptions are connected with their physical referents and not their mental content. It is, therefore, difficult to say just what is meant by the claim that the relations between mental

---

[26] *EAE* 224, 'relevant descriptions' refers to those descriptions that capture the lawlike nomological generalizations, under which the causal connection falls.

content and action are causal. Indeed, the theory as it stands seems to embody an implicit rejection of the inherent explanatory force of mental ascriptions *qua* their mental content.[27]

Further problems attend the supervenience claim. Davidson denies both that mental descriptions confer any explanatory force on the subvenient physical states and that there is any taxonomic congruence between physical states and mental ascriptions. These denials make it quite unclear what the supervenience claim achieves. It cannot introduce causality into the mental connections and it cannot operate by reducing the pattern of connections to dependence on physical laws. We therefore lack an account in which mental terms are both irreducible and genuinely explanatory.

### iii. The Defects of a Causal Account of Action

I have argued that a physicalist could easily refuse to be swayed by the speculative intractability of the norms of rationality and go on to claim that a developed causal theory will supersede mental terminology. The mentalist complaint is that Davidson accounts for the explanatory force of reasons in terms which have nothing to do with their reasonableness. Kant, by contrast, definitely preserves the explanatory force of reason, but identifies defects in the view that it is causal.

### 1. Defects in Connections and Relations

Kant's 'spontaneity' poses a serious challenge to a causal account: 'By freedom . . . I understand the power of beginning a state spontaneously . . . a causality . . . which can therefore begin a series of events entirely of itself' (B 561-2). This apparently implausible libertarian intuition grows more attractive the closer one looks at it.

First, 'making up one's mind' is an essential feature of both practical and theoretical reason.

In respect of aims and ambitions and that which I want to achieve, an uncertainty in giving a correct account . . . usually amounts to an uncer-

---

[27] The argument is summarized by Louise Antony in 'Anomalous Monism and the Problem of Explanatory Force', *Philosophical Review*, 98 (1989), 153-87, but used by her to recommend a functionalist view.

tainty of aim . . . there are many situations in which I do not know which of two things I believe about something and therefore no one else can know what I believe until I make up my mind and thereby come to know what I believe.[28]

Hampshire argues, as does Kant, that in coming to a belief or an intention—in making up his mind in a certain way—a subject has immediate, non-inferential and non-evidential knowledge of his own thoughts.

Second, as noted above, prescriptive norms are implicit in mental ascriptions: 'one cannot infer what one's beliefs are to be, starting from now. Either one already knows, or one has to answer a normative question, to form a belief on the evidences of truth as one takes them to be.'[29] Thus 'acts and inner determinations' (Kant) are essentially reason-governed; they do not just arise within or impinge upon the subject but are 'spontaneous', in the sense that their relation to the concept-using subject is different from that of physical states of affairs.

Third, a *reason* is something I can accept or reject, as I will, and, on that basis, act as I decide is best. Because reasoning is this way, the mental subject (indicated by Kant's 'I think') has an active role in the operation of reasons. The subject *determines* the way that a given reason will guide his conduct; the reason does not mechanically produce a belief or an action but depends for its effect on the way the subject makes up his mind. And, as Hampshire notes, one makes up one's mind in the light of prescriptive norms (or "oughts"—Kant). A *cause*, by contrast, explains events in such a way that rational decision is not required. Indeed, we only understand causal relations in nature when we stop anthropomorphizing them (by invoking djinns, demons, or spirits). Therefore, in contrast to causal explanations which are impersonal, mental explanations are ineliminably personal.[30] Thus the claim that mental ascriptions denote *causes* of action overlooks the requirement that rational subjects should not figure in a genuine causal explanation.

Fourth, Davidson claims that the indeterminacy of rational causes is secured by the *holism of the mental*. Nomological laws cannot

---

[28] S. Hampshire, 'Some Difficulties in Knowing', in T. Honderich and M. Burnyeat, eds., *Philosophy as it is* (Harmondsworth, 1979), 290.

[29] Ibid. 294.

[30] This claim is defended at length in, among other places, P. Winch, *The Idea of a Social Science* (London, 1958).

hold because one must always take account of all the relevant propositional attitudes of the agent. This seems to be more than just a claim about causal complexity or particularity, in that the mental scheme answers to norms of rationality. The state/event descriptions and their assembly into mental explanations are anomalous—they do not form a closed realm of explanation answering only to physical laws. But Davidson claims that this open and 'messy' scheme of explanation is nevertheless causal.

Thus the anomalous monist must provide some conception of the type of causality operating between mental descriptions and ascriptions (which are, *ex hypothesi*, not individuated in terms of spatio-temporal conditions[31]). And the prospects for anomalous causation do not look good. It is not the normal conception of relations between states and events that bases a singular causal explanation (e.g. the brick hit the window), nor is it based on lawlike generalizations. What is more, the fact that it is up to me as agent to determine the effect that conditions have on my behaviour so that they have no moment or vector of efficacy apart from the weight or significance I confer upon them makes it look decidedly unlike any 'kosher' causal account we possess.[32]

Kant agrees; he claims that descriptions of "states", "events", and "causal relations" are ill-grounded in the case of mental ascriptions/rational determinations. These terms all function properly only in relation to spatio-temporally specified objects and events.

## 2. *Defects in Description*

Kant complains that state and event terms are unsuited to the discussion of rational activity because spatio-temporal conditions are irrelevant in the individuation of mental content ascriptions. For instance, a subject can employ the concept ⟨red⟩—or exercise the function of unity among judgements expressed by 'red'—

---

[31] One could say that propositional attitudes are, in general, infected by 'the autonomy of meaning' which Davidson defends in 'Thought and Talk' in his *Inquiries into Truth and Interpretation* (Oxford, 1984).

[32] J. P. Sartre, *Being and Nothingness*, tr. H. E. Barnes (London, 1943), 572. This claim needs to be weakened from any implication of extreme libertarianism by a plausible story about unconscious states (on this see my 'Multiple Personality and the Concept of a Person', *New Ideas in Psychology*, 4 (1986), 178–84).

equally well in the judgements ⟨this is red⟩, ⟨this is not red⟩, ⟨I can imagine a red flag⟩, or ⟨this blue step might have been red⟩. Thus, once one has mastered a concept, its use is not causally tied to any physical state of affairs.

A presupposition of both thought and action is that the thinker is a competent user of the concepts embedded in the mental ascriptions which characterize her activity. This gives us further reason to hold that actions are different in kind from things that just happen. An action is individuated by the conception with which the thinker acts, and the concepts comprising this conception are subject to pervasive prescriptive norms. I have noted that the agent as concept-user is not merely a locus of dispositions but must appreciate that there is a right and wrong way of applying the term 'red' and thus grasp that certain things *count* as being red (i.e. that there are prescriptive norms governing the application of a concept in experience[33]). These prescriptive norms govern both the use of concepts and the formation of beliefs. Thus mental content draws on responses to the world which are essentially not causally produced according to the laws of nature. This, in turn, entails that the dependence of the content of reasons on 'norms for persons to follow'[34] distinguishes reasons from states evoked by certain inputs. Thus we understand human actions as *things we do* when we make sense of them according to the prescriptive norms followed by agents and as *mere things that happen* when we see them as caused events in space and time produced according to physical laws.

We can now assess the idea that causal explanations apply to our actions in virtue of their descriptions in some non-mental— perhaps physical—terminology. It is clear that bodily movements, muscle-cell action patterns, nerve firings, or the motion of molecules and physico-chemical structures in space are all causally explicable, in principle at least. But as such they are not actions; such descriptions do not individuate actions because they make no essential reference to the conceptions of the agent. Physical descriptions and explanations conceptualize the world in ways not adequate to explain meaningful human behaviour. The event and state descriptions of physical theory (or quantification sets

---

[33] On this see P. Pettit, 'The Reality of Rule Following', *Mind*, 99 (1990) 1–21.
[34] Peacocke, *Thoughts*.

of such states) serve our interests in understanding nature as a realm of mechanical and causal relations obeying laws linking spatio-temporal entities. Thus the physical events occurring when I act are not the basis on which rational explanations have coherence and explanatory power; they are merely one way of conceptualizing certain events and do not tell us about the mental activity of human subjects.

Kant argued that 'reason ... must also be described in positive terms as the power of originating a series of events' (B 582), because it involves the reasoned decisions of an agent which obey non-causal rules.[35] He insists that the rational agent is precisely *not* compelled by causal antecedents.

> When we say that in spite of his whole previous course of life the agent could have refrained from lying this only means that the act is under the immediate power of reason, and that reason in its causality is not subject to any conditions of appearance or of time. (B 584)

Kant takes the "ought" (either of morality or thought in general) as further indication of the fact that a lawlike causal connection between events located in space and time does not explain actions. If the content of mental ascriptions is derived from rules followed by thinkers and not dispositions to respond, then the judgements of the agent cannot be eliminated from mental explanation. The fact that judgements (which obey "oughts"—conceptual, mathematical, logical, and moral—and are not fixed by antecedent causes) essentially determine the conceptions according to which one acts, suggests that Kant is right. Mental ascriptions do not denote referents which would also 'fit' descriptions of the type underpinning causal laws.

## iv. An Alternative Account

I have argued that an action can only be explained by the reasons or "rational determinations" of the agent. An action *qua action* does not appear to be the type of thing that could (under any description) be causally explained by antecedent non-mental conditions without overriding the normal constraints on both mental

---

[35] Note that this is a "power of originating" and not an event which is the first of or origin of a series of events.

and physical discourse. This leaves us with two problems for an alternative theory of action:

1. We need a non-causal account which tells us how to pick out the PAs that actually explain a given action.
2. If an action is an event as well as being a mental phenomenon then surely it must fall within the causal nexus.

1. The need to explain the "operativeness" of PAs in a given action-explanation demands that we specify how to decide which reasons are relevant to an agent and why. But this need not (*pace* Hume) begin with the view of an agent as an inert object who must be moved to act. Only in inanimate matter are all changes mere occurrences produced by adequate antecedent causes. The "spontaneity" which characterizes the activity of rational subjects recommends a different view.

Active judgement and the use of concepts are the keys to rational activity, because reasons guide and direct that activity by means of the conceptions that structure it.[36] Actions are differentiated from mere things that happen because the conceptions, inferences, and judgements which make up a subject's reasoning involve rule-following. Therefore 'we can get as far as the intelligible cause, but not beyond it' (Kant), in that rule-following is an intentional activity governed by "oughts" and not merely a set of dispositions.

To explain why certain bodily events count as actions and not mere occurrences (like hair blowing in the wind, legs twitching, or eyes blinking) we show how the activity in question is guided and directed by rational determinations. But this explanatory story does not link what an agent is doing to antecedent spatio-temporal conditions (the conceptions may concern hypothetical or other non-actual situations); the rules governing concept-use link our thoughts to conditions in which various judgements have been warranted. These warrants forge diverse connections between actions and situations and determine how a given content relates to a range of possible conditions. For instance, if I am following someone because I take him to be my brother and then I meet my brother coming the other way, I *ought* to stop following the original man.

[36] I have discussed the implications of this approach for brain science in 'Representations and Cognitive Science', *Inquiry*, 32 (1989), 261–76.

A mental explanation explains behaviour because certain reasons "PAs" are those that the agent adopts as determinants of his activity at a given time. Therefore the agent's commitment to those PAs (which, of course, she may conceal), accounts for their "operativeness" in a mental explanation. They contribute to aberrant mental explanations when she lacks commitment to them as determinants of her behaviour (thus, in Davidson's famous example, the climber feels and is caused to behave by his fear, although he does not endorse it and therefore does not intentionally let his friend fall[37]). Only when we construe reasons as internal causal entities acting to *cause* behaviour or thoughts do we need a causal story about causal operativeness as a principled "moving" of an agent. Thus the motivation for the causal underpinning of operativeness is internal to an impersonal or causal theory of mental content.

I have argued that mental explanations focus on the self-determining agent and her making up of her mind. On this account, her free adoption of and commitment to reasons gives us the only way to account for operativeness that coheres with the rational explanation of behaviour. Thus the principled basis for judging that certain ascriptions are "operative" reasons for an agent's behaviour is that they forge illuminating explanatory links (in terms of the norms governing mental content) between different aspects of the agent's behaviour and the world in which it occurs.[38] For instance, the concept ⟨door⟩ is (prescriptively) tied to a means of entrance to and exit from a space, and we may only be able to explain an agent's behaviour when we realize that he is acting on the judgement that a certain rectangular panel in the wall is a door.

2. Kant remarked, 'Every action, [viewed] as appearance, in so far as it gives rise to an event, is itself an event or happening' (B 571). I have pursued his characterization of action as the 'power of originating a series of events' (B 582), which avoids slipping into a discussion of the actual (physical) event that *is* the action. The term "event" only has meaning when applied to what can be specified spatio-temporally. I would therefore argue that an action is not a physically identifiable event but is a relational description

---

[37] Davidson, *EAE*, 79.
[38] On this see A. Morton, 'Because he Thought he had Insulted him', *Journal of Philosophy*, 72 (1975), 5–15.

of the efficacy of the rational agent in the world. And a mental ascription is not an event or a state, although, when conceived as part of the causal order, the action it causes may begin a sequence of events. When we make mental ascriptions to a subject, we subsume that subject's pattern of relations to her context under a structured set of prescriptive norms. Admittedly, mental content must be ascribed to an identifiable agent before it explains behaviour, but this ascription is to a subject of experience *qua* rational being and not a spatio-temporal object.[39]

## v. Summary

I have used Kant's analysis to explain actions in terms of the rational determinations of a concept-using subject and to attack a causal theory of mental explanation. Kant argues that "oughts" govern mental content and that this (prescriptively) normative feature distinguishes "rational determinations" from things that merely happen according to (descriptive) causal laws. I have developed his claim by appealing to the rules governing concepts as showing that mental ascriptions could not denote causal states antecedent to action.

I have then examined the strongest reconciling thesis (Davidson's) in which a causal theory of action is linked to irreducibility claims about mental content. I have found this account wanting for several reasons:

1. The connections articulating mental explanations are not merely distinct from physical-causal relations (as between spatio-temporally specifiable events) in being non-lawlike, but have a different character altogether in that they involve competence in following prescriptive norms, making up one's mind on the basis of those norms, and they are of a piece with our understanding of persons. Thus action-explanation cannot help itself to the causality operating between spatio-temporal states and events antecedent to an occurrence.

2. Not only do we lack a conception of causality apt for mental explanation but, if we ground rational connections on underlying

---

[39] I have defended this claim in Disembodied Persons', *Philosophy*, 61 (1986), 377–86.

physical states, we are left without an analysis of the explanatory force of mental ascriptions *qua* their mental or reason-giving content.[40]

3. The idea that mental ascriptions denote states which move an agent to act is an inappropriate (Humean) conception based in the principle that subjects are like inanimate objects and must be caused to do what they do. But it is implicit within mental ascriptions that the subjects to whom they apply intentionally follow certain norms in the activity which supports those ascriptions.

A neo-Kantian account contends that the subject is active and that action-explanation reveals the conceptions (and their connections) which form and guide a subject's behaviour. These conceptions are not antecedent productive causes of movements in an impersonal body. Thus mental ascriptions map a person's behaviour onto a framework of rule-governed practices which confer content on the concepts structuring their intentional activity. The network of rule-governed practices normatively relates mental ascriptions to things in the subject's environment and also articulates a subject's activity in different situations. In this way it tells us the conditions to which a subject's behaviour is sensitive in the world in which the agent is acting. Both the structured sensitivity revealed by mental ascriptions and the rule-following implicit within them characterize a human being as a subject whose activity cannot be accommodated within spatio-temporal transactions and causal principles of explanation. Thus physicalist theory is lacking in one of its central desiderata—the provision of an explanation of actions.

[40] This is a conclusion that Davidson might well endorse and retain much of his account. If he tends toward a weak supervenience and a stringent denial of causation as operating between mental ascription *qua* their mental content then he would be a far less appropriate target for my critique than a more pretentious monist, but it would seem that his claims do not tolerate an overly weak reading and that he is not merely a stalking-horse for my theory but indeed one of its quarries.

# 5

# Materialism and the Logical Structure of Intentionality

*George Bealer*

This paper begins with a brief history of the thesis of intentionality and a review of some contemporary views. Following that, we present a problem for materialism that arises in connection with the possibility of a *general* materialist analysis (or reduction) of intentionality: if no such analysis (reduction) is possible, intentional phenomena would have at least one non-physical property, namely, their intentionality—this materialistically unanalysable general property. With this problem in mind, we will then suggest a general analysis of intentionality. We close by arguing that any satisfactory general analysis of intentionality must share a certain central feature with the proposed analysis and that this feature entails the existence of an *objective level of organization* that is non-physical. This is enough to show that the traditional materialist world view is mistaken. One way in which this argument against materialism is novel is that it would go through even if, *per impossibile*, every particular type of mental phenomenon (pain, belief, etc.) had a materialist analysis (reduction).[1]

## i. A Brief History

Contemporary philosophical discussions of intentionality may be traced to the following famous passage by Franz Brentano (1838–1917) in a chapter of *Psychologie vom empirischen Standpunkt* (1874) entitled 'The Distinction Between Mental and Physical Phenomena':

---

[1] Our intention is to use "materialism" in conformity with its traditional meaning. Some contemporary philosophers use the term in a diluted way. In consequence, some of the philosophers who now call themselves 'materialists' might accept the views defended in this paper.

Nonetheless, psychologists of an earlier period have already directed attention to a particular affinity and analogy which exists among all mental phenomena, while the physical do not share in it. Every mental phenomenon is characterized by what the scholastics of the Middle Ages called the intentional (and also mental) inexistence (*Inexistenz*) of an object (*Gegenstand*), and what we would call, although in not entirely unambiguous terms, the reference to a content, a direction upon an object (by which we are not to understand a reality in this case), or an immanent objectivity. Each one includes something as object within itself, although not always in the same way. In presentation something is presented, in judgement something is affirmed or denied, in love [something is] loved, in hate [something] hated, in desire [something] desired, etc.

This intentional inexistence is exclusively characteristic of mental phenomena. No physical phenomenon manifests anything similar. Consequently, we can define mental phenomena by saying that they are such phenomena as include an object intentionally within themselves.[2]

According to this passage, a mental phenomenon is one that includes an object that is not a 'reality' but exists merely 'immanently' or 'intentionally'. However, in a 1911 paper 'Genuine and Fictitious Objects',[3] Brentano gave up the doctrine that the objects of mental acts have a special kind of existence or being—intentional inexistence: 'And so it holds true generally that nothing other than things (*Dinge*), which fall entirely within the same concept of real entity (*Reales*), can provide an object (*Gegenstand*) for mental reference. Nothing else can ever be, like a real entity, the thing to which we mentally refer as an object' (p. 74). In this, he agreed with his student Edmund Husserl (1857–1938), who introduced the term "intentionality": 'It is a serious error to draw a real (*reell*) distinction between "merely immanent" or "intentional" objects, on the one hand, and "transcendent", "actual" objects, which may correspond to them on the other . . . It need

---

[2] In a lengthy footnote, Brentano traces his doctrine of intentional inexistence to a view he attributed to Aristotle and Thomas Aquinas (i.e. the view that the item that is experienced is *in* the one experiencing, the item that is thought is *in* the one thinking, etc.). In a remark about Anselm, he makes it clear that intentional inexistence is supposed to differ from actual existence. Brentano's intentional inexistence is what Descartes called objective existence in his notorious argument for the existence of God in *Meditations*, III.

[3] Reprinted in R. Chisholm, *Realism and the Background of Phenomenology* (New York, 1960).

only be said to be acknowledged *that the intentional object of a presentation is the same as its actual object, and on occasion as its external object, and that it is absurd to distinguish between them.*[4]

When purged of the doctrine of intentional inexistence, Brentano's thesis becomes:

1. (*a*) All mental phenomena make reference to or are directed upon an object.
   (*b*) Only mental phenomena make reference to or are directed upon an object.
2. No physical phenomenon makes reference to or is directed upon an object.

Alexius Meinong (1853–1920), another famous student of Brentano, accepted thesis 1(*a*)–(*b*)in a 1904 essay, 'The Theory of Objects'[5]: 'To put it briefly, no one fails to recognize that psychological events so very commonly have this distinctive "character of being directed to something" (*auf etwas Gerichtetsein*) as to suggest very strongly (at least) that we should take it to be a characteristic aspect of the psychological as opposed to the non-psychological' (p. 77).

The term "intentionality", which derives from the Latin *intendere*, meaning to point, was introduced by Husserl, not for this general property of being directed upon or making reference to, but for a property explicitly restricted to certain *conscious experiences*: 'The qualifying adjective "intentional" names the essence common to the class of experiences we wish to mark off, the peculiarity of *intending*, of referring to what is objective, in a presentative or other analogous fashion.'[6] Thus, Husserl ruled out, by definition, non-mental intentional phenomena (according to some philosophers, linguistic phenomena, for example, are intentional but non-mental) and mental phenomena that are intentional but non-conscious (e.g. standing beliefs, long-term ambitions, habituated likes and dislikes, etc.). Moreover, Husserl did not accept the thesis—entailed by Brentano's thesis—that *all* mental phenomena

[4] E. Husserl, *Logische Untersuchungen* (Halle, 1900–1), tr. J. N. Findlay (New York, 1970), 595.
[5] Reprinted in Chisholm, *Realism*.
[6] *Logische Untersuchungen*, tr. Findlay, 562.

are intentional: 'That not all experiences are intentional is proved by sensations and sensational complexes.'[7]

## ii. Contemporary Views

Contemporary philosophers, especially those writing in English, would accept something like the following informal definition: a phenomenon (state, event) is intentional if and only if it is 'directed toward' or 'makes reference to' something. Quotation marks are added to emphasize that the indicated phrases are used metaphorically. Evidently these spatial and linguistic metaphors can be eliminated in favour of a literal use of the term "about", yielding the following informal definition:

> A phenomenon (state, event) is intentional if and only if it is about something.

Thus, intentionality is the property of aboutness possessed by certain phenomena. In contemporary philosophy Brentano's original theses 1–2 have become the following:

    I. (*a*) All mental phenomena are intentional.
       (*b*) Only mental phenomena are intentional.
    II. No purely physical phenomenon is intentional.

Contemporary philosophers, somewhat inaccurately, call the conjunction of I and II Brentano's thesis of intentionality. I is often referred to as (Brentano's thesis of) intentionality-as-the-mark-of-the-mental. II is referred to as (Brentano's thesis of) the irreducibility-of-the-intentional.

On the contemporary formulation, an intentional phenomenon need not be about an *object* (i.e. an individual particular). For example, the phenomenon of judging that every man is mortal is not about any particular *object*; nevertheless, it would be counted as intentional because it is about something, namely, mankind and mortality. Brentano, by contrast, was inclined to restrict the range of the 'directed toward' relation to *objects*. (Accordingly, he would

---

[7] *Logische Untersuchungen*, tr. Findlay, 556.

have treated a judgement that every man is mortal as a rejection of men that are non-mortal. This treatment becomes ever more awkward for more complex examples.) Furthermore, the term "mental phenomena" is now almost universally understood to apply to not only conscious ('occurrent') mental phenomena but also 'standing' mental phenomena (e.g. standing beliefs), which need not be conscious.

As indicated, Husserl[8] used the term "intentional" in a more restricted way to pick out an explicitly psychological property, thereby rendering trivial the proposition expressed by the sentence, 'Only mental phenomena are intentional.' According to standard contemporary usage, by contrast, intentionality is not an explicitly psychological property; it is simply the general property of aboutness possessed by certain phenomena. Consequently, the above sentence expresses a highly non-trivial philosophical thesis—namely, thesis I(*b*).

By using the term "intentionality" for the general property of aboutness of certain phenomena (rather than for an explicitly psychological property), contemporary philosophers have been able to use the term to formulate a closely related substantive philosophical question: are intentional phenomena *fundamentally* linguistic or psychological? This was the main question under debate in the famous Sellars–Chisholm correspondence, 'Intentionality and the Mental',[9] wherein Sellars adopted the linguistic thesis and Chisholm, the psychological thesis. With the advent of H. Paul Grice's intention-based analysis of linguistic meaning,[10] Sellars's linguistic thesis has lost the support of most philosophers writing in English. In contemporary French critical theory, a number of philosophers still find it fashionable to reject the psychological thesis; however, these philosophers evidently have not come to terms with the power and elegance of the Gricean analysis. On that analysis, linguistic meaning is defined in psychological terms (intending, believing, etc.); accordingly, intentional linguistic phenomena turn out, upon analysis, to be complex phenomena

---

[8] And Searle, *Intentionality* (Cambridge, 1983): 'Intentionality is that property of many mental states and events by which they are directed at or about or of objects and states of affairs in the world' (p. 1).

[9] In H. Feigl *et al.*, eds., *Concepts, Theories and the Mind–Body Problem* (Minneapolis, 1958).

[10] 'Meaning', *Philosophical Review*, 66 (1958), 377–88.

concerning co-ordinated psychological states of relevant groups of people.[11]

## iii. Assessment of the Theses

*Thesis I(a)*. A number of contemporary epistemologists and philosophers of science are drawn to thesis I(*a*) in connection with the doctrine of the 'theory-ladeness' of perceptual experience, the doctrine that all perceptual experience is 'interpreted'. However, it is difficult to see how in perceptual experience there could fail to be a further element, namely, the element that is subjected to 'interpretation'—what Husserl calls the *hyle* (matter) of an experience, for example, mere tickles or mere sensations of colour. Arguments in recent philosophy of mind concerning the irreducibility of *qualia*—pure phenomenal qualities—lend support to this view. An attractive moderate position, therefore, is the following: all perceptual experience is intentional, although there is always a separately identifiable element in perceptual experience that has no intentionality.

*Thesis I(b)*. Linguistic phenomena provide the most likely candidate counter-examples to thesis I(*b*). For example, the production of a linguistic token of "Out of Order" by a vending machine *means* that the machine is out of order and, hence, is *about* the machine even though this does not seem to be a *mental* phenomenon. However, as already indicated, H. Paul Grice's analysis of linguistic meaning has convinced most philosophers that all such linguistic phenomena depend, by definition, on certain co-ordinated psychological states of people in the relevant language group and, hence, must be counted as partly psychological. In the vending machine case, it is the communicative intentions of the manufacturer that give the machine its intentionality.

---

[11] It should be mentioned that a distant relative of the linguistic thesis survives in the form of the 'language-of-thought' hypothesis in philosophy of mind, namely, the thesis that the ranges of all fundamental psychological relations—belief, desire, etc.—are comprised of sentences belonging to a hypothetical non-public 'language', where 'tokens' of these sentences are somehow inscribed in or realized in the brain. See e.g. J. Fodor, *The Language of Thought* (New York, 1975), and id., *Psychosemantics* (Cambridge, Mass., 1987). However, because this sort of 'language' is not a genuine public language, this position is not a version of the linguistical thesis, which is that public linguistic phenomena are the primary intentional phenomena. See nn. 15 and 30.

*Thesis II.* Contemporary thought is deeply divided over thesis II, the irreducibility-of-the-intentional. It is ironic, therefore, that most philosophers participating in the contemporary debate have—either implicitly or explicitly—abandoned the prospect of giving a general analysis of intentionality. (For example, Searle declares without any argument: 'In my view it is not possible to give a logical analysis of the Intentionality of the mental . . . There is no neutral standpoint from which we can survey the relations between Intentional states and the world and then describe them in non-Intentionalistic terms. Any explanation of Intentionality, therefore, takes place within the circle of Intentional concepts.'[12]) The importance of this issue for thesis II is seldom realized. Suppose that there does not exist a general analysis (physicalistic or otherwise) specifying what intentional phenomena have in common. Then, intentional phenomena would have a property—namely, their intentionality (this general unanalysable property)—that is not a purely physical property. Accordingly, intentional phenomena would not be purely physical. Therefore, thesis II would be vindicated. The possibility of a general analysis of intentionality is thus a pressing question.

Virtually no philosophers have attempted a general analysis of intentionality. One exception is Fred Dretske,[13] who gives an analysis in probabilistic terms (using the 'information theory' of Hartley, Weaver, Shannon, Wiener, *et al.*). However, there are several counter-examples showing that his analysis provides neither necessary nor sufficient conditions. For example, the general analysis of intentionality (ch. 7) does not provide a necessary condition; for, according to the analysis, something has the intentional content that *t* is F only if *t* is *in fact* F. However, intentional contents need not in general be true, as the phenomenon of false belief illustrates. In connection with his solution to this problem, Dretske adopts an etiological account, according to which a being has an intentional content that *t* is F only if the being, or its ancestors, were causally acted on by Fs in the right way. But this further restriction does not yield a necessary condition. For example, by a fantastically improbable but nevertheless causally possible coincidence, a being physically indistinguishable from me could arise spontaneously

---

[12] *Intentionality*, 26.
[13] *Knowledge and the Flow of Information* (Oxford, 1981).

without any relevant causal interaction with the things in its environment. According to the etiological analysis, such a being would in that case have *no* intentional contents. But this is absurd. Although the being would not (let us assume) have familiar natural-kind intentional contents, the being could have at least *some* intentional contents. For example, the being could be aware that it is in pain, that its experiences are changing, that everything is self-identical, that it is logically possible for there to be other things besides itself and its experiences.[14] The following counter-example shows that Dretske does not provide a sufficient condition: it is logically (or metaphysically) possible for there to be a world in which there is an etiological system that fits Dretske's analysis and in which *nothing* ever has been or ever will be (or ever has had or ever will have the capacity to be) *conscious* in any fashion—to have sense experiences, pleasures, pains, realizations, fears, wishes, and so forth. In such a situation, the envisaged etiological system would, intuitively, not have genuine intentional states.[15]

---

[14] Although Twin-Earth style arguments might be used to show that the being would not have any familiar natural-kind intentional contents, such arguments provide no motivation whatsoever for the radical thesis that the being could not have intentional states that are about such things as pain, experience, change, identity, logical possibility, etc. On the contrary, there is strong prima-facie reason to think that the being would have some intentional contents. In addition to my having colour sensations, smell sensations, sound sensations, etc., I have various purely cognitive phenomenological episodes (e.g. the episode of spotting a new logical connection or the idea behind a new proof). When one of these episodes occurs, I undergo a marked phenomenological change, even though there need be no change in the phenomenal qualities I am experiencing. And, of course, there need be no relevant objects in my environment that are causing the episode; I might like thinking about logic in a sensory deprivation chamber. Given that the envisaged being is physically indistinguishable from me, it should also be phenomenologically indistinguishable from me: each time I undergo a phenomenological change, the being ought to undergo a phenomenological change as well. Consider one of my purely cognitive phenomenological episodes whose occurrence is accompanied by no change in the phenomenological qualities I am experiencing. Since the occurrence of this episode constitutes a phenomenological change in me, there should be a corresponding phenomenological change in the envisaged being. But that change would not consist of a change in the phenomenal qualities that the being is experiencing. Thus, there is nothing that the phenomenological change in the being could be except a cognitive change: the being must be thinking. So there must be an intentional content.

[15] Besides these types of counter-examples to the analysis there are many technical difficulties. For example, the counter-example given in Bealer, 'Mind and Anti-Mind: Why Thinking has No Functional Definition', *Midwest Studies in Philosophy*, 9 (1984), 283–328; the problem mentioned in n. 30 below; and

Roderick Chisholm has shed light on the possibility of a general analysis of intentionality. In his early work on intentionality,[16] Chisholm offered extremely insightful logical criteria for intentional language (i.e. sentences that report intentional phenomena).[17] These criteria were found to be deficient in various ways,[18] but they nevertheless constituted promising suggestions. In later years Chisholm abandoned his effort to give purely logical criteria for intentionality. Indeed, he implicitly adopted the 'circle-of-intentional-concepts' posture, pursuing a definitional strategy that tries to define certain basic logical notions (e.g. the notion of one property's involving another) in terms of certain intentional notions (e.g. the notion of a person's conceiving something). Within this scheme he then attempts general definitions of intentionality and of the psychological. While not formally circular, this way of proceeding is far less illuminating philosophically, for it uses intentional notions in the very definition of intentionality and of the psychological. Moreover, within this scheme the prospect of a satisfactory logical theory is very unlikely, given that some of the ultimate primitives in Chisholm's logical theory would be psychological notions which are resistant to the sort of rigorous theoretical treatment expected in a logic.

## iv. An Analysis of Intentionality

On the face of it, the term "about" does not seem to be a psychological term; on the contrary, it seems topic neutral and, if

---

problems that arise in connection with the non-causal origins of our temporal concepts, spatial concepts, numerical concepts, modal concepts, etc. Jerry Fodor, *Psychosemantics*, offers a more complicated etiological theory of mental content. However, like other etiological theories, Fodor's theory falls prey to the two counter-examples given in the text. It also falls prey to pretty much the same sorts of technical difficulties.

All these problems aside, it is doubtful whether either Dretske or Fodor really is in a position to produce a *general* analysis of intentionality, one equipped to deal with *every* logically possible type of intentional phenomenon (see sect. v). Their proposals are aimed only at certain familiar types of intentional phenomena (primarily, perceptual experience and belief).

[16] *Perceiving: A Philosophical Study* (Ithaca, NY, 1957) and 'Intentionality', in P. Edwards, ed., *The Encyclopedia of Philosophy* (New York, 1967), 201–4.

[17] Daniel Dennett, for example, adopts Chisholm's criteria: *Content and Consciousness* (London, 1969), 22–32.

[18] See e.g. G. Bealer, *Quality and Concept* (Oxford, 1982), 229–31.

anything, belongs to logic, broadly construed. In view of this, it would not be implausible that an analysis of the notion of an intentional phenomenon could be stated within an appropriate logical theory. Such an analysis was ventured by me in earlier work.[19] A streamlined version is presented below.

By logic, we understand intensional logic, the sort of logic in which equivalent expressions cannot always be substituted for one another without changing the truth value of the sentences in which they occur. Intensionality in language results from reference to intensional entities, entities that can be equivalent without being identical. Properties, relations, and propositions are the paradigmatic intensional entities. Among all the various properties and relations, certain ones stand out as 'basic' or 'natural' (e.g. green and blue), whereas others are derivative (e.g. grue, bleen, being identical to green, being distinct from blue, etc.).[20] There are very strong intuitions supporting such a distinction. In addition, such a distinction proves useful, and perhaps essential, for dealing with a diverse family of important philosophical problems—for instance, clarifying the notions of objective similarity, supervenience, real (v. Cambridge) change, real (v. Cambridge) individuals and kinds, inductive inference, causation, causal law, scientific explanation, and so forth. The basic or natural properties and relations are called, respectively, qualities and connections. Derivative intentions can be obtained from these distinguished properties and relations (and perhaps subjects of singular predications) by means of fundamental logical operations (conjunction, negation, existential generalization, singular predication, etc.). The intensions that can be so obtained may in that sense be considered complex.

Notice that propositions (and other complex intensions) just on their own, independently of whether anyone believes (or otherwise employs) them, are said to be *about* things. For example, the

[19] *Quality and Concept* and id., 'The Logical Status of Mind', *Midwest Studies in Philosophy*, 10 (1986), 231–74.

[20] An increasing number of contemporary philosophers, especially philosophers of mind, accept a distinction between properties and relations that are basic or natural and mere grue-like "Cambridge" properties and relations. A survey of ways in which this distinction proves useful philosophically may be found in Bealer, *Quality and Concept*, ch. 8, 'Qualities and Concepts', and D. Lewis, 'New Work for a Theory of Universals', *Australasian Journal of Philosophy*, 61 (1983), 343–7. See also H. Putnam, 'On Properties', in his *Mathematics, Matter and Method* (Cambridge, 1970), 305 and Bealer, 'Theories of Properties, Relations and Propositions', *Journal of Philosophy*, 76 (1979). 634–48.

proposition that Socrates is wise is about Socrates and wisdom; and this would be so even if no one had ever considered the proposition. The aboutness of a proposition (or any other complex intension) has a realist (*v.* representationalist) analysis exclusively in terms of familiar logical relations holding between the proposition and its constituents.[21]

Our main thesis is this. The aboutness of all intentional phenomena derives from individuals' bearing relevant connections (namely, *intentional connections*) to complex intensions that, just on their own, are about things. We suggest the following definitions:

1. A connection is *hyperintensional* if and only if it can contingently connect some individual to some complex intension without connecting the individual to some necessarily equivalent complex intension and without the original intension's having veracity.[22]

2. A connection is a *mediating intentional* connection if and only if it is—or is necessarily included in—a hyperintensional connection whose range is necessarily restricted to complex intensions.

3. A connection is a *mediated intentional* connection if and only if, necessarily, it connects an individual to an item only if some mediating intentional connection connects the individual to a complex intension that is about the item.

4. A connection is a *direct intentional* connection if and only if it is a hyperintensional connection that is neither mediating nor mediated.

Seeming, believing, knowing, and deciding are examples of mediating intentional connections; looking for and seeing objects are examples of mediated intentional connections; acquaintance is an example of a direct intentional connection. (These examples are heuristic only; settling which intentional relations are genuine connections and which intentional connections are mediating,

---

[21] For a discussion of this sort of analysis and an examination of the differences between realism and representationalism and the advantages of the former, see Bealer, *Quality and Concept*, sect. 42, 'Realism and Representationalism' and pp. 225 ff.

[22] A complex intension has veracity if it is a true proposition or a complex property or relation that applies to something actual. In symbols, the definition of hyperintensional connection is: $c$ is hyperintensional iff $\Diamond(\exists x)(\exists i)(\exists i')(x$ is an individual & $i$ and $i'$ are necessarily equivalent complex intensions & $\Diamond(c$ holds between $x$ and $i$ and not between $x$ and $i')$ & $\Diamond(c$ holds between $x$ and $i$ and $i$ has veracity) & $\Diamond(c$ holds between $x$ and $i$ and $i$ lacks veracity) & $\Diamond(c$ does not hold between $x$ and $i)$ ).

mediated, or direct is ultimately a matter of theory.) Intuitive
motivation for these definitions and discussion of some of these
examples will come in a moment.

With these definitions in place, we venture a purely logical
analysis of the notion of an intentional phenomenon. Intentional
phenomena are either basic or derived. A phenomenon $e$ is a basic
intentional phenomenon if and only if, for some individual $x$, some
mediating, mediated, or direct intentional connection $c$, and some
item $y$, $e$ is the phenomenon of $x$'s bearing $c$ to $y$. Derived intentional phenomena are phenomena whose analysis depends in
some essential way on basic intentional phenomena.[23]

If this analysis is correct, we can also say what it is for something
to be an object of a basic intentional phenomenon: $z$ is an object
of a basic intentional phenomenon $e$ if and only if, for some individual $x$, there is a mediated or direct intentional connection $c$
such that $e$ is the phenomenon of $x$'s bearing $c$ to $z$, or there is a
mediating intentional connection $c$ and a complex intention $i$ that
is about $z$, such that $e$ is the phenomenon of $x$'s bearing $c$ to $i$.

Hyperintensional connections are the key to our analysis. Such
connections have three distinguishing features: contingency, independent veracity, and hyper-fine-grained discrimination. Contingency reflects the fact that when an individual stands in one of
these connections to something, there occurs a genuine *phenomenon*—a real *episode*—rather than, say, a logical or mathematical
fact. Independent veracity reflects the fact that in thought we can
do all sorts of things that are about (or at least purport to be
about) items in the world, even though these things we do need
not correspond to the actual conditions of these (purported) items
in the world. Hyper-fine-grained discrimination reflects the fact
that within the tide of naturalistic 'information', we intentional
beings exercise a capacity to be connected to subtly distinct (i.e.
hyperintensional) aspects of that brute flow, and, indeed, we pursue our lives in these terms. Whenever a basic intentional phenomenon occurs, an individual is related to something by a connection
that is contingent, independent, and hyper-discriminating in these
ways.

To get a better feel for the analysis, let us go through some

[23] The notions of psychological connection, basic psychological phenomenon,
and derived psychological phenomenon can be analysed along somewhat analogous lines. See Bealer, *Quality and Concept* and id., 'The Logical Status of Mind'.

examples. The relation of believing is evidently a hyperintensional connection. First, believing seems to be a natural relation, not a grue-like Cambridge relation. Second, relative to some individual $x$ (e.g. me), some complex intension $i$ (e.g. the proposition that I have 2 shoes on), and some necessarily equivalent complex intension $i'$ (e.g. the proposition that I have $\sqrt[7]{128}$ shoes on), believing has the three features: (a) contingency, (b) independent veracity, and (c) hyper-discrimination. (a) It is a contingent matter whether $x$ stands in the belief relation to $i$ (i.e. it is a contingent matter whether I believe that I have 2 shoes on). (b) $x$ can stand in the belief relation to $i$ independently of whether $i$ has veracity (i.e. I can believe that I have 2 shoes on whether or not I do have 2 shoes on). (c) $x$ can stand in the belief relation to $i$ without standing in the belief relation to the necessarily equivalent complex intension $i'$ (i.e. I can believe that I have 2 shoes on without believing that I have $\sqrt[7]{128}$ shoes on). These considerations show that believing is hyperintensional. Because the range of the belief relation is necessarily restricted to complex intensions—namely, propositions—believing is a mediating intentional connection.

Next, consider propositional knowing—the relation expressed by "know" in "that"-clause sentences such as "I know that I have 2 shoes on." Knowing is necessarily included in believing—that is, necessarily, for all $x$ and $p$, if $x$ knows $p$, $x$ believes $p$—and knowing is a natural, non-grue-like relation. Therefore, knowing is a mediating intensional connection.

Analogous considerations show that propositional seeming—the relation expressed by "seems" in "that"-clause sentences such as "It seems to me that I have 2 shoes on"—is a hyperintensional connection. Because the range of the relation of propositional seeming is necessarily restricted to complex intensions (namely, propositions), propositional seeming is a mediating intentional connection. Now propositional seeing—the relation expressed by "see" in such sentences as "I see that I have 2 shoes on"—is necessarily included in the relation of propositional seeming. For example, it is necessary that, if I see that I have 2 shoes on, it seems to me that I have 2 shoes on. Thus, propositional seeing is a mediating intentional connection. Propositional seeing is to propositional seeming as propositional knowing is to believing.

If I bear any of these four relations to the proposition that I have 2 shoes on, the associated phenomenon is an intentional phenomenon that is *about* me. For example, the phenomenon of its seeming to me that I have 2 shoes on is about me. This is so because, as a logical fact, the proposition that I have 2 shoes on is about me, regardless of whether I stand in any intentional relation to it. On the realist (*v.* representationalist) approach this proposition is about me because I am a constituent of the proposition. This notion of constituent can be made fully precise in a suitable intensional logic.

Let us now say a word about direct intentional connections. There is controversy over whether a person can be acquainted with an item (e.g. a colour, a taste, a proposition) without standing in *any* mediating intentional connection to *any* complex intension that is about the item. On Russell's view, such a thing is possible: for a certain narrow class of items, one can be *directly* acquainted with those items without the mediation of any complex intension. Let us suppose that Russell's view is right. Then, acquaintance would qualify as a direct intentional connection on our analysis; after all, countless complex intensions are possible objects of acquaintance on the Russell view. On the other hand, suppose that Russell's view is mistaken. Then, acquaintance would qualify as a mediated intentional connection on our analysis; for *ex hypothesi*, an individual could be acquainted with an item only if the individual stood in some mediating intentional connection to some complex intension that is about the item. Suppose that this generalizes; that is, suppose that every candidate direct intentional connection turns out, upon more careful examination, to be a mediated intentional connection. This is entirely consistent with our analysis. After all, the analysis makes no commitment to the existence of direct intentional connections; the analysis merely tells us what it would take for there to be one. The analysis is deliberately designed so that we can remain neutral on this issue.

One of the main challenges for a purely logical analysis of intentionality is to accommodate objectival perceptual phenomena. For example, the sort of phenomenon reported with formulas of the form "*x* sees *y*" and "*x* sees *y* F-ing". To be satisfactory, our analysis must be able to accommodate such phenomena. We have just noted that our analysis of intentionality is designed to be neutral on the question of whether acquaintance is a direct intentional connection. It is an advantage of the analysis that it does not ride on any one theory of this sort of issue. Our strategy is much the same concerning the vexed question of objectival perceptual phenomena. That is, our general analysis of intentionality is designed to accommodate a wide range of competing analyses of objectival perceptual statements. It will then be a matter for subsequent theorizing to decide which of these competing analyses is best. At the heart of the controversy is the logical form of these statements. Let us illustrate the point by examining a few of the leading analyses.

Let us first consider formulas whose surface form is "$x$ sees $y$", where the values of $y$ are physical objects or physical events. On one analysis, such formulas are treated as syntactic transformations from "that"-clause constructions. For example, "$x$ sees $y$" might be treated as a transformation from "For some $F$, $x$ sees that $Fy$". In this case, objectival seeing would be definable in terms of propositional seeing and, hence, would present no special challenge to our general analysis of intentionality. Suppose, however, that this easy approach is mistaken and that the logical form of "$x$ sees $y$" is just what it appears to be on the surface. That is, suppose that "$x$ sees $y$" has the form "$x \ R^2 \ y$". We would then hold that the relation expressed by "sees" in this formula—namely, the relation of seeing an object—is a mediated intentional connection. By definition, a connection is a mediated intentional connection if and only if, necessarily, it holds between an individual $x$ and an item $y$ only if some mediating intentional connection connects $x$ to a complex intension that is about $y$. Evidently, the relation of seeing an object satisfies this definition. If $x$ sees $y$, then intuitively one (or more) of the following holds: *either* it seems to $x$ that $y$ is present, *or* it seems to $x$ that $y$ is there, *or* it seems to $x$ that $x$ sees $y$, *or* it seems to $x$ that $x$ is aware of $y$, *or* $x$ sees $y$ there, *or* $x$ sees $y$ in the vicinity, *or* something else of this sort. (The latter items—$x$ sees $y$ there and $x$ sees $y$ in the vicinity—belong on this list of mediating intentional phenomena as long as one of the treatments discussed in the next paragraph is correct.) Unlike the syntactic-transformation approach, the present approach merely imposes an indefinitely specified necessary condition: there must be *some* appropriate mediating intentional connection and *some* appropriate complex intension. Just which ones is not something written into syntax; it all depends on the facts of the specific psychological episode in question. This gives our analysis a great deal of leeway. If someone doubts that this necessary condition is always met, let that person give us a concretely spelled-out candidate counter-example, and it shall then be our obligation to find some plausible candidate mediating intentional connection and complex intension that would play the indicated role in the example. It is our opinion that we are able to meet this obligation. Of course, there is no way to be certain in advance of actually trying.

We come next to formulas whose surface form is "$x$ sees $y$ F-ing". On one analysis, such formulas are treated as syntactic transformations of associated "that"-clause constructions. For example, "$x$ sees $y$ F-ing" is treated as a transformation from "$x$ sees that $y$ is F-ing". In this case, these objectival constructions would already have been dealt with in connection with our treatment of propositional seeing. But let us suppose that this easy approach is mistaken and that the logical form of "$x$ sees $y$ F-ing" is closer to what it appears to be on the surface. For example, let us suppose that "$x$ sees $y$ F-ing" has the form "$x \ R^2 \ y$ F-ing", where "$y$ F-ing" is a complex singular term. In this case, what does the singular term "$y$ F-ing" denote? A plausible answer is that it denotes a kind of complex intension—$y$ F-ing—one of whose constituents is $y$ and the other, the property F-ing. It is also plausible that in formulas of the form "$x$ sees $y$ F-ing" the verb "sees" expresses a relation $R^2$ whose range is necessarily restricted to complex intensions of the indicated sort. (There is considerable linguistic evidence for the view that "sees" in "$x$ sees $y$ F-ing" expresses a different relation from that which "sees" expresses in "$x$ sees $y$". For example, we can say "$x$ sees Tom, Dick, and Harry" but not "$x$ sees Tom running, Dick, and Harry".) Finally, suppose that this relation $R^2$ is necessarily included in a relation of appearing; that is, suppose that, necessarily, if $x$ sees $y$ F-ing, then $y$ F-ing is something that appears to $x$. In this case, this relation $R^2$ would straightforwardly satisfy our definition of a mediating intentional connection. Accordingly, "$x$ sees $y$ F-ing" would fit neatly into our general analysis of intentionality. (Incidentally, the present treatment of "$x$ sees $y$ F-ing" can easily be extended to formulas like the following: "$x$ sees $y$ there", "$x$ sees $y$ here", "$x$ sees $y$ in the vicinity", and so forth. For example, "$x$ sees $y$ there" could be treated as having the form "$x \ R^2 \ y$ there", where "$y$ there" would be a singular term denoting a relevant type of complex intension.)

Suppose, however, that neither of these two treatments of "*x* sees *y* F-ing" is correct. We can always deal with the associated kind of objectival perceptual phenomenon as follows. Notice that, necessarily, if *x* sees *y* F-ing, then *x* sees *y*. We have seen that our general analysis of intentionality accommodates the phenomenon of *x*'s seeing *y*. Therefore, to accommodate the phenomenon of *x*'s seeing *y* F-ing, we need only relax slightly our definition of the notion of a basic intentional phenomenon: a phenomenon *e* is a basic intentional phenomenon if and only if, for some individual *x*, some mediating, mediated, or direct intentional connection *c*, and some item *y*, the occurrence of *e* entails that *x* bears *c* to *y*.[24] Given this definition, the phenomenon of *x*'s seeing *y* F-ing would qualify as a basic intentional phenomenon. So even if the two original suggestions (discussed in the previous paragraph) do not work, statements of the form "*x* sees *y* F-ing" can easily be made to fit into our general approach of intentionality.

We have certainly not exhausted all the candidate analyses of the logical form of objectival perceptual statements. Nevertheless, our brief survey provides provisional evidence that, whatever the correct analysis, it can be made to mesh with the proposed general analysis of intentionality or, at least, with some suitably adjusted variation on that analysis.

Finally, we should say something about the role played in the proposal analysis by *connections*—natural, non-grue-like relations. Suppose that throughout the analysis we replaced "connection" with the less restrictive term "relation". The resulting analysis would be subject to a host of counter-examples. Consider, for example, a clearly non-intentional relation *R* that is defined as follows: *x* R *y* iff$_{def}$ *x* is a particular, and *x* is green if and only if *y* = the proposition that *x* is green, and *x* is not green if and only if *y* = the proposition that *x* is blue. It is easy to check that, according to the new, less restrictive analysis, *R* would qualify as a mediating intentional relation. So *R* is a clear-cut counter-example to the new analysis. Fortunately, *R* is plainly a grue-like

---

[24] Incidentally, suppose someone were to advocate treating "*x* sees *y* F-ing" as a three-place relational formula "$R^3(x, y, F\text{-ing})$" whose third argument is the gerund "F-ing". Even if this were right, the phenomenon of *x*'s seeing *y* F-ing would qualify as a basic intentional phenomenon on the definition just proposed; for, as we have noted, it is necessary that the occurrence of the phenomenon of *x*'s seeing *y* F-ing implies that *x* sees *y*.

relation. So *R* does not satisfy our official definition of a mediating intentional connection. Thus, the original analysis is in the clear.[25] Evidently, the only systematic way to avoid problems like this is to stick to our original strategy, namely, to define the narrower notion of an intentional connection (*v.* relation) and then to use this notion to define the notion of a basic intentional phenomenon and, in turn, the notion of a derived intentional phenomenon. This strategy certainly does not seem *ad hoc*; believing, knowing, seeming, perceiving, acquaintance, and so forth do not seem to be grue-like relations.

Several indirect intuitive considerations also support this assessment. For example, we mentioned that qualities and connections (i.e. natural properties and relations) play an essential role in analysing the difference between real change and mere Cambridge change. There is a real change in a situation over an interval if and only if the qualities and/or connections of some individual in the situation shift some time during the interval. As an illustration, consider what constitutes a real change in our conscious mental lives. One kind of real change is that involving a shift in the phenomenal qualities of which one is aware. Suppose, however, that the phenomenal qualities of which you are aware during a given interval remain the same. There are nevertheless other kinds of real change that can occur in your conscious mental life during that interval. For example, suppose that just before a given time *t* in the indicated interval you were contemplating, say, one of de Morgan's laws for the very first time. Suppose that this proposition struck you neither as true nor as false, that you had no response to it one way or the other. Suppose, however, that at *t* you realized that this proposition is true. Before *t* the relation of contemplating held between you and the proposition, but at *t* this relation was replaced by another relation, namely, the relation of realizing. Given that contemplating and realizing are genuine connections (natural relations), this shift constitutes a real change (*v.* a mere Cambridge change) in your conscious mental life. Of course, there are infinitely many shifts in your Cambridge relations, but these do not qualify as real changes.

---

[25] For a more thorough examination of this sort and other sorts of candidate counter-examples, see Bealer, *Quality and Concept* and 'The Logical Status of Mind'.

Considerations like these are essential to any adequate phenomenology of consciousness and, in turn, to any satisfactory theory of empirical knowledge. Indeed, our theoretical decisions about what hypothesized physical properties and relations to accept as genuine qualities and connections depend at least implicitly on our having first identified which of our mental properties and relations are genuine qualities and connections. Failing this, the indicated aspect of our physical theorizing would be at sea.

### v. An Obstacle for Materialism

We saw that materialists who deny thesis II have a pressing need for a general analysis of intentionality. What is it that intentional phenomena have in common that makes them intentional? Suppose that (except within the 'circle of intentional concepts') there does not exist a way to say what intentionality is. Then, intentional phenomena would have a property—namely, their intentionality (this general unanalysable property)—that is not a purely physical property. Accordingly, intentional phenomena would not be purely physical. Therefore, thesis II would be vindicated.

To avoid this outcome, materialists might claim that there exist physicalist analyses of all the familiar types of mental phenomena—e.g. beliefs, desires, etc.—and that these piecemeal analyses can be assembled into a 'disjunctive analysis'. There are several problems with this approach. Here are four.[26] First, in order for a 'disjunctive analysis' to be statable, there must be *finitely* many *logically possible* types of intentional phenomena. However, there is evidently no argument that a materialist could give to show that this finiteness assumption is met.[27] It looks like a mere article of faith. Second, how could materialists ever tell whether they had succeeded in finding the 'last' disjunct for their 'analysis'? How could they tell that they had dealt with *every* logically possible type

---

[26] There are, I believe, decisive obstacles to these individual physicalist analyses. The purpose of the argument in the text is to show that materialism would face difficulties even if the familiar types of mental phenomena could be analysed individually.

[27] In English alone there are hundreds of names for distinct types of intentional phenomena—regretting, pinning, suspecting, mistrusting, . . . Is there an argument ruling out the logical possibility of there always being additional types of intentional phenomenon, if only in new logically possible types of creature?

of intentional phenomenon? Evidently, there is no way to tell. A declaration by materialists that they had found the 'last' disjunct would be akin to a declaration by a species of blind and deaf creatures that they were acquainted with every logically possible type of sensation. For this reason materialists would never be justified in asserting a 'disjunctive analysis'. Third, suppose that, besides the types of intentional phenomena that actually occur, there is at least one further logically possible type of intentional phenomenon. How could materialists discover, and justify, the correct physical analysis of a non-actual type of intentional phenomenon? The task seems hopeless. Fourth, if materialists could not discover, and justify, a physical analysis of a non-actual but logically possible type of intentional phenomenon, it is difficult to see how they could ever justify their claim that all logically possible types of intentional phenomena have physical analyses.

As if these problems were not enough, the disjunctive approach is beset with still another sort of problem. Suppose we ask what it is about a person's believings, desirings, seemings, decidings, etc. that makes them intentional phenomena. Our own answer is that each of these phenomena consists of the person's standing in a certain kind of natural relation to a complex intension that all on its own is *about* things. Certainly, this answer is at least plausible. Suppose, however, that someone were to reject this answer and to propose the following instead: what it is about a person's believings, desirings, seemings, decidings, etc. that makes them intentional is that each of these phenomena is either a believing, a desiring, a seeming, a deciding, or ... Plainly this would not even begin to answer the question. But given that this does not constitute an answer, the following certainly would not, either: what it is about a person's believings, desirings, seemings, decidings, etc. that makes them intentional is that each of these phenomena is either $P_1$ or $P_2$ or $P_3$ or $P_4$ or ... (where $\ulcorner P_1 \urcorner$, $\ulcorner P_2 \urcorner$, $\ulcorner P_3 \urcorner$, $\ulcorner P_4 \urcorner$, ... are complex physical predicates that allegedly define "believing", "desiring", "seeming", "deciding", ... respectively). The conclusion is that there is a legitimate question about intentionality that *we* seem to be able to answer but that materialists cannot answer, at least by means of their disjunctive approach.

What about a functionalist approach? Suppose that $\ulcorner P_1 \urcorner$, $\ulcorner P_2 \urcorner$, $\ulcorner P_3 \urcorner$, and $\ulcorner P_4 \urcorner$ are correct functionalist analyses of "belief", "desire", "seeming", and "decision", respectively.[28] Then materialists might venture the following functionalist definition: $R$ is a mediating intentional relation if and only if $R$ can hold between individuals and complex intensions and there exists a system of causally necessary general propositions relating $R$ to $P_1$, $P_2$, $P_3$, and $P_4$. The hope would be that this analysis, perhaps together with some auxiliary analyses, could be assembled into a general analysis of the notion of an intentional phenomenon.

The most glaring flaw in this approach occurs at the first step: $R$ could be some grue-like Cambridge relation that is not intentional. For example, suppose we define a relation $R$ as follows: $x R y$ iff$_{def} x$ is an individual and $y$ is a proposition. This relation $R$ trivially satisfies the proposed functionalist analysis of the notion of a mediating intentional relation. However, $R$ is plainly not an intentional relation. Hence, a counter-example. Now there are various ways to try to tighten up the functionalist analysis. However, with a bit of cleverness, we can always concoct some new grue-like non-intentional relation $R$ that satisfies the tightened-up analysis. (The techniques for constructing these grue-like non-intentional relations are like those used in constructing counter-examples to Chisholm's early analysis of the notion of an intentional sentence.) Thus, there is evidently no way to rule out every grue-like non-intentional relation $R$ except by stipulating explicitly that $R$ is to be a natural relation (i.e. a connection). This is not surprising. Recall that, to rule out grue-like non-intentional relations, we were forced to organize our own analysis around the narrower notion of an intentional *connection* (*v.* relation). Evidently, advocates of the functionalist approach must, for the same reason, organize their analysis around this notion as well. Accordingly, they would be forced in the direction of something like the following: a connection $R$ is a mediating intentional connection if and only if $R$ can hold between individuals and complex intensions and there exists a system of causally necessary general propositions relating $R$ to $P_1$, $P_2$, $P_3$, and $P_4$. Our functionalists would then try to use this analysis, perhaps together with some auxiliary analyses, to analyse the general notion of an intentional phenomenon.

---

[28] I find it doubtful that there could be correct functional analyses of these terms. See e.g. Bealer, 'Mind and Anti-Mind'. It is also doubtful that, even if there were correct functional analyses, they would be consistent with materialism.

Similar considerations can, I think, be adduced to convince advocates of the functionalist approach to accept our full analysis (including, in particular, the contingency, independence, and hyper-discrimination features). However, for the point I wish to make against materialism, the previous conclusion suffices: it suffices that a satisfactory general analysis of intentionality requires that a family of intentional connections—natural intentional relations—be posited.[29] What is important for our purposes is that these natural relations are not among the natural relations posited in logic, mathematics, or the natural sciences (e.g. predication, identity; equinumerosity, isomorphism; gravitation, being located at, being a part of, being a descendant of, being fitter than, etc.). Thus to obtain an adequate general analysis of intentionality, one must accept the existence of a new family of natural relations (namely, intentional connections) above and beyond those posited in logic, mathematics, and the natural sciences.[30]

---

[29] We are supposing here that there exist at least some intentional phenomena. Even eliminative materialists (e.g. Sellars and the Churchlands) accept this, even though they reject the traditional theory of the propositional attitudes. For example, they accept that there is some knowledge, or at least some sentence, *about* physical objects.

[30] The indicated functionalist analysis of intentionality agrees with our own analysis on two points: first, it is committed to the existence of a genuinely new family of natural relations above and beyond those posited by logic, mathematics, and the natural sciences. Second, it recognizes that e.g. believing is a relation holding between individuals and relevant intensions, namely, propositions. There is an alternative functionalist approach that agrees with ours on the first point but not on the second. In particular, the notion of a 'token of a sentence in a language of thought' takes the place of the notion of a proposition. Our intensional logic approach is able to say what it is for a proposition to be about something in terms of intrinsic logical relations holding between the proposition and its constituents. The 'token in the language thought' approach throws away these realist tools and, therefore, must produce from scratch an analysis (usually it is an etiological analysis) of what it is for one of these 'tokens' to be about something. There are, I believe, insurmountable difficulties with this approach. For example, unlike the intensional logic approach, the 'token in the language of thought' approach provides a hopelessly disunified treatment of "that"-clauses as they occur in statements dealing with intentionality, logical necessity, causal necessity, probability, logical validity, definition, truth, and so forth. (See also the remarks on the etiological approach in sect. iii and in nn. 14 and 15.) But even if this approach were adequate, most of the points we are about to make in the text would still hold. For on the traditional materialist world view there is not an additional family of natural relations above and beyond those posited in logic, mathematics, and the natural sciences. Accordingly, this approach is committed to a new level of organization objectively distinct from the levels of organization recognized by the natural sciences.

(Recall, moreover, that we were able to give direct intuitive support for the thesis that the familiar intentional relations—believing, contemplating, realizing, and so forth—are in fact natural relations.)

The point I wish to make is that the existence of this additional family of natural relations goes beyond anything that traditional materialists would accept and, thus, is inconsistent with the traditional materialist world view.

According to the traditional materialist world view, the natural relations (besides those that are logical or mathematical) are those required for (a correct formulation of) the natural sciences. These natural relations are all *physical* in the following sense: they hold between physical particulars and physical particulars or between physical particulars and physical quantities or between physical particulars and locations or between physical particulars and times or between physical particulars and space-times. There is no room in the traditional materialist world view for the existence of an entirely new family of natural relations that hold between particulars and complex intensions (e.g. propositions). (There certainly is no room for natural relations with contingency, independent veracity, and hyper-discrimination.) We will show that such a family of natural relations entails the existence of a new objective level of organization above and beyond those levels of organization recognized by traditional materialists. To do this, we will discuss two pertinent issues: objective similarity groupings and levels of scientific explanation. It is important to realize that the question under discussion is independent of whether or not individual types of intentional phenomena have physical analyses; indeed, for the sake of argument, we will continue to assume that they do.

First, the issue of objective similarities. Possible situations are objectively similar to the extent that they—or their corresponding constituents—share natural properties and/or natural relations.[31] Let $s_1$ be a possible situation in which there exists a single agent $x_1$ who has intentional states; besides $x_1$ nothing else exists in $s_1$ except those things required logically or causally in order for $x_1$ to exist and to have the mental life that it has. Let $s_2$ be another possible situation in which there exists a single agent $x_2$ ($\neq x_1$) who has intentional states; besides $x_2$ nothing else exists in $s_2$ except those things required logically or causally in order for $x_2$ to exist and to have the mental life that it has. Suppose that $s_1$ and $s_2$—and the particular objects in $s_1$ and $s_2$—have very little in common by way of natural physical properties and natural physical relations. (For example, suppose that $x_1$'s body and its various parts share relatively few natural physical properties and natural physical relations with $x_2$'s body and its various parts.) Nevertheless, $s_1$ and $s_2$ could be such that $x_1$ and $x_2$ stand in exactly the same mediating intentional connections to all the same logical and mathematical propositions. (For example, $x_1$ and $x_2$ could be mathematical logicians who, throughout their lives, have exactly the same thoughts about logic and mathematics.) In this case, despite their relative physical dissimilarity, $x_1$ and $x_2$—and, in turn, $s_1$ and $s_2$—would nevertheless qualify as having a significant objective similarity to one another. However, according to traditional materialism, $s_1$ and $s_2$ would not have a significant similarity to one another; on the contrary, they would be rather dissimilar. For if materialism were correct, all natural properties and relations (besides those that are logical or mathematical) would be physical; therefore, $s_1$ and $s_2$—and the particular objects in $s_1$ and $s_2$—would have in common little by way of natural properties and relations. Consequently, $s_1$ and $s_2$ would be rather dissimilar. To the materialist, the fact that $x_1$ and $x_2$ bear exactly the same mediating intentional relations to all the same logical and mathematical propositions does not make $s_1$ and $s_2$ objectively similar situations. To the traditional materialist, these relations are just arbitrary Cambridge relations; they are no more distinctive than any number of other Cambridge relations that hold in objectively dissimilar situations. The presence or absence of such relations does not signal the presence or absence of objective similarities.

Given that this family of natural intentional relations exists above and beyond natural physical relations, and given that people often bear these relations to the same things, there exists a realm of phenomena that have objective similarities that would not exist if the traditional materialist world view were correct. The existence of this additional realm of objective similarities signals the existence of a non-physical level of organization.

An analogous point regarding scientific explanation can also be made. This point is more controversial; our conclusion does not depend on it. We assume that scientific explanations invoke *laws*.

Laws are causally necessary general propositions.[32] If *F* is a natural family of natural properties and natural relations, and every non-logical constituent of a given law *L* belongs to *F*, then *L* is said to be an *F law*. For example, a physical law, a psychological law, an economic law, and so forth. Traditional materialism recognizes only one kind of law, namely, physical laws. However, given that there are natural psychological properties and relations above and beyond natural physical properties and relations, and given that they form a natural family of natural properties and relations, laws involving only these natural properties and relations are psychological, not physical, laws. The following is an example of a psychological law: if a being is consciously and explicitly thinking that if *A* then *B* and if the being is consciously and explicitly thinking that *A* and if the being is carefully and attentively considering the question of whether *B* and if the being recognizes that he has no reason for thinking that not *B*, then it is probable that the being will think that *B*. There are some phenomena that can be explained without invoking physical laws but instead by invoking only psychological laws. For example, the phenomenon that I will probably think that *B* is explained by the above psychological law together with the fact that I presently satisfy the conditions specified in the antecedent of that law. (This is not to say that such a phenomenon does not also have a physical explanation. Given the assumption that every particular type of intentional phenomenon has a purely physical analysis, presumably intentional phenomena have both physical and psychological explanations.) In so far as scientific explanations impart understanding and in so far as there are scientific explanations that are non-physical, there is something more to understand even after all physical explanations have been given. Indeed, the totality of all physical explanations yields an incomplete understanding of reality.

As we have indicated, natural physical relations are categorically distinctive. They hold between physical particulars and physical particulars or between physical particulars and physical quantities or between physical particulars and locations or between physical particulars and times or between physical particulars and space-times or between locations and locations or between times

[32] We assume here that, not only are non-probabilistic laws causally necessary, but so too are probabilistic laws.

and times or between space-times and space-times. Natural physical relations—the sort of natural relations with which physics and the other physical sciences are concerned—do not hold between particulars and complex intensions (and they certainly do not exhibit hyperintensionality). To call the latter sort of relations *natural physical relations* would be to violate established usage. In the materialist tradition, however, there has been an unfortunate hidden assumption at work, namely, an assumption to the effect that, if a natural relation can be analysed in terms of natural physical properties and natural physical relations, then *ipso facto* it too is a natural physical relation. But this is an uncritical dogma plainly at odds with the way in which we talk: we simply would not call a relation that holds hyperintensionally between individuals and complex intensions a natural physical relation regardless of whether and how it might be defined. The possibility of physicalistic analyses is an independent issue. The obsession with this issue of physicalistic analysis, however, has caused many traditional materialists to overlook the standard intuitive criteria for how to classify natural physical relations, natural psychological relations, natural social relations, and so forth. As a result, these traditional materialists have been led to misconceive the question of objective levels of organization and the principles upon which the answer to that question depends.

Let us sum up. We saw that intentionality poses a challenge to materialism. If there does not exist a general analysis of intentionality, then intentional phenomena would have a property that is not physical—namely, their intentionality (the general unanalysable property itself). We then argued that, even if the familiar types of intentional phenomena, taken individually, have materialist analyses, we cannot have a satisfactory general analysis unless a family of natural intentional relations is posited. We argued, finally, that the existence of such a family of natural relations is incompatible with the traditional materialist world view: if there is such a family of natural relations, there is an objective realm of non-physical similarities, laws, and explanations. Hence, an objective level of organization above and beyond the physical. It is as though the world is a Seurat painting, and materialists wish us to be blind to everything but the individual points of colour.

# 6

# Truth, Physicalism, and Ultimate Theory

## Steven J. Wagner

Amongst the doctrines of Tlon, none has merited the scan-
dalous reception accorded materialism. Some thinkers have
formulated it with less clarity than fervor, as one might put
forth a paradox. In order to facilitate the comprehension of
this inconceivable thesis, a heresiarch of the eleventh century
devised the sophism of the nine copper coins . . .

> Jorge Luis Borges, *Tlon, Uqbar, Orbis Tertius*

I'm doing things that haven't got a name yet.

> The Jefferson Airplane, *After Bathing at Baxter's*

I believe that the ideas behind physicalism are poorly understood.
A better grasp of them encourages a position with significant
physicalist elements. How one may reach that destination, then
step far off the physicalist path, is recounted here. I will also shed
light on the concern, found in Quine and elsewhere, with *ultimate*
theories as standards of epistemic merit.[1]

Central to my project is the clash between Quinian epistemology and its pragmatic critics. This formulation may be surprising,
since Quine ushered in the half-century by identifying the rational
with the pragmatic,[2] in opposition to Carnap and C. I. Lewis.
But Quine in turn is charged with insufficient pragmatism. He

---

[1] This is the skeleton of a much longer essay, to appear in a projected book
(working title: *Truth, Pragmatism, and Ultimate Theory*). I hope the argument will
be useful in spite of my editorially mandated concision. Readers will find a host
of points at which more needs to be said; it will be, but not here. They are also
asked to tolerate the exploratory character of these reflections. I thank Hartry Field
and Stephen Schiffer for their comments on a first draft (presented at the American
Philosophical Association meetings in Portland, 1988) and Howard Robinson for
his editorial advice.

[2] In 'Two Dogmas of Empiricism', *Philosophical Review*, 60 (1951), 20–43, repr.
in *From a Logical Point of View* (2nd edn., Cambridge, Mass., 1961), 20–46.

emphasizes a distinction between 'seriously acceptable' and 'grade B' doctrines: statements that may limn the true and ultimate structure of reality versus those that will not.[3] Sentences of the former kind promise to appear in (or 'reduce to') a comprehensive, advanced physics. Notably placed in the latter category are intentional doctrines, whose practical necessity Quine grants even while banishing them from serious science. This is the doctrine of the double standard. A thoroughgoing pragmatist cannot easily follow Quine here. What is the point of calling statements grade B when they are essential to our life[4]—as intentional discourse is? Indeed, how could a pragmatist, of all people, come to speak of 'limning the true and ultimate structure of reality'? One point will be a partial defence of Quine. Dissatisfaction with a straightforwardly pragmatic account of epistemic acceptability may naturally lead to Quine's distinction.

For reasons of space, however, I will here simplify by opposing Quine not to the (ordinary) pragmatist, but to an ordinary empiricist. In brief, empiricists aim to accept whatever theories best organize or explain the data of sense. Their difficulty over physicalism then arises from a clash with empiricist principle: one would expect empiricists to accept empirically successful theories without insisting, in addition, on physicalistic credentials. If the empirically best (most simple, adequate, . . .) account of the data is not physicalistic, then the worse for physicalism. Or so a consistent empiricist should apparently hold. Nor does the business of coping with the data visibly motivate any Quinian concern with theories that are, in some sense, *ultimately* adequate. Those appear rather as creatures of rationalist fancy, without empirical interest. Since such empiricist objections evidently parallel the pragmatist's, I will avoid complications arising from the possible differences between pragmatism and empiricism. The argument would be much the same either way. It will, however be useful to have a more specific label for Quine's empiricist opponent. I will contrast Quine's physicalist empiricism with *vanilla* empiricism. The

---

[3] This and the following lines draw on *Word and Object* (Cambridge, Mass., 1960), esp. ch. 5. For the double standard, see sect. 45; for talk of ultimate structure or categories, see pp. 161, 221; for Quine's ideal language of science, see esp. sect. 33 and 54–5.

[4] A question Hilary Putnam attributes to Donald Davidson in *The Many Faces of Realism* (La Salle, Ill. 1987), 70.

vanilla empiricist has no principled preference for advanced physical theory, holding instead to the simple aim of finding empirically
adequate explanations in any language or style that does the job.

The physicalist's attack on intentional concepts provokes a
distinctive kind of reaction. A main theme of philosophy in this
century has been the idea of pragmatic incoherence or self-defeat
for philosophical ideologies. Positivism, for example, was charged
with being neither analytic, nor empirically confirmed, hence
unwarranted by its own lights. Similarly for physicalism: since the
notion of *physicalistically acceptable theory* is thoroughly intentional, physicalists seem forced to reject it, thus rejecting their own
philosophy. Indeed (the challenge proceeds), physicalist strictures
would all but abolish our language, leaving us to wag our fingers
in the market-place. Conclusion: physicalism is unbelievable.[5]

Evaluating such arguments will be a main goal of this paper.
We will find that self-defeat may typically be avoided via Quine's
distinction between serious and grade B acceptability. A theory
calling itself nothing worse than grade B can survive its self-
demotion, remaining acceptable in a lower-grade way. Yet Quinian
physicalism does collapse. The difficulty will arise from the clash
of two separately plausible elements: empiricism and a modest
realism.

I am as much concerned with (referential) semantic as with
intentional concepts. The two categories are customarily linked:
Quine has challenged both, and other writers have shown deep
connections. Davidson, above all, has argued that the (sometimes
implicit) use of semantic terms pervades our attempts to understand
rational behaviour.[6] Moreover, our semantic discourse is at once
intentional. Such predicates as 'true' are applied to beliefs, statements, and the like; if these objects were banished from science,

---

[5] e.g., Lynne Rudder Baker, *Saving Belief: A Critique of Physicalism* (Princeton,
1987). See also Terence Horgan and George Graham, 'How to be Realistic about
Folk Psychology', *Philosophical Psychology*, 1 (1988), 69–81, and eid., 'In Defense
of Southern Fundamentalism', *Philosophical Studies*, 62 (1991), 107–34.

[6] *Inquiries into Truth and Interpretation* (Oxford, 1984). See also, e.g., H.
Putnam, 'Reference and Understanding', in *Meaning and the Moral Sciences* (London,
1978); Hartry Field, 'Tarski's Theory of Truth', *Journal of Philosophy*, 69 (1972),
347–75; Stephen Schiffer, 'Truth and the Theory of Content', in H. Parret and J.
Bouveresse, eds., *Meaning and Understanding* (Berlin, 1981).—It will be clear that
the semantic notions of interest in the present essay are 'transcendent', that is,
applicable to languages other than one's own. (The term is Quine's from *Philosophy
of Logic* (Englewood Cliffs, NJ, 1970).)

how would semantic predicates survive? Yet the semantic concepts require separate consideration for two reasons.

On the one hand, intentional concepts are part of a largely pre-scientific or proto-scientific body of doctrine. Following common practice, I will call this *folk psychology*. Since semantic discourse might, conceivably, be separable from folk-style explanation of behaviour, it might survive the elimination of folk psychology after all. Talk of reference and truth is not obviously tied to a particular explanatory framework in the way that belief and desire seem to be.

On the other hand, an acceptability result for intentional concepts might not transmit to semantic concepts. The empirical utility of the latter is widely taken to reside in their role in intentional explanation. Within a broadly empiricist framework, this is taken to show their acceptability—they do useful empirical work. But a familiar pragmatist idea suggests a difficulty here. Although Quine agrees that any enquiry involves the use of a truth concept *of sorts*, he proposes a surrogate for classical truth.[7] Following Dewey, he lets 'true' simply mean 'now justified' in some sense; the truth predicate is indexed to present theory and defined in purely epistemic terms. Now suppose that Quine is right about the kind of truth concept indispensable for enquiry in general. Suppose further that our applications of 'true' in intentional explanation could similarly be replaced without loss by a Quinian, quasi-semantic predicate (QT). Then the vanilla empiricist (henceforth V) might reject classical semantic terms even while keeping folk psychology. She would employ a combination of intentional and quasi-semantic terms. Semantic discourse would hence need a justification of its own.

I argue elsewhere that something like this situation arises.[8] QT suffices both for the intentional explanations Davidson and others have studied and for the regulation of enquiry: using only QT and related epistemic notions (such as empirical adequacy), one can formulate adequate concepts of error, objectivity, and the like. Thus one makes sense of oneself as an enquirer without

---

[7] *Word and Object*, 23–5.

[8] In 'On Some Concepts of Truth', a chapter of my aforementioned book (see n. 1 above). For another view, see Hartry Field, 'The Deflationary Concept of Truth', in G. MacDonald and C. Wright, eds., *Fact, Science, and Morality* (Oxford, 1986), 55–117.

recognizing a distinction between truth and empirical adequacy or a goal of progress toward truth. Key elements of classical truth are dropped. This is not, however, a case for the full dispensability of standard semantic concepts. For the use of QT turns out (I argue) to involve an ordinary notion of reference. Any validation of folk-psychological explanation would therefore save reference, although not a full truth concept. But this is a somewhat provisional outcome. Further analysis may show that everyday purposes require only a watered-down concept of reference to go with Quinian watered-down truth.

For the reasons of the past three paragraphs, I will end with a complex resolution. Although physicalism is wrong, a species of eliminationism may be right—there is a good sense in which folk psychology plus referential discourse may be only practically indispensable. I suspect that full-blown semantic concepts are, in contrast, fully dispensable. Yet there are grounds for keeping these, regardless of our verdict on folk psychology.

i

The tensions of interest to me surface in Quine's discussions of canonical notation in *Word and Object*. Quine maintains that the best theory is the one that will best 'get us around'.[9] Yet mentalistic discourse counts as second best, although it is practically indispensable—now and perhaps forever. This apparent inconsistency is to be resolved within a framework that posits dual goals of enquiry. One goal of the Quinian enquirer is to construct the best theory of the moment, the one that will let us organize our present data as best we now can. The other, dominant, one is to describe, and approach as nearly as possible, an acceptable *ultimate* theory. Taking the first goal to be clear for the sake of argument, let us more carefully consider the second.

A main project of *Word and Object* is to find a language for a regimented and comprehensive scientific theory. The first condition means that the theory is to be written out in the language of extensional, first-order logic. The second aims, in part, at unification: an ultimate theory uses a physical vocabulary plus other terms defined from that as needed via set theory. Intuitively,

[9] p. 161. See again n. 3 above.

everything is reduced to an advanced physics. Now the language alone (which for Quine is not 'merely notation' but an essential part of the theory) would prevent actual human beings from using such a theory. Our difficulties with predicate notation are notorious. It is also very doubtful that the human scientific community as a whole (let alone any single member) could grasp the sum of its scientific beliefs as a totality in any meaningful sense. We constantly struggle to connect and integrate the myriad, ever-changing bits of scientific information that see the light of day. And certainly, a Quinian ultimate theorist would need superhuman capacities for gathering data. For example, Quine's serious science of behaviour is supposed to be neural, yet it seems clear that no neuroscience could ever provide *us* with more than a few of the predictions we need. Combining these observations, I suggest (without pretending to be precise) that an ultimate theory is one we might hold had we radically idealized cognitive abilities. We would need unbounded (finite) resources for memory, attention, and computing speed; plus extensive powers to observe things large and small. (Perhaps an ultimate theory would be responsive to what Quine, in another context, calls 'all possible observations'.[10]) This notion of ultimate theory does not, of course, commit us to the possibility of a unique, perfect science. For any ultimate theory, there might be a stronger one, and ultimate theories might conflict. However, any ultimate theory would far surpass our theories (or, presumably, any humanly attainable ones) in its empirical adequacy and power.

In terms of the ideal of an ultimate theory, we may define serious acceptability for present theories: a theory is seriously acceptable if an ultimate theorist might hold it—as part of her larger view. Of course we can only guess at the contents of any ultimate theory. But seriously acceptable sentences are, as far as we can tell on our present evidence, good candidates for inclusion. They contrast with low-grade empirical theory: theory that is visibly unsuited for ultimate acceptability in spite of its present use. Intentional doctrine is one intended example of the latter.

---

[10] e.g., 'On Empirically Equivalent Systems of the World', *Erkenntnis*, 9 (1975), 313–28. For other uses of the idea of ultimate theory, see my 'The Rationalist Conception of Logic', *Notre Dame Journal of Formal Logic*, 28 (1987), 3–35, and 'Logicism', in M. Detlefsen, ed., *Proof and Knowledge in Mathematics* (London, 1992).

*V* divides sentences of theory into the acceptable and the unacceptable. (These labels may come in degrees, but that will not matter here.) For this Quine substitutes a tripartite scheme. We recognize the seriously acceptable, the unacceptable, and the grade B—the good, the bad, and the (useful but) ugly. The puzzle is why Quine should amend *V*'s simpler taxonomy and in what sense grade B status is supposed to be a significant condemnation.

## ii

Nancy Cartwright's account of physical theory is interesting in this connection.[11] In brief, physics as she sees it opportunistically uses a hotchpotch of jointly inconsistent models. We might use one model to obtain rough solutions to a large number of equations, another when we need less, but more precise, information. A certain model might yield good predictions, but require data that are hard to obtain. Sometimes the accuracy may seem worth buying, while at other times we use a competitor. How are our competing models related to reality? A natural idea is that at most one can be right; that perhaps none is, although some messy synthesis would be correct. But Cartwright rejects such reactions. To paraphrase her (rather freely), they have no empirical warrant. Physics is in the business of empirical prediction, and empirical goals are best served by continuing to work with an irreducible plurality of stories. The faith in a single best model is empirically and practically unmotivated—it is metaphysics in a bad sense.

Our set of models will evolve, but there is no reason to claim that just one present or future model will turn out to be the best. Nor would accepting unification as an ideal serve any purpose. Physics (or any science) will progress as much as it can through the attempt to find better and better pluralities of models, developing and superseding each set in turn. A future science may unify phenomena we now cannot, but it will proliferate new stories in its own way. Thus, our total view of the world—if we can even be said to have one—turns out to be thoroughly and irremediably inconsistent for Cartwright.

Realists will counter that unified, comprehensive accounts must

[11] *How the Laws of Physics Lie* (Oxford, 1983).

be possible in principle, even if they are practically unattainable. But how can that be maintained without begging the question? The issue may turn on the legitimacy of a seemingly minimal realist intuition.

Cartwright connects the value of a model to our interests and powers. Our choice of a model in any particular context depends on our resources, and on the kinds of predictions needed: what computers we have, what applications we intend, how expensive (in one sense or another) an error would be, and so forth. One may gloss this by saying that pragmatic considerations influence our choice, but it would be wrong to conclude that Cartwright is talking about pragmatic *as opposed* to empirical worth. She is concerned with the value of theories *as* scientific theories; one may call that value pragmatic if one likes, but then her point is that our empirical purposes have an irreducible pragmatic component. We want explanations and predictions, but the explanation or pre- diction we count as best in a context depends on what we need there, and on what we think we can get. Yet while our interests and powers determine, in a shifting way, what counts as best, it is hard—here the unguarded realist speaks—to think that reality likewise depends on us. More circumspectly, it is very natural to posit a standard of 'best theory' that abstracts from our changing, highly contingent purposes and abilities. It is tempting to think that how things are does not depend on, say, what kinds of equations we can now most efficiently solve. Thinking along these lines, one might try to distinguish empirical value that depends on our particular, accidental histories and characteristics from that which does not.

All our theories were obtained by us under the constraints of our interests and limits. We may be unable to factor out our contribution—but sometimes we can. Regarding a model whose merits depend heavily on our contingent situation, we may judge that it is not intrinsically superior to the rivals we eschew for one reason or another. Cartwright shows how such situations can arise. To take a contrasting case, the hypothesis of curved spacetime might be wrong, but *we* have no reason to suppose that smarter computers, different predictive goals, or better techniques of ob- servation would lead us to think so. Our best present guess is that this hypothesis would be empirically warranted even for scientists with quite different interests and powers. One might therefore give it a higher status, claiming that it is not only acceptable but remains so even when we abstract as best we can from our subjective position. If this is metaphysics, still it is hard to resist.

Our reflections on Cartwright have led to a Quinian position. The starting-point was a vanilla empiricism—the aim of accepting the empirically best theory. Cartwright's detailed study of empirical enquiry then suggested a distinction. Some theories are accepted for highly context-dependent reasons, while the merits of others appear more absolute. Thus we may naturally distinguish two grades of acceptability. Empirical acceptability of the higher kind would seem to remain stable under changes in our practical interests, computing powers, techniques of observation and experimentation, and the like.

This line of thought makes Quine's progress intelligible. The pragmatic factors governing enquiry, and our awareness of our limits, make *V*'s perspective unsatisfactory. Science gives us the world as an inconsistent hotchpotch. While we are forced to use this picture, we may envision, alongside it, a picture reached by more ideal means. And the elements of our present views that might fit into the latter picture are deemed acceptable in a way the rest are not.

The connection of Quine's abstract epistemology to Cartwright's material is admittedly not straightforward. The two philosophers are drawing different morals from rather different cases. Cartwright studies situations in which conflicting models are opportunistically employed. Since it would be inconsistent to believe them all, and arbitrary to select any one, she recommends an instrumentalist stance. Quine, however, allows us to believe grade B theories. Since his primary target, intentional psychology, does not suffer from serious competition within its own domain, believing it involves no straightforward irrationality. We may, as far as Quine is concerned, believe that we have beliefs and desires, as long as we concede that this is grade B thinking. In contrast, the Cartwright theories are not even candidates for Quinian grade B status: they are not sensible objects of belief.

Further, Quine's grade B label must subsume various cases. A plausible critique of intentional psychology is that its concepts are vague and ambiguous, it is riddled with exceptions, its nomic endowment is minimal, and it yields imprecise predictions or none in many central cases. The standard quantum theory would also plausibly count as grade B, but for quite different reasons: it combines empirical success with foundational ills of the first order. The best accounts of microphysical reality are, in a sense, incomprehensible; they certainly fail reasonable standards for conceptual clarity. (Cf. the calculus in the eighteenth century.) This catalogue of diverse failings leading to grade B status could no doubt be extended.[12]

Although these qualifications are important, they leave the underlying picture intact. The point about Cartwright was the ease with which a vanilla empiricist may come to a Quinian epistemology. Reflection on the nature of empirical theorizing leads naturally to a distinction between contextually acceptable doctrines and those more absolutely warranted. What we have just added is that, on the one hand, theories may fall short of ultimate acceptability in diverse ways, while on the other hand, some theories required for empirical purposes are not even grade B. This is significant, but it does not affect the motivation for complicating *V*'s scheme.

What now appears problematic is the nature of grade B acceptance for Quine. Grade B theory is empirically best in its domain, yet unfit for inclusion in ultimate theory. But this characterization is supposed to induce us to take up a different attitude: grade B, not serious, acceptance. Since this distinction is not, for Quine, a matter of belief versus non-belief, its content is unclear.

A natural question is why Quine would admit grade B *beliefs*, since they seem to clash with a fundamental epistemic value of his. His first aim, unlike *V*'s, is to evaluate beliefs from the viewpoint of ultimate theory. The primary question about a sentence is its potential for *ultimate* acceptability. So grade B belief seems to violate Quine's epistemic ideal. We commit ourselves to sentences taken to be ultimately unacceptable. To understand grade B acceptance, therefore, one thing we want to know is why it need *not*, for Quine, involve disbelief.[13]

There is a natural but fallacious attempt to show that any grade B belief must be irrational. Since grade B statements are ones we would ideally do without, it may seem that the object of a

---

[12] Hartry Field emphasized the diversity of the grade B category in his comments.

[13] To simplify the present discussion, I will follow Quine in setting aside the possibility of replacing belief by belief-like alternatives (e.g. 'acceptance').

grade B belief is a proposition that better-placed theorizers would probably reject. But then why shouldn't we, too, reject it? The recognition that our view would eventually be overcome seems to undermine our present stance. This reasoning, however, confuses the assignment of grade B status with negation. If I call *P* a grade B proposition, I claim that it would not appear in an ultimate theory. Still, *P* is my best present guess, so I affirm it. In general, I will certainly not suspect that its *negation* might ultimately be acceptable. It is one thing for ultimate theorists to fail to assert a proposition, quite another for them to deny it. This distinction is familiar from discussions of radical theoretical change, and we have here a special case of its commonplace application. When new theories significantly vary their predecessors' conceptual frameworks, the later attitude toward earlier claims is often neither assertion nor denial: consider how we now regard Newtonian statements about motion and time or Cartesian statements about perception. Similarly, to hold that ultimate theorists will not accept a certain doctrine is not to say that they will deny it. It may, rather, receive no simple evaluation from their refined viewpoint. So belief in grade B propositions leads to no simple inconsistency. Even if there is a general problem about combining belief with an awareness of our fallibility (as instrumentalists impressed by the history of error maintain), grade B propositions raise no special problems in this connection. The difficulty arises, rather, within Quine's particular stance. Why hold grade B beliefs, when our main goal is to occupy an ultimate theorist's viewpoint as best we can?

I believe Quine's resolution would be that a belief may serve the ideal of ultimately acceptable belief either directly or indirectly: by being suitable for inclusion in ultimate theory (which makes it seriously acceptable), or through its heuristic value with respect to ultimate theory. That is, a grade B theory might serve well as a starting-point for successive revisions and extensions leading toward a seriously acceptable descendant. In such a case, believing it is a ladder up to believing serious theory, and hence is reasonable.[14] It is justified pragmatically with respect to the dominant goal.

[14] The simplification of n. 13 enters here: I will not ask why we should *believe* grade B doctrines, as opposed to employing them in some instrumentalist way. The fuller version of this paper will show that the complications make no difference to the critique of Quine's physicalism.

Diverse grade B theories may have heuristic value of this kind. Folk psychology is one example: even a fairly strong eliminativist may hold that clarifying, testing, and modifying folk beliefs is a good route toward a more ultimately acceptable view. It is less obvious how grade B theories might *lack* such redeeming character. I suspect that there have been theories that were not only heavily wrong, but that—worse—were actually dead ends. Alchemy and behaviourism come to mind. Another example will follow shortly. Then we will also see how the requirement of heuristic value for grade B belief can be a significant constraint.

These remarks illuminate the possibility and nature of grade B belief for Quine. To accept a sentence as being grade B is to accept it merely in a temporizing way: understanding that it is not what one ultimately wants but that its acceptance will lead one closer to the ideal. One regards it as a concession—ideally temporary, actually perhaps eternal—to one's epistemic limits.

### iii

Quinian ultimate theory is physicalistic. But does only physical theory merit serious acceptance? And what are the boundaries of 'physics'?

I sympathize with the view (long Chomsky's) that 'physics' as employed by physicalists is too vague for any critical use. Also, the physical character of much unquestionably reputable science is doubtful: theories of computer architecture, for example, or population biology. Claims that these 'reduce to' physics seem to involve a notion of reduction unconstrained even by the standards of reductionist literature. Yet a critique of folk psychology in the physicalist spirit is still possible. The question is not whether folk psychology is physical (whatever that means) but whether cognitively ideal theorists would retain it. It seems reasonable (however vague) that an ultimate theory would include a recognizable form of physics. But an eliminationist argument might do without this assumption and without any bias toward the 'physical'.[15]

---

[15] Quine's tendency in recent years has been to base physicalism on a principle of the dependence of everything on physics (e.g. in 'Goodman's Ways of World-making', in *Theories and Things* (Cambridge, Mass. 1981). I doubt that anything

Let us consider a strictly limited eliminationism: folk psychology disappears from ultimate empirical theory. An eliminationist should not claim that actual humans could dispense with (all forms of) folk psychology. No good case for that has ever been made. She should also not assert that folk theory is empirically unjustified *simpliciter*. That is a position Stephen Stich may hold.[16] He argues that any work done by the folk theory is done better by a theory discussing only the computational, non-representational properties of mental states. But no one has a working scientific account of what 'mental syntax' is, or of our specific mental syntax. And certainly, no one can replace the useful generalizations we now state in folk terms. Although Stich can conceive their replacement in an advanced state of knowledge, there is, as things now stand, no empirical case for eliminating belief. Folk psychology is at least grade B acceptable and may always remain so. The eliminationist's best strategy is to argue that it is at most grade B, and to infer appropriate morals.

The problem lies in folk psychology's empirical limitations. To repeat: its concepts are vague and ambiguous, it is riddled with exceptions, its nomic endowment is minimal, and it often yields imprecise predictions or none. The predictive failures occur throughout the cases of great importance—whether someone will fall in love, choose engineering over painting, defect or stay loyal, serve to the backhand or the forehand, and so on. I am stating this without argument, but it is not really controversial. Critics have backed up these judgements in detail, and defenders have hardly contested them.[17] Such facts as that folk psychology is indispensable, that it is often illuminating, or that it guides research do not remove its defects.

of methodological interest follows from this (itself problematic) metaphysical premiss. The present section is intended to save as much of physicalism as can reasonably be saved.

[16] *From Folk Psychology to Cognitive Science: The Case against Belief* (Cambridge, Mass., 1983).

[17] A main critic is Patricia Churchland. The influence of her *Neurophilosophy* (Cambridge, Mass., 1986) will be clear, even though my position is, in part, radically opposed to hers. See also Stich, *From Folk Psychology*, and D. C. Dennett, *Brainstorms* (Hassocks, 1978). Some principal opponents are cited in note 5 above. Of course I am here discussing only some of the considerations that bear on physicalism. Notably omitted are problems about *qualia*, particularly as addressed in the literature reacting to Thomas Nagel's 'What Is it Like to be a Bat?', *Philosophical Review*, 83 (1974), 435–50, repr. in Nagel, *Mortal Questions* (Cambridge, 1979).

It is widely agreed that a computational neuroscience would be superior—if it were sufficiently advanced, and if we had access to enough data. A systematic theory of processing in the brain should illuminate a range of now mysterious cases, as well as handling those we find intelligible. But that science would not be folk psychology. It would discuss kinds of storage, processing, and representation that we are now only beginning to describe.

A main point is that the brain is viewed as a vast number of systems passing information among each other according to complex schemes. This abandons the folk viewpoint. Behaviour here depends not on attitudes attributed to the thinking system as a whole (as in folk description), but on just where, and on what causal paths, specific pieces of information are located. Moreover, although this cognitive-scientific use of 'information' is not yet clear (there are likely to be several relevant construals), we certainly do not want to attribute propositional attitudes to neural assemblies in general. Neural states must have representational content in some sense, but ultimate theory would not explain an organism's behaviour by attributing *beliefs* to bits and pieces of its brain. Indeed, residual talk of explaining the actions of functional subsystems of the brain in terms of their desires, expectations, beliefs, and so forth will clearly be left behind.

Such considerations have been rehearsed at length elsewhere, notably in Dennett's discussions[18] of personal versus subpersonal description. They may be expanded on in a variety of ways, leading to a radical condemnation of folk psychology as *science*. To add one familiar, central difficulty, consider the semantics of belief sentences. If we are required to give a recognizably plausible semantics in terms that bring fewer troubles than they remove, then there is some reason to judge the problem unsolvable. But the lack of an accepted semantics means—by definition—that we cannot even agree on what follows *immediately by logic* from a belief attribution. This fact has not always been sufficiently appreciated: *what kind of a language for serious theory is that?*

A rejoinder is that the concepts and patterns of folk explanation would, nearly enough, be implicit in an advanced neuroscience. As one says, the intentional psychology would reduce to its ultimate successor. Approximations to folk concepts would be definable,

---

[18] In *Brainstorms*.

perhaps with the help of set theory and parameters, from the ultimate theorist's terms. And this, one may hold, is enough. Seriously acceptable doctrine need not be a candidate for explicit inclusion in an ultimate theory; the prospect of reduction suffices.

This raises complex issues about reduction and the character of an ultimate theory. But these can be passed over here, since the prospect of reduction has simply not been made out.[19] A common observation in the philosophy of science is that only fairly good theories end up being reduced. The weak are replaced. Given the massive empirical weakness of folk theory, the folk psychologist would have to assert reducibility not for her present theory, but for some highly evolved descendant.[20] But why should progress yield a sufficiently advanced *intentional* psychology? The needed evolution may remove just what distinguishes folk theory. Indeed, this appears to be the tendency in cognitive science. To maintain that the folk theory would reduce to an ultimate neuroscience effectively begs the question by assuming the long-term viability of just the concepts at issue.

Of course, something in folk psychology may be partially reducible in some reasonable sense. That is a very weak claim, compatible with grade B status or worse. All kinds of grade B theories—e.g., the calculus in the eighteenth century, Newtonian mechanics, our foundations for quantum mechanics—do or will (presumably) admit partial reductions to seriously acceptable theories. Intuitively, this means that they are not *totally* wrong. For the eliminationist to grant such a claim on behalf of folk psychology is no concession.

This situation needs more study. But I am relying on the empirical defects of folk theory, plus the contrast between folk explanations and those found in the study of neural information-processing. These factors should make the argument for grade B status robust. It does not turn on which detailed interpretation of the grade B label we settle on, or which precise account of the relation of folk theory to an ultimate psychology. Note that although we have

---

[19] These remarks should also apply, with changes, to the more Davidsonian position of Terence Horgan and James Woodward, 'Folk Psychology Is Here to Stay', *Philosophical Review*, 94 (1985), 197–226. My general idea is to put epistemology first: to base our attitude toward folk theory on its strengths and weaknesses as theory. And I propose that the defects we find cast doubt on the possibility of *any* reasonable mapping of is objects onto those of an advanced science.

[20] Cf. Churchland, *Neurophilosophy*.

rejected physicalist bias, an echo of the preference for physics remains. Ultimate theorists would use comprehensive, systematic, rigorous theories whose observational bases are largely inaccessible to us, and whose application introduces formidable complexities. An ideal physics would be one such theory. Although an ultimate theory of behaviour would not be physics in any good sense, it would share these features and would thus have virtually no use for folk concepts. A grade B status for folk psychology follows; and that is a significant, albeit limited, condemnation.

One familiar reaction to the empirical critique of folk psychology is that scientific standards are out of place here. Folk psychology is not science nor a step towards science. Folk explanations of action (the objector continues) do not, even implicitly, subsume actions under general laws or appeal to models of an agent's causal organization. They neither resemble scientific explanations closely nor compete with them. Perhaps the very properties that are defects from a scientific viewpoint, such as the vagueness of folk predicates or the ways in which an interpreter's interests might colour her interpretations, are virtues given the actual role of folk psychology in our lives.

Although I will not evaluate such claims here, they seem plausible. They do not, however, remove the empirical defects of folk doctrine. A mediocre television set is not redeemed by the discovery that it is an excellent piece of modern sculpture—not, that is, if it is needed to receive television signals. And clearly, one does use folk psychology empirically: to explain and predict the behaviour of agents, oneself included. Given its weakness in this respect, an ultimate enquirer interested in good empirical results would use something else.

This last remark clarifies an eliminationist presupposition: that ultimate enquirers will be purely empirical theorists rather than pursuing the other ends folk psychology might serve. Otherwise they would not necessarily dispense with folk psychology. Of course this is no problem for Quine, who judges total views just by their success in organizing the data of sense. But someone who would favour the pursuit of non-empirical goals even under cognitively ideal conditions might seriously accept folk doctrine. It would be taken to serve those goals regardless of our imagined facility in predicting, say, neural computations.

This line cannot be evaluated apart from details about the

hypothesized non-empirical purposes of folk psychology. That is a matter for other occasions. Note, however, that finding such purposes is not nearly a sufficient defence against the eliminationist. In addition one must show, first, that these purposes are not largely parasitic on our empirical applications. Perhaps folk interpretation serves its various social or personal ends poorly to the extent that its predictions are unreliable and its explanations weak. (In that case the analogy might be with a family car, which has many functions besides simple transportation, but which does badly at all of them if it won't run.) Second, one needs to argue that an empirically superior theory would not serve the assorted ends of folk psychology just as well. Otherwise ultimate theorists could anyway dispense with folk descriptions and gain a good theory into the bargain. These two arguments will not easily be made. For the moment, we lack clear reason to believe that folk psychology would survive the transition to ultimate theory. Its serious acceptability remains in doubt.

Section v will return to these issues, although without offering anything near a resolution. Let me remark in passing that the considerations of the past two sections may shed light on instrumentalist tendencies in the philosophy of mind, indeed on the general empiricist tendency toward instrumentalism. One might, similarly, apply them to questions of ontology—of whether to assert the existence of belief and consciousness. But of these things another time. I turn to the status of Quinian physicalism within Quine's own framework.

iv

Quinian epistemology, like any other, uses the intentional vocabulary of belief, reason, and so forth. Its characteristic further notions, such as those of a physical or physicalistically acceptable theory, are also intentional (and semantic). A grade B status for his epistemology does not follow at once, since epistemology is normative; we previously defined grades of acceptability for descriptive theories. An ultimate theorist would, however, state her norms using her descriptive vocabulary. So she would apparently not be a Quinian epistemologist. If we extend our definition to normative doctrines in an obvious way, then Quinian epistemology is also grade B. So, indeed, is any epistemology. If I am right, ultimate theorists would avoid anything close to our notions of science, evidence, and ultimate theory itself. Our descriptions of ultimate enquiry would not be the enquirers' own.

This brings no immediate self-defeat. Since grade B doctrine is believable for Quine, he can allow belief in a grade B physicalism that admits its own non-physicalistic character. This may seem odd, but it is straightforward on reflection. Once we permit grade B belief in general, there is no special problem about a grade B theory that happens to be our theory of epistemic status. Intuitively, a grade B theory is an ultimately inadequate but best available answer to certain questions. (Remember: ultimate theorists are not presumed to *deny* any theory, such as physicalism, that we label grade B.) But as it is now the best available answer, it is sensibly acceptable. In particular, physicalism can stand as our present epistemological programme, even as we recognize its limitations in principle.

We see an effect of Quine's trichotomy. A danger of self-defeat arises for epistemologies dichotomizing the acceptable and the unacceptable. These cannot call themselves unacceptable, on pain of pragmatic incoherence. But as long as grade B status is a form of acceptability, self-classification as grade B is not automatically disqualifying. And this is quite generally relevant to the question of physicalism. The dichotomous epistemology precludes any even prima-facie reasonable physicalist thesis. One is forced to put good physical science (in any sense) on one side and everything else on the other, thus grouping the human sciences with astrology and demonology. Only a scheme like Quine's gives proper weight to the distinction between good and bad non-physics. So self-defeat arguments that fail to take Quine's division into account attack a physicalism Quine himself does not hold and that is too plainly unreasonable to make subtle undermining worth bothering with. When we move to the tripartite division, however, the self-defeat argument loses force.

Yet I think Quine's epistemology collapses after all. Recall that for Quine, grade B beliefs should bring us closer to an ultimate theory. When is an epistemology grade B acceptable? A necessary condition is that applying its categories and following its prescriptions should aid empirical progress. And physicalism fails on just this count. We will not approach better theories via the use of physicalist classifications and strictures. Indeed, although I will address the following argument to a physicalist specifically, Quine's bias toward physics will play no role. It is his trichotomy—the very element that blocked the standard self-defeat challenge—that is heuristically useless. Quinian epistemology fails because the scheme of serious versus grade B acceptability serves no empirical purpose.

Enquiry as we understand it requires a distinction between acceptable and unacceptable belief. Agents must see themselves as seeking acceptable rather than unacceptable belief in some rule-governed way. The question is whether replacing this picture with one based on Quine's trichotomy would lead to superior empirical results. To pursue this, consider two enquirers. The first is *V*, who accepts empirically confirmed theory, rejects the rest, and continuously updates her views in the light of new data. The second, *Q*, is a Quinian physicalist. Aiming for a comprehensive, unified physical theory, she seriously accepts what might belong to one; other empirically useful doctrine is labelled grade B. Will *Q* empirically outperform her vanilla counterpart in the long run?

The two are identical in certain respects. Both reject empirically unsupported sentences—vanilla empiricism is not distinguished by lax standards of evidence. Both also accept good physical theory— vanilla empiricists value physics as much as anyone. The possible differences would lie in their treatments of empirically acceptable, non-physical doctrine. Here I know of two arguments on *Q*'s behalf.[21]

1. Since the serious acceptability of apparently non-physical doctrine turns on physical reduction, *Q* will have stronger reason to seek reductions—they are needed to vindicate working grade B theories. Thus *Q* will tend to gain a more unified science.

2. Since doctrine that does not reduce to physics is unacceptable in the long run, *Q* will surpass *V* in hostility toward theories that resist reduction. *Q* is less likely to tolerate theories, such as those of ESP, that seem irreducible yet have some measure of empirical support. And such theories merit no tolerance. So at any time, *V* is likely to accept dubious sentences that *Q* avoids.

---

[21] I owe both to Hartry Field. 'Tarski's Theory of Truth' emphasizes the first; other lectures and comments have emphasized the second.

These are really two aspects of one idea: that physicalism pushes
$Q$ toward a science that is more unified, and less cluttered with
epistemic debris.

But, to begin, (1) is simply wrong. Reductions are valuable
independently of any reductionist programme. They do have a
special, additional meaning for reductionists: they show acceptability, or a higher grade of it. But their empirical value is a
sufficient reason for $V$ to seek them in every case in which $Q$
does. Any survey of the usual examples—from thermodynamics,
genetics, physiological psychology, and so on—will show that the
reductions led to tremendous empirical progress. Knowledge of
underlying mechanisms brings deeper understanding of the reduced
theory (including its limits and generalizations); at the same time,
we discover fruitful questions for the reducing theory. And a successful reduction explains formerly primitive laws, which is agreed
on all sides to be an explanatory advance. The empirical benefits
of reduction are uncontroversial. But then $V$ will not lack reductive
ardour.

More generally, $V$ will have every bit as much reason as $Q$ to
improve theories that the latter deems grade B. Relegation to grade
B status results from *empirical* deficiencies, as we have seen. Such
features as excessive vagueness, lack of generality, *ad hoc* elements,
and conceptual unclarity reduce the empirical success of a theory
in a sense that is fully accessible to $V$. Since $V$ wants the best
empirical theories she can get, she will constantly aim to clarify,
refine, and otherwise improve all of them. Declining to call any of
the lesser ones grade B will not lead to any complacency. Hence
$Q$'s distinguishing interest in judgements of ultimate acceptability
does not translate into a difference in ongoing empirical practice.
So far, then, $Q$ and $V$ behave indistinguishably.

(2) is a more complex case. We may have either the mere illusion
of a difference or a difference that cuts *against* $Q$.

If the claim is that $Q$ will have better reason to reject theories
inconsistent with established physics, this is again wrong. $V$, like
$Q$, accepts established physics. Something that conflicts with it (or
seems very likely to) would need greater independent confirmation
in order to be acceptable. Since fanciful cases of this kind are
presumably not at issue (they would, among other things, force
reconsideration of any physicalism), $V$ will be equally ready to
condemn offences against physics.

Would $Q$ more easily reject doctrines that, although perhaps consistent with existing physics, appear to resist any future reduction? I do not think this attitude is obligatory for physicalists. But if $Q$ assumes it, her performance will indeed differ from $V$'s—for the worse.

$Q$'s gain will be an easier rejection of theories ultimately irreconcilable with physics. Whereas $V$ must wait for clear empirical failure to defeat doctrines of (say) ESP, $Q$ will be able to dismiss these near the start. But this advantage of $Q$'s is small, and the cost is high. The empirical inadequacies of a theory like ESP appear soon enough; good experimental practice will bring their dismissal as surely as rejection on physicalist principle. It takes just a little more patience. On the other hand, $Q$ is going to inhibit theories whose appearance of ultimate irreducibility reflects only the limits of current physical theory. This may significantly retard progress, since empirically valuable theories may be proposed in the absence even of vague prospects for reduction. And when such prospects do obtain, it often appears accidental in a way that encourages no confidence in $Q$'s strictures.

Consider Chomskyan linguistics. Even now, we have no understanding of how innate mechanisms of Chomsky's kind could arise; and at best a vague idea of how the requisite learning machinery could be realized in the brain, questions of innateness aside. If his ideas had been introduced before the advent of modern digital computers and brain theory—as might easily have happened, given small changes in the evolution of science—its physical reducibility would have been hardly less mysterious than ESP's. Yet it should in any case have been developed as a treatment of data in its own psychological and linguistic domain, just as happened in reality. There are many other examples. Darwinian theory was rightly accepted before anyone knew how the needed mechanisms of variation could be implemented. The law of valences was mysterious before quantum chemistry. Economics is an entire science with no prospects of reduction at all—not even, at the moment, to psychology. Shelving theories that we have no idea how to reduce would cripple enquiry. Nor does science obey any such rule. Better to keep a few poor bets around until they fail on their own terms than to kill ideas born early.

Given a useful, unreduced theory, $Q$ will reasonably be concerned about its reducibility. But since $V$ values reductions equally, this element of scientific practice is preserved either way. Of course the lower-level theories may offer no hope of reduction in a given case. $V$ will then not worry about constraints and demands that might restrict $Q$. We improve our various theories as best we can, waiting for possible connections to develop. The physicalist's real worry may be this: what if an empirically successful theory posits interactions for which there seems to be no hope of physical reduction at all? Suppose that something like ESP seemed empirically sound. Shouldn't we still insist that the data must be wrong, instead of overthrowing our picture of physical reality?

As far as I can tell, such challenges (however fanciful) add nothing new. What if some brilliant Stoics had discovered the theory of formal grammars, then invented a version of Chomskyan linguistics? The necessary psychological mechanisms could not have been sketched by any theory, materialist or immaterialist, for two millennia. So, what? Our Stoics would have been right to proceed in blithe disregard of the primitive state of their lower-level sciences. Similarly, solid evidence for telepathy would just be one more sign of how much we have to learn.

So physicalism offers no methodological advantage, no improved ability to find good empirical theory. What Quine adds to vanilla empiricism is a piece of metaphysics—just as his talk of ultimate structures and categories lets us suspect. His metaphysical addition may be extremely natural, but it is gratuitous by his own empirico-pragmatic lights. Since his epistemology is, on his terms, warranted only if empirically fruitful, it is unwarranted—not even grade B, not even instrumentally or pragmatically valuable. It does defeat itself.

Note that the serious–grade B distinction has not been under attack. On the contrary, I earlier tried to make it seem natural. But we now see that it is a departure from pragmatism and empiricism, hence not an option for Quine. I have likewise left open—indeed, also sympathetically presented—the possibility that intentional discourse is deficient for essentially the physicalists' reasons. Folk psychology is, probably, low-grade empirical doctrine, to be radically superseded in the limit of enquiry for all empirical purposes. (More on this below.) So I am conceding much more than most critics of physicalism. Yet the result is not physicalism. First, *physicalism* has simply not been defended. Even if a theory-transcendent notion of 'physics' could be made out, why should an entire ultimate theory reduce to physics in any half-way constrained sense? I have suggested only that ultimate theorists would favour computational neuroscience over folk psychology. Second, physicalism grows out of an exclusive preference for good empirical science. Yet making the serious–grade B distinction is inconsistent with this underlying motivation. Combining these two points, observe that ultimate theorists need not, for all we have said, limit themselves to empirical theorizing, or to pragmatically mandated efforts. Their interests may go well beyond scientific perfection and the pursuit of well-being in any obvious sense. (More on this, too, below.)[22]

The fundamental physicalist ideas are scientific hegemony and the epistemological trichotomy. The first leads to collapse, and I see no reason to keep it in any form. The second hardly suffices for physicalism, even with the demotion of folk psychology thrown in. But given that physicalism fails, we need a closer look at the remaining options.

v

One consistent stance is, presumably, some form of vanilla empiricism: we rigorously avoid empirically superfluous concepts and beliefs. The precise commitments of this kind of position are unclear. Considerations favouring theoretical *belief* need to balanced against those favouring instrumental treatments; the admissibility of a priori justifications must be settled; there are Kantian questions about the need for a basic, in some sense non-empirical, framework of concepts underlying empirical enquiry. But however these issues may turn out, V may have to live with some disquieting omissions.

Recall that Quine's position was deeply motivated. Understanding what empirical justification means for us, we may naturally measure our theories by a more absolute kind of acceptability. This motivation is accessible to V: she can accept the epistemic terms (belief, acceptability, . . .) needed to formulate it and can recognize the role of pragmatic considerations in our theorizing.

---

[22] I offer a complementary discussion of physicalism in 'Why Realism can't be Naturalized', in Steven J. Wagner and Richard Warner, eds., *Naturalism: A Critical Appraisal* (Notre Dame, Ind., 1992). See also the introduction to that volume.

Yet following out the argument will land her in $Q$'s self-defeating
view. For if she is still fundamentally empiricist, she will be unable
to justify the Quinian trichotomy. She will therefore fall back to
vanilla empiricism. If these are the only two options, our epistemology may be profoundly unstable, ever vacillating between the
points represented by $V$ and $Q$. The former tends to lead out of
itself into the latter, which then collapses back. Now reflective
beings may simply be doomed eternally to retrace such Kantian
loops. But one does hope for an escape.

I also conjectured, in section i, that $V$ can restrict herself to a
Quinian truth concept. Both the general conduct of enquiry and
intentional explanation may get by with a notion of truth as present
acceptability. If so, $V$ would at least in part eliminate traditional
semantic concepts. Yet one may, even while granting the consistency
of $V$'s stance, prefer a more conservative option. What Quine
notably surrenders is reflection on the possible falsity of our best
present theories; lost with that is any reasonable way of regarding
the future course of enquiry as progress. These costs are perhaps
not lightly accepted. The possibility of presuming (justified) present
views to be false, and the hope of correction by future enquiry,
may seem fundamental to our view of ourselves as theorists.

One recourse is to stipulate that the use of a (classical, non-
Quinian) truth concept shall be part of any acceptable total view.
Not that the stipulation should be arbitrary—on the contrary. We
may hold the reflections Quine eschews to be intrinsically
worthwhile—to embody a perspective on our enquiring that we
wish to retain, as long as we enquire. The point of the stipulation
is to free the relevant truth concept from empirical obligations: we
would keep it, even if it does not serve our empirical purposes.
Thus we maintain, in addition to $V$'s empiricist goals, the aim of
asking (classical) semantic questions as enquiry continues. That
aim will stand alongside coping with the data of sense as a fundamental epistemic value.

Since space prohibits an adequate treatment of this proposal, I
will merely sketch some main difficulties and implications. To this
end, let us explore the perspective of a philosopher $T$, who wishes
to preserve some form of classical semantic thought; who would
escape $V$'s expressive limitations and do justice to $Q$ without
falling into the latter's inconsistency. My sympathies will be clear.

To begin with, $T$'s stipulation is very strong. What if future discoveries invalidate semantic discourse? What, for instance, if empirical or logical investigations reveal such confusions and false presuppositions as beset the lore of witchcraft? For example, any application of semantic terms might lead to paradox.[23] Or, learning theory might show that the linguistic structures semantics requires are illusory. *T* replies that since these doubts cannot absolutely be ruled out, her proposal is conditional. She requires the use of semantic terms as long as possible: as long as it is consistent with good science. In this connection, *T* introduces a distinction between the empirically *necessary* (or useful) and the empirically *tolerable*. With *V*, *T* accepts empirically necessary doctrine. Like *V*, she gives empirical claims priority: doctrine inconsistent with good empirical science must go. But she insists on using semantic terms provided no such clash arises. In so far as it seems unlikely that 'true' should actually be empirically illegitimate, not just superfluous, this modification of her stance will look small.

Yet doesn't *T* overlook facts about conceptual evolution? No one would stipulate that any future theorist must employ our notions of force, say, or justice. We admit that these may be superseded. Semantics, too, does not stand still. The paradoxes have changed how we think about truth; while we may still describe ourselves as investigating traditional semantic concepts, we must concede both the change and the possibility of further developments. Semantic concepts are, further, tied to intentional ones, as remarked early on. Truth is predicated of beliefs, statements, and such. All sides concede that such psychological and linguistic notions are open to at least some revision. Why must truth as we understand it still be a useful predicate when the revisions are done?

In view of such considerations, some writers suggest that future theories must contain not truth but an as yet unknown 'successor concept'.[24] But this is unhelpful. *T* is better off insisting (conditionally) on the appearance of *translations* of our semantic terms in any future theory. Since translation in the relevant sense applies

---

[23] This worried Tarski in 'The Concept of Truth in Formalized Languages', in *Logic, Semantics, Metamathematics* (Oxford, 1956). The next worry is arguably Quine's in *Word and Object*.

[24] e.g., Paul Churchland, in Z. Pylyshyn and W. Demopoulos, eds., *Meaning and Cognitive Structure: Issues in the Computational Theory of Mind* (Norwood, NJ, 1986), 244 and 252. I owe the reference to H. Putnam's *Representation and Reality* (Cambridge, Mass., 1988).

to inter-theoretic contexts, this claim involves notorious difficulties. Yet we still do speak of inter-theoretic translation. Although some claims about translatability appear too problematic to evaluate, we find ourselves definitely able to accept or reject others. And a difficult but somewhat understood notion of translation is better than a thoroughly unconstrained notion of successor concept. (We do better to use the notion of translation forthrightly, warts and all, than to obscure our commitments with a new label.) T therefore maintains that conceptual evolution will not keep future enquirers from using a truth concept recognizable to us; and that they, being in a position to use one, shall indeed do so.

Of course this is no attempt to impose a binding requirement on our descendants. *T* is, rather, recommending a vision to *us*. We are to regard a classical truth concept as essential to an acceptable world view; we should hence aim to retain it as theory changes. But now *T* confronts a difficulty.

*T* will distinguish between grade B and serious acceptability. The distinction is well motivated, and *T*, being uncommitted to holding only empirically (or pragmatically) useful beliefs, may indulge in metaphysics. So *T* will give folk psychology a grade B status, for the reasons of section iii. The dependence of semantic concepts on folk-psychological (and linguistic) concepts then seems to make semantics dispensable. Even if any human enquirer must use a form of folk psychology, we have reason to think that ultimate theorists would proceed otherwise. And, not speaking of beliefs and other propositional attitudes, they would lose the objects of which we predicate truth. Hence the semantic predications, too, would presumably disappear. A truth predicate will be of no use to an ultimate theorist who has nothing to apply it to. Why, then, should we give semantic discourse any distinguished status now? Why insist on preserving it, even should it lose empirical utility? More intelligent theorists would, anyway, not posit the mental states to which a truth predicate applies.

Here *T* can try two lines of defence.

(*a*) *T* might deny that semantic predication would end with the demise of folk psychology. The latter may ultimately disappear,[25]

---

[25] Here and in similar contexts, 'ultimately' means 'in an ultimate theory'. I emphasize that there is no suggestion of our ever actually reaching such a theory.

but current cognitive neuroscience is shot through with talk of representations. Since such talk is ultimately acceptable as far as we know, it seems that objects of semantic predication would still be around: ultimate theorists would predicate truth of neural states or structures, not of propositional attitudes. The problem, however, is that the representations of neuroscience may be unsuitable for semantic evaluation in the relevant sense.

Many writers have tried to explicate various notions of representation used in cognitive science.[26] The result has been failure— *if* success means that representation as explicated should fundamentally resemble belief. For no one has shown how to give 'representations' determinate, non-arbitrary content of the kind beliefs are taken to have.[27] To use an overworked example, does the frog's neural system represent bugs, or black dots, or . . .?[28] Moreover, the contents in cognitive science are naturally assigned subpersonally: to units much smaller than the whole system. (Indeed, this is absolutely central to the cognitive-scientific revolution, as Dennett has long seen.) But of course these points signal failure only if cognitive science is required to preserve the language of folk psychology. They obstruct neither ongoing research nor the attempt to formulate a satisfactory theoretical vocabulary.[29] Whether the content of the frog's state is taken to concern bugs, or black dots, or . . . does not really matter to cognitive science. The natural moral is this: there is now no reason to believe that an ultimate theory of brain and behaviour would use a fundamentally folk-psychological notion of representation. Athough neural representations are analogous to beliefs in certain respects, they also differ crucially: in the units to which they are assigned and, above all, in the nature and determinacy of their contents. Nor is there any clear reason to expect a

---

[26] e.g., Dennett, *The Intentional Stance* (Cambridge, Mass., 1987); F. Dretske, *Explaining Behavior* (Cambridge, Mass., 1988); R. G. Millikan, *Language, Thought and Other Biological Categories* (Cambridge, Mass., 1984) and 'Biosemantics', *Journal of Philosophy*, 86 (1989), 281–97; R. Cummins, *Meaning and Mental Representation* (Cambridge, Mass., 1989).

[27] Jerry Fodor describes the problem very well in ch. 4 of *Psychosemantics* (Cambridge, Mass., 1987)—before falling to it himself.

[28] Recent lectures by Fodor have stressed the force of this question against the popular teleological approaches to content.

[29] This is a main point of Cummins, *Meaning*, who dwells on the difference between representation in an ordinary, folk-psychological sense and the notion that seems most useful for cognitive science.

folk-psychological notion of representation to be constructible from, or reducible to, these others.

If cognitive science will not save *T*'s concept of representation, it will not save her concept of truth. Our use of 'true' presupposes determinately true or false bearers of truth values, and this determinacy rests on a presumed determinacy of content. If the cognitive theorist does not offer determinate representational content, then she provides no foothold for semantic evaluation. Folk contents are determinate; if hers are not, then theory has introduced a distinct notion of representation, unsuitable for folk purposes. Let us call folk representation, with its determinacy of content, Representation. Our speculation, then, is that although an ultimate science might trade in representations, it will abandon Representation.

*T* can try to turn this situation to her advantage. Our notion of belief gets its meaning from its folk applications. Ultimately, it would be dropped as part of a primitive vocabulary. But why tie the notion of truth to the specifics of human psychology, let alone to our inadequate present picture of them? We may also have, apart from that picture, a more general—yet ill-articulated—notion of Representation: Representations are states susceptible of (determinate) truth and falsity. This notion subsumes belief, yet one might posit Representation only. One might largely reject the framework within which belief appears (perhaps a functional theory articulating our present understanding), while leaving room for a state that is generally belief-like. Thus, while *T* lets folk psychology be eliminated in principle, she may hope to exploit a distinction between everyday psychological thought and the use of a concept of truth. The latter may be general enough to admit separation from an ultimately dispensable theory of the types and interactions of our inner states.

*T*'s commitment to truth now further limits her eliminationism: she posits ultimate detention of a belief-like notion, an echo of the folk vocabulary. But as noted earlier, an ultimate theory can hardly fail to keep *something* of the folk scheme. And this bit of conservation is small. Since we characterize Representations just as states susceptible of truth and falsity, we are explicitly committed only to one element in a rich description of our inner life. We abstract from our belief concept until only a rather formal property remains: of saying, determinately, 'this is how things stand.'[30] Anything in the folk conception of belief and other mental states that goes beyond this may still—but only ultimately—be eliminated with indifference.

I earlier noted a possible gap between folk psychology and (classical) semantic thought—empirical utility for the former might not save the latter. But this may, as we now see, cut both ways. The empirical critique of folk psychology might not impugn the concept of truth. Thus also, a general notion of Representation would need no neuroscientific validation.

*T*'s proposal is not—I emphasize—that ultimate theorists would, after the fall of folk psychology, speak of Representation and truth for *empirical* purposes. We grant that ultimate empirical theory posits representations, not Representation. But *T*, remember, only needs Representation to be empirically tolerable. As long as science fails to rule out Representational states, *T* holds that any adequate total theory should consider the truth and falsity of Representations. Thinking about truth and Representation, but not belief, is stipulated to be a desirable feature of enquiry, hence immune to empirical developments. Unless, of course, such developments should show that semantic thought is positively wrong, not just empirically dispensable. But nothing I know of points in that direction.

(*b*) *T*'s second defence would be to accept the positive result of (*a*) while taking a much less conciliatory, defensive stance toward empiricism. Keeping truth and Representation regardless of the fate of folk psychology is well and good, but why surrender the psychology? (*a*) violates empiricism by insisting on the use of truth for non-empirical purposes. Ultimate theorizers are thus permitted non-empirical goals. So why not let them also retain the empirically sub-optimal folk language for such ends? As noted in Section iii, the grade B classification of folk psychology derives from an empiricist view of ultimate theory. Yet (*a*) has already modified that. Making one exception, for truth, opens the door to others.

---

[30] Wittgenstein, *Tractatus* 4. 5 and *Investigations* 1. 136. In moving from the *Tractatus* to the *Investigations*, Wittgenstein turned from a highly formal notion of proposition to an exploration of the folk scheme. My distinction between belief and Representation is analogous to ones used by Stich (*From Folk Psychology*, e.g. 217–19) and others, although there are differences both of detail and, notably, of intended application. (Stich's remarks, ibid., on the richness and cross-cultural diversity of folk notions undermine our convenient pretence of a unique reference for 'folk psychology'.)

Section iii also recorded the uncertainties attending this line of thought. Neither the non-empirical benefits of folk psychology nor the absence of alternative routes to these have been established. Yet suppose we assign intrinsic, non-empirical value to a view of ourselves as Representing. If that seems important, what about the view of ourselves as subjects of wish, enjoyment, love, imagination, desire, and courage? Such folk terms make possible a family of descriptions we may want to apply even if an ultimate theory of brain and behaviour were also available. An intrinsic attachment to a conception of human beings as capable of Representation, without an analogous view of love, would be curiously (pathologically?) intellectualist. But if a rich folk vocabulary is to be retained for what might be called personal and moral reasons, then the empirical limits of this language do not entail grade B status. So the language of propositional attitudes on which semantic discourse seems to depend is not in danger of ultimate elimination, and $T$'s commitment to that discourse is safe. This is defense (*b*).

I find this a powerful argument. It is essentially compatible with (*a*), since the effect of the latter is to add an extra line of resistance if the grade B label for folk psychology turns out to stick. The difficulty with (*b*) is that it is not, after all, very clear just how much of our folk picture we should be wedded to. Ideal knowledge might lead us willingly to revise our self-descriptions and, with them, the forms of human behaviour and attachment. The eliminationist is not (as the Churchlands like to stress) necessarily condemning ultimate enquirers to a barren regimen of perception and ratiociation.

Perhaps (*a*) and (*b*) ultimately lead to similar questions. (*a*) exploited the presumed gap between belief and the general notion of a truth-valued state. Thus we envisioned keeping the latter without the former's numerous specific elements. Of course this calls for a clear and informative way of drawing the distinction, which I have not given. The question for (*b*) is how much of such concepts as love and imagination is to be deemed ineliminable from our view of ourselves as persons, how much open to revision or replacement, at least in principle. To make progress, one would have to spell out these concepts more precisely and judge the extent of their ties to our present, limited, viewpoint. That would amount to judging which elements in our folk scheme are ultimately acceptable, on the understanding that empirical criteria alone would not be decisive. This is a forbidding task. In the meantime, $T$ can leave this possibility open while opting at least for the conservative defence (*a*). As long as $T$ is just committed to defending truth, she need insist only on keeping the notion of a belief-like state in the broadest sense: a state that represents in some prepositionally determinate way. Even ultimate theorists can call such states true or false.

$T$'s position is vague in any case. One question is what it is for an ultimate theory to contain a translation of 'true'. To answer that would be to explain the general notion of a truth concept—a task obstructed by the paradoxes and by the connection of truth to such problematic concepts as meaning and predication. Another, closely related question is how far our present psychological concepts can be revised while preserving a notion of Representation. To what minimal assumptions about our inner workings does semantic discourse commit us? For obviously, it must be something about a state's location in a web of other states that makes it susceptible of truth or falsity. A precise identification might enable us to say just how much—or little—of folk psychology $T$ needs the ultimate theorist to preserve.[31]

It is hardly surprising that these questions should remain. They amount simply to asking what truth is; yet I have tried not so much to analyse that concept as to consider how far its acceptability is tied to the course of empirical theory.

## vi

We have found support for Quinian epistemology—for recognizing epistemic standards higher than the pragmatic ones forced on limited beings. Although saying that these favour *physics* is a gross over-simplification, they do not favour folk psychology. Belief, desire, consciousness, and the like are concepts that more adequate empirical enquirers would probably avoid, hence that are, at least from an empirical viewpoint, grade B for us now.

Yet Quine's own stance is incoherent. Although self-demotion

---

[31] 'Might', because we would also need to know how folk psychology characterizes belief—otherwise the two stories could not be compared. The explication of folk notions has proved troublesome.

158 *Steven J. Wagner*

to grade B status is not generally self-defeating—a common objection to physicalism fails—Quine's constraints forbid empirically fruitless theorizing. And his epistemology offers no empirical gain. One response is to retreat to the project of simply accepting empirically useful doctrine and nothing else. That saves folk psychological concepts for now and possibly for always. An alternative lets us retain both Quine's trichotomy and the old idea of a distinguished place for semantic concepts. Although countenancing the abandonment—if only in principle—of folk psychology, we build semantic discourse into our conception of any satisfactory, comprehensive theorizing. Notably, we demand continued reflection on our own Representational successes and failures. One concession to the empiricist here is to keep open the possibility, however improbable, of an empirical refutation of semantic discourse. Another is to admit the vagueness of the general notion of Representation that this alternative employs. To regard truth as a non-empirical notion is to regard as unessential the specific constraints imposed by our present empirical uses of this term, hence to leave the limits of the concept less clear. As noted, one might also extend this line by insisting on a permanent place for folk concepts generally, as long as empirical enquiry does not invalidate them outright.

I endorse the alternative and would not rule out the extension. But I doubt that arguments could force a choice here. *V*'s goal of coping with the data may indeed be a basic epistemic imperative. Beyond that, however, it may be up to us how many more questions to ask; what concepts, and what conceptions of ourselves, to retain through the flux of enquiry. These questions fall outside of epistemology and semantics, into the province of ethics. Thus I would, in the end, argue that even if a form of empiricism is logically and pragmatically tenable, it is wrong.[32]

---

[32] The ultimate primacy of an ethical viewpoint on questions of physicalism and realism is also a theme of Hilary Putnam's recent writings, although his overall position is very different from mine.

# 7

# The Anti-Materialist Strategy and the 'Knowledge Argument'

*Howard Robinson*

i

There is an argument (which is generally called the 'knowledge argument') which has been used to show that physicalism faces a serious problem. Versions of this argument, in slightly different forms have been much discussed and criticized in recent years.[1] My purpose in this paper is to present the strongest version of the argument and then defend it. Put informally, the argument can be expressed as follows.

A deaf scientist (*DS*) might become the world's leading expert on the physical aspects of sound and hearing. Assuming science to be more advanced than at present, *DS*'s knowledge of the physiology, physics, chemistry and AI-style cognitive psychology of hearing might be complete. But there remains something which he does not know. The information he lacks concerns what might variously be characterized as *what it is like to hear* or *what things sound like*, or *the phenomenal nature of sound* or *the qualitative nature of sound*. Since he knows all there is to know about the physical process of hearing, that about which he does not know must not be a physical state of affairs: so *what it is like to hear, what things sound like*, and *the phenomenal and qualitative natures of sound* must be non-physical features of hearing.

[1] e.g. F. Jackson, 'Epiphenomenal Qualia', *Philosophical Quarterly*, 32 (1982), 127–36, and 'What Mary Didn't Know', *Journal of Philosophy*, 83 (1986), 291–5; T. Nagel, 'What is it Like to be a Bat?', *Philosophical Review*, 83 (1974), 435–50; H. M. Robinson, *Matter and Sense* (Cambridge, 1982), 4; Paul M. Churchland, 'Reduction, Qualia, and the Direct Introspection of Brain States', *Journal of Philosophy*, 82 (1985), 8–28; repr. as ch. 3 of id., *A Neurocomputational Perspective* (Cambridge, Mass., 1989), 47–66; R. Warner, 'A Challenge to Physicalism', *Australasian Journal of Philosophy*, 64 (1986), 249–65; D. Lewis, 'What Experience Teaches', in *Mind and Cognition: A Reader*, ed. W. G. Lycan (Oxford, 1990), 499–519. See also works cited in n. 11 below.

The various expressions which can be used to say what *DS* lacks all concern the subjective properties of hearing, but the first two of them pick out the character of the experiencing, whilst the last two mention the character of the phenomenal objects of sense. For our purposes, this is a distinction without a serious difference, for the character of sensory experience is given by its internal phenomenal object: hence *what it is like to hear* for a given subject is a direct function of the phenomenal nature of sound in his experience—that is, of the way sound seems to him. Saying this does not involve denying that there is a distinction between the act and the object of experience, for such a distinction is compatible with the introspectible character of the former being dependent on the latter.

For purposes of close discussion, the argument needs to be put in a more formal manner.

1. *DS* knows all those facts about hearing which can in principle be expressed in the vocabulary of physical science.
2. Unlike those who can hear, *DS* does not know the phenomenal nature of sound (etc.).

Therefore:

3. The phenomenal nature of sound in principle cannot be characterized using the vocabulary of physical science.
4. The nature of any physical thing, state, or property can be expressed in the vocabulary of physical science.

Therefore:

5. The phenomenal nature of sound is not a physical thing, state, or property.

One objection that has been made against this argument is that it is not valid.[2] Propositional attitude verbs such as 'know' create opaque contexts and perhaps the above argument ignores this fact and moves from two things not being known to be the same to the conclusion that they are not the same. The following argument is not valid because of such opacity.

6. *S* knows that Cicero was an orator.
7. *S* does not know that Tully was an orator.

---

[2] Churchland, 'Reduction, Qualia, and the Direct Introspection of Brain States' is the best attack on the deaf scientist argument. He uses this objection, but it is not the one on which he puts most weight.

Therefore:

    8. Cicero is not Tully.

The opacity of 'knows' does not, however, affect our argument, though not for the reason sometimes suggested. It has been suggested that the argument is invulnerable to this objection because 'knows about' or 'knows, concerning' is transparent, not opaque.[3] If we were to argue:

    9. Concerning Cicero, *S* knows that he was an orator.

    10. Concerning Tully, *S* does not know that he was an orator.

Therefore:

    11. Cicero is not Tully.

then the argument would be valid. The error would lie in (10) because, given that Cicero is identical with Tully, then *S* does know *about* or *concerning* Tully anything he knows about or concerning Cicero, because knowledge *about a* does not imply one knows that what one knows is in fact about *a*: the 'that' which introduces the propositional content of *S*'s knowledge follows the name and hence does not include it within its scope. The relevance of this to our original argument would be brought out by rewriting (1) and (2) as

    1′. Concerning hearing, *DS* knows everything which could in principle be expressed in the vocabulary of physical science.

    2′. Concerning hearing, *DS* does not know the phenomenal nature of its object, sound.

The knowledge referred to in both (1′) and (2′) concerns hearing, and that which is said to be unknown in (2′) must fall outside the class of things said to be known in (1′). As the latter includes everything encompassed by physical science, the former must fall outside that class. Hence (3) follows. This explanation, however, shows that it is not the transparency of 'knows about' which saves the argument, but the proviso that *DS* knows *everything* that physical science could tell him about hearing.

This is in fact the crucial point. Opacity is created by the fact that things can be objects of mental states under many different aspects or descriptions. What (1) asserts is that *DS* knows every physical aspect of the system, and hence any aspect under which

---

[3] See e.g. K. Campbell, 'Abstract Particulars and the Philosophy of Mind', *Australasian Journal of Philosophy*, 61 (1983), 129–41.

he does not know it cannot be a physical one. We can see how this would modify the other argument.

12. *S* knows everything about Cicero, including that Cicero was an orator.
13. *S* does not know that Tully was an orator.
Therefore:
14. Cicero is not Tully.

The argument is valid, because if *S* knew everything about Cicero he would know that he was Tully, if he were Tully. On the other hand, the transparency of 'knows about' would not alone save the argument, for if we replace (12) by

15. *S* knows most things about Cicero, including that he was an orator.

the argument to (14) by (15) and (13) would not be valid, for that Cicero was Tully might be one of the things *S* did not know. Similarly it would be invalid to argue

16. Concerning hearing, *DS* knows *most* of the facts which could in principle be expressed in the vocabulary of physical science.
2′. Concerning hearing, *DS* does not know the phenomenal nature of its object, sound.
Therefore:
3. The phenomenal nature of sound cannot be expressed in the vocabulary of physical science.

This is not valid because *the phenomenal nature of sound* may be one of the physical features *DS* does not know about. Hence it is the completeness of *DS*'s knowledge in the relevant area which makes the argument a good one.

This very fact may open the way to a new objection to the argument, namely that no one ever could know everything that could *in principle* be expressed in the vocabulary of physical science, and perhaps that the very notion of knowing all such facts is a bogus one, because there are indefinitely many. This is a somewhat tedious objection, merely forcing one to make the argument more indirect, for the notion of *knowing everything* is merely an aid to easy exposition of the argument. It can be expressed without it. The crucial idea behind the argument is that no possible knowledge of a physical sort would constitute or entail knowledge of the subjective dimension. This can be expressed as follows.

17. Take any set of facts of the sort in principle expressible in the vocabulary of physical science such that the facts in that set could be known, at one time, by a given subject, and suppose DS to possess knowledge of that set.
18. Whichever set as above DS knows, he, unlike those who can hear, does not know the phenomenal nature of sound.
Therefore:
19. Knowledge of the phenomenal nature of sound cannot be strictly derived from the knowledge of any set of physical facts, as above.
Therefore:
20. Either (*a*) knowledge of the phenomenal nature of sound can only be derived from knowledge of some set of physical facts which no individual could ever know at one time, or (*b*) the phenomenal nature of sound cannot in principle be expressed in the vocabulary of physical science (i.e. (3) ).
21. 20(*a*) lacks any plausible rationale.
Therefore:
3. The phenomenal nature of sound cannot in principle be expressed in the vocabulary of physical science.

I shall discuss the argument in its original formulation.

(18) parallels (2), and the issues that arise for (2) arise in the same way for (18).

## ii

Given that the argument is valid, is it sound, or are some of the premisses defective? I have already dealt with objections to (1), and the principal problems concern (2); but some remarks may be required in defence of (4). It may be objected to (4) that there are a lot of facts about physical objects that are not expressible in scientific jargon—for example, that penknives are useful for getting stones out of horses' hooves. Many of such cases will bring in human purposes and perspectives at least indirectly, and may, therefore, be judged dubious as instances of uncontroversially physical properties. Notwithstanding this, such examples are irrelevant to the present issue. Physical science concerns itself with bedrock description and explanation, and those facts which fall outside of it concern larger and looser and more informal perspectives on things. Sensory consciousness will only be thought to come into this latter category if one accepts a reductive social-cum-behavioural analysis of it. Such theories are not, at the moment, in play, and we can accept that sense experience is involved at a more fundamental level in the operation of the human organism. I shall assume, therefore, that (4) applies at the relevant level of description and that any reasonable controversy concerning this will resurface when I discuss the physicalist strategies relevant to (2).

A physicalist who accepts the validity of the argument must challenge the truth of one of the premises, presumably (2). If *DS* knows everything physical which is relevant to hearing, then, from a physicalist perspective, there cannot be anything that he does not know: hence (2) must be rejected. Everyone agrees that *DS* lacks something and that what he lacks could be called the *experience of hearing*. What he lacks is certainly something to do with knowledge. It might concern knowledge in either of two ways. It might be that the hearer possesses a state about which *DS* cannot know. As knowledge of physical states is, in principle, open to anyone, such a state would not be physical. This is the consequence of saying that what *DS* lacks is access to some *object* of knowledge. Alternatively, *DS* might lack a *mode* of knowing rather than access to an *object* of knowledge. The latter is, for obvious reasons, the option a physicalist must choose.[4]

There are a variety of forms that this choice can take. The simplest is to follow the behaviouristic intuition that what *DS* lacks is knowledge *how* and not knowledge *that*. There are certain things that *DS* cannot do—most obviously, he cannot respond spontaneously to sound—but it is these dispositions and abilities that he is lacking, not any sort of information about how the world is. (2) is replaced by

2″. Unlike those who can hear, *DS* lacks the ability to respond directly to sound, and certain consequent abilities.

Nothing interesting follows from (1) and (2″) and the argument is neutered. The price is high, however. The intuition driving the

[4] This is the argument employed by Churchland, 'Reduction, Qualia, and the Direct Introspection of Brain States'.

argument is that, on gaining his hearing, *DS* would learn something about empirical reality. Even if his new knowledge is not propositional, but knowledge by acquaintance, it is still real information that he had previously lacked about states and properties in the world. There is, therefore, pressure to think of what *DS* lacks as more than knowledge *how*. If one is to be consistently physicalist, one must do this whilst retaining the idea that it is merely a different mode of access to the same truths as he had previously known in propositional form. This gives

2′′′. Unlike those who can hear, *DS* does not know the nature of sound phenomenally.

The assumption is that knowing something phenomenally is *not* just a matter of possessing certain abilities; it is a different mode of access to some of the facts that *DS* knows scientifically. Again, nothing interesting follows from (1) and (2′′′).

Asserting that what *DS* lacks is a mode, rather than an object, of knowledge does not, however, solve the problem. The problem is that, given the truth of physicalism, *DS* is supposed to know *everything* relevant to hearing. If this is so, the fact that there may be some *ways* of knowing that he lacks should make no difference to the content of his knowledge. In Frank Jackson's words: 'What is immediately to the point is not the kind, manner or type of knowledge [*DS*] has, but *what* [he] knows.'[5] Richard Warner illustrates the point: we may either see or hear that a certain person is in the room, and which we do is indifferent to the content of our discovery.[6]

It is not difficult to appreciate the prima-facie appeal of the idea that a difference of mode in knowledge could explain *DS*'s case. The idea behind the 'mode' theory is, presumably, that if the phenomenal is merely another mode of access to respectable physical facts, then it does not itself constitute an extra fact: it is not an addition to ontology, but an extra mode of access to part of the previously accepted ontology. A moment's reflection will, however, show this to be sophistical. Call the set of physical facts *P* and the scientific modes of access which *DS* has to these facts *S*, and the experiential mode of access he lacks *H*. If we regard *S* and *H* as external to *P*, then the addition of a new mode of access will

---

[5] 'What Mary Didn't Know', 293.     [6] 'A Challenge to Physicalism'.

not alter *P*. But the physicalist hypothesis is that everything relevant is included in *P*: modes of access to physical facts are themselves simply physical processes and are included in physical facts. Therefore, if *DS* knows all the relevant members of *P*, he should know all the facts about *H*, including the fact of what that mode of access is phenomenally like.

Paul Churchland, in his most recent reply to Jackson, seems to think that the boot is on the other foot.[7] He thinks it obvious that what *DS* lacks is just a different way of knowing, and that 'the resources of modern cognitive neurobiology already provide us with a plausible account of what the difference in the two kinds of knowledge amount to, and of how it is possible to have the one kind without the other' (p. 69). In his first sketch of this difference it turns out to be that between knowing *how* and knowing *that*, but Churchland is not content to leave the characterization of what *DS* lacks in these crudely behaviouristic terms.

While the approach is well motivated, this binary distinction in types of knowledge barely begins to suggest the range and variety of different sites and types of internal representation to be found in a normal brain. There is no reason why we must be bound by the crude divisions of our pre-scientific idioms when we attempt to give a precise and positive explication of the equivocation displayed in Jackson's argument. And there are substantial grounds for telling a somewhat different story concerning the sort of nondiscursive knowledge at issue. Putting caution and qualification momentarily aside, I shall tell such a story. (p. 69)

The issue between Churchland and Jackson is set up, not in terms of a deaf scientist, but in terms of one who lacks chromatic vision. Churchland's story concerns how chromatic vision works, from retinal cones to synaptic activity in different areas of the brain, and explains how these bits of machinery enable normal people to do things that the chromatically blind cannot.

At first sight, it is difficult to see the relevance of Churchland's story. It never was disputed that those with a perceptual defect lack a mechanism that, in others, realizes the capacities they lack. This does not seem to show that they lack more than abilities or dispositions. The crucial difference is meant to consist, I think,

---

[7] 'Knowing Qualia: A Reply to Jackson', which is ch. 4 of Churchland's *A Neurocomputational Perspective*, 67–76.

in the fact that these states are described as *representations* of external properties.

> Her representational space within the relevant area of neurons would contain only the subspace for black, white, and the intervening shades of gray . . . there is a complex representation—a processing framework that deserves to be called 'cognitive'—that she either lacks or has in a reduced form. (p. 70)

The question is whether this sort of 'representation' is sufficient to constitute what Churchland is prepared to call 'knowledge by acquaintance', and so avoid being either propositional or merely behavioural. On Churchland's view, the fact that the language of computation and artificial intelligence can be used, rather than the jargon of behaviourism, to describe *DS*'s deficit is sufficient to make it the case that what he lacks is more than *knowledge how*. This is not meant to push it back into a form of *knowledge that*, in which *DS* is supposed to be complete. Rather it is a form of representation which is 'not remotely propositional or discursive, but is entirely real' (p. 70). Propositional knowledge is restricted to information stored in language:

> These same assumptions are entirely consistent with the further assumption that elsewhere in [the chromatically blind scientist's] brain—in the language areas, for example—she has stored a detailed and even exhaustive set of discursive, propositional, truth-valuable representations of what goes on in people's brains during the experience of color . . . (p. 70)

Whether this account does constitute a middle way between behavioural and propositional knowledge, and succeed in giving a physicalist sense to 'knowledge by acquaintance' will depend, in part, on how one interprets the language of artificial intelligence. The only serious physicalist interpretations of 'representation' and 'information' are causal and, hence, functional. In Churchland's own terms, non-linguistic brain states are representations of external states by being 'calibrated' to respond to them (p. 43). This seems to trivialize the distinction between the behavioural-functional and the informational accounts of what *DS* lacks. 'Representations' just turn out to be nodal states in the possession or exercise of an ability. But this is not the most serious objection.

Talking the language of information theory, there are many states in the world that can be said to represent others, and this has nothing, as such, to do with experience. No one disputes that what *DS* is lacking is experience of a certain sort. What makes certain kinds of neural representations, and not others, constitute experiences? Churchland's account of *qualia* in terms of 'state spaces' (pp. 102 ff.) does not seem to touch this problem. It is difficult to see how any of his neurology could be relevant unless there were a covert assumption that having one sort of representation *felt different* from having another. But this, of course, is what the physicalist is trying to analyse. The only other path is to say that they count as experiences because of the role they play in producing behaviour, but then Churchland will be agreeing with Lewis, that lacking experience is simply lacking (neurally grounded, of course) sets of abilities to respond.

Churchland's confusion—as I believe it to be—about what representations count as experiences is perhaps explained by the way that he and Patricia Churchland talk about qualia.[8] *Qualia* are, of course, essentially connected with experience, and the Churchlands' willingness to talk about *qualia* should be a sign that they take seriously the problem of distinguishing real experiences from other representations. The Churchlands define *qualia*, uncontroversially enough, as follows.

'Qualia' is a philosophers' term of art denoting those intrinsic or monadic properties of our sensations discriminated in introspection. The quale of a sensation is typically contrasted with its causal, relational, or functional features . . . (p. 21)

Because of the connection with experience, the natural way of understanding 'discriminated in introspection' is to take it as meaning that in introspection one is aware of, such that one can recognize, the qualitative nature of the *quale*. The point of *qualia* is that they constitute the qualitative content of experience: *qualia* are qualitative entities and being introspectively aware of them would seem to imply being aware of their qualitative natures. The Churchlands, however, are using 'discriminate' in a purely extensional sense, in which one can discriminate something without being in a position in principle to recognize what it is that one

---

[8] 'Functionalism, Qualia, and Intentionality' was co-authored by Paul and Patricia Churchland and originally appeared in *Philosophical Topics*, 1 (1981). It is reprinted as ch. 2 of P. M. Churchland, *A Neurocomputational Perspective*, 23–46, and page references are to this edition.

is discriminating. The intrinsic properties of the sensations turn out to be such things as 'the spiking frequency of the signal in some neural pathway, the voltage across a polarized membrane, the temporary deficit of some neurochemical, or the binary configuration of a set of direct-current impulses' (p. 30). As such different physical realizations are not experientially discernible as such, and yet they are supposedly the *qualia* themselves, it follows that one cannot tell by experience what *quale* one is experiencing. In the Churchlands' own words, they are only 'opaquely discriminated'. If two different physical states played the role of the same kind of sensation in the same brain they would be totally different *qualia* (because their monadic properties are different) but no difference would be available to introspection, for the physical properties are not themselves discernible. But if the term '*qualia*' has any use at all it is to designate *experientable* differences; significantly different *qualia* can, in principle, be recognized as different. The point is not purely verbal. If *qualia* do not constitute the available content of experience they make no contribution to explaining the difference between experiences and other so-called representations; and if they fail in that it is difficult to see what purpose they serve.

A further confusion in the Churchlands' understanding of experience is relevant. They are emphatic about the plasticity of experience, by which they mean that the content of experience is relative to descriptions and not 'given'. If we were taught to report on our experiences using such expressions as 'the spiking frequency in pathway $x$ is $n$' then we could be said to be directly aware of such processes as the spikings. However, they also say—and obviously correctly—'our mechanisms of sensory discrimination are of insufficient resolution to reveal on their own' such detailed facts as what goes on in the brain (pp. 30–1). Far from showing either that experience is relative to whatever theory one happens to hold, or that it is of whatever micro-process happens in fact to be its cause, what this suggests is that experience is most faithfully expressed by a description or conceptualization that has just the same grain of accuracy as the sensory or introspective mechanism that realizes it. A description at this level is bound to be topic neutral about what the actual process is. The only plausible candidates for this are the functional ones used by Smart and Armstrong, of the general form 'something is going on of the sort that goes on when there is a certain stimulus', or '. . . that is apt to cause a certain response'. One is not now discriminating a monadic property opaquely, but discriminating functional properties explicitly. As we shall see in the final section, the topic neutralist approach to experience is impotent against the knowledge argument.

### iii

I argued above that, if physicalism is correct, DS should know all the facts about hearing, including the fact concerning what hearing is phenomenally like. Michael Tye seeks to overcome this problem by denying that what something is phenomenally like is a fact about it.[9] He claims both that what the missing mode of knowledge is phenomenally like is not a further fact over and above the physical facts, and that if DS were to gain the ability to hear he would learn something new. Against the obvious response that this 'something new' would be a new fact, he makes two points. The first is that learning how to balance a pencil on one's nose is learning something new but not learning a new fact. If this comparison is to shed any light it must be interpreted as saying that if DS gained his hearing he would gain knowledge *how* and not knowledge *that*. This approach, to which we shall return, is fundamentally the behaviouristic one that lacking experience is no more than lacking the ability to do something—presumably the ability to respond spontaneously to the environment. Tye's other response is less reductive, and shows that he does not wish to assimilate the new knowledge to knowledge *how*. He claims, in effect, that provided that the new knowledge were connected by *de re* necessity to the old, then the new knowledge could just be a fresh mode of presentation of an old fact.

He compares knowing the brain state but not knowing the phenomenal nature of the experience with knowing of some liquid that it is water, but not that it is $H_2O$. Just as the water is the same thing as some $H_2O$, so the phenomenal state could be the same thing as a brain state.

[9] M. Tye, 'The Subjective Qualities of Experience', *Mind*, 95 (1986), 1–17. The arguments cited below are mainly from pp. 9–16. They are also found in his *The Metaphysics of Mind* (Cambridge, 1989).

It is not irrelevant, however, that water is a substance or stuff, not a property, state, or feature. There are many facts about water other than the fact that it is $H_2O$. Indeed, as Kripke points out, that there are other such facts concerning, for example, how it looks or feels is why the identity of water and $H_2O$ can only be known *a posteriori* and hence why one can know of some liquid that it is water without knowing that it is $H_2O$.[10] Water presents a qualitative front which does not reveal its inner structure. But (again as Kripke argues), for the explanation of the identity of brain states with experiences to parallel the explanation in the case of water and $H_2O$, brain states would have to possess a mode of presentation other than those captured by the physical descriptions.[11] If our senses were different, water would look and feel differently, whilst still being $H_2O$. So how water looks and feels are facts over and above the fact that it is $H_2O$. Why, therefore, is not the fact that a certain brain state has a certain phenomenal mode of presentation a fact over and above facts about its physical structure and powers? It may be argued that the phenomenal mode of presentation associated with perceiving water is only a feature of the fact that it is a perception of something external, which introspection of our brain is not. This objection misses the point. It is undoubtedly a fact that the brain presents itself to introspection in a way that does not reveal it to be the brain—if this were not so the supposed truth of materialism would be obvious and not require discovery. That it presents itself in such and such other way (whatever that way may be) must be a fact over and above the facts expressive of its physical structure—on at least one natural sense of 'fact'—otherwise we would not know how it introspectively seems without explicitly knowing something of how it neurologically is. *What* we know when we know how it seems—whether it is a Cartesian datum or topic neutral knowledge or something else—is a further question.

Without denying the distinction between how the brain seems and how it is, it might be argued that the connection between the two is a *de re* necessity, such that the physical state must have just that presentational aspect. But this would not justify the claim that they are the same fact, in any useful sense. A necessarily

---

[10] S. Kripke, *Naming and Necessity* (Oxford, 1980), 142 f.
[11] Ibid. 151–2.

supervenient property or feature cannot simply be the same property or feature as that on which it supervenes, otherwise the claim that there is anything supervenient becomes vacuous. If one chooses to use the word 'fact' in such a way that the presence of the supervenient feature is the same fact as the presence of that on which it supervenes, one will then require a different word from 'fact' to explain what the difference is. The difference is not just a verbal one—two ways of saying the same thing—for it is genuinely different aspects of the object that are presented by neurology and sensation. *DS* could not compensate for his deafness (make it the case that he would learn nothing new by coming to hear) by further linguistic education. It is this difference *de re* which is salient, and it is immaterial for present purposes whether we say that the difference consists in an extra fact, aspect, situation, feature, property, or state of affairs.

iv

It seems that all physicalist attempts to avoid the 'abilities' analysis of what *DS* lacks have failed. What he lacks is simply the ability to *do* certain things. This was the theory expressed as

2″.  Unlike those who can hear, *DS* lacks the ability to respond directly to sound, and certain consequent abilities.

Lewis[12] says that he lacks the abilities to remember and imagine what sound is like. This is to employ psychological language, rather than to talk in a reductive, behaviouristic way.[13] Nevertheless,

[12]  D. Lewis, 'Knowing What it's Like', *Philosophical Papers*, 1 (New York, 1983), 130–2.
    [13]  L. Nemirow, in 'Physicalism and the Cognitive Role of Acquaintance', in W. G. Lycan, ed., *Mind and Cognition: A Reader* (Oxford, 1990), says that '[k]nowing what an experience is like is the same as knowing how to imagine having the experience' (p. 495). This formula combines an 'abilities' analysis with the heavily mentalistic notion of *imagining*, in that sense which is close to *imaging*. If Nemirow, like Block ('Mental Pictures and Cognitive Science', also in Lycan, ed., *Mind and Cognition*) intends a purely functionalist sense for mental images, then the arguments that follow in the text apply to him. If he does not mean that, I do not know what physicalistically respectable sense he would hope to give to the notion of a mental image. Furthermore, I do not see that there is a necessary connection between knowing what an experience is like and being able to imagine or image; one may know intellectually that one will recognize something when it comes along again, and so know what it is like whilst being very weak at imagining. Janet Levin, 'Could Love be Like a Heatwave?' in the same volume, argues that what

in the context of the present argument, these notions must be intended in a physicalist sense, which means, in effect, that they must be interpreted in a functionalist sense. Functionalists are proud of the ways that their theory, by permitting psychologists to think in terms of what is going on inside the subject, improves on behaviourism. But functionalism is still a very behaviouristic theory, because the psychological value of a functional state consists entirely in its potential for modifying behaviour, even if only indirectly, through other functional states. This is not importantly different from allowing that a disposition is modified by the presence of another disposition.

There are at least four lines of argument that constitute serious challenges to behaviouristic theories of mind in general, that is, to both functionalism and classical behaviourism. The first concerns the difficulties such theories have coping with *qualia*. We are in the middle of one version of this argument now, and I cannot appeal to it in response to those physicalists who are prepared to accept a counter-intuitive behaviouristic treatment of experience, and so deny the intuition on which it rests.

The second strategy exploits the tension that exists between functionalist criteria for the identity of mental states and the need in certain circumstances to invoke structural criteria. Just as we believe that 'super Spartan' could feel pain without showing it, thus embarrassing the behaviourist, we believe that a brain in a vat, or someone entirely paralysed could have experiences, though his central states had been deprived of their usual functional significance. In these latter cases, the presence of states *structurally* like those that usually possess the functional role is deemed logically sufficient to constitute the presence of mental states. Under pressure, this seems to lack a non-arbitrary rationale. This argument is discussed extensively elsewhere, and I cannot pursue it here.[14]

The third and fourth arguments are less well known. According to the third, functionalism evacuates all our empirical concepts of content. The functionalist provides a relational and topic-neutral

---

*DS* lacks is not a concept but the ability to apply a concept; he knows what sound is, he just cannot tell whether sound is present in some circumstances when others can tell. This, too, seems to me to come to the simple behavioural ability account.

[14] See e.g. J. Owens, 'The Failure of Lewis's Functionalism', in L. Stevenson, R. Squires and J. Haldane ed., *Mind, Causation and Action* (Oxford, 1986), 49–63; H. M. Robinson, 'Un dilemme pour le Physicalisme', *Hermes*, 3 (1988), 128–50.

analysis of the mental, whilst failing to notice that our physical concepts are themselves topic-neutral. So, if the functionalist is correct, we have no empirical concepts that are not relational and topic-neutral. We in fact rely upon the qualitative content present in experience to give intrinsic content to our interpretation of the world, and the functionalist proposes to abolish this qualitative content.[15] Realization of the disastrous nature of this predicament is just beginning to dawn.

The fourth argument is the one I shall develop here. It rests on a common intuitive objection to behaviouristic theories which seems not to have been worked up into a formal argument in the way that it might have been.

A constant complaint about behaviouristic approaches is that they are viciously third-personal; that is, that they present a third-personal perspective on something which is essentially first-personal, namely, the viewpoint of the conscious subject. As with many fundamental disagreements—especially in the philosophy of mind—there is great difficulty in turning what appears to be a clear intuition into a demonstrative argument—that is, into an argument that does not rest on a premiss which is more or less equivalent to, and just as contentious as, the initial intuition. I am going to try to turn the intuition that behaviouristic theories are viciously third-personal into an argument by showing that such theories cannot be applied to the first-personal perspective without a vicious circularity.

The problem can be brought out by considering the sort of situation that gave rise to behaviourism. It seems fairly natural to interpret the understanding of the world possessed by a rat in a maze as being no more than its ability to react to the barriers it encounters: one need not think of anything else inside the rat constituting its understanding other than those dispositions.[16] But

---

[15] For the view that our conception of the physical world is topic neutral, see Lockwood's chapter, below, and for an argument that the dispositional powers conception of the world is incoherent, see Robinson, *Matter and Sense*, ch. 7, and also Lockwood, below.

[16] Those influenced by cognitive science will probably think that there are representations in the rat's head. Giving a functionalist account (as is the norm) of what makes these into representations brings such theories within the scope of functionalism and, hence, makes them behaviourist in the sense I have explained above. In the sense relevant to this argument, the mental states of the cognitive scientist-cum-functionalist are dispositional.

we can only make sense of the rat's understanding in these reduced terms by interpreting those dispositions against a background picture of how the world around the rat really is: we have a non-reductive grasp on how the world really is and how the rat actually behaves, and against this background we can see the rat's grasp on the world as no more than its dispositions to move in certain ways. It would make no sense to try to understand the rat's dispositions in abstraction from a general conception of the physical world, for the notion of a behavioural disposition is locked into that conception. It involves concepts such as body, motion, and spatial location, which are constitutive of our conception of the physical. We can see the rat's cognition as merely dispositional because we take our own cognition naïvely.

The situation of a rat is no different from the way we stand with regard to other minds in general; we employ our non-reductive grasp on the world to set up the framework in which we can make the reductive interpretation of others. But we are no different from others, and if the reductive theory were true we ought to be able to apply it to ourselves. Yet, as the case of the rat clearly shows, seeing cognitive grasp in terms of dispositions necessarily presupposes a direct grasp on the world to form the background of which notions essential to the concept of disposition are part. One could not reduce that apprehension to dispositions without a regress, for 'disposition' is a concept which only makes sense as part of a general conception of the physical world. So I can never make the reductive interpretation of my own understanding, paraphrasing my conception of the physical in dispositional terms.

The intuition behind these thoughts can be expressed more rigorously. It should be uncontroversial that, for any philosophical analysis, understanding the analysans is sufficient for, and logically independent of, understanding the analysandum. For example, if we assume for purposes of argument that knowledge can be analysed as justified true belief, then we would expect that (a) an understanding of the notion of justified true belief will be sufficient for understanding the notion of knowledge; and (b) there is no conceptual necessity in understanding the notion of knowledge prior to, or as a necessary means to, understanding 'justified true belief'; the latter concepts are autonomous relative to 'knowledge'.

If these conditions are not met it would seem that an analysis is either incomplete or circular. Using $U$ to mean 'understanding', this can be expressed as:

1. $U$(analysans) is sufficient for, and does not conceptually presuppose, $U$(analysandum).

The analyses we have called 'behaviouristic' analyse mental states in—broadly—dispositional terms. For present purposes I am concerned with cognitive mental states. Their common feature is propositional and conceptual content; they all, that is, involve understanding propositions and/or concepts. The behaviouristic theories can, therefore, be represented as presenting an account of understanding. Using $c$ as a variable ranging over anything conceptual—which includes propositions and single concepts—they can be expressed in the form:

2. Understanding $c$ $[Uc]$ is analysed as having a certain disposition $D$.

Employing the analysis presented in (2) to instantiate (1) we get the idea that we ought to be able to understand understanding something by *understanding* having the appropriate disposition:

3. $U$(having $D$) is sufficient for, and does not conceptually presuppose, $U(Uc)$.

This should still be uncontroversial. But it is at this point that the feeling comes in that what seems initially plausible when taking the third-personal perspective on a rat will not apply to oneself. I cannot understand my own understanding, complete with its content, in purely dispositional terms. I must always think of my own cognition as being genuinely of the world, and I would lose the world if I could think of it simply as a causal tendency within myself. Once the transparency of contact with the world that intentionality gives is reductively analysed in terms of some physical tendency within myself, then the contact with an object—which is the whole purpose of cognition—is lost. But I cannot even think of my cognition reductively, for the very idea of a causal tendency to behaviour makes sense to me only if I allow myself a non-reduced understanding of such basic empirical concepts as *body*, *space*, and *motion*.

The question of whether this intuition is sound is the question of whether a reductive analysis of understanding also affects our grasp on what is understood. The physicalist who rejects this intuition objects that when he presents an analysis of what it is to understand *c*, it is the *understanding* he is analysing, not *c*, its content; so, he argues, saying that our understanding of the concept *body*, for example, is simply a disposition has no consequences for what we understand by, or in, that concept. By contrast, the intuition on which the argument rests is founded on the claim that, for cognitive states, *the essence of which is their content*, this distinction cannot be made; a reductive account of understanding involves thinking of the content understood in a reductive way. This can be proved if we apply to this reductive analysis the principle that was illustrated with respect to the 'justified true belief' analysis of knowledge. This gives the idea that understanding *understanding c* is sufficient for, and does not conceptually presuppose, understanding *c*.

4. $U(Uc)$ is sufficient for and does not conceptually presuppose $Uc$.

This will be defended shortly. Accepting it for the present, together with (3) and the fact that the relation 'is sufficient for and does not conceptually presuppose' is transitive, it entails.

5. $U(\text{having } D)$ is sufficient for, and does not conceptually presuppose, $Uc$.

In other words, an understanding of the reductive account of understanding some particular content should be sufficient for understanding that content, without requiring an independent grasp on that content.

The requirement in (5) cannot be met. Suppose we substitute for *c* a concept fundamental to our grasp on the physical world, such as the concept of body, thus

6. $U(\text{having } D')$ is sufficient for, and does not conceptually presuppose, $U(\text{the concept 'body'})$.

Then (6) says that an understanding of the appropriate disposition should be *autonomously* sufficient for an understanding of the concept 'body'. But the situation is just the reverse: the concept 'body', and a variety of other fundamental concepts, are essential for an understanding of the concept of a behavioural disposition. So, in contradiction to (6), we have

7. $U(\text{having } D')$ presupposes $U(\text{the concept 'body'})$.

As (6) and (7) are incompatible, we have a *reductio* of (2), which stated the behaviouristic account. Therefore

8. Understanding cannot be analysed simply as having a disposition.

Everything turns on (4). It divides into two parts, which it is convenient to discuss separately. They are

4*a*. $U(Uc)$ is sufficient for $Uc$;

and

4*b*. $U(Uc)$ does not conceptually presuppose $Uc$.

The rationale of (4*a*) is that one cannot *fully* know what it is to understand a proposition or concept without understanding—or, at least, having the materials to understand—the concept or proposition itself: hence understanding what it is to understand something is sufficient for actually understanding it. I could know in general terms what it is to know, for example, a language—that is, what, in general, is involved in knowing any language, without knowing a particular language; but I could not have a specific and precise analysis of what understanding French sentence by sentence is without thereby understanding French. (This might be compared with knowing the Davidsonian theory for a language, which involves knowing the meanings of the individual sentences in the language.) Similarly, if the dispositional analysis of cognitive states is not only presenting a theory about understanding in general, but about understanding *this* concept or *that* proposition, then the corresponding disposition must be sufficient to determine the content. This is only to be expected: if a certain state contains a certain piece of information—as, presumably, cognitive states do—then an adequate analysis of that state must preserve that information. And the information a cognitive state contains is its conceptual and propositional content.

In sum, we can say that the rationale for (4*a*) is that a cognitive mental state has two elements: (i) its content, which is conceptual, and (ii) the appropriate attitude, e.g. belief or desire, which will involve understanding. An analysis must cover its analysandum as a whole, and so, in this case, must be sufficient to account for both elements.

Resistance to this rationale can only come from denying that content is strictly intrinsic to the mental state; one believes, etc., in a manner appropriate to a certain content, but the content is not in any further sense part of the mental state. It is this *appropriate manner* that is to be analysed dispositionally.

The phrase 'appropriate manner' is loose. It might merely be a way of signifying the fact that content, though intrinsic to the state, is adverbial not objectual. This would not affect (4). Or it might signify that content is extrinsic to the mental state. This is what my opponent requires, if content is not to fall within the scope of an analysis of mentality. I discuss externalism elsewhere, but it is doubtfully relevant here, for, even if content is external to the *brain*, it is not external to the *broad disposition*.[17]

The impossibility of such radical externalism is the task of the second main argument of this chapter, which begins in the next section.

(4*a*) would have to be met by any account of understanding that avoided externalism of content. (4*b*) is different because it applies only to reductive accounts of understanding, and the fact that the dispositional analysis is reductive is essential to its having the disastrous consequences it does. Anything that would normally be called an 'analysis' is reductive, just in the sense that it provides an account which is free of the concept being analysed. If the 'justified true belief' analysis of knowledge were correct, one could think always in terms of justified true belief instead of knowledge. The logical independence of the analysans is a feature of anything which is an analysis in this sense. A non-reductive account of understanding will not, therefore, be an analysis in this full sense. If one understood understanding simply as the holding of a *sui generis* relation to a proposition, with the notion of proposition also understood non-reductively, then the analysans would not be logically independent of the analysandum, for the *sui generis* relation would not be some idea which was graspable independently of the idea of understanding, in the way that belief is independent of knowledge. A non-reductive account would present no problem for our grasp on the external world, for the nature of the world is represented directly in the content of the propositions which constitute the mental content: construing the world from concepts realized in it and from propositions about it does not

---

[17] 'Physicalism, Externalism and Perceptual Representation', in *New Representationalism*, ed. Edmond Wright (Avebury Press, forthcoming, 1993).

face problems in the way that construing it from dispositions does. The argument shows that there cannot be a full or reductive analysis of understanding a content, where that means cutting free from a certain circle of intellectualist ideas, for those ideas are basic and cannot be replaced by physicalist ones, in the way that the concept of knowledge could (perhaps) be replaced by that of justified true belief.

Michael Martin has objected to (4*b*) on the grounds that it is absurdly strong. (4*b*) is much stronger than the ban on presupposition in (1). (1) only states that the understanding of an *analysans* must not presuppose an understanding of the *analysandum*: this merely rules out circularity of analysis. (4*b*) says that a reductive understanding of understanding a concept must not presuppose understanding that concept itself. If it were the case that no true, reductive analysis of understanding a notion could presuppose actually understanding it, then a reductive understanding of what it is to understand concepts in general would have to be given in terms that did not presuppose an understanding of concepts, which would require that the account did not employ concepts, and this is ridiculous.

This criticism forces a further clarification of (4*b*). What the reductive understanding of understanding some concept must not presuppose is a naïve or non-reductive grasp on the concept understanding of which is being reductively analysed. What cannot be the case is that it is a conceptual requirement that you can grasp the reductive account of understanding the concept only if you have already understood the concept naïvely. When applied to Martin's case of the reductive understanding of our understanding of concepts in general this does not require that such an account be possible without understanding concepts, but only that such understanding could—conceptually—be had in the reductive form alone. This requirement can be expressed in two conditions. First, that there could be a creature that had never explicitly possessed the notion of concept, or having a concept, but had always explicitly operated in the terms given in the reduction. Second, that such a creature could, by acquaintance with our reductive account, come to see what we naïvely mean by 'having a concept'. *For any correct reductive analysis it cannot be an absolute conceptual requirement that understanding that analysis presuppose the prior possession of the concept in its non-reduced form.* This is so because reductionism is like eliminativism in that it is a condition on its adequacy that one be able to conduct all one's business, in principle, in the preferred terms. The reductionist looks at his analysans and sees that it entails that which he is reducing: the eliminativist considers his preferred theory and sees that it does everything legitimate that was done by the eliminated theory, but that it does not entail it. They are equal in finding their preferred discourse omnicompetent. The problem on which my argument rests arises because one could not have a creature whose understanding of the concept body was solely through the medium of the behaviouristic account of what it is to have that concept, for that account conceptually presupposes an understanding of 'body'. If one tried to make a reductive reading of *that* understanding, one would end up with the same problem. Just as with the rat, where we can see its understanding behaviouristically only by taking our grasp on the world naïvely, so in our own case, we are forced to presuppose a contentful and direct grasp on the world as a conceptual priority to our reductive reading. It does not make sense, therefore, to think of the reductive reading as giving all there is to our understanding.

There is reservation of a different sort that might be felt about this argument. It is directed against an across-the-board behaviouristic analysis of cognition. What we were discussing was (2″), the behaviouristic analysis of the sort of state that *DS* lacks—that is, of sensation. The falsehood of a general behaviouristic theory does not entail that such a theory is not correct for sensation and perception. Could it be that (2″) is correct, although the argument in this section is sound? Reflection on the nature of that argument, however, reveals that it refutes the behaviouristic treatment of sensation in particular. That argument showed that knowledge of the external world cannot be reduced to dispositions because the very idea of a disposition functions only in the context of an unreduced grasp on the physical world. But there is nowhere else that we might get our conception of the physical world from, other than perception. It is the content specifically of perception that must be taken non-reductively, if the contrast required by our concept of disposition is to be maintained.

v

*Conclusion and Comments.* Sections i–iii show that there is no physicalist account of what *DS* lacks except a very reductive and behaviouristic one; and section iv shows that such a treatment of perception is unsuccessful. The physicalist is, therefore, unable to propose a version of (2) which prevents the argument from proceeding and refuting him. There are, however, various aspects of the argument that require further comment.

(a) *The status of 'the knowledge argument'.* Jackson, Nagel, and others present the argument as a refutation of physicalism, and it is as such that Churchland challenges it. Churchland, in a variety of places, has generously cited me as one of those who use the argument in this way, but this is only half true. At the beginning of *Matter and Sense* I use it to show what the physicalist is up against, and then consider the various physicalist theories as ways of coping with it. I now think that I was not entirely clear about the force of the argument. The argument is somewhat more powerful than I had thought. I had, for example, discussed the 'topic neutral' analysis of sensations as if saying that our knowledge of our sensations is topic neutral were a way of explaining what *DS* lacked consistently with physicalism. The topic neutral analysis of sensations does not, however, touch the knowledge argument. The fact that we had only neutral knowledge of the nature of our experiences would explain how we are able to have those experiences without realizing that they are brain states. This is the phenomenon the analysis was concocted to explain. But it would not at all explain how knowledge of the brain state might be insufficient to give knowledge of the nature of experience. Scientific knowledge of the brain is topic specific and is more detailed than topic neutral experiential knowledge of the brain: the scientific knowledge, therefore, includes everything the experiential knowledge contains. It cannot, therefore, explain why *DS* lacks any knowledge.

Nevertheless, the knowledge argument itself is not a complete refutation of physicalism. The completion of the argument as I presented it required that behaviouristic theories be independently refuted—independently in the sense that no appeal is made to the knowledge argument or the situation of *DS* in that refutation. All that the knowledge argument shows is that a reductive physicalist is forced to adopt a hard-line behaviouristic view of experience. In that way it brings out more strongly than a simple appeal to intuition how implausible such theories as functionalism are. But the claim that what *DS* lacks is more than a mere ability is not something that the argument proper proves, rather it presupposes it. As the example of Lewis suggests, a clear-headed behaviourist, functionalist, or causal theorist would always have realized that he was obliged to treat experience as no more than a dispositional state, and not a state characterized by knowledge of *what it is like* in any sense stronger than knowledge how.

(*b*) *The argument and dualism.* Churchland tries to undermine the motivation for the argument by pointing out that it would work equally against dualism: knowledge of the nature of ectoplasmic stuff would be no more use to *DS* than knowledge of brain states in informing him of what it is like to hear.[18] The suggestion is that an argument which works equally against the two alternative theories must have something wrong with it. Jackson points out that this response does not touch property dualism, which is all that the argument proves.[19] But neither does it touch a sensible substance dualism. 'Mental substance' is not something composed of 'ghostly atoms'—whatever that would mean—but something that is not *made of* anything at all. In so far as it has a structure, that structure would be entirely psychological—that is, would consist of the faculties, beliefs, desires, experiences, etc. There would be no autonomous sub-psychological stuff. Such a notion faces many problems, of course, but this is the Cartesian conception, not the ectoplasmic one; and against this conception the knowledge argument is irrelevant. One cannot know the nature of the faculties, thoughts, and experiences that are part of someone's mind without thereby knowing what the experiences are like. There is no purely scientific perspective on such a mind.[20]

---

[18] *A Neurocomputational Perspective*, 71–2.

[19] 'What Mary Doesn't Know', 295.

[20] I am grateful to many people who have commented on various drafts of this paper, but especially to Nicholas Nathan and Michael Martin for astringent criticisms of versions of the argument in sect. iv. I fear I have not overcome all their reservations.

# 8

# Incorrigibility

## Richard Warner

I will defend the spirit of the traditional doctrine of incorrigibility. The letter, I abandon. The spirit is that there is a fundamental epistemological difference between the mental and the physical. The letter is that the difference consists in having or lacking immunity to error; more fully: certain beliefs about mental items are immune to error, while beliefs about physical items exhibit no such immunity.[1] One source of this view was the now discredited doctrine of the given. Traditional epistemology held that certain mental states could be 'given' to the mind.[2] 'Givenness' involved no 'conceptual interpretation', and for this reason it was thought that certain beliefs about the given were immune to error. I will stand the traditional doctrine on its head: incorrigibility is the result of conceptual interpretation—or, more accurately, the result of the exercise of a recognitional ability. So conceived, incorrigibility turns out to be a kind of conditional immunity to error.[3]

The idea is that a *certain kind* of mistake—possible in the recognition of physical things—is *not* possible in the case of (certain) mental items. To illustrate, suppose your ability to recognize foxes is completely unimpaired, and that, as a result of using this ability, you believe a particular item to be a fox. You might be mistaken—the "animal" might be a hologram, for

---

[1] The letter still has adherents; see C. McGinn, *The Subjective View* (Oxford, 1983), 45. Many, however, have abandoned both the letter and the spirit: see e.g. P. M. Churchland, *Matter and Consciousness* (Cambridge, Mass., 1984), 76–9. Donald Davidson is another abandoner—in 'First Person Authority', *Dialectica*, 38. 2–3 (1984), 103.

[2] I have in mind such figures as C. I. Lewis. For criticisms of the doctrine of the given, see Michael Williams, *Groundless Belief* (New Haven, Conn., 1977).

[3] Some may object to calling this 'incorrigibility'—insisting that the term be reserved for absolute immunity. I use the term because it is convenient and, more importantly, because conditional immunity preserves the spirit of the traditional doctrine: conditional immunity is a fundamental epistemological difference between the mental and the physical.

example. Mistakes of this sort are impossible in the case of (certain) mental items—pain, for example. That is (suppressing one qualification): *necessarily*, if your ability to recognize pain is completely unimpaired, and, as a result of using that ability, you believe you are in pain, then you are in pain. This is a modal property of pain. No physical thing has this property.[4]

For reasons I will explain later, I prefer to put the conclusion this way: pain is not an objective phenomenon, but a subjective one. The physical is, of course, the exemplar *par excellence* of the objective, and, in recognizing pain as non-physical, we are recognizing it as subjective. This theme is familiar from Thomas Nagel's work;[5] however, there is a crucial difference between Nagel's approach and mine. Nagel contends that (at least certain) mental states are fully understandable only from a certain "point of view": e.g. one can know what it is like to be in pain only from the point of view of a pain-feeler. It is this fact that makes pain a subjective phenomenon and blocks its identification with any physical state. In developing this position, Nagel self-consciously avoids appeal to traditional notions like incorrigibility: part of his intent is to provide a new perspective on the mind–body problem. Illuminating as this project has been, it is misguided. Incorrigibility is the central notion, the key to understanding the subjectivity of the mental and to deriving anti-physicalist results.

## i. The Traditional View

The place to begin is with the traditional view of incorrigibility. The view asserts a necessary connection between belief and truth: for at least some mental states, necessarily, if one believes that one is in that state, then one really is.[6] The assertion is not without plausibility. Imagine you have, or at least that it seems you have,

---

[4] I argued against physicalism in 'A Challenge to Physicalism', *Australasian Journal of Philosophy*, 64 (1986), 249–65. The present essay works out of the view of incorrigibility suggested in that article and offers a different but related argument against physicalism.

[5] See T. Nagel, 'Subjective and Objective', in his *Mortal Questions* (Cambridge, 1979).

[6] As formulated, the thesis concerns only beliefs about mental states, and such beliefs will be my exclusive focus throughout; I will not consider other beliefs that might qualify as incorrigible (e.g. the belief that I exist). McGinn, *The Subjective View*, contains a discussion of the incorrigibility of 'indexical beliefs' such as 'I exist', 'I am not you', 'I am here', and so on.

a pounding headache: it seems as if someone were relentlessly
pounding with a hammer on the inside of your skull. Your attention is riveted remorselessly on the sensation; you complain about
your pounding headache—manifesting your belief that you are in
pain. Could your belief be false? It certainly seems that it could
not.[7]

Despite its plausibility, the traditional view is indefensible. It
falls foul of the fact that, in taking something to be of a certain
kind, one commits oneself to the claim that the thing is relevantly
similar to other things of that kind. The difficulty is that—in
general, at least—it can happen that the relevant similarity does
not really hold but merely appears to. Why should this not happen
in the case of the mental? Suppose you believe a certain sensation
to be a pain. You take the sensation to be of a certain kind—a
pain—and hence are committed to the claim that the sensation is
relevantly like other things of that kind. Why should it not turn
out that the similarity is merely apparent?

The traditional view rests on the idea that, at least for some
mental states, at the very least for sensations, an apparent similarity is *eo ipso* a real similarity. The problem is that there are clear
counter-examples. Suppose you believe that you have a magenta
after-image. However, when you project the after-image alongside
a standard colour sample of magenta, you see that there is clearly
not enough purple in the after-image for it to count as magenta.
The reason you formed the false belief is that, although you can
reliably identify most instances of magenta, you are confused about
just how much purple a red has to have to count as magenta, so
you still make mistakes on borderline cases.[8]

---

[7] This example also illustrates another virtue of the traditional view. Consider
that you do not merely believe that you are in pain, you know you are. You know
non-inferentially. You do not, for example, observe yourself holding one hand to
your head, reaching for the aspirin with the other, and then conclude that you are
in pain. Your belief qualifies as knowledge without such inferential backing, and
the traditional view explains why. The point of demanding a backing would be to
have evidence that the way things seem really is the way they are. But things must
be the way they seem, so there is no point in demanding inferential backing, and
your belief qualifies as knowledge without it. This explanation of non-inferential
knowledge is an important feature of the traditional view. The thesis of incorrigibility does not merely assert a necessary connection between belief and truth; it
also explains a fundamental sort of self-knowledge: our non-inferential knowledge
of our mental states.

[8] There are interesting questions here about the distinction between having a
concept—like the concept of magenta—but having mistaken beliefs about its ap-

False beliefs are possible even in the case of pain—often taken to be a 'best case' for the traditional view. Imagine you are at the dentist but are not paying any attention to what the dentist is doing; instead you are consumed with worry about whether you will be on time for the very important appointment you have afterwards. You are snapped back to your current situation when a particularly hard probe makes you complain, 'That hurt!' Since you should be completely anaesthetized, the dentist is perplexed and asks if you will submit to the same probe again. This time, attending carefully to the sensation, you recognize it as qualitatively identical to the sensation you felt before; and you also realize that the present sensation is not painful at all. It is just a sharp sensation of pressure—as was, you now realize, the previous, qualitatively identical sensation. You thought the previous sensation painful because the suddenness of the sensation so startled you that immediately, without attending at all carefully to the sensation, you took it for a pain.[9] You did so because, for you, dentistry is an ordeal of anxiety and fear, and your agitation and apprehensiveness predispose you to take almost any sudden sensation to be a pain. To have managed to lose yourself in worry about the appointment was a blissful release.

Considerations such as the foregoing have led some to the view that self-ascriptions of mental states are—in general—not incorrigible. Incorrigibility, they contend, is enjoyed only by a very special kind of belief: for example, 'It seems to me as if I see this colour', where 'this' refers to the colour of a sensation one is currently having.[10] This retreat is the wrong reaction. We can give an account of incorrigibility that represents a wide range of our ordinary, everyday beliefs about mental items as capable of incorrigibility—beliefs like 'I am in pain', 'I want coffee', 'I believe the book is on the table'. I will, however, focus exclusively on pain in what follows—leaving aside questions about generalization from pain to other mental states.

---

plication, and having a concept different from, but similar to, e.g., the concept of magenta. Children's versions of adult concepts may raise this issue. I am indebted here to Jennifer Berry.

[9] P. M. Churchland offers a similar example, *Matter and Consciousness*, 77.

[10] e.g. John L. Pollock, *Knowledge and Justification* (Princeton, NJ, 1974), 75–6.

The key lies in certain connections between false beliefs and recognitional abilities. A few remarks about recognitional abilities are in order. The ability to recognize *F*s is the capacity reliably to form true beliefs as to whether or not a given item is an *F*. I will, because it is natural and convenient, talk of the exercise of a recognitional ability; however, I do not mean to imply that the activation of the ability is always or even usually under one's voluntary control. An ability, for instance, to recognize foxes by sight may be causally and non-voluntarily activated by a fox's coming in to view. Such a non-voluntary activation counts as an exercise.

Now let us turn to the relation in question between false beliefs and recognitional abilities. This relation is a special case of a relation between failures to *know* and recognitional abilities. False beliefs are, of course, failures to know; however, as we will see, one can truly believe, for example, that one is in pain, yet fail to know that one is. It is illuminating to set the false belief cases in the broader context of failures to know; indeed, the essential step to a defensible incorrigibility thesis is to distinguish two ways in which one may fail to know: failures due to lack, impairment, or misuse of a recognitional ability; and failures that arise from other sources.[11] My claim will be that, for a wide range of mental states, the false belief that one is in that state can arise only from the first source.

## ii. Recognitional Abilities

To distinguish the two ways in which one may fail to know, let us focus initially on a belief, not about a mental state, but about an ordinary physical object. Suppose that you see—or at least, think you see—that the animal in the field is a fox. You claim to know, based on what you see, that it is a fox. Now, it really is a fox, a paradigm fox, in plain view in good light. However, even in such conditions, you may fail to know. There are three cases to distinguish.

---

[11] J. L. Austin draws a similar, if not entirely explicit, distinction in 'Other Minds', in his *Philosophical Papers*, ed. J. O. Urmson and G. J. Warnock (Oxford, 1979), 79–80.

1. *Lack of ability.* You mistakenly believe that you have the ability to recognize foxes by sight. For a joke, we told you that the only small, pointy-eared animals around are foxes, when in fact the area is full of small, pointy-eared dogs. In fact, you are ignorant of the colour, size, and shape of a fox, and hence lack the ability to recognize a fox by sight. So, since it is by sight that you claim to know, you do not know that the animal is a fox.

2. *Impaired ability.* You have the ability to recognize foxes by sight; however, the ability is impaired: you do not have your glasses on; or you have been drugged (so that your vision is blurred); or you have been hypnotized (so that you will misidentify dogs as foxes); and so on. If your ability is sufficiently impaired, you do not know that the animal is a fox.

3. *Improperly used ability.* You have the unimpaired ability to recognize foxes by sight, but you do not employ it properly. You merely glance for a second at the animal—not nearly long enough to see what you need to see to determine if it is a fox; none the less—because you are being careless—you form the belief that it is a fox. Given the way in which you employed (or tried to employ) your recognitional ability, you do not know that the animal is a fox.

The distinction between impairment and improper use needs clarification. Improper uses arise from various forms of lack of careful attention—carelessness, over-hastiness, distraction, and so on. One can avoid these pitfalls simply by paying careful attention to the matter at hand. Impairments are not avoidable in this way. If one is drugged or hypnotized in a way that makes foxes look exactly like dogs, paying careful attention to what one sees is unlikely to avoid a misidentification. This difference provides a rationale for distinguishing between improper uses and impairments.[12]

(1)–(3) are exhaustive of the ways in which failures to know can be laid at the door of recognitional abilities. If you have the unimpaired and properly employed ability to recognize foxes by sight, how could you fail to know because of something wrong with the recognitional ability? There is nothing wrong.

---

[12] If one insists on thinking of misuse cases as cases of impairment, the result is merely to simplify my scheme of classification.

The fox case also illustrates the distinction—crucial for our purposes—between failures to know due to lack, impairment, or misuse of a recognitional ability; and failures that arise from other sources. As an example of the latter sort of failure, suppose you exercise your unimpaired, properly employed ability to recognize foxes by sight; as a result, you form the belief that a certain item is a fox. In response, I tell you that earlier, as a practical joke, I placed holograms of foxes in various spots; the holograms are indistinguishable by sight from real foxes. I ask you how you know that the apparent fox is not just a hologram. You are at a loss to answer, revealing that you do not know that the object is a fox.[13] Here your recognitional ability is entirely in order. It is unimpaired—you are not drunk, drugged, hypnotized, fatigued, or any such thing; and, it is properly employed—you have not been inattentive, careless, or any such thing. The problem is not your ability; it is the holograms.[14]

Now let us return to the mental—specifically to pain. Subject to one qualification which I will suppress for the moment, my claim is: *necessarily*, if one believes that one is in pain, and that belief results from properly exercising one's unimpaired ability to recognize pain, then one is in pain. This claim is true if and only if all false beliefs that one is in pain arise either from the lack, impairment, or misuse of the ability to recognize pain. Let us examine each case in turn.

[13] You fail to know because I have given you good reason to think that what you see might be a hologram; having been given such a reason, to know that what you see is a fox, you have to know that it is not a hologram. The reason you fail to know is not that to know that *p* (that the animal is a fox) one must know whatever is entailed by *p* (that it is not a hologram). Indeed, it is probably not true that to know that *p* one must know everything entailed by *p*; see e.g. Robert Nozick, *Philosophical Explanations* (Cambridge, Mass., 1981), ch. 3. However, to know that *p* one must know that not-*q*, in those cases in which *q* and *p* cannot both be true, and one has (at least in the light of certain considerations) good reason to think *q* might be true. See Austin, 'Other Minds'.

[14] Some may object that all the example shows is that you lack the ability to recognize foxes: if you really had the ability, you would be able to tell a fox from a hologram of one. This objection overlooks the fact that one can have the ability to recognize *F*s without having the ability to recognize *F*s in all circumstances. Suppose, as we are about to go out fox-hunting, I ask you, 'Can you recognize a fox when you see one?' Your 'yes' answer means that—in normal circumstances—you are a reliable detector of foxes. Your inability to distinguish the real foxes from the holograms does not show that you lack the ability you attribute to yourself.

1. *Lack of ability.* Suppose the people from Alpha Centauri arrive. They never feel certain sensations—among them pain and nausea. However, one of the Alpha Centaurian neurophysiologists discovers a way to modify the Alpha Centaurian nervous system so as to allow Alpha Centaurians to feel pain, and she finds a volunteer who wants to feel the sensation that humans call 'pain'. That there is a sensation with that name is all the volunteer knows about pain. With the volunteer in place, the experimenter flips the switch, but the volunteer experiences nausea instead of pain. However, the volunteer, not realizing that the experiment has failed, believes that he is in pain; he infers that the feeling must be pain since he has never felt it before, and since it is the sensation produced by the experimenter. The volunteer's false belief is explained (at least in part) by his lack of an ability that we all have: the ability to recognize—*non-inferentially*—that one is in pain. This ability is the capacity reliably to form beliefs as to whether or not one is in pain—where the belief is not the result of an inference. If the volunteer had this ability, he would recognize that he was not feeling pain. I will focus on this non-inferential recognitional ability in what follows; it is this ability that is involved in incorrigibility.[15]

[15] It is worth noting that lack of the non-inferential ability also explains how one can fail to know that one is in pain even when one *truly* believes one is. Suppose the experimenter's every attempt to cause pain has so far produced only nausea. Having hooked up a new volunteer who has not participated at all in the experiments, the experimenter flips the switch, and this time the volunteer feels pain. The volunteer knows of the long series of failures, but he is an optimistic sort and believes that this time the experiment is a success and that he is in pain. The belief is true, but it does not qualify as knowledge. Knowing of all the past failures, the volunteer has every reason to think that what he is feeling is nausea, and virtually no reason to think that he is feeling pain. His failure to know is explained—in part—by his lack of the ability non-inferentially to recognize pain. Lacking that ability, he has to rely on the dubious inference that what he feels must be pain since it was produced by the experimenter. There is no possibility of his knowing non-inferentially. Such cases of true belief without knowledge are not confined to situations in which one lacks the relevant ability; both the impairment and the improper use of an ability also give rise to such cases, cases that would be well worth investigating in a full treatment of the relation between recognitional abilities and the knowledge of mental states.

Some have objected (in conversation) that necessarily, since the volunteer feels pain, he knows he is in pain. He knows—so the objection goes—that he feels *that*, and since 'that' is pain, he knows that he is in pain. This is like arguing that, since I know I see that, and since 'that' is a sea-lion, I know I see a sea-lion. This inference is obviously fallacious; I may be totally unable to tell a sea-lion from a seal, or even an otter for that matter. The example in the text shows that the similar inference about pain is equally fallacious.

2. *Impaired ability.* Consider a variant of the earlier dentist example. This time you are not lost in thought and worry about your appointment; rather, since dentistry is for you an ordeal of fear and anxiety, you are fully focused on what the dentist is doing and what you are feeling. You see the sharp prong of the hard silver instrument as it approaches your mouth, and you feel the scraping on your teeth and hear the peculiar sound it makes. Suddenly, one of these sounds lasts longer than the others as the instrument abruptly slides off your tooth. You feel it strike the soft surrounding tissue, and you protest, 'That hurt!' as in the original example, you should be completely anaesthetized, so the dentist is perplexed. After some apologetic and reassuring words to the effect that it will never happen again, the dentist, to test the anaesthesia, probes the tissue once more. Calmer now, all you feel is a non-painful sensation of pressure; moreover, you recognize your present sensation as qualitatively identical to the sensation you felt before. The reason you thought that previous sensation painful was that, in your anxiety, you would have taken virtually any sudden, unexpected sensation to be a pain. Your anxiety impaired your non-inferential ability to recognize pain.[16]

3. *Improperly used ability.* The original, consumed-with-worry dentist example illustrates this possibility. In that example, you mistakenly believe a sensation to be a pain because the suddenness of the sensation so startles you that immediately, without attending at all carefully to the sensation, you take it for a pain. You do not properly employ your non-inferential recognitional ability.

Do (1)–(3) exhaust the possible sources of the false belief that one is in pain? The claim that they do has considerable plausibility. Recall the example in which your attention is focused on what seems to be a pounding headache. You have the ability to recognize pain. The ability is in no way impaired—you are not drugged, subject to post-hypnotic suggestion, delusional, deranged, or any such thing; and, carefully attending to your sensation, you are properly exercising your ability—you are not careless, distracted, over-hasty, or the like. Could your belief that you are in pain be false? The answer, it would seem, must be 'no'. That is:

[16] P. M. Churchland's example mentioned in n. 9 is perhaps best regarded as an anxiety example—although this is not entirely clear.

(\*) Necessarily, if one believes that one is in pain, and the belief results from properly exercising one's unimpaired ability non-inferentially to recognize pain, then one is in pain.[17]

This (or, more accurately, a suitable generalization of it) is the incorrigibility thesis I propose.

It is essential that the recognitional ability referred to in (\*) be a non-inferential one. (This is the qualification I suppressed earlier.) Otherwise, there are counter-examples. Thus: the experimenter is working with her one-thousandth volunteer. She has—as this volunteer knows—produced pain in 999 volunteers in a row. The experimenter flips the switch, but the result is nausea instead of pain. The volunteer, however, infers—given the experimenter's success rate—that what he feels must be pain. The volunteer's belief is false even though his ability inferentially to recognize pain is unimpaired and properly employed.[18]

There is an objection to consider—one raised with surprising frequency. The objection is that one can dream that one is in pain and hence believe falsely that one is in pain even though one has the unimpaired and properly employed ability to recognize pain.[19] In reply, we should distinguish three cases.

1. I am observing myself in the dream—observing myself from 'outside' as if I were another person. As a result of an inference

[17] Are there problems about causal deviance? Suppose at $t$ that you believe, as a result of using your unimpaired, properly employed ability to recognize pain, that you are in pain. An evil genius ensures that the belief will persist for 5 minutes past the time you are in pain. Is this a counter-example to (\*)? It is not clear how the evil genius makes the belief persist without impairing your ability to recognize pain, but, if this is possible, addition of temporal references in (\*) will avoid the example. I am indebted to Alfred Mele here.

[18] (\*) explains—or, at least, provides the basis for explaining—how one can count as knowing non-inferentially that one is in pain. The explanation is basically the same as the traditional view: there is, in the headache case for example, no need for inferential backing since your belief cannot be false—*given* that the belief results from properly exercising your ability non-inferentially to recognize pain. And this ordinarily is given. Ordinarily, the question of whether your belief results from the proper exercise of your unimpaired ability does not arise. We take it for granted that you have the ability to recognize pain. We also take it for granted that your ability is unimpaired, since an impairment that would make one unable to recognize pounding headaches as pain would be extraordinary. Improper employment would be equally extraordinary; after all, the pounding headache rivets your attention on the sensation. Why we take this much for granted is an interesting question, but not one I will treat here.

[19] This objection has been raised frequently in conversation. A version of it also appears in B. O'Shaughnessy, *The Will* (Cambridge, 1980), 2. 163.

based on observations of 'my' behaviour, I believe, of that observed person who happens to be me, that he is in pain. The belief is false, but this is not a case of exercising the non-inferential ability to recognize pain.

2. I am not in my dream as if I were another person; my point of view is my normal point of view, from 'inside'. I exercise my non-inferential ability to recognize pain and, as a result, believe—falsely—that I am in pain. The falsity of the belief is explained by the fact that I am confused and disoriented, as one can be in dreams; the confusion and disorientation impair my ability to recognize pain. This is consistent with (*).

3. I believe that I am in pain, and my ability non-inferentially to recognize pain is unimpaired and properly employed. In this case, I do feel pain. This is the case in which one wakes up and realizes that one was, and perhaps still is, in pain. (*) does not deny this possibility.

Carefully distinguishing these cases shows there is no defensible version of the 'dream objection' that is really inconsistent with (*).

### iii. The 'Neural Hologram' Objection

The dream objection is easily answered, but there is another, far more serious, objection that goes to the heart of the matter. Recall the anxiety version of the dentist example. In that example, you mistakenly believe a sensation of pressure to be a pain. I claimed that your anxiety impaired your ability to recognize pain. But *why* view the matter this way? Is it not possible that your ability to recognize pain is unimpaired and properly employed?

To make the point more graphically, suppose—to engage in some neurological science fiction—that your anxiety operates this way. Let $N$ be neural activity sufficient for the occurrence of pain. $N$ includes a sequence of neural events $e_1, \ldots, e_n$ involving interactions between the brain stem and the frontal cortex. The final event in this sequence is (or is the cause of) the belief that one is in pain. Suppose that your anxiety in the dentist case causes the sequence $e_1, \ldots, e_n$ to occur even though the rest of $N$ does not occur. The result is that you believe you are in pain even though you are not. What appears to be pain is really just a kind of hallucination, an anxiety-produced 'neural hologram', as it were. The hallucination consists in the occurrence of the sensation of pressure in conjunction with $e_1, \ldots, e_n$. After all, the objection goes, the combination of the sensation with $e_1, \ldots, e_n$ is surely as much like pain as a hologram of a fox is like a fox. Nothing in this story requires that we regard your ability as impaired. Why not regard the case as analogous to the fox/hologram case? Why not regard it as a case in which a 'neural hologram' makes your belief false even though your ability is unimpaired and properly employed?

It may seem that there is an easy reply here.[20] Consider: what makes the fox hologram indistinguishable by sight from a real fox is that it looks like a fox. Similarly, what makes a purported neural hologram indistinguishable from pain is that the hologram feels like pain. But—in a case in which one properly exercises one's unimpaired ability non-inferentially to recognize pain—if a sensation feels like pain, then it is pain. Thus, if—as the neural hologram objection asserts—one's ability is unimpaired in the anxiety version of the dentist example, then the sensation is a pain, not a neural hologram.

This reply may seem attractive, but it is not adequate. The difficulty arises when we ask what 'feels like' means. An 'epistemic' reading is one possibility. Roughly: a sensation $S$ feels like pain if and only if, as a result of having $S$, one believes or is inclined to believe that $S$ is a pain. On this reading, the reply asserts that, in a case in which one properly exercises one's unimpaired ability non-inferentially to recognize pain, a sensation that feels like pain— that is, a sensation one believes (or is inclined to believe) is pain— must be pain. This 'reply' is merely a disguised reassertion of (*). A second possibility is the 'phenomenal' reading: a sensation feels like pain if and only if the sensation has a felt quality relevantly like the felt quality of pain. The problem, of course, is what 'relevantly like' means. One possibility is that the two felt qualities are relevantly like just in case they are indistinguishable (on introspection) by a person with the unimpaired and properly employed ability non-inferentially to recognize pain—where 'indistinguishable' means 'believes or is inclined to believe'. But then the 'phenomenal' reading collapses into the 'epistemic' one.

---

[20] I am indebted to Brian Loar for pointing out the possibility of this reply.

However, if 'relevantly like' does not mean something like this, it is completely unclear what it means. I claim that there is no non-question begging explanation of what 'feels like' means in this context. The neural hologram objection is not so easily answered.

My answer is that (\*) must express a necessary truth, since the supposition that it is false yields a contradiction: if (\*) is false, one cannot know—non-inferentially or otherwise—that one is in pain; but one can, and does, know this.

Suppose, then, that (\*) is false; suppose, that is, that one can falsely believe that one is in pain even when the belief results from properly employing one's unimpaired ability non-inferentially to recognize pain. For the sake of definiteness, imagine that there are neural holograms of pain. Now let us return once again to the headache case. It seems as if your head is being hammered open from the inside, and you believe that you are in pain. Your belief is the result of your properly employed and unimpaired ability non-inferentially to recognize pain. But how do you know that what seems to be pain is not just a neural hologram? I claim: (1) you have no way of knowing whether or not your apparent pain is merely a neural hologram; and hence (2) you do not know that you are in pain.

To argue for (1), it is useful first to reconsider the case in which I have placed holograms of foxes in various places. This example has important analogies and disanalogies to the pain/neural hologram case. In the fox/hologram example, you claim to know, by sight, that a certain animal is a fox; I point out that the area is filled with holograms of foxes, indistinguishable by sight from real foxes, and I ask you how you know the apparent fox is not just a hologram. You cannot rule out the possibility of a hologram; here 'rule out' is convenient shorthand for 'know that the possibility does not obtain'. Since you cannot rule out the possibility, you fail to know whether what you see is a fox—even though your belief is the result of your properly employed, unimpaired ability to recognize foxes by sight.

To develop the analogy with the pain/neural hologram case, suppose that, after I raise the hologram possibility in the fox case, you want to determine whether what you see is a fox or a hologram. A natural way to do this would be to look at the apparent fox from another perspective; if it is a hologram, it may not seem as fox-like from some perspectives. Or you could try to touch the apparent fox; if your hand goes through it, it is a hologram. But suppose you are not allowed to change your perspective; you have to stay exactly where you are; and the 'fox' does not move either. Suppose also that you are not allowed to touch, smell, or do anything but look at the apparent fox. In this situation, you will never know whether you are looking at a real fox. Or that is almost right. You might, after an hour, infer that the apparent fox is not real on the ground that real foxes do not stand still for so long; or if it suddenly vanished into thin air, you might, on the ground that real foxes do not simply vanish, reasonably infer that someone turned off the machinery generating the hologram. The point is that, without exploiting knowledge of some sort of empirical regularity (such as: real foxes do not stand still for so long; or, real foxes do not vanish), you will never be able to tell whether the apparent fox is real—the holograms being indistinguishable by sight from real foxes.

Compare the headache case. You cannot change your perspective on the pain; there is no relevant sense in which you can move in relation to it. Moreover, you are confined to one form of sensory experience of the pain; you feel it.[21] It follows, by parity of reasoning with the fox/hologram case, that you cannot rule out the possibility that what seems to be pain is just a neural hologram —unless you have some suitable empirical regularity to rely on. But there is no such regularity. To see why, consider any type of sensation $S$ that one would believe to be a pain—where the belief results from properly exercising one's unimpaired ability non-inferentially to recognize pain. You discover that a regularity $R$ is true of $S$. Is $R$ a regularity that holds for pains or for neural holograms? To settle that question you have to know whether $S$ is a pain or a neural hologram, but you cannot know this unless you appeal to some appropriate regularity. Appeal to $R$ will not do, of course, and if you appeal to some other regularity the problem begins all over again.

---

[21] Of course, if pain were to turn out to be an electro-chemical state of the brain, and the relevant parts of your brain were exposed (in neurosurgery, say), you might see your pain. This would give you a different sensory experience of the pain from a different perspective. Let us stipulate, however, that the relevant parts of your brain are not exposed. I will argue later that pain cannot be an electro-chemical state—provided such states are physical in the relevant sense; but I am not entitled here to the assumption that pain cannot be an electro-chemical state.

One may object that I have tacitly assumed that, to establish the appropriate regularity *R*, pains and neural holograms must be 'observationally distinguishable'—distinguishable on introspection without appeal to any empirical regularity. The objection is that, even if pains and neural holograms are observationally indistinguishable, it does not follow that we cannot distinguish between them. For example, two chemical compounds may be indistinguishable within the limits of ordinary, everyday observation, yet chemical theory may provide us with grounds for holding that they have different chemical compositions and obey different laws. Why should not the same thing happen in the case of pain and neural holograms? Have I not simply ignored the holistic, theoretical sorts of inferences that allow us to distinguish between what is indistinguishable within the limits of ordinary, everyday observation? In particular, could not a neurological theory discover how to distinguish between pains and neural holograms?

Suppose it could. It still does not follow that you can *now*—in your present state of knowledge—rule out the possibility of neural holograms. After all, you do not have the theory now, so you have no way of knowing now whether or not your apparent pain is merely a neural hologram.

Now I claim that it follows that *you cannot know now—in the present state of our knowledge—whether you are in pain.* To see this, consider what we require for knowledge in cases *not* involving mental states. Suppose a scientist discovers a disease—pseudo-measles—which, although it is not a kind of measles, manifests all the observable symptoms of measles. Pseudo-measles differs from measles in its underlying pathology and can be detected by photographic images generated by rotating the patient through a powerful magnetic field. The drug that cures pseudo-measles causes severe brain damage if one has measles, and vice versa. Imagine you have the observable symptoms the two diseases share. There are three cases to consider.

1. We know that 50 per cent of the cases with these symptoms turn out to be pseudo-measles; 50 per cent, measles. We have not yet tested you in the magnetic field. Do we know which disease you have? Certainly not; for all we know, you could have either.

2. We know that 99 per cent of the cases are measles. We believe, on this basis, that you have measles, and without testing

*Richard Warner*

you in the magnetic field (which is prohibitively expensive), we give you the drug for measles. No brain damage occurs, so you did in fact have measles. Did we know you did? Almost certainly; we had excellent grounds for our belief that you had measles. Of course, in this particular case, some may insist on extremely high standards for knowledge—since the consequences of being wrong are so drastic. But let us suppose the standards, however high, are fulfilled; suppose a vanishingly small percentage (far less than 1 per cent) of cases exhibiting the symptom are cases of pseudo-measles.

3. We do not know—even approximately—the relevant percentages. All we know is that some cases with the symptoms are pseudo-measles, and some are measles. Without testing you in the magnetic field, do we know which disease you have? No, for we do not know if the measles/pseudo-measles ratio more or less approximates case (1) or case (2). We would *merely be guessing* if we were to claim that you had one disease or the other. Were we to recommend that you take the drug for measles, you could— and should—reject the suggestion on the ground that we do not know you have measles. To know that you have measles would be to have a good reason for choosing the drug for measles instead of the drug for pseudo-measles; since we clearly have no such reason, we do not know that you have measles. In such cases, genuine knowledge provides a good reason for a choice.

One may object that the foregoing argument ignores reliability theories of knowledge.[22] Such theories are popular enough for the objection to merit an answer. The root idea behind the theories is that it is a sufficient (if not also a necessary) condition for knowing that $p$ that one's true belief that $p$ be the result of a reliable process of belief formation. Theories differ as to what counts as a reliable process, and what they add (if anything) to the root idea. However, on some theories, we could count as knowing which disease you had in case (3). Thus, suppose that we claimed, on the basis of your symptoms, that you had measles; and, suppose that, unbeknownst to us, 99 per cent of the cases with your symptoms are cases of measles. The inference from the symptoms to the disease is reliable—in a probabilistic sense of 'reliable';

---

[22] The reliability theory is discussed and evaluated (negatively) in R. K. Shope, *The Analysis of Knowing* (Princeton, NJ, 1983).

hence, on versions of the reliability theory that interpret 'reliable' in this probabilistic way (and add nothing to the root idea), we would count as knowing that you had measles. This result may make it appear that we were wrong to conclude above that we do not know which disease you have. However, this appearance is deceptive. It is case (3) that counts against reliability theories, not the other way around. It is clear that we do not know which disease you have, so we should reject those reliability theories that entail that we do know.[23]

*The assumption that there are neural holograms places us in a situation analogous to case (3).* To see this, note first that we lack any way to tell the difference between real pains and neural holograms. This may seem obviously false. Didn't we examine several cases in which what seems to be pain turns out not to be? But these were all cases in which one lacked the ability non-inferentially to recognize pain, or in which that ability was impaired or improperly employed. The present question is whether we can tell the difference between a real pain and what only seems exactly like pain *to one whose ability to recognize pain is unimpaired and properly employed.* It is clear that we have no way to tell the difference. The seeming pain feels exactly like pain, so there is no difference as far as feeling is concerned. And, given that it feels exactly like pain, the apparent-pain feeler will behave just as if he felt pain. A pain hologram will lead one to take aspirin as surely as a real pain. One may object that these considerations are not decisive. Could you not feel a seeming pain at one time, and then later recognize it as qualitatively identical to a non-painful sensation? We claimed that this was possible in the dentist example, and that it showed that the first sensation was not a pain. But this will not do. What makes the dentist example intelligible is the supposition that your ability to recognize pain is impaired. Here we are being asked to think that one whose ability is *un*impaired will first think a sensation is a pain and then later think—correctly—that it was not a pain. The supposition that the ability is unimpaired deprives us of any way to explain why the sensation should later be—correctly—recognized not to have been a pain.

Given that we now have no way to tell the difference between

---

[23] For a somewhat similar criticism, see R. E. Grandy, 'Ramsey, Reliability and Knowledge', in D. H. Mellor, ed., *Prospects for Pragmatism* (Cambridge, 1980), 197–209.

real pains and neural holograms, we do not now know the percentage of apparent pains that are really neural holograms.[24] It follows that, in the headache case, you do not know that you are in pain—despite the fact that it seems as if someone were pounding with a hammer on the inside of your skull. This yields the promised contradiction, for you *do* know that you are in pain. Thus, (*) must be true.

(*) expresses a property pain has—a modal property. It is the property of being a state $S$ such that necessarily if one believes that one is in $S$, and the belief results from properly exercising one's unimpaired ability non-inferentially to recognize instances of $S$ as pain, then one is in $S$. To deny that pain has this property is to deny that one can know that one is in pain.

## iv. A Principled Distinction

Some may be sceptical of the argument that (*) is true, for the argument relies heavily on a distinction between false beliefs due to lack, impairment, or misuse of recognitional abilities, and false beliefs arising from other sources. I have not shown how to draw this distinction in a principled manner, and some may doubt that it is possible to do so.

To still this doubt, we should first note that the discussion of the fox/hologram example distinguishes two cases: one in which you can alter neither your perspective on, nor your type of sense experience of, the fox; and one in which you can change your perspective on the fox and have other types of sense experience of it. In the first case, the possibilities you can rule out include lack, impairment, and improper employment of the relevant recognitional ability. You can rule out the possibility that you lack the ability: you can remember past successful identifications. You can rule out the possibility of impairment: you can check if your glasses are on; you can, via memory and (in some cases) bodily sensation, rule out the possibility that you are over-fatigued, drugged,

---

[24] To make the cases exactly analogous, suppose we have just discovered a way—using the magnetic field—to detect neural holograms; the technique is so new that we do not yet know, even approximately, the percentage of apparent pains that are really holograms. Suppose the drug that cures holograms causes brain damage if one has a pain, and vice versa.

hypnotized, etc.[25] You can rule out improper employment by paying careful attention. What you cannot rule out are possibilities that can be realized when the recognitional ability is entirely in order—for example, the possibility illustrated by the fox hologram. This suggests the following: where a belief results from the exercise of a recognitional ability $R$,

> The falsity of the belief is due to lack, impairment, or improper use of $R$ if and only if the belief is false due to the realization of a type possibility that one who had $R$ could (in those cases in which the possibility is not realized) rule out without any relevant change in perspective or type of sense experience.[26]

This definition is not arbitrary. It rests on the distinction between cases in which you can alter neither your perspective nor the type of sense experience; and cases in which such changes are possible. Our cognitive access to the world divides along these lines, as the discussion of the fox and pain cases shows.

What counts as a relevant change in perspective or type of sense experience is a function of the recognitional ability. In the fox example, the recognitional ability in question is the ability to recognize a fox by sight. A relevant change in type of sense

---

[25] Touching your glasses and attending to bodily sensations may involve changes in perspective and/or type of sense experience, but they do not involve any change in perspective on the apparent fox, nor any change in type of sense experience of the apparent fox. These latter changes are what we are not allowing.

[26] What about false logical and mathematical beliefs? Do they not all come out false due to lack, impairment, or misuse of an ability—change of perspective or type of sense experience being irrelevant to forming true logical and mathematical beliefs? I think this is a correct result, but if one wants to avoid it, one may restrict the definition to empirical beliefs. I have argued that the result is correct for first-order logic in "Why Is Logic A Priori?", *The Monist*, 72. 1 (Jan. 1989), 40–50.

Some may want to relativize the definition to a given set of recognitional abilities—e.g. the abilities normally possessed by human beings (or this or that group of human beings). To see why, suppose that, although we believe it to be infinite, the universe is in fact finite. Since we lack the ability to recognize infinite extension by sight, it would follow, unless the definition is applied relative to the set of human recognitional abilities, that our belief is false due to lack of the ability to recognize infinite extension by sight (if we had the ability, we could see that the universe was finite). Some may find this an undesirable result on the ground that what explains our arriving at a false belief is a complicated story about our cosmological theories, not the lack of an ability we do not, and could not, have.

I explain the principled distinction differently and more fully in 'Is the Body a Physical Object?', in Steven J. Wagner and Richard Warner, eds., *Naturalism: A Critical Appraisal* (Notre Dame, Ind., 1992).

experience would be a change to something other than visual experience. A relevant change in perspective would be a change that would reveal something previously unseen about 'the fox'— either the real fox, or the merely apparent one (in some cases the change in perspective will be a change in perspective on the real fox; in other cases, on the hologram of the fox—that is, on that portion of the world in which there appears to be a fox).

This completes my argument that (*) is true.

## v. The Subjectivity of Pain

It follows from (*) that pain is not a physical state—or, as I prefer, that pain is a subjective, not an objective, phenomenon.

The essential point is that the nature of an objective item is not determined by what this or that particular person does or would believe about it: objectivity is a matter—at least in part—of *mind-independence*. An item is objective only if its being the way it is does not, in any essential way, depend on our beliefs about it or the way in which we come to know about it.[27] It is, of course, problematic to say, in any more precise way, what mind-independence consists in; however, the following is—I submit—at least a necessary condition. Being F is an objective phenomenon only if: there is *no* necessary connection of the sort illustrated by (*) between the exercise of the ability to recognize Fs and the truth of the resulting belief that a given item is an F. If there were such a connection, being F would, in an essential way, depend on one's beliefs about whether something is F.

Now the physical is, on current conception at least, certainly mind-independent. We certainly do not think that a physical item's being the way it is depends, in any essential way, on our beliefs about it or the way in which we come to know about it. On this conception, pain is not a physical state. (*) holds for pain, and nothing analogous holds, or can hold, for anything physical.

One may object that all I have shown is that pain is not a physical state—given our current conception of the physical. However, even if our current conception should change, a dichotomy remains—between that which does, and that which does

[27] See e.g. I. Scheffler, *Science and Subjectivity* (Indianapolis, 1976).

not, have a belief-independent determinate nature; between, for example, pain, and the electro-chemical activity of the nervous system that subserves the occurrence of pain. We should focus not so much on whether pain and other mental states are 'physical', but on what relations obtain between the two sides of the objective/subjective dichotomy. The recognition of this dichotomy is the spirit behind the traditional doctrine of incorrigibility.

# 9

# Weak Materialism[1]

## N. M. L. Nathan

### i

It is often said that although some mental properties are irreducibly non-material, not open to any behavioural or functionalist analysis, still every mental property is or even has to be owned by a material substance, by a brain or body. And from this the conclusion is drawn that a certain vestigial materialism can be preserved, property irreducibility notwithstanding. If a material (or mental) substance is just a particular which instantiates a material (or mental) property, then the thesis that every mental property is or must be owned by a material substance can be joined without inconsistency to the parallel thesis that every material property is or must be owned by a mental substance. There is no priority for the material in this conjunction, no reason to call it materialism even of the most vestigial kind. But probably the idea is to affirm either the modal thesis

1. Every instantiation of a non-material mental property must be by a particular which also instantiates a material property, but not all instantiations of material properties must be by particulars which also instantiate non-material mental properties,

or the non-modal thesis

2. Every instantiation of a non-material mental property is by a particular which also instantiates a material property, but some instantiations of material properties are by particulars which do not instantiate any non-material mental properties.

These two doctrines, which are indeed weakly materialist, are the ones now to be discussed.

[1] My thanks to Paul Snowdon, Kevin Mulligan, and Howard Robinson for their comments on a previous version.

We can argue against a position, and we can argue against arguments for a position. With (1) and (2), the latter task seems easier than the former. In the next section I consider and reject an attempt to dispose of both (1) and (2) by deriving a dilemma from the disambiguation of 'material property'. In Section iii I present an argument just against those who uphold (1). This is that (1) cannot comfortably be reconciled with the neutrally acceptable thesis that at least some volitions are caused by changes in brains or bodies. In Section iv nominalist considerations are invoked to show that if this objection to (1) did work it would hardly matter to us, as critics of weak materialism, if we had no objection at all to (2). In the fifth and last section, feeling myself finally on rather firmer ground, I criticize what I take to be the chief arguments for (1) and (2). A premiss which these arguments have in common is that experiences must have subjects and volitions must have agents. I think, however, that we have no reason to accept this, in the relevant senses of 'subject' and 'agent'. We would have reason to accept it only if introspection revealed that in experience there is a something to which a content is presented, and in volition an agent by which an event is willed. But the something which introspection seems to reveal, in these cases, may well be nothing more than the quality of a volition.

ii

One way to attack both the (1) and the (2) versions of weak materialism is to press for an explanation of what precisely it is that 'material property' is supposed to mean. Call dispositional and relational properties complex, and all other properties simple. Are there simple material properties, and how do (1) and (2) fare if it is the latter that they are taken to be about? A weak materialist who upholds either (1) or (2) under this interpretation of 'material property' will not presumably want to say that a simple material property is just any simple property mentioned in natural science, with natural science taken to include reports of how things are for the experimentalist and of what the experimentalist does. For then probably all simple mental properties will also be material, and typically it is his admission that this is not the case which makes the weak materialist admit that some mental properties are not material. Is it then that simple material properties are those which our senses represent things outside us as possessing, as for example non-dispositional colour qualities? On that definition it does at least seem that some simple mental properties are not material. External objects are represented by my senses as being non-dispositionally scarlet, but nothing outside me is represented by my senses as having a visual experience as of something scarlet. But are simple material properties, on this new definition, ever actually possessed by any of the particulars, such as brains or bodies, which according to (1) and (2) also possess non-material mental properties? Are brains really non-dispositionally greyish-pink? Is it not rather that they have merely the power to produce experiences as of something non-dispositionally greyish-pink?

Confronted with these questions, the weak materialist may prefer to assert that it is complex rather than simple material properties which are possessed by whatever has non-material mental properties. The material properties of brains and bodies are of a relational or dispositional kind. But surely brains and bodies have *some* simple properties. And if, as we are now to suppose, these simple properties are not material, what can they be but mental, or, perhaps, 'spiritual', characteristic of those entities which one recent writer has rather unappetizingly described as 'indivisible chunks of soul-stuff'.[2] But a doctrine on which the simple properties of brains and bodies are all mental or 'spiritual', and which is therefore presumably compatible even with the immortality of the individual mind, is surely hardly worth calling materialism at all.

It seems to me that this line of objection is in fact quite inconclusive, popular though elements of it are with idealist writers anxious to turn the tables on topic neutral analyses of the concept of mind. For why should we accept that simple material properties, defined as those which our senses represent things outside us as having, are none of them possessed by the particulars, such as brains or bodies, which according to the weak materialist instantiate non-material mental properties? No good arguments have yet been produced for that conclusion. It has in particular (I am glad to say) never been shown that mind-independent objects do not have non-dispositional colour qualities. It may have been shown that

[2] R. G. Swinburne, *The Evolution of the Soul* (Oxford, 1986), 154.

we do not know what colour qualities they have. It may even have been shown that we do not know that they have colour qualities. But it has never been shown that they do not have colour qualities. And until some convincing argument has been produced to exclude that possibility, the present objection to weak materialism cannot be sustained.[3]

### iii

I will now try to develop a different objection, which applies only to

1. Every instantiation of a non-material mental property must be by a particular which also instantiates a material property, but not all instantiations of material properties must be by particulars which also instantiate non-material mental properties.

It is that if he upholds (1) then the weak materialist cannot easily believe, as we might expect him to, that there can be no volitions without brains or bodies which are their agents, unless he also rejects something which it is independently reasonable to accept, namely, that at least some volitions are caused by changes in these brains or bodies. For it turns out that if he does accept this last thesis about the causation of volitions, and also that volitions are existentially dependent on brains or bodies which are their agents, then it will be difficult for him not to accept that possibly some brains or bodies have always existed and have never begun to exist. And one should be uneasy about accepting that as a possibility.

There is a ... curious asymmetry in our intuitions. Something infinitely old makes the mind boggle in a way in which something with an infinite future does not. Wittgenstein in a lecture once asked his audience to imagine coming across a man who is saying '... 5, 1, 4, 1, 3— finished!' and, when asked what he had been doing, replies that he has just finished reciting the complete decimal expansion of π backwards— something he has been doing at a steady rate from all of past eternity.

---

[3] For criticisms of some current arguments against the mind-independent realization of non-dispositional colour qualities, see my 'Simple Colours', *Philosophy*, 61 (1986), 345–53, and *Will and World* (Oxford, 1992).

There is a special way in which this story strikes us as absurd, a way in which the corresponding story about a man beginning to recite the complete decimal expansion of $\pi$ and carrying on forever does not strike us as absurd.[4]

Let us say that $a$ is causally derived from $b$ if $b$ either causes a, or causes a cause of $a$, or causes a cause of a cause of $a$, or . . . , and so on. And suppose we accept the Humean principle that if one event is causally derived from another event, then either event can occur without the other.[5] Suppose now that volitions are caused by changes in brains or bodies. It will then be reasonable to suppose that if even $E$ were the beginning of the brain or body, changes in which actually cause some volition $V$, then $V$ would be causally derived from $E$. Now on our Humean principle about causality, if $V$ were causally derived from $E$, then it would be possible for $V$ to occur without $E$. And if $V$ occurred without $E$ then the brain or body, changes in which actually cause $V$, would either not exist or have existed forever. But the type 1 weak materialist thinks that every instantiation of a non-material property *must* be by a particular which also instantiates a material property, and, as we are assuming, thinks more particularly that volitions *cannot* occur without the brains or bodies which are their agents. So either the type 1 weak materialist must deny that some volitions are caused by changes in brains or bodies, or he must deny our Humean principle about causation, or he must concede, uneasily, that it is possible that there are brains or bodies which have always existed. In each case he would I think be paying quite a heavy price for his weak materialism, and perhaps too heavy a price, if, as I show in Section v, there are defects in the chief positive argument in favour of his doctrine. I do not say that the weak materialist cannot consistently deny that some volitions are caused by changes

[4] A. Moore, *The Infinite* (London, 1990), 44.
[5] Suppose I am sad that Mary is in London. Doesn't my judgement that she is in London cause this sadness, even though this sadness couldn't occur without my judgement? But maybe my being sad that Mary is in London is my being sad, after judging that she is in London, and whilst believing that my sadness is caused by this judgement. In this case it will be impossible for me to be sad that Mary is in London without my judging that she is. But if my judgement does cause my sadness, it is only my feeling that it causes, and not the whole complex of states and events which is my sadness that Mary is in London. Since my judgement is part of the whole complex, it cannot cause the whole complex without causing itself. What is caused, in the example, is not the same as what cannot occur without that cause; the Humean principle seems therefore to survive.

in brains or bodies. Nor do I say that this thesis is entailed by the premisses of some argument he is likely to adduce in his own favour. He will not claim that the dependence of instantiations of non-material mental properties on instantiations of material properties itself derives from the fact that mental events are caused by changes in brains or bodies. My point is rather that it would be far-fetched for anyone to deny that some volitions are caused by changes in brains or bodies, and that, because of the modality of his doctrine, it will be difficult for the type 1 weak materialist not to deny this unless, what would be almost as uncomfortable, he is prepared either to deny Humean principles about causation in general, or to assert that beginningless brains or bodies are a possibility.

This reasoning, for what it is worth, does not apply to the type 2 weak materialist. (2) is a non-modal doctrine. It says only that every instantiation of a non-material mental property is by a particular which also instantiates a material property; it does not say that every instantiation of a non-material mental property must be by such a particular. There is, accordingly, no reason to expect the type 2 weak materialist to maintain that volitions *cannot* occur without brains or bodies. And so no inconsistency need afflict the type 2 weak materialist even if he also maintains that all volitions are caused by or causally derived from the beginnings of brains or bodies, and that although it is indeed possible that these brains or bodies should not have existed, it is not possible that any brain or body should always have existed.

iv

It is only to version 1 of weak materialism that I have so far found even a remotely promising objection. But I will now try to show that if this objection does work, then little more remains for the critic of weak materialism to do.

(1) and (2) both presuppose the traditional ontology of instantiated universals and instantiating particulars. But what, we may ask, *are* the particulars that instantiate? Are they bare, or do they have natures? If they are bare, how can there be more than one of them? If they have natures, then presumably they already instantiate properties, and their postulation cannot therefore help to explain what property instantiation is.[6] We may well prefer

an alternative scheme, often called tropist, in which multiply instantiated universals are replaced by sets of non-instantiating particulars which exactly resemble each other, and multiply
instantiating particulars by bundles of dissimilar non-instantiating
particulars. And for the critic of weak materialism one agreeable
by-product of the move to a tropist ontology would be a less
diversified target. On a tropist ontology, it is not (1) and (2) which
the critic of weak materialism needs to consider, but the tropist
analogues of (1) and (2). But (2)'s closest tropist analogue, unlike
(2) itself, and unlike (1)'s closest tropist analogue, is a thesis which,
as we shall see, it is pointless to call materialism even of the
weakest kind. The critic can accordingly concentrate wholly on
(1)'s analogue. But if the beginninglessness objection to (1) does
work, a parallel objection works also against (1)'s tropist analogue.

There are in fact various alternatives to the traditional ontology
of instantiated universals and instantiating particulars. In one
alternative scheme, which Russell at one stage advocated, multiply
instantiated universals and multiply instantiating particulars are
replaced by bundles of universals.[7] But in the alternative which
I want to invoke, multiply instantiated universals are as I said
replaced by sets of non-instantiating particulars which exactly resemble each other, and multiply instantiating particulars by bundles
of dissimilar non-instantiating particulars. Thus, this apple is not
a particular instantiating various universals including red, but a
whole partly composed of a particular redness, a redness which
cannot be shared even by another apple whose component particular redness is precisely similar.

Non-Russellian anti-instantiationism is compatible with various
theses about the nature and interrelations of the replacement entities.
Let a substance be defined as an entity which can exist even though
no other entity exists which is not one of its proper parts, and let
a moment be defined as a non-substance.[8] Let a simple entity be

[6] The questions are Campbell's. See K. Campbell, *Abstract Particulars* (Oxford,
1990), 53–7.
[7] Russell, *Human Knowledge: Its Scope and Limits* (London, 1948), pt. 4,
ch. 8.
[8] For a detailed exploration of the varieties of ontological dependence, see. P.
Simons, *Parts* (Oxford, 1987), ch. 8. Simons moves forward from Husserl's theory
of dependent and independent parts. For an excellent account of the nature and
influence of Husserl's theory, see B. Smith and K. Mulligan, 'Pieces of a Theory',
in B. Smith, ed., *Parts and Moments* (Munich and Vienna, 1982), 15–109.

defined as an entity with no parts and let a complex entity be defined as one with parts. The non-Russellian anti-instantiationist may or may not believe that this apple is a substance. He may or may not believe that the redness of this apple, in addition to being one of the parts of this apple, is a moment which cannot exist if this apple does not exist. And he may or may not believe that the redness of this apple is infinitely divisible, or that any of the parts of this apple are simple entities. Equally, non-Russellian anti-instantiationism is distinguishable from abstract particularism. According to the latter doctrine, the world is composed of abstract and concrete particulars.[9] Abstract particulars, though in the view of some not moments,[10] are parts of concrete particulars. This apple is a concrete particular; its redness, like its shape, is an abstract particular. All particulars are spatio-temporally located, a particular is concrete if not abstract, and abstract only if some other particular which is not one of its proper parts can be simultaneously located at the same place.[11] A non-Russellian anti-instantiationist might reject abstract particularism on the ground that mental particulars have no spatial location at all. He might even reject it on the ground that uninstantiated universals exist. If nominalism is the doctrine that there are no universals, instantiated or otherwise, then the anti-instantiationist may or may not be a nominalist.[12] Donald Williams called abstract particulars tropes.[13] But, following Campbell, I take a tropist ontology as one which also allows there to be non-spatio-temporally located non-instantiating particulars.[14]

    [9] See D. C. Williams, 'The Elements of Being', in his *Principles of Empirical Realism* (Springfield, Ill., 1966), 74–109; id., 'Universals and Existents', *Australasian Journal of Philosophy*, 64 (1986), 1–14; and Campbell, *Abstract Particulars*.
    [10] See e.g. Williams, 'Elements of Being', 97.
    [11] Williams, like Campbell, thinks that a particular which is abstract in the sense that another particular which is not one of its proper parts can be simultaneously located at the same place is also abstract in the sense that it is abstracted by the mind from the bundle to which it belongs. Neither writer makes it entirely clear which kind of abstractness enters into his actual definition of 'abstract particular'. The advantages seem to lie with a non-psychological definition.
    [12] Campbell (*Abstract Particulars*, 27) prefers to define nominalism as the denial that there are properties. He then claims that since abstract particulars *are* properties, abstract particularists are necessarily not nominalists. But properties need owners, and, like Williams, Campbell recognizes (p. 59) that some abstract particulars may exist all by themselves rather than in bundles, throngs, or stacks.
    [13] Williams, 'Elements of Being', 78.
    [14] Campbell, *Abstract Particulars*, 53–7.

Let me now show in more detail how acceptance of a tropist ontology can help the critic of weak materialism.

(1) can be contrasted with:

3. For every instantiation of a non-material mental property, there has to be a certain particular instantiation of a material property, but for no instantiation of a material property must there be any one instantiation of a non-material mental property.

(1) requires that when a non-material mental property is instantiated, the very same particular which instantiates it must also instantiate a material property. (3), on the other hand, allows the material property, which has to be instantiated if the non-material mental property is instantiated, to be instantiated by a different particular from the one which instantiates the non-material mental property. There is a parallel contrast between (2) and

4. Every instantiation of a non-material mental property goes specially together with a certain particular instantiation of a material property, but some instantiations of material properties do not go specially together with any instantiations of non-material properties.

Although (3) and (4) do both give some kind of priority to the material, their materialism, if that is what we are to call it, is in one way even more vestigial than that of (1) and (2). Since (3) and (4), unlike (1) and (2), do not require the particulars which instantiate non-material mental properties to be the same as those which instantiate material properties, they do not require there to be such an intimate relation between non-material and material properties. But actually there is no point in calling (4) a version of materialism at all. The relation it postulates of going specially together could just be a causal relation, and in this case (4) would be perfectly consistent with what is generally called epiphenomenalist dualism. Now consider the closest tropist analogues of

1. Every instantiation of a non-material mental property must be by a particular which also instantiates a material property, but not all instantiations of material properties must be by particulars which also instantiate non-material mental properties,

and

2. Every instantiation of a non-material mental property is by a particular which also instantiates a material property, but some instantiations of material properties are by particulars which do not instantiate any non-material mental properties.

For (1) we have

1'. For each non-material mental trope, there is some material trope or other without which it cannot exist, but some material tropes are not similarly dependent on the existence of any non-material trope.

And for (2) we have

2'. Every non-material mental trope goes specially together with some material trope, but some material tropes do not go specially together with any non-material mental tropes.

(2'), however, seems also to be the closest tropist analogue of (4). And like (4), (2') seems not to be a thesis to which there is any point in attaching the label even of weak materialism. Because it eliminates the instantiating particular, the tropist ontology does not allow for a contrast like that between (2) and (4). And since it is as pointless to call (2') weak materialism as it is to apply that label to (4), the critic of weak materialism can if he accepts the tropist ontology ignore (2') and concentrate his attacks on (1'), which, thanks to its modality, is still distinctively materialistic. If, however, the beginninglessness objection to (1) is sound, then it will be easy enough for the critic to adapt it against (1'). Anyone who believes (1') can also be expected to believe that there can be no volitions without bodies or brains which are agents, the volitions being moments and the bodies or brains on which they depend parts of complex entities of which the volitions are also parts. And he too will find it difficult to make room for volitions to be caused by changes in bodies and brains unless he is prepared to believe it possible that these bodies or brains have always existed.

There is not much space here actually to defend tropism or to rehearse its merits. Nor for that matter is it easy to find plausible objections to the doctrine which have not already been refuted. But in the rest of this section I will briefly consider some objections of Armstrong's which, though directed against abstract particularism, also apply to the broader tropist view.

Some but not all classes of abstract particulars have a unity: the class of rednesses, for example, has a unity, and there is no similar unity in the class formed by the union of the class of particular smells and the class of particular triangular shapes. What makes for such unities? According to Armstrong, the abstract particularist has no plausible answer to this question other than that the unity of, for example, the class of rednesses consists in the fact that each redness resembles a paradigm redness. But this lays him open to three at least of the objections which are fatal to Resemblance Nominalism. According to the latter, '*a* has the property *F*' is analysed as '*a* suitably resembles a paradigm case (or paradigm cases) of an *F*.'[15] The first objection is that 'the relation of resemblance . . . depends on the nature of the object, not the nature of the object on the relation.'[16] Secondly, 'the Resemblance analysis is involved in vicious regress.'[17] And thirdly, '. . . it is perfectly intelligible that a particular may be the only one of its kind, and so have nothing to resemble . . .'.[18] As to the regress, if the special unity of the class of rednesses consists in the fact that each resembles a paradigm redness, then a further question arises about the special unity of the class of relations of resemblance between rednesses and the paradigm redness. In what does *that* unity consist? Presumably, in the fact that each of its members resembles a paradigm relation of resemblance between a redness and the paradigm redness. But the class of relations of resemblance between relations of resemblance between rednesses and the paradigm redness also has a special unity. In what does *that* consist? And so on, *ad infinitum*.

It would I suppose be possible for the abstract particularist to admit a regress but ask for some evidence that it is infinite. It will not be infinite unless the number of rednesses is also infinite. For the question to arise as to what constitutes the unity of the class of first-order relations of resemblance between rednesses and a paradigm redness, there must be at least two such first-order relations. And this requires that there are at least three distinct rednesses, including the paradigm. But equally, for the question to arise as to what constitutes the unity of the class of second-order relations of resemblance between first-order relations of resemblance between rednesses and a paradigm redness, there must be at least

---

[15] D. M. Armstrong, *Universals and Scientific Realism*, 1. 15.
[16] Ibid 85.   [17] Ibid.   [18] Ibid.

two such second-order relations, which requires at least four rednesses, and so on. So if there is a limit to the number of rednesses, there is some order of relations of resemblance between lower-order relations of resemblance such that there is only one relation of that order, and in this case no question can arise as to what constitutes the unity of the class of relations of resemblance of that order, and the regress has come to an end.

But as Armstrong himself acknowledges, in his more recent book *Universals*, the abstract particularist can in any case say that the unity of the class of rednesses rests on nothing but the nature of each redness.[19] If this is what he says, he will not need to deny that the relation of resemblance depends on the nature of the object, rather than the other way about. He can agree with the later Armstrong that the facts that there are relations of resemblance between rednesses *a* and *b*, relations of resemblance between those relations of resemblance, etc., are not facts additional to the actual natures of *a* and *b* themselves.[20] Nor need he deny that an abstract particular may be the only one of its kind. If his problem were to explain how, say, a redness has the property red, and his explanation was that for a redness to be red is for it to resemble another and paradigm redness, then there would be a difficulty. But the abstract particularist need not claim that any particular redness has the property red. For a particular to be red, is, he thinks, for a redness to be part of that particular. Nor, contrary to the first point, need the abstract particularist say that it is on its relation of resemblance to some other abstract particular that the nature of an abstract particular depends.

Though retracting his earlier objections, Armstrong still prefers 'Realism about universals (. . . in a substance attribute from)'.[21] Why? So far as I can see, he has only two new arguments against abstract particularism. One is that abstract particulars or tropes 'are not really suited to be the substances of the world'. For example, 'a trope of a particular mass or a particular charge seems nearly as insubstantial, as incapable of independent existence, as the corresponding universal.'[22] This objection, however does not apply to nominalist anti-instantiationism in general, nor even to abstract particularism in general, but only to those versions of

---

[19] D. M. Armstrong, *Universals* (Boulder, Col., 1989), 46.
[20] Ibid. 56.    [21] Ibid. 120.    [22] Ibid. 114–15.

anti-instantiationism which maintain both that there is at least one substance, and that any substance is a particular which is not a bundle of particulars. It is perfectly consistent with nominalist anti-instantiationism to maintain that all particulars are moments, or that all substances have parts, or even that the only substance is the universe. The other new objection is a recondite conundrum about 'swapped tropes' on which he himself does not seem to place much weight. It is effectively dealt with by Campbell in chapter 3 of his *Abstract Particulars*, as are various further difficulties raised by other authors.

v

If there were a strong positive argument for (1) or its tropist analogue, the weak materialist might be willing to pay the price exacted by the considerations about beginninglessness which I expounded in Section iii. I turn then in this final section to a scrutiny of what seem to be the main arguments in favour of these doctrines.

(1)'s tropist analogue is

1'. For each non-material mental trope, there is some material trope or other without which it cannot exist, but some material tropes are not similarly dependent on the existence of any non-material trope.

The main argument for (1') depends on the premiss that experiences must have subjects and volitions must have agents. With that assumed, it is then claimed that subjects and agents can only be brains or bodies, and, given a tropist ontology, it is a manageable step from there to (1') itself. Obviously we could meet this by insisting that there is no actual incoherence in the idea that the subject and agent is a 'spirit', or trope of 'soul-stuff'. But we can also challenge the initial premiss. And if that works we will also have an objection, independent of any general pro-tropist considerations, to the principal argument for

1. Every instantiation of a non-material mental property must be by a particular which also instantiates a material property, but not all instantiations of material properties must be

by particulars which also instantiate non-material mental properties.

For it is hard to see how (1) can be defended except by inference from the same two premisses. We would, furthermore, have a non-tropist objection to the main argument for

2. Every instantiation of a non-material mental property is by a particular which also instantiates a material property, but some instantiations of material properties are by particulars which do not instantiate any non-material mental properties.

In this the first premiss is again that experiences must have subjects and volitions must have agents, and the next move is to assert, not that these subjects and agents must be brains or bodies, but that probably this is what they are, because if they were not then we would have to suppose, 'uneconomically', that subjects and agents are entities of a new kind which we do not already know to be otherwise exemplified.

Support is needed for the premiss common to these two arguments, namely that experiences must have subjects and volitions must have agents. And I do not see how it can have this support unless introspection reveals that in experience there is a something to which a content is presented and in volition a something by which an event is willed. If this is revealed by introspection then we might go on to claim that in revealing it introspection makes it impossible for us to conceive that there is volition without an agent or experience without a subject, and that it is this inconceivability that 'must' expresses in 'volitions must have agents' and 'experiences must have subjects'.

But unless introspection does reveal an indeterminate something to which contents are presented and by which events are willed, there is not even the beginning of a reason to accept that there cannot be experiences or volitions without those subjects and agents which according to the weak materialist are or must be brains or bodies. And in fact introspection does not reveal this.

When I am aware of an experience as of something scarlet, what I am aware of is not precisely a something to which the content 'something scarlet' is presented, but only a something seemingly distinct from and yet somehow intimately linked to the content 'something scarlet'. And sometimes I conceive of this something as quite different from a something to which a content is presented, and without the existence of which there could be no experience. I conceive of it, not as a something which has the experience, but rather as a part of the experience. How can this be, given that experience is 'transparent', has no introspectible feature? The answer is that I conceive of the experience as an act of attention to the content, and acts of attention, like other volitions, do have a special and at least dimly introspectible quality. When I am aware of willing, things are a certain particular way for me, whatever it is that I will. If experiencing is attending, then the distinct something without which there can be no experience is a part of the experience, and so the dependence of the experience on this part does not make the experience a moment.

What now of attending itself, and of volitions more generally? How can an act of attention or any other volition be conceived of as existing without an agent? When I am aware of a volition, I am aware, not precisely of a something by which an event is willed, but only of a something which is distinct both from what is willed and from the quality of the volition. And sometimes I conceive that this distinct something is the quality of *another* volition. Sometimes it seems to me that the position is this. In awareness X of willing that p, a something is revealed which is distinct both from the idea that p and the quality of willing that p. 'Attention to . . .' replaces 'experience as of . . .', and likewise replaces 'awareness of . . .'. So awareness X of willing that p is replaced by attention X to willing that p. Attention X has however an introspectible quality. And the something, distinct both from the idea that p and the quality of willing that p, of which there is awareness when there is attention X to willing that p, is not an agent, but the quality of attention X. When there is attention X to willing that p, there is also attention W to attention X, and the quality of attention X which is part of the object of attention W is the something, distinct both from the idea that p and the quality of willing that p, that there is awareness of when there is attention X to willing that p. And since I can perfectly well conceive that there is a willing that p to which there is no attention X, I can conceive that there is a willing that p with no distinct something which could be regarded as an agent whose existence that willing requires.

*Objection (a)* It cannot be the case that all supposed presentations of content are really only acts of attention, for to attend is itself to focus or concentrate on part of an already presented content. If all presentations of content were acts of attention, there would be no act of attention without an infinite series of acts of attention, each with a narrower content than its predecessor. And that is absurd.

*Reply.* Attending to a content is not the same as focusing or concentrating on a content. By attending to a content I mean sustaining or keeping hold of a content, and this need not involve any selection from a wider content previously attended to.

*Objection (b).* There can be no willing without a previous or simultaneous idea or image. If, for example, I will my arm to go up I must have, or have had, an idea or image of its going up. The idea or image must however be simply presented to a subject rather than actively attended to, otherwise there could be no willing without an infinite series of acts of will. So it cannot be the case that all supposed presentations to subjects are really just acts of attention.

*Reply.* Suppose that the necessary image is presented to the subject at the very time of the act of will, and that the act of will has an agent who is identical to this subject. How could the agent act at all, if at precisely the time of his action he was occupied with the reception of a presentation? It seems then that if the idea or image were presented to the subject at the very time of the act of will, then this act would either have no agent, or it would have an agent who was not identical to the subject. Neither alternative can be reconciled with the weak materialist doctrine that the brain or body is both subject and agent. Suppose then that the idea or image is presented to the subject before the act of will. Its presentation would then presumably stand in a causal relation to the subsequent act of will. But the act of will has its own content, and cause and effect are distinct existences. So we can conceive of the act of will occurring with its own content and without the previous presentation.

*Objection (c).* If there were no presentations of content but only acts of attention, then there would be no veridical perception. The content of an act of attention would be produced by the act rather than by those parts of the mind-independent world which the content represented.

*Reply.* We are concerned only with what it is possible to conceive, and maybe it is possible to conceive that there is no veridical perception. And anyway, a whole act of attention could still be caused by those parts of the mind-independent world which were represented by the content of the act.

*Objection (d).* Attention has no introspectible quality. There is nothing to be aware of, in attention to a content, which is distinct from both content and possible attender, nothing by describing which we can give a fuller description of what is distinct from the content than we give when we say merely that the content is presented to something.

*Reply.* I am myself aware of a special quality in acts of attention, as in other volitions. For evidence that I am not alone in this see the numerous protocols of conative phenomena assembled and discussed by Michotte, Ach, and other introspectionist psychologists of the first forty years of this century.[23]

Weak materialism may yet be true, even if there is no reason to think that it is. But if it is thus left without any rational support, and if we accept that some mental properties or tropes are non-material, we do not have to agree with the weak materialist that persons are brains or bodies which have non-material mental properties or that they are partly physical entities whose mental parts are moments. And if we further accept that experiences are volitions, there are several voluntarist theories of the person which deserve further exploration. A person could be a series of volitions connected causally or by their contents, or, what seems on the evidence of his *Philosophical Commentaries* to have been Berkeley's view, a single continuous activity in which all succession and variety belongs to the content of that activity.[24] Equally, a person could be a set of entities consisting partly of a content-connected series of volitions, or single continuous activity, and partly of a causally related brain or body, or immaterial spirit. Possibly serial voluntarism is best. That there are continuous people in the

[23] See A. Michotte and E. Prüm, 'Étude expérimentate sur le choix volontaire', *Archives de Psychologie*, 10 (1910), 113–320; N. Ach, *Analyse des Willens* (Berlin, 1935); H. M. Wells, 'The Phenomenology of Acts of Choice', *British Journal of Psychology*, monograph suppl. 4 (1927), 1–155; and the discussion of these writers in my *Will and World*.
[24] See A. C. Lloyd, 'The Self in Berkeley's Philosophy', in J. Foster and H. Robinson, eds., *Essays on Berkeley* (Oxford, 1985), 192.

Berkeleian sense seems to run counter to the fact that there are different kinds of volition. Perhaps attention is never interrupted by periods in which there is no volition of any kind, and unconsciousness in sleep is always absence of awareness of volition rather than absence of volition. But still attention is sometimes interrupted by volition of a different kind, by effort or decision. And that makes it difficult to maintain that all succession and variety belongs to the content of a single continuous activity, and that there is no series of distinct acts of will.

# 10

# Non-Reductive Physicalism?

## A. D. Smith

For though the Democriticks and Epicureans did indeed suppose all human cogitations to be caused or produced by the
incursion of corporeal atoms upon the thinker, yet did never
any of them arrive to such a degree either of sottishness or
impudence as a modern writer hath done, to maintain that
cogitation, intellection and volition are themselves really
nothing else but local motion or mechanism in the inward
parts of the brain . . .

Ralph Cudworth[1]

The argument of the present paper is simple and as follows: there
is no such thing as non-reductive physicalism; but all reductivist[2]
accounts of consciousness are misguided and unacceptable; therefore
physicalism is false. I shall not argue against reductive accounts of
conscious states and processes: it is, I believe, sufficient for any
sensible person simply to read them in order to see their inadequacy.
I shall, however, say something about what reductionism means in
this context. The central argument of this paper is, therefore, that
physicalism is essentially reductionist.

i

First, a few remarks on the title. I choose the term 'physicalism',
rather than 'materialism', since it is in one way weaker and in
another way stronger than the latter, at least in certain philosophical circles. It is weaker in that it does not restrict its ontology to
things composed of matter. This is desirable in so far as the main
motivation for physicalism is a desire to establish a comprehensive

---

[1] *The True Intellectual System of the Universe*, pt. 1 (London, 1678).
[2] Or 'reductionist': I shall use the two terms interchangeably.

ontology that is consonant with scientific knowledge; and current science is not, of course, restricted to dealing with matter. (Indeed, this widening of the notion of the physical to embrace more than matter and its modifications may render physicalism somewhat less intuitively objectionable: for many who are repulsed by the idea that conscious experience is nothing more than the cavortings of little billiard balls may be happier with the idea of, say, souls being special forms of energy.[3]) On the other hand, materialism is sometimes taken to mean only that whatever substances exist possess some physical properties—or that all (non-abstract) properties are properties of physical individuals. Such a position rules out various radically non-physicalist theories such as idealism, a Cartesian dualism of substances, and neo-Humean dualism; however, it is compatible with property dualism and even certain forms of epiphenomenalism. By 'physicalism' I intend a strong metaphysical theory that is incompatible with such positions. By this term I mean the view according to which everything non-abstract, every individual, property, relation, event, state, or process, is physical and wholly physical.[4] I shall say something later about how we are to understand the notion of what is purely physical.

At this point, however, I wish to say something about reductionism. What the opponents of reductionism in this area are against is, of course, reducing conscious states of awareness to the realm of the merely physical. In this paper I shall oppose physicalism by focusing on just one aspect of (some) conscious states: on the intrinsic, qualitative, sensory character of experiences, or on *qualia* as such characteristics are now commonly termed. This is not because I endorse what may be termed *radical psychological empiricism*: the view that all conscious states wholly consist in the awareness of sensory or quasi-sensory (i.e. imagistic) items, supplemented at most by an apperceptive appreciation of mental operations. In my view this theory is totally inadequate. Perhaps

---

[3] In his useful survey of 17th- and 18th-cent. literature on this topic, *Thinking Matter* (Oxford, 1983), John Yolton stresses the way in which a growing appreciation of the 'active principles' at work in the physical realm changed the nature of the controversy over physicalism. As will emerge, the precise nature of the physical world will not be relevant to the argument of the present paper.
[4] Thus Wilfrid Sellars, who has repeatedly argued that a truly adequate physical science must contain ineliminable reference to *sensa*, will not count as a physicalist: see e.g. 'Science, Sense Impressions, and Sensa: A Reply to Cornman', *Review of Metaphysics*, 24 (1970–1), 391–447.

it is true, as such widely differing philosophers as Aristotle, Leibniz, and Husserl have held, that there must be some sensory aspect to any (finite) state of consciousness; but the capacities of the human mind certainly outstrip the mere registering of sensory data—and the exercise of such capacities can be conscious. Indeed, a focusing on the qualities of mere sensation may be thought a singularly prosaic way of demonstrating the inadequacy of physicalism to a world containing the wonder of self-conscious spiritual beings. However, sensory features of conscious states, both perceptual and somatic, *are* indisputably genuine features of reality, ones that have received considerable philosophical scrutiny, and ones to which physicalism is, I shall argue, demonstrably incapable of doing justice. Thus I am, in this paper (to employ an idiom from that Americanized English that bids fair to become the lingua franca of analytical philosophy) adopting the position of the "*qualia* freak".

But what, more precisely, will reductionism with respect to *qualia* amount to? There is initially something of a problem here, since the notion of reduction has been clearly articulated only in relation to scientific theories; and although accounts of reduction in science have come a long way since the days of Nagel, Woodger, and Kemeny and Oppenheim, what all such accounts have in common is that there is an actual reduction of one property[5] to "another"[6] only in so far as there is a reduction of one theory to another; and to assert reducibility is to claim that such an inter-theoretic reduction will, or at least in principle could, be achieved. (Marshall Spector has argued that there are indeed reductions in the absence of theory. Thus he claims that we know that atomic nuclei reduce to more elementary particles, even though we lack an adequate theory of the latter.[7] However, if we do know this, it is only in virtue of knowing that such an adequate fundamental theory will, or in principle could, be forthcoming—one by which an actual reduction will be effected.) The initial problem that now

---

[5] Recall that *qualia* are properties, not mental objects: they are the various intrinsic characteristics of certain conscious experiences.

[6] The scare-quotes are to indicate that on most current accounts such reductions issue in synthetic *identities*. See e.g. D. Lewis, 'Psychophysical and Theoretical Identifications', *Australasian Journal of Philosophy*, 50 (1972), 249–58; R. L. Causey, 'Attribute Identities in Micro-Reduction', *Journal of Philosophy*, 69 (1972), 407–22; C. Hooker, 'Towards a General Theory of Reduction, 2. Identity in Reduction', *Dialogue* (Canada), 20 (1981), 201–36.

[7] *Concepts of Reduction in Physical Science* (Philadelphia, 1978), 90.

faces us is that there is not much of a theory about *qualia*, or
sensation, in the "manifest image"—"folk psychology" is mostly
silent here. There are, indeed, a few law-like generalizations relating
to sensations: for example, relating (at least moderately severe)
pains and aversive behaviour, itching and scratching; but not many.
How, in purely general, theoretical terms, are we supposed to
distinguish, or indeed say anything illuminating about, mild pains,
queasiness, mild physical irritation, and a host of other distinguishable, unpleasant physical sensations? We actually distinguish
them, of course, just by how they feel.[8] The same goes for perceptual *qualia*: there may be a modicum of everyday "theory"
about, for instance, all those who see something to be red—but
nothing relating to the (possibly divergent) *qualia* such persons
thereby enjoy. This point does not depend upon the possibility of
an intersubjective discrepancy of *qualia* that is undetectable in
principle; the point is, rather, that folk psychology has little or
nothing to say about the generally admitted possibility of such a
discrepancy that is simply non-obvious. Moreover, even if one
could establish, by general philosophical considerations, that there
could not possibly be an intersubjective discrepancy of *qualia* that
was indeed undetectable in principle, this too is no part of folk
psychology.[9] Conversely, several of the attempts to establish
physicalism that are explicitly patterned on the theoretical identifications that are found in inter-theoretic reduction in science are
presented as *non-reductive* accounts of the mental.

The anti-reductivist convictions that most of us hold have a
simpler source: it is the thought that the accounts in question just
leave something out. Physicalism excludes *qualia* from its account;
*qualia* are genuine features of reality; physicalism pretends to be
a comprehensive inventory of the world; so physicalism is false.
Perhaps a better term than 'reductivism' would be *bowdlerism*. The
trouble with physicalism is simply that it is a bowdlerization of
our world. Such an attitude may be found in the writings of some
proponents of the Identity Theory who are at pains to present it

---

[8] If the Private Language Argument really does imply that this is false, so much
the worse for the Wittgensteinians.

[9] I suppose first-year philosophy undergraduates are fairly good representatives
of enlightened common sense. I have yet to encounter one who is not wholly
convinced of the Lockean possibility that a violet looks to me the way a marigold
looks to you.

as non-"reductive". Thus we find Richard Brandt and Jaegwon
Kim writing:

> We are unhappy, however, with current statements of the theory. For one
> thing, we are unhappy with formulations in which such events as something
> looking red to me or my being in pain, in the ordinary sense of these
> terms, disappear from the actual world, as they appear to do in the
> proposals of Smart and Feyerabend.[10]

Let us pause to consider these two bowdlerizers, since their positions are instructively different from one another. Feyerabend, like
Richard Rorty, was a progenitor of what has come to be known
as *Eliminative Materialism*. This theory is explicitly bowdleristic:
there just aren't any sensations (or thoughts, desires, etc.), and
when science finally Gets Things Right such will be seen to be the
situation. Such a theory does not even need to countenance psycho-
physical identities: there is nothing psychological to identify physical
things with: thoughts and sensations are on a par with witches
and phlogiston. I shall not address this form of physicalism here;
it is explicitly bowdleristic, and I just cannot take it seriously.[11]
However, Smart's view warrants closer attention, since it was
explicitly presented as a form of the Identity Theory; and one
advantage that is commonly thought to attach to such a theory is
that it need not deny the genuine existence of the psychological
states and processes that it identifies with physical items. As Brandt
and Kim put it: 'Identity is a symmetric relation; it does not favor
one of its terms at the expense of the other.'[12] Identity Theorists
are supposed not to have to feign anaesthesia, as was the common
complaint against the behaviourists whom they superseded, and in
contrast to whom Smart himself, like D. M. Armstrong, initially
characterized his position. It is significant to note, therefore, that
right from the beginning Smart (again, like Armstrong) felt himself
constrained theoretically to deny the intrinsic sensory character of
ordinary perceptual states, and to specify them, in his view adequately, in "topic-neutral" terms. Smart was so constrained by
Max Black's objection to his purported physicalism (implicitly
echoed in Brandt and Kim's point about the symmetricality of

---

[10] 'The Logic of the Identity Theory', *Journal of Philosophy*, 64 (1967), 515.

[11] Should an argument be needed, the paucity of everyday theory concerning
*qualia* will serve as a fruitful premiss.

[12] Brandt and Kim, 'The Logic of the Identity Theory', 537.

identity) that Smart seemed saddled with 'irreducibly psychic properties'. Smart's response was simply to eliminate such *qualia* from his account; so that, for example, seeing a yellowish-orange after-image is supposedly adequately rendered in terms of 'something going on which is like what is going on when . . . I really see an orange'.[13] Similarly, we find Armstrong, in his analysis of perceptual experience in terms of the acquisition of beliefs, attempting to capture the phenomenology of perceptual experience, and to distinguish it from mere belief, by claiming merely that the content of perception is more detailed than that of mere belief, that visual perceptions are accompanied by us feeling our eyes move, and that we believe that our perceptual beliefs are acquired as a result of the use of sense organs.[14] All reference to the sensuous character of perceptual experience is studiously excluded. I hope it is not necessary to argue for the pitiful inadequacy of this. My claim is that no form of physicalism can avoid such an elimination of *qualia*. The notion of topic-neutrality will play a central role in the argument to this effect.

It is commonly said that a version of physicalism is reductive just in case it asserts type–type identities between the physical and the psychological. Now it may well be the case that the type–type Identity Theory is an unnecessarily strong position for a physicalist; but it seems to me that the mere assertion of a two-way strict implication between mental and physical characteristics is not, by itself, any more intuitively "reductionist" than other weaker forms of physicalism. It *is* reductionist, as we shall see: but only because such a position is implicitly bowdleristic—like all the weaker forms of physicalism, as I hope to show.

It is perhaps worth saying something briefly here about functionalism, since the early work of Armstrong and Smart contributed to its establishment as arguably the currently dominant account of the mind. Functionalism is typically paraded as an acceptably non-reductive account of the mind: chiefly, I suppose, because it is non-committal on the nature of the "hardware" that may realize the functional organization which is claimed to be the essence of mentality. Surely any theory of the mind that is compatible with Cartesian dualism is non-reductive? But when we understand this

---

[13] 'Sensations and Brain Processes', *Philosophical Review*, 68 (1959), 149.
[14] *Perception and the Physical World* (London, 1961), 112–14.

last notion, as I have suggested we should, in terms of the theoretical elimination of *qualia* from the world, the answer to this question must be a firm NO. Functionalism is just topic-neutrality run riot. It is thus not necessary for *qualia* freaks to oppose functionalism by attempting to demonstrate the possibility of in principle undetectable intersubjective differences in *qualia*. It is, indeed, obvious why attacks on functionalism have taken this form: for should the possibility in question be demonstrated, then functionalism would indeed be refuted. But it is not necessary for opponents of functionalism to attempt to demonstrate such a problematic possibility. Even if there cannot, for general philosophical reasons, be such a radical intersubjective discrepancy, the fact remains that functionalism simply leaves the subjective character of conscious states out of account, and therefore is not a fully adequate, comprehensive theory of mind. For it is not only theories that restrict their characterization of the world to specifically physical features that are objectionable: any supposedly exhaustive account of the world that supplements such narrowly physical notions with more abstract, formal ones—such as functional role and causal relations—will be equally, and equally unacceptably, bowdleristic in leaving out the intrinsic qualitative character of conscious states.

Before moving on to the main argument, I should like briefly to draw attention to one extraordinary bit of philosophical prestidigitation that has bedazzled certain members of the philosophical community.[15] The trick begins by pointing out that there are severe problems for physicalism if one adopts an act–object analysis of perceptual consciousness. For on such a view, whenever one, say, seems to see something red when there is nothing relevant before one, one will have to recognize the existence of some nonphysical item, a sense-datum, that either is red or, more plausibly, has some property analogous to red; and the physicalist will be hard pressed to include such properties of sense-data in his inventory of the world. However, if we opt for a unary characterization of perceptual states in terms of sensing, we no longer have the

---

[15] It is first found explicitly in T. Nagel's 'Physicalism', *Philosophical Review*, 74 (1965), 339–56. He says that it is 'a somewhat altered version of a device employed by Smart, and earlier by U.T. Place' (p. 341); sadly this is true. The disappearing trick is also performed by James Cornman in his *Materialism and Sensations* (New Haven, Conn., 1971).

problematic internal objects and their problematic properties. This is ludicrous. It is just a fact that certain conscious states have intrinsic phenomenal character: *qualia* are manifest features of reality—specifically of sensory states. To deny this would be to bowdlerize our world. If these states are not analysed in terms of an act and an object, but in terms of a sensing, then *qualia* are intrinsic characteristics of those sensings. The issue between sense-datum theorists and adverbialists is of considerable importance in giving a philosophical account of perception; in the present context, however, the dispute is wholly irrelevant.

ii

Surely, it will be objected, most physicalists do not deny that experiences have their intrinsic sensuous character; there *are* such qualities as the stingingness of an experience of being stung by nettles, phenomenal redness, and so on: it is just that such features have a wholly physical nature. Thus to take a (closely) analogous issue: when George Pitcher, in his development of David Armstrong's account of perception as the acquisition of beliefs, comes to consider the phenomenal character of perceptual experience, he does not follow Armstrong's patently bowdleristic route, but comes clean:

> It will doubtless be objected that what is left out of this account is the very essence of seeing—namely, the sensuous visual presentation or manifold. But the answer to this might well be that to be aware of, or to have, that visual presentation or manifold just *is* to know, by means of using one's eyes, that . . .[16]

Now one way to undermine physicalism would be to attack the suggestion that the instantiation of sensuous properties is nothing but the instantiation of various physical and/or functional properties. Surely we are at least dealing with different *properties* here. Unfortunately, for such a discussion we should need an agreed account of universals, their instantiation and cognition.[17] For

---

[16] *A Theory of Perception* (Princeton, NJ, 1971).
[17] Frank Jackson's much-discussed recent argument against physicalism can be properly assessed only in the light of such a general theory. See his 'Epiphenomenal Qualia', *Philosophical Quarterly*, 32 (1982), 127–36.

example, the physicalist who wishes to identify physical and phenomenal properties must individuate properties more coarsely than predicate-meanings or general concepts. What is required by such a physicalist is something like a sense/reference distinction for properties: my enjoying an experience of a certain character is to enjoy a certain mode of presentation of a physical property that may also be scientifically specified. There is, however, a problem with this which I do not see the physicalist surmounting. It is not that such a sense/reference distinction for properties is clearly untenable; it is rather that once such a distinction is deployed in this context, the sensuous features with which we started will re-emerge as characterizing the mode of presentation itself. A discussion of this topic will not be undertaken here: not only because it would involve agreeing on a general theory of universals, but also because the physicalist does not, perhaps, even need to *identify* physical and phenomenal properties, but can settle for a weaker relation. I propose, therefore, to approach the general issue of physicalism from a rather different angle: one which, as I hope will be seen, embodies the simplest intuitive reaction against the theory, and one which also will implicitly refute the foregoing suggestion that the physicalist can satisfactorily encompass phenomenal properties in his ontology by a device weaker than identity.

Since the aim is to refute all forms of physicalism, we need to consider the weakest monistic theory that counts as such. It is commonly held that a type–type psycho-physical identity theory is both stronger than is necessary for a robust physicalism, and also independently implausible—the chief objection to it being the possibly multiple kinds of physical realization of any given type of psychological state. There have, indeed, been attempts to deflect such criticism—typically by making the psychological states in question species-specific; but since this question is far from having been settled by the physicalists themselves, we should agree in looking for a weaker form of physicalism.[18] The common reaction to the perceived weakness of the type–type identity theory was the

---

[18] David Lewis attempts so to defend the theory in 'Mad Pain and Martian Pain' in N. Block, ed., *Readings in Philosophy of Psychology*, 1 (London, 1980); the manœuvre is criticized by Michael Tye in 'Functionalism and Type Physicalism', *Philosophical Studies*, 44 (1983), 161–74. (A different kind of attempt to defend the type–type theory is criticized by Jennifer Hornsby in 'On Functionalism, and on Jackson, Pargetter and Prior on Functionalism', *Philosophical Studies*, 46 (1984), 75–95.)

embracing of a merely token–token identity theory. According to this, each individual psychological state, process, or event is as a matter of fact identical with some physical state, process, or event; but there is no implication either way concerning the type of psychological or physical items in question.

However, despite the frequency of talk about the "token identity theory", such a theory, by itself, is wholly inappropriate for a physicalist: it is much too weak, and, moreover, of dubious intelligibility. For on such a view there is no restriction whatever on the possible physical realizations of psychological states: I may be racked with pain, and you may be in a type-identical physical state to me and yet be feeling nothing at all; and a stone may be feeling pins and needles. By lacking any sort of determination of the psychological by the physical, a mere token–token theory wholly fails to do justice to the central physicalist claim that the mental is nothing "over and above" the physical.

Conversely, a number of physicalists have found the token identity theory in another way too strong. Some have felt this because of a worry about the possibility in principle of determining *the* physical state of affairs with which a given psychological phenomenon is to be identified—even though it is admitted that the mental is wholly realized by the physical.[19] Others have felt that the relation of the physical to the mental should be construed in terms of constitution—and the problem in identifying a composite entity with its constituents is well known.[20]

The form of physicalism that solves both of these problems at one stroke is the thesis that the mental *supervenes* on the physical: for supervenience explicitly specifies a determination of the mental by the physical (and thus is not too weak), and also, since it applies to wholes and their parts, does not require the postulation of identities (and is thus not too strong). Supervenience is the notion that is designed to capture, while not going beyond, the idea that the psychological is "nothing over and above" the physical. However, since there are several varieties of supervenience, we

[19] e.g. Jennifer Hornsby in 'Which Physical Events are Mental Events?', *Proceedings of the Aristotelian Society*, 81 (1980–1), 73–92; John Haugeland in 'Weak Supervenience', *American Philosophical Quarterly*, 19 (1982), 93–103; and Bradford Petrie in 'Global Supervenience and Reduction', *Philosophy and Phenomenological Research*, 48 (1987), 119–30.

[20] Thus Richard Boyd in 'Materialism Without Reductionism: What Physicalism Does not Entail', in Block, ed., *Readings*, 101–2.

need to establish which precise supervenience relation is the weakest that is adequate to physicalism.[21] My claim will be that any theory of the supervenience of the mental on the physical will be either too weak to embody physicalism, or so strong that it is false.

### iii

The notion of supervenience has a long philosophical history: the Latin term was used by the medievals, and by Leibniz; in English we find Robert Boyle speaking of 'the supervening of a higher form' in *The Origin of Forms and Qualities*; but the term gained currency this century as a result of the ethical writings of R. M. Hare (though G. E. Moore, while himself not actually employing the term, had earlier in the century applied the notion to the sphere of ethics); and its current widespread application to the issue of physicalism seems to derive from the writings of Donald Davidson. As will soon emerge, the supervenience required by physicalism is in general considerably stronger than the notion that was popularized by Hare (though in one respect it may be weaker).

The general notion of supervenience may be introduced in the by now standard fashion as follows: one family of properties supervenes on another (the family of *base properties*) if and only if:

1. It is not possible for two objects to be indiscernible with respect to base properties while yet differing in any way with respect to the other, supervening, properties;[22]
2. Necessarily, an individual possesses a property superveniently only if it possesses some positive, intrinsic base property; but the converse does not hold.[23]

[21] There is by now a considerable body of literature on supervenience. *Southern Journal of Philosophy*, 23, suppl. (1984) is given over to the topic, and contains extensive bibliographies.

[22] 'Property' is to be taken as including what would intuitively be regarded as a change in properties.

[23] The qualification 'positive' is intended to rule out a wholly non-physical entity counting as instantiating physical properties in virtue of possessing negative properties. As John F. Post has pointed out, Jaegwon Kim's influential account of supervenience fails to avoid this problem of vacuous supervenience ('Comment on Teller', in *Southern Journal of Philosophy*, 23, suppl. (1984)). Relatedly, 'non-relational' is in there to exclude properties such as *being related to something that has mass* sufficing for an individual to count as physical.

Thus, to take an example from the sphere of aesthetics, where supervenience is generally admitted to hold: if it is given that, say, the *Virgin of the Rocks* is a beautiful object, then necessarily any object that is exactly like this picture physically is also (indeed, equally) beautiful. Moreover, each of these objects is beautiful only because it has some physical nature: you need something to *be* beautiful. Finally, such a picture could cease to be beautiful or change its degree of beauty only if it changes in some physical respect. (Perhaps a family of properties can supervene on different families of base properties. Thus someone might hold that beauty sometimes supervenes on the physical (as with paintings), and sometimes on the psychological but non-physical (as with mental images). All that is required here is that supervenient properties have at least one base family.)

A few remarks on this definition. First, John Haugeland[24] has criticized use of a clause such as (1) to formulate supervenience, for entailing token identities. However, this would be true only if the domain in question were that of physical and psychological states, events, and processes; whereas the individuals in question here are physical organisms. (The assumption that such individuals are the genuine subjects of experience is not, of course, wholly uncontroversial; I shall, however, make it for the purposes of the present discussion, since physicalists will have no reservations about it.) Second, the modality is required in clause (1) so as to rule out mere *de facto* correlations—for such would fail to embody the idea of determination that is central to the notion of supervenience. Thus we want our account of supervenience to allow us to say that if a perfect replica of a beautiful picture were to be produced, it would be as beautiful as the existing original. (William E. Seager has recently argued, in effect, that (1) unmodalized 'is not an altogether incredible form of supervenience', illustrating his claim by pointing out that although economic properties of communities supervene on material and human conditions, there are possible worlds containing interfering non-human intelligences where 'this supervenience will not hold at all'.[25] However, such a possibility does not at all show that the modality in (1) is unnecessary, but merely raises a question about the nature of the

[24] 'Weak Supervenience'.
[25] 'Weak Supervenience and Materialism', *Philosophy and Phenomenological Research*, 48 (1988), 700.

necessity that is in question. That there is a possible world where supervenient indiscernibility fails does not in any way cast doubt on the claim that there is a principled set of ("closer") worlds where such indiscernibility does hold. And there must be such a relevant set of worlds: for, as I have said, removing the modality in (1) altogether will leave us with mere matters of fact, and no notion of determination whatsoever. The nature of this modality will concern us shortly.) Third, clause (2) brings out the original meaning of 'supervene': any supervening property is possessed only by something that has a nature independently specifiable by the base or subvening properties. It brings out the fact that supervening properties are dependent, resultant properties.[26] Many formulations of supervenience are defective by not going beyond clause (1): indeed, Jaegwon Kim terms such a definition 'canonical'.[27] One reason for this is that it is commonly, and correctly, held that Moore developed a theory of the supervenience of ethical properties; and in a *locus classicus* Moore lays down a principle that is close to (1).[28] However, in that passage Moore is concerned to define merely a notion of *intrinsicness*—one that applies equally, as he says, to the (for him) non-supervening property of being yellow. Moore did indeed hold that goodness was a supervenient property—but only because such a property is *both* intrinsic *and* non-natural. He says of the latter:

I should never have thought of suggesting that goodness was "non-natural," unless I had supposed that it was "derivative" in the sense that, whenever a thing is good (in the sense in question) its goodness (in Mr. Broad's words) "depends on the presence of certain non-ethical characteristics".[29]

[26] The first occurrence of the word in Hare's *The Language of Morals* (Oxford, 1952) is as follows: 'It is a feature sometimes described by saying that "good" and other such words are the names of "supervenient" or "consequential" properties' (p. 80). Similarly, Donald Davidson introduces the term into the debate over physicalism as follows: '. . . mental characteristics are in some sense dependent, or supervenient, on physical characteristics': 'Mental Events' in *Essays on Actions and Events* (Oxford, 1980), 214. However, he then goes on to spell out such supervenience in a way that fails to embody (2).
[27] '"Strong" and "Global" Supervenience Revisited', *Philosophy and Phenomenological Research*, 48 (1987), 316. (This formulation is different from the one criticized by Post ('Comment on Teller')—though it too, by neither including nor entailing (2), allows vacuous cases of supervenience.)
[28] *Philosophical Studies* (London, 1922), 261.
[29] *The Philosophy of G. E. Moore*, ed. P. A. Schilpp (Evanston, Ill., 1942), 588.

Without this component of consequentiality, not only would we not exclude unwelcome vacuous cases of supervenience (equivalent mathematical equations or logical systems would supervene on chemistry); but also, and more importantly, supervenience would then have no ontological import, since it would imply no ontological priority: we would, for example, have to take a type–type identity as involving mutual supervenience.

The above definition of supervenience is, however, too weak to embody physicalism (or, indeed, any interesting example of supervenience). This is because all that is so far ruled out are $n$-tuples of objects that are indiscernible with respect to base properties, but superveniently diverse. It is compatible with such a ruling that you and I should actually be in the same physical state, and be thereby in pain, but that if things had differed only in the world containing one more penguin, we would both have been wholly free of pain—even though physically we remained exactly the same. Moreover, in restricting its scope to coexistent $n$-tuples, it warrants no inference at all to the supervenient properties of entities that have no exact replica; whereas physicalism would licence the claim that if I were in the above physical state, I would, *ceteris paribus*, be in pain even if neither you, nor any other replica of me, ever existed. In other words, we have so far failed to embody the idea that *which* supervenient properties an individual possesses is in some way determined by its base properties. It is for this reason that the notion of supervenience spelt out so far is now termed *weak supervenience*. One way to achieve a needed strengthening is to state that no possible world identical to a given one at the base level differs at the supervenient level. This account of supervenience, now known as *global supervenience*, is, however, still too weak: for although such a formulation is not restricted to co-existent $n$-tuples of objects, since it fails to put any restrictions on the psychological properties that are instantiated in worlds that are not physically identical, it is compatible with there being a situation differing physically from the actual one only in the existence of an extra penguin, but where the psychological facts are as different as you like from the actual ones.[30] We need,

---

[30] Indeed, global supervenience even fails to entail mere weak supervenience: since the only restrictions it imposes are on physically identical worlds, I may be as different psychologically as you please from someone in my world who is physically type-identical to me.

somehow, to narrow down to the *relevant* base properties that determine the supervenient ones. The only way to achieve this is to embrace what is called *strong supervenience*: we reformulate (1) so that what is ruled out is any *possible* pair of objects being indiscernible at the base level while differing at the supervenient level.

Unfortunately, such a specification of the *general* notion of supervenience either is too strong, or reduces to global super-venience. It is too strong if the base properties are intrinsic properties of the individuals in question, since many admittedly supervening properties of a given object depend upon that object being situated in a wider context. Thus, for example, *being a fulcrum* would commonly be held to supervene upon physical properties; but it is not true that anything intrinsically type-identical at the physical level to a given fulcrum would necessarily be a fulcrum: for to be such depends on its relations to other physical objects. Again, no doubt *being a politician* supervenes upon the physical and the psychological; but it is not true that any possible person physically and psychologically type-identical to, say, Margaret Thatcher, is a politician: in some possible contexts such a person would be merely a raving lunatic. On the other hand, if we unrestrictedly allow relations into our family of base properties, we shall revert to mere global supervenience. There is thus a problem, for each claim of supervenience of one family of properties on another, of specifying the relevant scope of the subvening properties. Fortu-nately, however, this is not a problem for the physicalist with respect to *qualia*. This is because *qualia* are *intrinsic, qualitative* characteristics that do not at all depend on physical facts external to the subject in question. We can (and must) therefore settle for strong supervenience as an adequate expression of physicalism.[31]

We now need to face the important question of the nature of the necessity involved in strong supervenience. For it is often said that although conceptual necessity is perhaps appropriate for the supervenience of aesthetic and moral properties, nothing stronger

---

[31] Harold Noonan has pointed out that strong, but not weak, supervenience will fail for another class of properties that are not exactly either relational or non-qualitative. The properties in question are those to which Robert Nozick's *best instantiated relation* theory applies: H. Noonan, 'Supervenience', *Philosophical Quarterly*, 37 (1987), 78–85. It is obvious, however, that Nozick's theory does not apply to *qualia*. *Qualia* are, as we might say, *irrelative*.

than nomological necessity is needed for physicalism. This is incorrect, because an epiphenomenalist, a neo-Cartesian, and a neo-Humean could admit that it is nomologically (i.e. psycho-physically) impossible for mental states to differ independently of subjects' brains. The idea of mere causal (or, more generally, nomological) determination does not do justice to the idea of the psychological being nothing over and above the physical. However, the considerations adduced in favour of the suitability for physicalism of a modality weaker than metaphysical necessity do require a minor qualification to the account of supervenience employed thus far.

One recent writer has defended the appropriateness of the weaker modality for physicalists as follows:

interpreting the modality as logical or "metaphysical" necessity seems too strong. Most people would agree that the mental supervenes upon the physical, but there is not any *contradiction* in the idea of a world which is physically exactly like our world but differs from it in what mental properties it exemplifies. Dualism is not incoherent . . . [32]

This remark forms part of a discussion of global supervenience; so let us momentarily focus on that issue. Let us agree, for the sake of argument, that physicalists can coherently allow the possibility of dualism being true. So there is a possible world that contains immaterial souls at best causally related to physical bodies; a world, moreover, which may differ not at all from our own physically. However, what is not compatible with physicalism is the suggestion that such a world should not at least contain counterparts of every actual psychological item. A world physically type-identical with ours could, compatibly with physicalism being actually true, differ psychologically from this world only by comprising a *surplus* of psychological fact. This is because physicalism holds that experience is *nothing over and above* the totality of physical fact. Reproduce that physical totality and necessarily you reproduce such experiences—since there is no psychological extra that could possibly get omitted. It is thus a mistake to suppose that the contingency claimed for the truth of physicalism requires a modality weaker than metaphysical necessity. What such contingency requires, rather, is that supervenience be construed not as the impossibility of worlds being at

[32] Petrie, 'Global Supervenience', 120.

all discernible with respect to the psychological if they are not so physically, but the (absolute) impossibility of any world physically type-identical to ours failing at least to reproduce this world psychologically.

The same point carries over to the strong form of supervenience that I have claimed to be demanded by physicalism. It is metaphysically impossible for there to be a body type-identical to mine that does not at least enjoy just the kind of psychological life that I actually do, since, once again, according to physicalism, my psychological attributes are nothing over and above my physical attributes: they could not possibly get omitted in an exact physical replication of me. The only way in which an exact physical replica of me could differ from me psychologically is, if this makes sense, by enjoying extra non-physical experiences. As the case of composition shows, the nothing-over-and-above relation is certainly weaker than identity: if in some possible world you assemble just the atoms that now make up my body in just the way that they are now assembled, you will not necessarily have reproduced exactly me, let alone the numerically identical experiences that I am now having. Yet when we restrict attention to intrinsic, non-formal, irrelative properties, the nothing-over-and-above relation carries across metaphysically possible worlds as rigidly as identity. Here we have an absolutely necessary coexistence in every world where the physical base is instantiated—or, rather, even more than that, since, according to physicalism, there are not here two independent items to *co*exist: the psychological is nothing over and above the physical. Spooks, Cartesian souls, and ectoplasm there may well be in such worlds; but as I have said, this affects the newly formulated issue of supervenience not a jot. Nomological necessity is too weak for physicalist supervenience, since physicalism is not about mere causal determination. We may perhaps dub this relation which interprets strong supervenience in terms of metaphysical or "broadly logical" necessity *metaphysical supervenience*.

There is, finally, an issue concerning the nature and scope of the modality in (2). By the very meaning of the term, a property can supervene only given certain base properties possessed by the individual in question; so the modality read as taking wide scope truly expresses a conceptual necessity. However, there is a real question as to whether properties that are actually supervenient are necessarily or essentially so. In the ethical and aesthetic realms they certainly seem to be: nothing (save, perhaps, God) could *only* be good or beautiful: things are good or beautiful in virtue of being or behaving a certain way. However, a physicalist who, as above, wishes to countenance the metaphysical possibility of Cartesian souls, must allow it to be a contingent matter whether a given property is supervenient or not: in this world phenomenal redness supervenes on some neurological state, in a Cartesian world it does not supervene on anything; in one world the property is consequential or resultant, in the other basic and underived. It is in this respect that the supervenience required by physicalism may be weaker than that suitable to express the nature of ethical or aesthetic properties. However, it must be said that the idea that the ontological status of an identical intrinsic, qualitative, irrelative property should vary from world to world is of dubious coherence. (In fact it strikes me as being absurd.) If this really is so, then physicalists should, as still only a minority do, present their claims as necessary truths.

We should be quite clear about the position we have now reached. Even if we leave aside the last point about the non-contingency of the physicalist's theory, we now see that it is an extremely strong claim indeed. For physicalism is committed to the view that an individual's possessing certain physical properties *entails* the possession of certain definite psychological properties. Supervenience is, as it were, simply one-half of the type–type Identity Theory. This is certainly a much stronger notion than that intended by Hare[33] (though not stronger than Moore's notion[34]). It is also, it is clear, a much stronger claim than many self-styled physicalists have recognized or desired. They ought, therefore, to think again.

---

[33] As he has recently made clear: 'Supervenience', *Proceedings of the Aristotelian Society*, suppl. vol. 58 (1984), 1–16. (However, Hare's objection to employing a notion of necessity in analysing ethical supervenience is that we might have commended different kinds of things; hence Hare's opposition to strong supervenience is grounded on his rejection of ethical realism, and is thus not pertinent to the present discussion.)

[34] In *The Philosophy of G. E. Moore*, ed. Schillp, Moore says, 'if a thing is good (in my sense), then that it is so *follows* from the fact that it possesses certain natural intrinsic properties . . .' (p. 588). He later (p. 607) makes clear that by 'follows' he means 'logically follows'.

iv

So far I have attempted to show how strong a theory physicalism is—something that by itself will be sufficient to refute it in the eyes of many. However, there will not be wanting those to defend even such extreme claims. And one knows by now how their defence will go. What grounds, they will ask, could we have for denying entailments from physical to psychological types? Surely only that we can imagine an instance of relevant physical properties in the absence of anything psychological; but we now know that imaginability is not an infallible indicator of real possibility. However, if we sever our beliefs in possibility entirely from conceivability, we shall simply land ourselves with an extreme Megareanism, where the possible and the necessary collapse into the actual. Indeed, many physicalists admit that the onus of proof is on them to explain away the apparent contingency of psychophysical co-presences; and none of the proffered explanations strikes me as having any plausibility whatever. (Note that what is arguably the most plausible of such explanations—that we cannot guarantee that we are conceiving of numerically the same individuals when we suppose a token-identity claim to be false—is inapplicable here.) However, as Descartes so clearly saw, we do need to make sure exactly what the natures are of the items that we seem to be able to conceive apart, so as to make sure that there is no possible covert necessary connection between the items in question. In particular, in the present context, we need to be clear about what it is for something to be physical. Moreover, recall that metaphysical supervenience has been brought into the discussion simply in order to try to express the central tenet of physicalism that the psychological is *nothing over and above* the physical. Now there will be those for whom even such a strong supervenience relation will be too weak to embody this principle of the ontological exhaustiveness of the physical. I have in mind those who hold that causal determination involves the highest degree of necessity. If we took such a view, even certain forms of epiphenomenalism would require that the psychological metaphysically supervene on the physical. It should be noted, therefore, that the by now standard explication of physicalism in terms of supervenience will be acceptable only to one who does not hold an extreme Rationalist theory of causality. The essential issue is thus not supervenience itself, but the principle of ontological exhaustiveness, which, for some, even metaphysical supervenience would but partly capture. With this in mind, let us turn to consider what it means to speak of something as being purely physical, since my contention is that when this is made clear, it will emerge that the claim that experience is nothing over and above the physical is simply preposterous.

It is in fact astonishing how little is said by physicalists themselves on the presumably crucial question of what it is to be physical.[35] Frequently the attempt to delineate the physical is confined to identifying it with what the physical sciences deal with—where these are specified by enumeration. But it is clearly neither necessary nor sufficient for an item to be purely physical that it be describable in the vocabulary of *current* physical science; and who knows how future, or ideally completed, science will pan out?[36] In any case, our conception of such a perfect science, in so far as we have one, is just one of a systematic body of theory that gets everything physical right—which already assumes the notion of the physical. Space-occupancy won't serve as an adequate, non-controversial criterion, since, although perhaps the majority of dualists have regarded mental items as not being located in space at all, there have not been wanting dualists who have affirmed just that.[37] It is true that no dualist (or idealist), so far as I am aware, has ever held that mental entities are extended. However, extension will not serve as a sufficient index of physicality: for on the one hand, we should not forget Boscovich's point-centres of force; and on the other, a non-physicalist might grant a non-extended mental entity an extended *sphere of influence*. Neither will perceptibility serve, since we do not and could not perceive quarks or photons; nor will a weaker notion of being manifestable, perhaps

[35] Indeed, the problem of specifying the nature of physicality has led Hugh Mellor to conclude that physicalism cannot even be precisely stated: 'Materialism and Phenomenal Qualities', pt. 2, *Proceedings of the Aristotelian Society*, suppl. vol. 47 (1973), 107–19.

[36] Recall Wilfrid Sellars's contention that any adequate physical science must incorporate items that correspond to the qualities of perceptual sensations.

[37] Thus John Yolton (*Thinking Matter*) cites John and Samuel Clarke from the early 18th cent.; and the position does not lack its defenders today: see D. H. Mellor and T. Crane, 'There is No Question of Physicalism', *Mind*, 99 (1990), 185–206.

indirectly, to the senses, since anger, for example, is at least that. (Of course a physicalist will insist that anger is physical; however the point is that we need a non-question-begging criterion of physicality before we are in a position to assess, or even understand, the physicalist's contentions.)

In fact, the physical can only be defined negatively: as that which in a way contrasts with the mental and conscious realm. But obviously the contrastive definition cannot simply be that the purely physical is that which is wholly non-mental: for this clearly rules out physicalism *ab initio*. Rather, we need to proceed in two stages.[38] First, let us define a *merely physical* individual as any (non-abstract) individual that lacks consciousness, or sentience. A merely physical property is any property that could be possessed by a merely physical individual.[39] A merely physical state of affairs is any that consists in the instantiation of a merely physical property. A *purely physical* state of affairs may now be defined as one which either is merely physical or else is just a complex of merely physical states of affairs. As before, a purely physical property can be defined as any property the instancing of which would be a purely physical state of affairs. A purely physical individual is one which possesses only purely physical properties. This captures the physicalist claim that the psychological is nothing "over and above" the physical: the psychological is nothing but a certain complexity of the physical. The psychological is purely physical because it is nothing but a complexion of items which taken individually are clearly physical because "merely" so. (This definition may seem to beg the question against panpsychism: the view that there are physical things, but no merely physical things. In fact the question is not begged, unless panpsychism is held to be metaphysically necessary—since a merely physical property is here defined as one that *could* be possessed by an insentient individual. I must confess, however, not to be able to give a definition of physicality that would be acceptable to such a radical panpsychist except by a possibly problematic appeal to a *per impossibile* clause.

---

[38] The following definition diverges from, but is similar to, one given by J. Cornman, *Materialism and Sensations*, 12.

[39] While, of course, remaining merely physical—i.e. the modality takes wide scope. I here, once again, gloss over as irrelevant the distinction between specifically physical properties and formal and functional ones.

The pertinent point here, however, is that the present account must be accepted by any physicalist.)

The above brings out the way in which the psychological truly *supervenes* on the physical—implying, as this notion essentially does, the idea of the determination of the former by the latter. For on the present account, the psychological, being purely, but not merely, physical, arises only when and because physical elements, otherwise bereft of any psychologicality, come together in a certain way. Without this idea of a set of base properties which, taken individually, have no subvening role whatever, the crucial idea of determination is lost.[40]

With this account of physicality in hand, I believe we are in a position fully to appreciate the enormous implausibility that almost everyone at least initially finds in physicalism. The intuitive reaction to such a theory is surely this: if you start with a bunch of non-conscious items, and then simply put them together into some spatio-temporal and causal configuration, however complex, then, on the physical level, that is all you have: a load of non-conscious things buzzing around. A complex of non-conscious elements can, as such, at most constitute a complex non-conscious individual. The sensory qualities of experience—*qualia*—don't get a look in at this level of reality. Perhaps it is true that when an appropriately complex physical state of affairs arises, then some conscious parousia takes place; but that is a different issue not compatible with physicalistic monism, according to which the only levels of (non-abstract) reality are those of the complexity of configurations of insentient elements. Sentience, to quote Ralph Cudworth again, 'could never possibly result from mere passive bulk, or dead and senseless matter, however modified and compounded; because nothing can come effectively from nothing'.[41] Thus, surely, is expressed the fundamental reflective resistance to physicalism. And, I believe, it is sound.

The only possible response to the above consideration is to point out that there are, after all, properties which are possessed

---

[40] Indeed, any theory embodying supervenience that is worth its salt should provide some informative general account of *how* the supervenient properties are determined—as in ethics we hear talk of 'good-making characteristics'. Physicalists presumably view this as being the job of neurophysiology.

[41] Cudworth, *True Intellectual System*, 849. The essential point, to repeat, is not tied to the identification of physicality with 'passive bulk'.

by complex wholes that are not to be found in the constituent elements. There are two types of case to consider. First, it is common for chemical compounds to possess qualities quite dissimilar to those of their constituent elements, so that there is no predicting, simply on the basis of the known properties of the elements, the properties of the compound. Such laws of generation that exceed the principle of the Composition of Causes, J. S. Mill termed *heteropathic laws*.[42] However, in many such cases the properties of the compounds are at least of a type that is also represented at the level of the constituents. Thus, to take one of Mill's own examples, 'the taste of sugar of lead is not the sum of the tastes of its component elements, acetic acid and lead or its oxide'; however, all three possess some taste—it is just that the taste of the compound is surprisingly and unpredictably different from those of the constituents, not a mere sum of them. What we need to sustain physicalism is the possession by a complex of a type of property that is not to be found at all at the level of its constituents. This brings us to the second type of case: that of *emergent properties*.[43] These are properties that are genuinely *novel*, in that they are manifested by a complex whose constituents, taken individually, wholly, and necessarily, fail to exhibit properties of that type. (It is for this reason that the notion of emergence characteristically goes together with a doctrine about the different *levels* of reality.) There certainly are such properties. Thus, for example, water is liquid, and (chemically pure) water is nothing over and above $H_2O$ molecules; but no such molecule is itself liquid. Similarly, being viscous, crystalline, or jelly-like are properties that only complexes of molecules can possess. To take a rather different kind of example, heat and temperature are notions that have direct applicability only in relation to a constellation of atoms: the kinetic energy of an isolated atom is not properly spoken of in such terms. Again, a living thing such as a plant is, if we take Drieschian vitalism to be false, nothing but a complex system of molecules; and yet a plant possesses life—something not to be found at the level of the constituent 'dead and senseless matter'.

---

[42] *A System of Logic*, 8th edn. (London, 1872), 3. 6.
[43] This term was popularized by C. Lloyd Morgan in *Emergent Evolution* (London, 1923), though he was consciously employing G. H. Lewes's distinction between resultant and emergent properties: *Problems of Life and Mind*, 2 (London, 1874), 412.

So may not consciousness and its distinctive qualities similarly be found only at the level of complexly organized biochemical structures? R. W. Sperry thinks so:

First, conscious awareness, in the present view, is interpreted to be a dynamic emergent property of cerebral excitation . . . Compared to the elemental physiological and molecular properties, the conscious properties of the brain process are more molar and holistic in character. They encompass and transcend the details of nerve impulse traffic in the cerebral networks in the same way that the properties of the organism transcend the properties of its cells, or the properties of the molecule transcend the properties of its atomic components, and so on.[44]

However, *qualia* are *a priori* demonstrably not emergent in this sense. The reason for this is that for any property that is emergent with respect to specified types of lower-level elements, there must be *a priori* available a sufficient specification of that property which either represents it as being but a certain organization of elements, or is *topic neutral*, thereby allowing it to be no more than a complexion of some suitable, independently specifiable, lower-level elements: for in no other way is it intelligible how the property in question could be non-causally, non-miraculously emergent, nothing over and above a configuration of lower-level elements. So, for example, liquidity is known *a priori* to be restricted to amounts of stuff where portions of the whole move in a certain way in relation to one another in specified types of circumstance. Such movement makes perfect sense at the level of the constituents: it is just that, given the molecular nature of matter, for liquidity we need a certain number of elements potentially mobile in relation to each other. Concepts of other emergent properties are not thus explicitly of configuration and organization. So, for example, heat is a matter of the movements of a body's constituent elements, though that this is so was an empirical discovery, and presumably had to be. However, our concept of heat (as opposed to sensations of heat) is just of that physical state, whatever it intrinsically may turn out to be, that is responsible for those phenomena that fix the reference of our term 'heat'. There is, in our concept of it, nothing *distinctive* about heat over and above its characteristic manifestations. Our concept of heat is thus topic-neutral, in that it leaves

[44] 'A Modified Concept of Consciousness', *Psychological Review* 76 (1969), 533.

open what precise physical nature lies behind its manifestations. Similarly with life; despite generations of resistance to the idea of a purely physical account of living organisms, it is surely clear *a priori* that to be alive is just to function in certain characteristic ways—thus leaving it open whether or not these ways are realizable by purely physical systems. Vitalism and other such oppositions to purely physical accounts of life were fuelled, rather, by the thought that, for one reason or another, the merely physical could not be so complexly organized as to manifest the intricate functions of living things. This claim is certainly not *a priori* evident, and seems to have turned out actually to be false.

When we turn to *qualia*, the situation is, of course, radically different, since for them above all is a topic-neutral specification wholly inadequate. A pain may be, and of necessity, a certain functional state; but it also feels a certain way, has its distinctive character, which only a bowdlerization of the world can omit from consideration. And, of course, nor is our appreciation of the character of a certain sensation *a priori* that of a certain configuration of lower-level elements—as was the case with liquidity. What we would require here is a kind of *radical emergence*: the instantiating by a complex, but by none of its constituents, of a type of quality with its own distinctive, homogeneous, qualitative character: one not exhaustively specifiable, in abstract or topic-neutral terms, simply as its being a matter of that complex having its elements configured and functioning in a certain way. But this is impossible. The notion of a radical emergent in the physical world makes no sense.[45] When we reflect on the notion of emergence, as spelled out, for example, by Sperry, we see that it is impossible that our concepts of the "holistic" properties in question should be other than topic-neutral and intrinsically characterless. Since *qualia* are pre-eminently not susceptible to such treatment, they cannot be emergent properties. It may well be that the distinctive psychological qualities "emerge" from the physical realm

---

[45] I have argued elsewhere that all of our knowledge of the physical world lacks qualitative character: necessarily, all adequate representations of the physical world are ultimately topic-neutral through and through; qualitative characteristics are to be found only within experience: 'Of Primary and Secondary Qualities', *Philosophical Review*, 99 (1990), 221–54. This is, indeed, the general reason why reductions, theoretical identifications, and nothing-over-and-above relations are to be found in the physical realm: by the same token, all such are necessarily precluded from applying to the sphere of consciousness.

in the non-technical sense that they are caused to appear by suitable physical processes. But that is another issue: for that is not physicalism.

The psychological does not therefore supervene on the physical in the strong sense required by even the weakest form of physicalism—in a sense that embodies the idea of the psychological being nothing over and above the physical. The physicalist's principle of exhaustion would be true only if *qualia* were emergent properties; but nothing with the distinctive intrinsic qualities of *qualia* can be thus emergent, for such emergence requires topic-neutrality. But any such claim of topic-neutrality for *qualia* would be bowdleristic. Physicalism needs to be reductivist in the sense I have given to this term. Physicalism is therefore false.

# 11

# Difficulties with Physicalism, and a Programme for Dualists[1]

*Peter Forrest*

Physicalism is not a precise and articulate theory so much as a programme for metaphysical speculation. It has at its core the *physicalist thesis*, which states that the world, including human beings, can be completely described in physical terms. In addition, the physicalist programme relies only on scientific and causal ways of understanding the world. So it concerns both description and understanding.

There are well-known difficulties with physicalism, which are ultimately based on our experience of ourselves. But because it is a metaphysical programme, and not just an isolated thesis, these difficulties are not, and ought not to be, persuasive until we have a satisfactory rival programme of metaphysical speculation. Now, there are equally well-known difficulties with most versions of dualism. And physicalists complain that these force dualists into a series of *ad hoc* responses. If so, then there is a stalemate. On the one hand, physicalism is charged with empirical inadequacy, because it ignores much of our experience. On the other hand, dualism is charged with theoretical incompetence, because of too frequent a resort to the *ad hoc*. As a result of this stalemate we would be forced to choose between the scientific and manifest images. The purpose of this paper is to argue that things are not so. We can reconcile the manifest and scientific, by defending a non-Cartesian dualist programme.

*One-category dualism*, as I call the programme which I am advocating, is based on three guiding principles. The first is respect

[1] I would like to thank the following for their helpful comments on various versions of this paper: Fred D'Agostino, Robert Elliott, Jim Franklin, David Londey, Jeff Malpas, Erle Robinson, all of the University of New England; David Armstrong; and the editor, Howard Robinson.

for introspection.[2] The second is respect for what I call the manifest understanding of persons, which I shall discuss below. These two principles entitle the programme to be called dualist in the broad sense. The third principle, the *one-category thesis*, states that an ontological theory which is adequate for the physical world already contains all the concepts and distinctions needed to describe the non-physical, without recourse to the mental as *sui generis*. The slogan of one-category dualism is that the mental and physical are different species of the one genus. Its positive heuristic is that we should be careful in describing the ontology of the physical world. For that is far richer than most physicalists think. And it is only because of this unacknowledged ontological richness that the mental need not be thought of as *sui generis*. Within the programme of one-category dualism I shall expound a further speculation, namely the *grand-property hypothesis*. It asserts that there are non-physical qualities[3] of the physical properties of brain-processes.

I shall begin by listing some of the well-known difficulties with physicalism and some of the equally well-known difficulties with dualism. Next I expound a central tenet of my proposed rival programme, namely, that we have what I call a manifest understanding of human beings. Because of the difficulties with dualism, we need a theoretical speculation such as the grand-property hypothesis to support our reliance on manifest understanding. In the last section, I show how this speculation avoids the various difficulties which I have listed.

The position which I shall defend, while contrary to the physicalist thesis, is compatible with the thesis that there are no non-physical contingencies. Everything which the physical description omits could well hold of necessity given the purely physical.[4] However, I think we tend to make rather over-confident claims about what is, or is not, necessary. And in this paper I shall not be relying on those claims. For that reason I merely note the compatibility.[5]

---

[2] I stipulate that introspection is not just inner perception (as in body-awareness or the sensation of pain) but includes a wide range of non-inferential beliefs about ourselves.

[3] By a quality I mean any non-relational property, and not merely one which can be experienced. But the experienceable ones are of greatest interest.

[4] As a special case of this, any non-physical being such as God would have to be metaphysically necessary.

[5] An argument to show that on the grand-property hypothesis the mental could

Space does not permit me to go into much detail, or to qualify my assertions or to provide caveats. What I am proposing is therefore very much a programme for dualists rather than a detailed theory.

i

I begin, then, by stating some of the well-known problems for physicalists. For a start there are the *qualia* of sensations. Physicalists may describe a sensation by giving a structural, neurophysiological description of the brain-states of the person having that sensation. Instead of, or in addition to, that structural description, they may characterize a kind of sensation functionally, that is, in causal terms, as likely to cause this, and as likely to be caused by that.[6] The missing-*qualia* objection is that even in combination, these two ways of describing sensations fail to acknowledge the occurrence of the *qualia*, that is, the introspectible character of sensations.[7]

I would like, however, to make a concession to the functionalists. The *qualia* are *appropriate* to the functional roles. For example, suppose one of the functional roles of pain is to cause us to avoid the situations which endanger us. Now a state with that functional role could simply fail to have any introspectible character. We could just find ourselves avoiding the situations which put us in that state, rather as compulsive hand-washers just find themselves washing their hands for no reason. However, in addition to the straightforwardly causal account, it can be pointed out that we have good *reason* to avoid the pain-producing situations.

be taken as supervenient on the physical is to be found in my 'Supervenience: The Grand-Property Hypothesis', *Australasian Journal of Philosophy*, 66 (1988), 1–12.

[6] The *this* and the *that* may be stimuli, behaviour, or other mental states. It is not enough to characterize a kind of mental state in terms of stimuli and behaviour.
[7] This objection has been presented by Block, Searle, and Jackson in different ways. See N. Block, 'Troubles with Functionalism', in *Perception and Cognition: Issues in the Foundations of Psychology* (Minnesota Studies in the Philosophy of Science, 9, ed. C. W. Savage; Minneapolis, 1978), 261–325, repr. in id., ed., *Readings in Philosophical Psychology*, 1 (London, 1980), 268–305; J. Searle, 'Analytic Philosophy and Mental Phenomena', in *Midwest Studies in Philosophy*, 5, ed. P. A. French, T. E. Uehling, and T. K. Wettstein (1980), 405–23; and F. Jackson, 'Epiphenomenal Qualia', *Philosophical Quarterly*, 32 (1982), 127–36. It is also discussed by David Smith, above.

What is that reason? It cannot be articulated further than to say that the *qualia*[8] of my pain sensations provide me with all the reason I need for deliberately avoiding pain. In this fashion, pain *qualia* are appropriate to the functional role of pain.

There are well-known difficulties with physicalism concerning representation and intentionality. I shall mention just one of these. Perceptual sensations *represent*, and it is not just that they can represent given a suitable interpretation—anything can represent anything given a suitable interpretation. Rather they carry their interpretation with them: *they are intrinsically meaningful*. For example, there is something about seeing a rock which makes the visual sensation invite interpretation as seeing an object of a certain shape and size.

Next on the agenda of difficulties is the distinction between reasons (for both beliefs and actions) and causes. I have no *a priori* objection to the speculation that reasons are a species of cause. But if they are causes, then they are causes of a special kind. For not every belief which causes another belief is a reason for that other belief. Phenomenologically, the difference between reasons and (other) causes is that my reasons are *my* reasons, whereas (other) causes are things that happen *to me*. Hence there is a connection between reasons and actions, where action is specified as behaviour of which I am the author, as opposed to that which merely happens to me. The difficulty, then, for physicalism is in giving an account of this difference.

An act is free, to some extent I believe, if it is an act done for reasons and not caused (in any other way). So free acts are causally undetermined unless reasons are causes. Physicalists can distinguish free acts from other behaviour in a phenomenologically adequate fashion only, I submit, if they can distinguish reasons from (other) causes.

The list of difficulties with physicalism could go on, but I shall conclude by considering the synchronic unity of a person. (Similar difficulties hold for diachronic unity.) Hume complained of the difficulty of finding the self as a further item of introspection. And, indeed, there is no direct evidence for a self separate from and

---

[8] It would be natural to talk of the *quality* of the pain sensation. But, because I mean by a quality a non-relational, non-structural property, this begs the question. I use the word *quale* for a property which is experienced without any experience of a relational or structural character to it.

alongside the various mental states which, intuitively, belong to that self. But I am aware of something of a rather different kind. It is the—admittedly fragile and imperfect—unity of the various mental states, with their various *qualia*. And the way in which these mental states are causally connected does not adequately account for this unity. For I can easily imagine the mental states of different people, with different beliefs and desires, being connected causally. Thus, given artificial nerves joining the brains of different people, your belief and my desire might result in a third person acting. Such an "action" would be unintelligible to any of the three people involved, precisely because they have different beliefs and desires. Yet the appropriate causal connections would be there. So the unity is not entirely due to causal connections. Therefore, in addition to the *qualia* of mental states, we are aware of a non-causal unity.

There are, then, difficulties with physicalism. But there are also difficulties with dualism.[9] First dualists as well as physicalists have problems with unity. We experience the fragile and imperfect unity of the mental life. Again, we experience ourselves not just as unified minds but as psychosomatic unities. Yet again, we may ask what makes two minds *two* minds—what differentiates them? Surely it is the fact that the totality of mental states for the two minds lacks the unity which each mind has. How can the dualist account for these unities? It is tempting to posit a spiritual substance to account for unity. But there is a dilemma here. Either saying that there is a substance is just to repeat that the mental states form a unity, and so is no explanation, or it amounts to positing a substrate (substance in the Lockean sense) which bears the mental states just as all the properties of a material object could be said to be born by a substrate. I have doubts as to whether positing a substrate is much of an explanation of the mere fact that the mental states form a unity of some sort or other, but it certainly goes no way towards explaining the precise kind of unity which we experience the mental as having.

The *problem of origins* occurs for any version of dualism in which suddenly, at some stage in the development of the embryo or foetus, a hitherto non-existent soul or self comes into existence.

---

[9] The first four chapters of D. M. Armstrong's *A Materialist Theory of Mind* (London, 1968) still contains, I believe, the best account of the difficulties which the dualist faces, and the problems which I mention are selected from those he lists.

If having a soul, or whatever the dualist proposes, is an all or nothing affair, then this gradual process of growth leads at one point to the sudden coming into being of a fully formed soul. Notice that this is not the problem of discovering when the mental comes into existence. Why should we be able to discover that? It is a problem of how something discontinuous could depend on something continuous.

Next there is the *problem of interaction*. Suppose, for example, that the intention to whistle causes certain brain processes. What would a psychosomatic interaction law relate? It would have to relate a type of brain process of incredible complexity to a type of mental state characterized in terms of some action. The sheer complexity of the *relata* prevents there being a correlating law which meets the standards of clarity and simplicity required of fundamental laws in scientific explanations. The problem, then, is of giving some account of the interaction which makes it comprehensible.

Finally, intentionality is not just a problem for the physicalist. The Brentano-inspired dualist orthodoxy is that some mental properties are not merely intentional, but irreducibly so. As such they are quite unlike familiar non-relational properties in that they cannot be described or understood without mention of the intentional object, which, if it exists, is typically a physical item. However, because the intentional object need not exist, intentional properties are also quite unlike familiar non-relational properties. According to the objector, the dualist requires some totally new basic category of entity, namely, that of irreducibly intentional properties. And it is a defect in a theory to resort to the *sui generis* in this way.

ii

I now expound the programme of one-category dualism, beginning with the feature which is most obviously dualist. I call it the *manifest understanding* of human beings.[10] First I shall expound it, then I shall consider its application to persons, distinguishing it

---

[10] Manifest understanding of the mental requires a realism about *qualia* which is incompatible with the physicalist thesis. I leave it to the reader to supply the details of the argument.

from folk psychology, and finally I shall reply to two objections to it.

Manifest understanding is that mode of understanding which is non-theoretical, and which requires neither generalization[11] nor articulation. When it occurs there is a single act of knowledge-cum-understanding rather than knowledge followed by understanding. It is not my present concern to discuss the limits of manifest understanding. Rather, I claim that there is much manifest understanding in our day to day way of thinking of persons as beings who perceive, who have memories, who have beliefs, whose behaviour is sometimes a case of action done for reasons, who have virtues and vices, and so on. Poetry, novels, drama, even ordinary conversation, educate us in this way of thinking. As a result, I submit, we have much manifest understanding both of ourselves, and of others.

The paradigm of manifest understanding is our understanding of pain. If someone reports being in pain and also complains about it, that is something we understand. The nature of pain is such that, to put it mildly, it is worthy of complaint. This, I claim, is something which we can understand, indeed can only understand, by experiencing pain. But, you say, could not someone actually seek pain for its own sake (and not for the sake of an associated sexual gratification)? At least, there are reports of those who say they are in pain but it does not bother them. So the connection between pain and our dislike of it (and hence the connection between pain and pain-behaviour) is contingent. I agree. None the less, I submit, we understand the unpleasantness of pain just by knowing it. By contrast, we find the lack of such unpleasantness in need of some further explanation, say in terms of lack of unity in the person.

That knowing certain mental states makes other mental states comprehensible is not itself a theory which helps us understand. Rather it is a claim about understanding. To defend this claim, I note that we sometimes have a 'sense' of having understood. A general scepticism about the reliability of our 'sense' of understanding would undercut even scientific understanding. For what other than this 'sense' of understanding can we rely on when

---

[11] That it is not to say that manifest understanding might not be of the general. All I mean is that no process of generalization is required to understand manifestly.

asked to justify the claim that scientific theories enable us to understand? Assuming that we reject such scepticism, we should allow that our 'sense' of having understood is an—admittedly fallible—guide to understanding.

The first three of the difficulties I listed for physicalism are cases in which, I claim, we do have a manifest understanding. The appropriateness of the *qualia* for behaviour, which I pretended was a concession to the functionalist, shows how we have a manifest understanding of that behaviour. Again, reasons are the sort of item which can make beliefs and actions immediately intelligible, without recourse to a scientific theory. (Other) causes are not. As regards representation, there is a similar situation. In some cases, we have only to know the nature of the representing state to understand how it represents.

That there is manifest understanding provides part of the answer to those who object that dualism does not result in a satisfactory alternative to the theoretical understanding of persons provided by physicalism. This partial answer is that manifest understanding is not theoretical. (It is only a partial answer, because it does not, by itself, solve all the problems which we have listed for physicalists and dualists.) In theoretical understanding, we generalize in order to understand. By contrast, manifest understanding requires no generalizations, although it permits them. Thus I can understand my avoidance of pain by considering the nature of my own pain, ignoring that of others.

That not all understanding requires generalization may be argued for by considering our knowledge of others as more than just things which behave in complicated ways. I come to know others only, I submit, by 'putting myself in their shoes'. By an exercise of imagination, I fit mental states to behaviour.[12] However, telepathy apart, I have only my own case to go on. How, then, do I come to realize that another person is in pain? An argument by induction from a single case is far too weak. What is required is something like an inference to the best explanation. More accurately, we rely on an interpretation of the behaviour of another based on an imaginative putting of oneself in the other's position. This interpretation is then justified by the understanding it provides. But if generalization were required in order to understand, then

---

[12] See Z. Vendler, *The Matter of Minds* (Oxford, 1984), ch. 1.

that justification would be circular. For we would require knowledge of other minds in order to infer the generalizations which would then enable us to understand. But surely we do know and understand other minds. Hence, I conclude, understanding need not involve generalization.

Another respect in which manifest understanding differs from theoretical understanding is that it is not hypothetical. The generalizations of scientific theories are, typically, hypotheses which, if they fit the facts, provide a way of understanding them. But it is characteristic of manifest understanding that we understand by knowing, without the need for hypothesis.

It is important to distinguish manifest understanding from folk psychology, which is the attempt to assimilate our pre-theoretic thought about persons to *scientific* understanding. But I say that much of this pre-theoretic thought just is manifest understanding, and so is to be contrasted with, rather than assimilated to, scientific understanding. Moreover, folk psychology is conservative in a way in which manifest understanding need not be. Just as new scientific theories can lead to the evolution of scientific understanding, likewise new insights can lead to the evolution of manifest understanding. Hence the objections to folk *psychology*[13] are not automatically reasons for rejecting manifest understanding.

I anticipate two objects to my reliance on manifest understanding. The first is that a way of understanding in which to know is to understand is too easy: the charlatans and obscurantists could go around saying that they too understand things merely by knowing them. I grant that we should exercise the greatest care in our appeal to manifest understanding. For it is an appeal which is easily abused. But, I insist, we should avoid the vice of the puritan, namely prohibiting good things just because they can be abused.

The second objection which I anticipate is based on the claim that there can only be one mode of understanding. I reject that claim. Even the understanding provided by the sciences combines an understanding by means of generalization with a further understanding of these generalizations, obtained by fitting them into

---

[13] See P. S. Churchland, *Neurophilosophy* (Cambridge, Mass., 1988), 299–310; P. M. Churchland, 'Eliminative Materialism and Propositional Attitudes', *Journal of Philosophy*, 78 (1981), 67–90 repr. in id., *A Neurocomputational Perspective* (Cambridge, Mass., 1989), 1–22; and S. Stich, *From Folk Psychology to Cognitive Science: The Case against Belief* (Cambridge, Mass., 1983).

suitably elegant or harmonious theories.[14] Yet again, the understanding of a result in mathematics derives, in typical cases, from the ability to prove it. So an independent case can be made for the plurality of modes of understanding.

### iii

I shall assume that we accept the thesis that we have considerable manifest understanding of ourselves and each other. If there were no difficulties with dualism there would, therefore, be no need for a dualist *theory*. For manifest understanding is not theoretical. However, we do need theory—or perhaps I should say speculation—in order to meet the difficulties with dualism. Without such a theory we could dismiss the 'sense' of manifest understanding as illusory because it commits us to dualism. To meet these difficulties I recommend the programme of one-category dualism. In accordance with this metaphysical programme, I shall begin by describing an ontology adequate for the physical world. I shall then point out just how little more is required to make it adequate for the mental as well.

Now there are different ways of discussing ontology. But for the sake of exposition, I shall adopt a traditional approach. Let us start, then, with an ontology of properties and relations. Ignoring a few details, an ontologist might claim that the physical world is made up of instantiated properties and relations. Is that adequate? I say not. Even an account of the purely physical needs to take into account, in some way or another, four further categories, namely quantity, quality, becoming, and unity.

First, there is quantity. Most physical properties admit of degrees of intensity. In some cases, this is unproblematic. Thus we might insist that having mass $N$ units is just a matter of being made up of $N$ disjoint parts each of mass one unit.[15] However, this account cannot be smoothly generalized to those quantities which take vector values. Forces, for example, are characterized by direction as well as strength. Our ontology must be enriched to take into

[14] See my 'Aesthetic Understanding', *Philosophy and Phenomenological Research*, 51, 3 (Sept. 1991), 525–40.

[15] See D. M. Armstrong, *Universals and Scientific Realism*, 2, *A Theory of Universals* (Cambridge, 1978), ch. 22.

account the fact that properties admit of varying magnitudes, where the degrees may be vector quantities. No doubt there are many metaphysical speculations which would be appropriate here. But one which is especially attractive is that we should include in our ontology various relations of comparative magnitude between physical properties. It is also a plausible speculation that such a relation between properties is internal, in the sense that it is essential to either property that it is related as it is to the other.[16] For example, consider two forces. My intuition is that the forces could not be the forces which they are, if they were not related as they are, both in the proportions of their strengths and in the angle between them. Thus, in many cases, the relations between physical properties are essential to their being the properties they are. Now, I concede that this is speculative. No doubt there are other accounts of magnitudes. However, it is a tenable speculation to extend our ontology of the physical to include some internal relations, without necessarily accepting the neo-Hegelian thesis that all relations are internal.

Next there is quality. Consider the following attempt to describe the physical world:

> There are various properties and relations some of which stand in relations of comparative magnitude to each other, and various combinations of them are instantiated.

Such a description leaves something out, namely the *qualia* of *physical* properties. Those properties of inanimate objects and those relations between them which we experience themselves have *qualia*, and our experience of them acquaints us with those *qualia*. By contrast, purely theoretical properties either lack *qualia* or have *qualia* with which we are not acquainted. My argument for these claims is an appeal to the phenomenology. There is a phenomenological difference between our understanding of those properties and relations which we experience, and those we know of only via a scientific theory. Thus the property of roundness and the relation of adjacency have *qualia* experienceable by humans, whereas simple electromagnetic properties do not. A natural speculation concerning such *qualia* is that they are non-relational properties of the physical properties and relations described by

---

[16] See J. Bigelow and R. Pargetter, 'A Theory of Structural Universals', *Australasian Journal of Philosophy*, 67 (1989), esp. 4–5.

the sciences. In that case they are purely physical, but not described by the physical sciences. This speculation will lead to the grand-property hypothesis when it is generalized to cover the *qualia* of mental states. Readers who are prepared to grant that even the properties of inanimate objects such as rocks have *qualia* not described by the physical sciences, but who give some other account of them, could be led to a rival speculation within the programme of one-category dualism. I ask them to treat the grand-property hypothesis as merely an illustration of how one-category dualism might be developed.

I have just appealed to the phenomenology of perception, but perhaps critics could likewise appeal to the phenomenology. Surely, they might say, the *qualia* are qualities of the things which have the physical properties, not qualities of the physical properties themselves.[17] The phenomenology of perception, I reply, supports the claim that qualities (and in some cases relational properties) are the direct objects of perception, but it tells us nothing at all about what they are properties of. Indeed, if we are prepared to countenance uninstantiated qualities, there is much to be said for the thesis that in a radical illusion what is perceived is an uninstantiated quality. Thus the phenomenology of perception is quite neutral of what the perceived qualities are qualities of, and so is compatible with my suggestion that they are grand-properties.

Then there is becoming. Much could be said of the metaphor—not myth—of passage. But I shall concentrate here on the anisotropy of time. There is a difference between *earlier than* and its converse *later than*, a difference which is not adequately described by pointing to the asymmetry of the relation, or by pointing to processes which just happen to proceed in one temporal direction but not the other. Following Grünbaum we may call this an intrinsic difference between *earlier than* and *later than*. Various attempts have been made to characterize this intrinsic difference.[18] Perhaps the commonest is to say that the overall direction of increasing entropy is from earlier to later. I ask readers to judge such attempts themselves. But, for what it is worth, I say that all

---

[17] I am indebted to David Armstrong for pointing out to me just how peculiar my proposal seems initially.

[18] A. Grünbaum, *Philosophical Problems of Space and Time* (Boston Studies in the Philosophy of Science, 12; Dordrecht, 1973).

such attempts rely on accidental accompaniments of the earlier/ later distinction, and are not intrinsic.[19] Thus it is not merely conceivable, but physically possible, for entropy to decrease. I submit that we need some further account of the anisotropy of time. As in the case of quantities and qualities, I present what I take to be a tenable speculation. It is that the difference between *earlier than* and *later than* is that at a later time, more is actualized than at an earlier time.[20] Some detail is required to make this speculation comprehensible. Each determinate way the physical world might be corresponds to a 'possible world'. And each of these 'worlds' is given by a physically complete spatio-temporal description. But, I say, what is actual at a given time $t$ is not determinate. So the actual at time $t$ is indeterminate between the members of the subset, $W_t$, of the set of all possible worlds, where $W_t$ is larger than a singleton.[21] If we reject backward causation, then, all the worlds in $W_t$ agree in their history up to $t$, but they do not agree in what happens after $t$. The 'passage of time' consists, I speculate, in the increasing determinacy of what is actual. That is, if time $t$ is later than time $s$, then the set of worlds $W_t$ is a proper subset of the set $W_s$.

Finally, there is unity. Consider a description based on the physical sciences, but which completely left out all considerations of unity. In particular consider the following three properties of an electron: *having mass $m_e$, having charge $c_e$*, and *having spin 1/2*. If we ignore unity, then we cannot distinguish (1) a single particle with a given path in space–time and with all three of those properties, from (2) three particles with the same path, the first having mass $m_e$, the second having charge $c_e$, and the third having spin 1/2. For the difference between (1) and (2) is that in (2) the three properties are merely instantiated at the same location, whereas in (1) they form a unity, which cannot, I submit, be adequately analysed in causal terms. To say that there is a substance (in the

[19] This is, of course, a far from original criticism. Grünbaum's defence against criticisms of this sort is to emphasize epistemological questions. I, however, am not concerned with how convinced we should be that the anisotropy of time is universal. Rather I experience the difference between past and future, and I seek an account of that difference which is adequate to my experience.

[20] See my 'Backwards Causation in Defence of Freewill', *Mind*, 94 (1985), 210–17, and my *Quantum Metaphysics* (Oxford, 1988), ch. 8.

[21] In the context of special and general relativity what is actual is relative not to a time but to a point in space–time.

Aristotelian/scholastic sense) amounts to no more than repeating that the properties do form a unity. An attempt at explanation is made by positing a substrate (substance in the Lockean sense) which bears all the properties. What other accounts are there? Perhaps for each individual there is a grand-property, that is, a property of properties, which is peculiar to that individual. Call such a property a grand-haecceity. Then it would serve both to unify the properties of the individual (by being a property of them all) and to individuate otherwise indiscernible objects. Or perhaps no further account provides any understanding and we should take unity as a basic category. In any case it suffices to say that some account has to be given of unity, if we are to have an ontology adequate to the physical world.

In a nutshell that is the Forrest theory of the physical world. It is a world of properties with *qualia*, internally related by comparative magnitude relations, forming unities, and in which the anisotropy of time is due to the anisotropy of increasing actuality. It is not important for my present purpose that this be the only tenable ontology for the physical world, merely that it is one which is not *ad hoc*, and is not significantly inferior to rivals.


iv


We now have all the ontological categories which we need in order to describe the mental. To illustrate this I shall go through the difficulties with physicalism and with dualism.

The *qualia* of sensations may be taken to be non-physical qualities of the physical properties of the brain-processes with which the sensation is correlated. I call this the grand-property hypothesis. We have already speculated that physical properties have qualities. All I am now doing is to posit more qualities than are required to describe the non-sentient. I am not introducing a new genus of items, merely a new species in a genus already required.

*Qualia* become a little more mysterious when we consider the appropriateness of the *qualia* for the functional role of the physical properties of which they are qualities. The problem here is not that of explaining why the *qualia* are appropriate given that there could be such appropriateness. There is a Darwinian/teleological explanation of *that*. Rather, the problem is that of understanding how there could be appropriateness. A partial solution to this problem is to rely on the manifest understanding of persons. Once you are aware of a given *quale*, then you know that it does provide a reason for acting in a way appropriate to the functional role. But this solution is only partial. For it raises a further ontological problem: what kind of relation is this *providing a reason for*?

The short answer is that *providing a reason for* is not exactly like any physical relation. But merely to give that answer would be an *ad hoc* appeal to the *sui generis*. To avoid the *ad hoc*, I recall the internal relations of comparative magnitude, which were relied on when providing an account of quantity. They were essential to their *relata*. Likewise, *providing a reason for* a certain action is essential to the quality of the mental state which provides a reason for the action. Thus *providing a reason for* is a further species of a genus already introduced in order to describe the physical— namely, relations essential for one or more of their *relata*.

The representative power of sensations is likewise partially understood manifestly, and partially by invoking the category of internal relations. Take the case of the sensation we have when we 'see' an after-image. To be more specific, consider the sensation which occurs when I 'see' an after-image obtained by looking at the setting sun. The sensation itself has the capacity to represent (intrinsically) something red and round. We understand this capacity to represent manifestly, that is, by experiencing it. But to what category does this capacity belong? We should avoid saying it belongs to a *sui generis* category of intentional properties. Instead I treat representation as a species of the genus of internal relations. Thus the quality[22] of the sensation is internally related to what it represents, namely, the quality of the property of being red and round. Furthermore, that there can be the capacity to represent something red and round without there being anything red and round there to be represented is not, *pace* Brentano, a feature peculiar to the mental. (What is peculiar to the mental is the capacity to represent *intrinsically*.) Rather it is a special case of a quite general feature of internal relations. For instance, the property of having mass 250 grams stands in a certain relation to

---

[22] If it is indeed a quality. We might analyse the experienceable character of the sensation relationally, namely, as the awareness of an image or sense-datum. For simplicity I ignore this possibility.

(and could be used to represent—though not intrinsically) the property of having mass 450 grams. And it would do so even if nothing ever had mass 450 grams. The possibility of a non-existent *relatum* is thus a characteristic of internality, not of the mental. And, for what it is worth, I handle it by appealing to uninstantiated properties.

The linked problems of reasons and of freedom require more than the combination of manifest understanding, on the one hand, and an appeal to qualities and internal relations, on the other. But first let us run through that combination. We understand what reasons are, and what freedom is, as a result of our experience of ourselves. I have already assigned *providing a reason for* to the category of a relation internal to various qualities which are its *relata*. But more needs to be said about that relation. Consider the case of pain and pain-behaviour. And suppose the pain-behaviour in question is indeed an action, not just a reflex. Then the pain and the action are related in that the quality of pain provides a reason for the action. In this case the relation of *providing a reason for* is internal to the quality of pain. As regards the associated problem of freedom, the explication of becoming as increasing actuality leaves room for categorical freedom of action, that is, for acts which are done for reasons and which are not determined causally. As I have said, this may conveniently be described using sets of possible determinate worlds. What is actual is indeterminate between these determinate worlds. The physical laws put constraints on the sets of worlds, but within those constraints we are free to ensure that what will be actual at a later time is indeterminate between the members of some smaller set of possible worlds. There is nothing *ad hoc* in this, for increasing actualization is already a feature of the physical world. All I have done is to exploit it.

Finally, there is the unity of a person. I have submitted that an adequate account of the physical world requires that there be unities which cannot be explained in purely causal terms. I rejected the hypothesis that the unity of a person is simply due to a substrate which bears the various properties, because positing a substrate does not account for the kind of unity we experience. Could we handle this difficulty by saying that the substrate has its own peculiar quality? No. For in that case the quality would be just a further property of the person and so an item to be unified rather than a kind of unity. Therefore, if we were otherwise committed to substrates as the best account of the unity of material objects, the failure of this account to generalize to the unity of the mental would be a serious difficulty for the dualist. However, the substrate account was merely one speculation concerning the unity of material objects. Let us compare it with the rival, higher-order haecceity account. Both speculations are subject to the same criticism, namely, that some new entity is posited in an *ad hoc* way just to account for unity. Either that criticism shows that our best policy is to reject both accounts and to take unity as a basic category, or we reject the criticism. In the former case, the special unity of the mental would then be a further species of the basic category of unity but not something *sui generis*. In the latter case, there is little to choose between the two speculations, so dualists are free to choose the one which fits in better with their dualism, namely, the higher-order haecceity account. As in the case of the substrate account, merely positing a higher-order haecceity fails to explain the kind of unity we experience the mental as having. But we may posit a special quality which the higher-order haecceity has without it becoming just another quality to be unified. Thus even if we decide not to treat unity as a basic category, dualists can treat the unity of the mental as a new species of a genus required to handle the unity of material objects.

I now turn to the difficulties for dualists. I have argued that an ontology adequate for the physical world enables us to account for the special unity of the mental, without being *ad hoc*. In addition, the unity of the whole person (non-physical and physical) is ensured by the grand-property hypothesis itself—the non-physical consists of properties of the physical. This handles the difficulties with unity.

On the grand-property hypothesis the *interaction problem* concerns the mysterious correlation between the physical properties of brain-processes and their non-physical qualities. While I do not pretend to have a complete understanding of this correlation, I propose two principles which greatly reduce the mystery. The first of these, the *principle of harmony*, states that none of the pieces of behaviour (including changes of mental state) which tend to happen as a result of the purely physical working of the brain should be incompatible with the acts (including mental acts) which we have reasons to perform. Since the non-physical qualities provide reasons for acts of various kinds, this principle constrains which physical properties of the brain have the non-physical properties in question. This constraint amounts to the requirement that the *qualia* of mental states be appropriate for the functional roles which they play.

The principle of harmony does not exclude Keith Campbell's 'imitation man' who completely lacks all *qualia*.[23] So it provides only a partial understanding of the interaction of the physical and the non-physical. But there is a further principle which leads to a fuller, although still incomplete understanding. It is that sufficiently similar physical properties have similar qualities. Call this the *continuity principle for qualia*. This principle excludes the case in which real people and imitation people are both actual.

Without the continuity principle, the problem of origins would evaporate. For we could say that various mental characteristics suddenly arise in the developing human some time after the physical conditions (i.e. brain development) are appropriate, but we know not when. So the fact that the problem of origins has intuitive appeal justifies my hypothesizing the continuity principle: I am not hypothesizing anything which is antecedently implausible.

Conversely, given the continuity principle there is an obvious argument to show that all *qualia* arise gradually, and hence that the problem of origins has not evaporated. For as the correlated brain-states change by small degrees so, by the continuity principle, should the associated *qualia*. In particular the coming into existence of some *quale* should be gradual. In order to reply to this argument, I first examine the phenomenology. I suggest that the introspectible quality of mental states neither seems to arise gradually nor seems to arise suddenly. The coming into existence of mental states is not introspectible in the way that the mental states themselves are. So we have as much reason to say that they occur gradually, but we are introspectively blind to their occurrence, as to say that they arise suddenly. Hence I could accept the conclusion that the mental arises suddenly. However, introspectible mental states such as having a pain in a toe are correlated not with instantaneous brain-states but with brain-processes. (Frequencies of spiking cannot be instantaneous.) As a consequence, the introspectible qualities do not have precise temporal locations. So

---

[23] See K. Campbell, *Body and Mind* (London, 1971).

we may deny that they come into existence by small degrees without asserting that they come into existence suddenly. This dissolves the problem of origins as usually stated. I leave it to the readers to decide whether various residual puzzles are genuine difficulties for those who reject physicalism.

## Conclusion

The well-known difficulties with physicalism become grounds for rejecting it, because there is, I have argued, a viable alternative metaphysical programme, namely one-category dualism, which avoids these difficulties, as well as those of Cartesian dualism. Unlike physicalism, one-category dualism is adequate to experience. Unlike Cartesian dualism, it is theoretically satisfactory. In short, the manifest and scientific images are reconciled.

# 12

# The Grain Problem[1]

## Michael Lockwood

> Think of what consciousness feels like, what it feels like at
> this moment. Does that *feel* like billions of tiny atoms wig-
> gling in place?
>
> (Carl Sagan[2])
>
> How can technicolour phenomenology arise from soggy grey
> matter?
>
> (Colin McGinn[3])

There is, today, no glimmer of a consensus amongst philosophers
about the mind–body problem. Nevertheless, an increasing number
of philosophers find themselves occupying a middle ground between
physicalist reductionism, on the one hand, and dualism on the
other. Physicalist reductionism I take to be the view that the physical
story about what is going on in the brain and the world with
which it interacts is in some sense the whole story. If there really
are such things as mental states and processes—which eliminative
materialists notoriously deny—then their existence must be logically implicit in facts statable in the language of physics. Space does
not permit a detailed rebuttal of reductionist physicalism; nor do
the arguments I have elsewhere presented[4] admit of brief sum-
mary. But the simple intuitive argument is that a being provided
with a description of you or me couched purely in the language
of physics—even if it possessed unlimited powers of ratiocination—
would have no way of deducing that our bodies were associated

---

[1] In writing this article, I have benefited greatly from an excellent critique of my
views—as set out in ch. 10 of my *Mind, Brain and the Quantum: The Compound
'I'* (Oxford, 1989)—which appears in J. A. Foster's *The Immaterial Self* (London,
1991), 119–30. My statement of the grain problem, in particular, owes much to
this discussion.

[2] *Contact: A Novel* (New York, 1985), 255.

[3] 'Can We Solve the Mind–Body Problem?' *Mind*, 98 (1989), 349.

[4] *Mind, Brain and the Quantum*, ch. 8.

with awareness at all, much less what specifically it was *like* to be you or me.[5] There is, of course, a lot more to be said on the matter; but attempts to disarm such intuitive arguments seem to me, in the end, uniformly unsuccessful. Indeed, for those not blinded by science, the falsity of reductionist physicalism will probably seem almost too obvious to require argument: Galen Strawson aptly describes it as 'moonshine'.[6]

Dualism, on the other hand, is unattractive to most philosophers because embracing such a doctrine seems more like giving up on the mind–body problem than providing a genuine solution to it. Dualism does little or nothing to satisfy our cravings for an integrated world view. It remains obscure, on the dualist theory, just how the material is supposed to dovetail with immaterial mind. For, on the face of it, there are no mind-shaped gaps in the material fabric; the material world offers no explanatory or descriptive slots into which immaterial minds could comfortably fit. (One pictures matter saying to Cartesian mind: 'This universe ain't big enough for both of us'!)

Anyway, I shall be assuming in this paper that, though reductionist physicalism is false, some form of materialism is nevertheless true. Conscious states and events are, on the view I favour, states of, or events within, the brain. But the very existence of consciousness shows that there is more to the matter of the brain (and hence presumably to matter in general) than is currently capable of being captured in the language of physics or physiology. How, then, is this 'more' to be conceived? Well, Bertrand Russell suggested, in the 1920s, that, in respect of the brain, awareness might be providing content, where science provides only form.[7] All that we really know of the physical world, on the basis either of sense perception or of physical theory, Russell argued, is that it possesses a certain *causal structure*. Any attribute of a physical system, whether it be shape, size, or electric charge, is really known to us only as whatever it is that occupies a certain logical niche within a causal-explanatory system. We have no way of knowing what the external world is like *in itself*; its intrinsic

    [5] See T. Nagel, 'What is it Like to be a Bat?', *Philosophical Review*, 83 (1974), 435–50; repr. in id., *Mortal Questions* (Cambridge, 1979), 165–80.
    [6] G. Strawson, 'Consciousness, Free Will, and the Unimportance of Determinism', *Inquiry*, 32 (1989), 3.
    [7] See esp. B. Russell, *The Analysis of Matter* (London, 1927).

character is systematically hidden from the gaze of ordinary observation or experiment. But now, the brain is itself a part of the physical world, and we are assuming that conscious states are brain states. We certainly seem to know, from introspective awareness, the intrinsic character of an itch or the sound of middle C, played on the piano, or a patch of phenomenal yellow. So if conscious states *are* brain states, do we not here have a corner of the physical world whose intrinsic nature precisely *is* made manifest to us, albeit in a very limited way? This was Russell's suggestion: that in consciousness, a fragment of physical reality is, so to speak, being apprehended from within.

This idea—which seems to me the only approach to the philosophical mind–body problem, currently on offer, that holds out the slightest promise—can be thought of as a neat inversion of a celebrated theory put forward some thirty years ago by J. J. C. Smart. Smart suggested that mental state terms were, as he put it, 'topic neutral'. According to Smart, when I say that I am experiencing a yellowish-orange patch in my visual field, I am saying something like this: 'There is something going on which is like what is going on when I have my eyes open, am awake, and there is an orange illuminated in good light in front of me, that is, when I really see an orange.'[8] This then leaves it open for the physiologist to discover what, in relevant respects, actually is going on under such conditions, physiologically speaking, and identify it with the occurrence of phenomenal yellow-orange. But of course this isn't at all what I am saying when I report that I am experiencing phenomenal yellow-orange; if it were, it would follow, absurdly, that there was nothing to prevent a congenitally blind person from having as rich and complete an understanding of such introspective reports as a sighted person. Russell's view turns this unworkable theory on its head: for him it is the *physical* descriptions, rather than the mental ones, which are topic neutral.

It is at this point that we encounter the *grain problem* (a difficulty attributed to Wilfrid Sellars[9]). For if the immediate objects of introspective awareness just are states of, or events within, the brain, seen as they are in themselves, why do they *appear to be* so

---

[8] J. J. C. Smart, 'Sensations and Brain Processes', *Philosophical Review*, 68 (1959), 141–56.

[9] W. Sellars, 'The Identity Approach to the Mind–Body Problem', *Review of Metaphysics*, 18 (1965), 430–51.

radically different from anything that a knowledge of the physiology of the brain would lead one to expect?

That rather vague intuitive thought may be resolved into three more specific difficulties, each of which can be regarded as an aspect of the grain problem, as I conceive it. First is the fact that the phenomenal objects of introspective awareness are far less finely structured than are any plausible physiological correlates. Consider, for example, a phenomenally flawless auditory experience, of a note, say, on a violin. Its physiological substrate, presumably, is a highly structured, not to say messy, concatenation of changes in electrical potential within billions of neurons in the auditory cortex, mediated by the migration of sodium and potassium ions across cell membranes, and of molecules of transmitter substances within the chemical soup at the synapses. How do all these microstructural discontinuities and inhomogeneities come to be *glossed over*, in such a way as to generate the elegant perfection of auditory phenomenology that we associate with the playing of a Yehudi Menuhin? How are we to make philosophical sense of such phenomenological *coarse-graining*?

The second problem is that the structure we do encounter at the phenomenal level seems not to match, even in coarse-grained fashion, that of the underlying physiology, as revealed by scientific investigation. The phenomenal contents of awareness don't appear to have the *right kind* of structure; what is ostensibly lacking, here, is even the most approximate isomorphism between states of awareness and the underlying physiological goings-on that, on my view, they are supposed to be mirroring. In particular, three-dimensional spatial arrangement, and changes therein, seem central to all physical structure. Where, then, are their phenomenological counterparts? Of course, there is the visual field, and auditory and somatic-sensory space. But these are local, modality-specific *representations*, merely, of regions of the external world. We search in vain for some global, overarching mode of phenomenological organization that could plausibly be equated with introspectively encountered spatial layout. It is all very well to insist that the scientist's characterization of the brain, as of the physical world in general, is ultimately topic neutral; so that the terms of the characterization are, in the final analysis, mere placeholders for unspecified intrinsic natures. The problem is that the phenomenal pegs, as John Foster neatly puts it, seem not to be the right shape to fit these holes in the topic-neutral characterization.[10]

Someone may see in these difficulties an argument for functionalism. The functionalist would regard the relation between a phenomenological description of the contents of consciousness and a physiological description of the corresponding brain-processes as analogous to that between a description of the workings of a computer in software terms, on the one hand, and in terms, say, of the electronic configuration of the underlying circuits, on the other. Thus, brain states, for the functionalist, impinge on awareness only *qua* possessors of certain high-level causal-functional roles. Precisely what, in physiological terms, are playing those roles, and how they do so, is, at the level of phenomenology, essentially irrelevant.

Functionalism, however, has its own problems—most notably its inability to explain why functional roles should be associated with any phenomenal qualities—*qualia*—at all. And in any case, it would seem, intuitively, perfectly possible for there to be a system functionally equivalent to a human mind, in which the corresponding functional roles were associated with different *qualia* from those associated with these roles in our own case.[11] Functionalism may have some plausibility in accounting for mental structure but, on the face of it, fails utterly to account for phenomenal *content*. Moreover, all arguments one could mount against reductionist physicalism apply *a fortiori* to functionalism; since if functionalism were true, reductionist physicalism clearly *could be* true also. If a physical system is, so to speak, running the right programs, then it follows, for the functionalist, that it has certain mental states; and this is something that a being with sufficient ratiocinative power could presumably read off from a description of the system couched in the language of physics. If, as I have been suggesting, reductionist physicalism is essentially a non-starter, then so too is functionalism—at least if put forward as a global theory of mind.

The third aspect of the grain problem that I wish to consider is raised by the profligate *qualitative diversity* of the phenomenal

[10] Foster, *The Immaterial Self*, 126.

[11] See N. Block, 'Troubles with Functionalism', in *Minnesota Studies in the Philosophy of Science*, 9, ed. C. W. Savage, Minneapolis, 1978), 261–325, and also my *Mind, Brain and the Quantum*, ch. 3.

realm, which seems flatly at odds with the comparative qualitative homogeneity of the physical ingredients out of which any corresponding brain state could realistically be composed. There are two levels at which this might be argued. Both visual and auditory information, according to the current wisdom, are encoded—albeit in different parts of the brain—by firing rates within certain batteries of neurons. But there is (as far as I am aware) nothing qualitatively distinctive about a neuron in the auditory cortex, or the corresponding action potential, to mark it out from a neuron, or the firing of a neuron, in the visual cortex. So how, on this basis, is one to account, say, for the fundamental phenomenological difference between a sound and a flash?

The other level at which the point could be argued is that of particle physics. The most promising currently available candidate for a so-called *theory of everything* (TOE) is something known as *superstring theory*.[12] According to this theory, everything is ultimately composed of incredibly minute loops—the 'strings'—with length and tension, but no thickness; everything that happens is ultimately a matter of the motion and interaction of these strings; elementary particles are strings in different vibratory states. These strings are held to inhabit a ten-dimensional space-time, in which six of the spatial dimensions are curled up in such a tight radius that they are effectively undetectable *as spatial dimensions*, though their presence manifests itself in the form of forces. The details of the theory scarcely matter, for our purposes. What does matter is that, once again, it seems incomprehensible that different combinations of collective or individual string states could generate the qualitative diversity that is manifest at the phenomenal level. It seems inconceivable in much the same way, and for much the same reasons, that it is inconceivable that an artist, however skilled, should conjure the simulacrum of a Turner sunset from a palette containing only black and white paints.

What is ostensibly lacking, both at the neuronal level and at the level of particle physics, is, most obviously, the requisite qualitative potential—just as black and white paints provide the potential for an infinite number of shades of grey, but not for a yellow or a red. But there is also (as John Foster has pointed out[13]) a subtler

---

[12] See M. B. Green, 'Superstrings', *Scientific American*, 255 (Sept. 1986), 44–56.
[13] Foster, *The Immaterial Self*, 127–8.

difficulty having to do with the possibility of securing, at the fundamental level, the required qualitative *flexibility*. One might, in speculative vein, attempt some wholesale enrichment of the physical microstructure—crediting the basic ingredients of the physicist's ontology with intrinsic attributes way beyond what are called for by their explanatory roles within physical theory, but which are specifically tailored to the demands of phenomenology. The trouble then, however, is that it seems scarcely deniable that, at some level, these fundamental ontological ingredients, whatever they are, must be broadly *interchangeable*. What, one may ask, is the use of attributing, say, embryonic colour to the ultimate physical components involved in the neuronal goings-on that are supposed to be constitutive of a phenomenal patch of red, if these self-same constituents are also to be capable of figuring in auditory or olfactory experiences which are wholly devoid of visual phenomenology? Little is gained if what one does in order to account for the *presence* of phenomenal qualities in one place has the effect of making a mystery of their ostensible *absence* elsewhere.

With regard to the first of these three difficulties, a concrete analogy may help to fix ideas. Consider a (monochrome) newspaper photograph. Seen at very close quarters, or through a magnifying glass, it stands revealed as a rectangular array of different-sized black dots on a white background. But casual inspection shows, rather, lines, edges, and patches of black, white, and varying shades of grey. Let the latter appearance correspond, in our analogy, to the phenomenal aspects of an experience, and the array of dots to the nitty-gritty of ion exchange and so forth, which is constitutive of the corresponding brain-process.

The very word 'introspection' invokes a supposed analogy with perception: the metaphor of the 'inner eye'. (Compare Kant's talk of an 'inner sense', complementary to the 'outer senses'.) Now if there really were a close parallel here, this first aspect of the grain problem would scarcely be troubling. Just as, with the photograph, the limited resolving power of the eyes ensures that, if we stand back sufficiently, we shall have the illusion of continuity, so we could envisage the mind, in introspection, as standing back from the underlying brain-processes—again, with consequent loss of resolution. Particulate and discontinuous physico-chemical activity will yield perceived continuity, just as the discrete patches of ink on paper give way to ostensibly continuous lines and patches of black, white, and grey. But of course, this picture is simply incoherent. For the mind is not supposed to exist *over and above* the relevant brain activity. And no literal sense can be attached to the notion of the conscious mind being distanced, in this fashion, *from itself*.

Coarse-graining within ordinary perception is ultimately to be explained via the concept of a *mental representation*. It is a mental representation of the external object, rather than the object itself, that is directly before the mind in ordinary perception. And this mental representation is linked to the external object by an information-conveying causal chain. Degree of resolution is largely a matter of *how much* information about the external object is conserved in transmission; though, more generally, it is also a matter of how the information is encoded and reprocessed. (Thus, 'smoothing' of the data is presumably, in part, a product of specific processing; it could hardly be accounted for on the basis merely of information degradation.)

But, as I say, there is no such story to be told in regard to introspective awareness. Introspection is not a distinct sensory modality whose objects differ from those of 'outer sense' by being internal instead of external to the conscious mind. Rather, it is distinguished by one's cognitive or intentional *focus*. Thus, any of the ordinary five senses may be exercised in introspective mode; and doing so is a matter of taking as one's cognitive focus the mental representations themselves, instead of the external objects (if any) which they represent. (Compare the way in which, while watching the Wimbledon men's finals on television, one could switch one's mental focus from the players themselves to the corresponding images on the screen—in the context, say, of wondering whether one should adjust the contrast.) Hence, there are no distinctively introspective meta-mental representations, which stand to introspection as do ordinary visual, auditory, etc. representations to sight and hearing—and whose separation from their mental objects could help us resolve this aspect of the grain problem. And even if there were, the original problem would simply re-emerge at the level of these meta-representations themselves. Our difficulties begin at the point where the perceptual buck stops.

The force of these arguments will, I suspect, be lost on some people. Clearly, someone might protest, there are macroscopic qualities, and there is macroscopic structure: consider liquidity, for example, or temperature, or sphericity. These are perfectly genuine features of physical reality; so why shouldn't it be correspondingly macroscopic features of brain activity that manifest themselves in awareness? But macroscopic features such as those cited are not genuinely *emergent* attributes of the physical world. On the contrary, high-level descriptions like 'liquid', 'hot', or 'spherical' apply—so it would seem—entirely in virtue of what holds true at the microlevel. And if so, it appears to follow that external physical reality can, in thought and perception, present itself to the mind in such high-level terms only by courtesy of the mediating role of mental representations.

I am not, of course, suggesting that the objects of direct awareness come unconceptualized. Thus the presence, within one's visual field, of a number of black dots—even if, in contrast to the dots in our newspaper photograph, they are individually perceived as such—may inescapably carry with it the interpretation *circle*. But that does nothing to explain how what is presented to awareness can, in another instance, just *be* a phenomenally continuous circle, when the physical substrate of the experience consists of a discontinuous array of, say, discrete centres of electrical activity.

Grover Maxwell (whose statement of the grain problem is the must lucid I have come across in the published literature) suggests that, if we are looking for physical structure that is isomorphic to the phenomenal structure encountered in awareness, we might find it at what he dubs the 'middle-sized' level.[14] What he has in mind is a level of structure intermediate between, and less familiar than, quantum microstructure and quasi-classical macrostructure: a level the better understanding of which might, he thinks, hold the key to the elusive goal of bringing together, into a consistent whole, quantum mechanics and general relativity. But there is a fundamental philosophical unclarity in Maxwell's proposal. For what exactly is 'middle-sized' structure supposed to consist in? Is it supposed to be structure which is, in the above sense, *high-level* with respect to electrons and the like—albeit low-level with respect

---

[14] G. Maxwell, 'Rigid Designators and Mind–brain Identity', in *Minnesota Studies in the Philosophy of Science*, 9, ed. C. W. Savage (Minneapolis, 1978), 399.

to, say, blizzards, buffaloes, ball-bearings, and bacteria, hamsters, ham sandwiches, and housing estates? If so, then all he's really talking about—so it's tempting to argue—is microstructure under a (relatively) high-level description. And all the considerations invoked in the past few paragraphs still apply; it will remain a complete mystery how direct introspective contact with brain activity—unmediated by intervening mental representations—can reveal middle-sized structure to the total exclusion of the microstructure which is ultimately constitutive of it.

Perhaps, however, what Maxwell means by middle-sized structure is not merely high-level structure, with respect to the quantum microstructure, but something genuinely *emergent*, in a sense in which liquidity, temperature, and the like are not. The only sense I can attach, in the present context, to Maxwell's middle-sized structure being emergent is that it is structure which is instantiated—in part or in whole—by *emergent qualities*. By emergent qualities, I mean intrinsic attributes which are qualitatively distinct from any attributes possessed either by the low-level constituents of physical reality, considered individually, or by any configurations of them that involve relatively small numbers of these constituents, or which have a relatively low level of organization or complexity. The idea is that, at a certain number/density/complexity (or whatever) *threshold*, new qualities emerge which are different in kind from any that are present in sub-threshold phenomena involving these same constituents; and *pari passu* with these new qualities, new behaviour also. One can imagine possessing a dynamical theory which is ostensibly equal to the task of describing the fundamental constituents, and explaining and predicting their behaviour, *up to the threshold*—at which point, however, the theory begins to prove inadequate.

Well, I daresay that something roughly along these lines may be true. Indeed, it is difficult to see how *awareness itself* could be anything other than an emergent phenomenon, in something like the above sense, assuming the truth of materialism. Nor does such emergence threaten to compromise the unity of physical science. Whatever emerged, at and above the associated threshold, would—by hypothesis—have been *latent*, all along, in the low-level constituents. Hence, a complete description of these constituents would have to include reference to dispositional properties, of which the emergent qualities and behaviour constituted a manifestation. If we assume—as is very plausible—that all dispositions must have a *categorical base* (as the disposition of a key to draw the bolt of a given lock has *shape* as its categorical base), then a description of these constituents need contain no reference to these dispositions as such. It would suffice to cite their intrinsic (non-dispositional) attributes, together with the fundamental laws; a disposition, on the part of any low-level constituent, would hold in virtue of the combination of its intrinsic, categorical attributes and laws which related these attributes to the emergent ones. And incidentally, even if awareness, say, is an emergent phenomenon in the sense just indicated (involving emergent properties and relations), it does not follow that the fundamental low-level constituents need possess any intrinsic, categorical attributes other than those which current physical theory would credit them with— at least, under the conditions prevailing in ordinary physics experiments. Their potential for generating awareness could be a matter of the application of certain currently unknown *laws* to their familiar physical attributes (in which laws, of course, there *would* be an essential reference to the emergent attributes). This fairly elementary point would appear to have escaped those authors who have argued that, if we are made out of electrons, quarks, gluons, and the like, then—given that we are conscious— electrons, quarks, and so forth must themselves be possessed of some sort of primitive proto-consciousness. As I see it, this is a complete *non sequitur*.

So, as I say, emergence in this sense seems to me wholly unobjectionable, philosophically speaking. But, having said that, I doubt very much whether such emergence could, realistically, be expected by itself to offer a solution to the grain problem. For we need to ask: is it really *scientifically* plausible to suppose that the distribution of these emergent qualities would possess any less microstructural complexity than that of the non-emergent ones? Let us go back to our earlier schematic example, involving a circular array of discrete centres of electrical activity in the brain. How, by appealing to emergence, might one explain how this array could present itself to consciousness as an *unbroken* circle? Well, one might suppose that, under the right conditions, such an array would give rise to an emergent field, in the immediately surrounding space, which was continuous, homogeneous, and bounded, in such a way as to match the associated phenomenal presentation, and

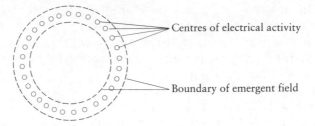

**Fig. 12.1.** *How a circular array of discrete centres of electrical activity in the brain might give rise to an emergent field*

the innate quality of which was registered in awareness. (See Fig. 12.1.)[15]

In short, we should have to suppose that the microstructural arrangement of the fundamental constituents was capable of giving rise to emergent distributions of qualities which were *truly* smooth and homogeneous, where their 'source' was anything but—in stark contrast to any actual field known to science, and in clear violation of the theoretical demands of quantum mechanics. Well I, for one, simply don't believe it; and I doubt if many people would. Where emergence may indeed come into its own is in accounting for the qualitative diversity that is in evidence within the phenomenal realm: McGinn's problem of how 'technicolour phenomenology [can] arise from soggy grey matter'. But as regards the problem of phenomenal coarse-graining, it seems to me that it has little or nothing to offer. A solution—if such is to be found within the confines of philosophical materialism—must be sought elsewhere.

Before we proceed further, I should make clear just what I take to be required of a solution to the grain problem. The premiss of the problem is that sensory phenomenology belongs, so to speak, to that tip of the neurophysiological iceberg which projects above the surface of awareness. We are to regard it as a part or aspect of the reality of the brain that is directly present to the conscious mind, without benefit of any intervening representation: in awareness, the intrinsic nature of some part or aspect of what is to be

---

[15] I am here imagining that phenomenal spatial relations, say within the visual field, reflect—indeed, in some sense just *are*—actual spatial relations within the appropriate region of the cerebral cortex. But this is only for the same of concreteness; I do not advance it as a serious hypothesis.

found within the skull stands revealed. From this it follows that the phenomenal objects of sensory awareness must be thought of as somehow *embedded* within that tract of physical reality consisting of the brain and its doings. Assuming this position to be correct, consciousness, at the phenomenal level, can only make selections from the underlying neurophysiology. There is, as we have seen, no possibility of interposing any further stage of reprocessing between awareness and the neurophysiological substrate of its phenomenal objects; for sensory phenomenology is located precisely at the point where the *output* of all processing of sensory data is delivered to the conscious mind. The challenge posed by the grain problem is, therefore, the challenge of showing how *mere selectivity*, as applied to the physical reality of the brain, can yield the form and qualitative content characteristic of sensory phenomenology.

It is often said that philosophers are better at asking questions than at answering them; and I fear that this philosopher is no exception. All that I shall try to do now (and all that space really permits) is to provide a few hints towards a solution.

Underlying the grain problem, it seems to me, are a number of tacit assumptions about the nature of reality and our relationship to it which, though intuitively natural, are philosophically far from compelling. First, I suspect that most people, when it is put to them that in awareness we are immediately aware of some part or aspect of our own brain states, will think that, on this view, the relation between what is going on in one's brain as a whole and the phenomenal contents of awareness must be something like that between a painting and a detail of that painting. But to suppose that is to make the natural but nevertheless unwarranted assumption that the *principle of selection* underlying consciousness must be purely spatial location. There is, *a priori*, no reason to assume that *any* purely *spatial* cordoning of the brain at a given time would capture all *and only* that of which the subject was directly aware. With respect to any spatially defined region, the subject could surely be aware of some but not all aspects or attributes of what lay within it. Secondly and relatedly, there is no good reason to assume that the contents of a given state of awareness correspond to *simultaneous* goings-on in the brain. Indeed, in the context of relativity, no absolute sense can be attached to the notion of spatially separated events being simultaneous. From a relativistic viewpoint, the brain corresponds to a four-dimensional *world-tube*. And it is as likely as not that what is, so to speak, *given together* in awareness is spread throughout a segment of this world-tube, rather than being confined to a time-slice. In some ways, that would square better, in any case, with the psychological phenomenon of the *specious present*—the fact that, subjectively speaking, states of awareness seem to possess a measure of temporal 'depth'.

These are assumptions relating to us in relation to the world. But there is, thirdly, an assumption about the nature of reality itself which one might wish to question. Kronecker once said, apropos of arithmetic, that the natural numbers were created by God and that everything else is the work of man. In a similar way, it seems to me, people are very apt to suppose that only micro-structure is, so to speak, God-given, and that any higher level of structure is, at best, ontologically or metaphysically derivative, and at worst, a mere conceptual artefact. That assumption, in effect, was the basis of our earlier attack on Maxwell's suggestions regarding 'middle-sized structure'. But perhaps, after all, this notion of the ontological primacy of the microstructural is a dogma which should be rejected; perhaps the dilemma on whose horns we attempted to impale Maxwell is a false one. (I shall shortly advance some considerations which suggest that it is.)

None of these observations, however, penetrates to what I conceive to be the real heart of the matter, which is that the grain problem is one manifestation of a more general philosophical puzzle having to do with *subjectivity* and *objectivity*. The world of modern science, it is sometimes said, is a *centreless* world, a world which abstracts from the *point of view* of any particular observer. As Nagel neatly puts it, science is in the business of describing 'the view from nowhere'.[16] Awareness, by contrast, is inescapably centred on a point of view. What is directly present to awareness must, therefore, be conceived as a *perspective* on the brain. I wish to argue that the apparent dissonance between a physiologist's description of brain activity and the contents of our introspective judgements is to be seen, in part, as a consequence of the (relatively) perspective-transcendent character of the former.

If what is true 'subjectively' is true relative to a point of view,

[16] T. Nagel, *The View from Nowhere* (Oxford, 1986).

then the only way of reconciling subjectivity and objectivity is by incorporating *points of view* within one's objective inventory of the world. Any metaphysical theory which does not somehow include points of view in its ontology is to that extent inadequate, as a comprehensive conception of reality. One philosopher who saw this very clearly was Leibniz, who went to the extreme lengths of supposing, in effect, that the universe was entirely composed of points of view—his *monads*.

What I have just said applies as much to physics as it does to metaphysics. Indeed, it is in some sense as much a condition of the explanatory adequacy of a physical theory that one be able to locate, within it, the point of view of the observer, as it is of the practical efficacy of a map that one be able to pinpoint, on the map, one's own position.

In classical physics it was unnecessary to address this requirement explicitly, since the associated conceptual scheme was essentially continuous with that of common sense. In the theory of relativity, however, the requirement is met quite explicitly via the notion of a *frame of reference*. The currently favoured language of space–time and four-vectors would be intuitively unintelligible without the auxiliary notion of an *observer* as situated at the origin of a set of spatial co-ordinates with respect to which he is invariably at rest, with a personal flow of time which corresponds to integration of the space–time *interval* along his own *world-line*. (Einstein sometimes put this very concretely, imagining the observer as carrying around with him an apparatus consisting of three rigid, mutually perpendicular measuring-rods, clutching it at the point where the three rods intersect—the 'origin'—to which is attached an ideal clock.)

Via this notion of a frame of reference, one comes to see how, from the observer's own point of view, space–time comes to be partitioned into the distinct space and time of common sense. Thus, the space–time interval (that is, four-dimensional separation) between two events comes to be decomposed into spatial and temporal intervals corresponding, respectively, to the *projections* of the space–time interval on to the three-dimensional space defined by the spatial co-ordinates (or the set of mutually perpendicular measuring-rods) and the one-dimensional space defined by the time co-ordinate (or the ideal clock). And, in general, a four-vector is decomposed into a three-vector and a scalar component—the four-momentum, for example, into a three-vector momentum and a scalar energy.

It is tempting to think of an observer, in the context of relativity, as the *concrete embodiment* of a frame of reference (rather than merely as 'carrying around' such a frame, à la Einstein). A description of objects and events *relative to* this frame of reference— couched, therefore, in the language of space and time, rather than of space–time—may then be thought of as corresponding to the observer's perspective: how things are from his own 'subjective' point of view.

The conception of physical science as giving us a centreless account of the world chimes well with its aim, in modern times, of finding things that remain *invariant* with respect to different ways of representing physical reality. (Einstein, it is alleged, originally wanted to call his theory the *theory of invariants*.) This notion of invariance is perhaps the single most powerful idea in modern physics and crops up everywhere—gauge invariance, in field theory, being one of its most prominent recent manifestations. But in particular, it crops up at the foundations of *quantum mechanics*. States of a physical system, in quantum mechanics, correspond to vectors in an abstract space known as *Hilbert space*. And just as the four-dimensional space of relativity can be seen through the eyes of any of an infinity of different *frames of reference*, so the Hilbert space of a quantum-mechanical system can be seen through the eyes of any of an infinity of different so-called *vector bases*. Every quantum-mechanical *observable*, that is to say, question one can ask of a quantum-mechanical system, susceptible of being answered by a suitable measurement—or more generally, every set of *compatible* observables, that is, questions capable of being simultaneously answered—corresponds to a vector basis for Hilbert space, known as the *eigenbasis* of the corresponding observable or set of observables. A set of observables, via its *eigenbasis*, defines a co-ordinate system for Hilbert space, just as a frame of reference defines a co-ordinate system for space–time. (The key things that remain invariant with respect to different bases are the respective probabilities of getting various outcomes, when carrying out measurements on the quantum-mechanical system in question.)

Quantum mechanics was discovered independently, in the mid-1920s, by Heisenberg and Schrödinger. But so different, in their mathematical formulation, were Heisenberg's *matrix mechanics* and Schrödinger's *wave mechanics*, that they were at first thought to be distinct, rival theories. Only subsequently were they found (by Schrödinger himself, in the first instance) to be essentially equivalent, the difference in form being due, in large part, to different choices of basis. Roughly speaking, Heisenberg chose the eigenbasis corresponding to the energy observable, and Schrödinger the eigenbasis corresponding to the position observable.

That said, I am now in a position to convey the essence of my own favoured approach to the grain problem. (Again, space does not permit more than a very approximate and compressed rendering.) First, the brain, I suggest, may legitimately be regarded as a quantum-mechanical system. (There is nothing in the formalism of quantum mechanics that prevents it from being applied to macroscopic systems.) As with most complex quantum-mechanical systems, the brain may be conceptually decomposed (doubtless, in several alternative ways) into *subsystems*, which can be treated as quantum-mechanical systems in their own right. One of these subsystems I take to coincide with the neurophysiological substrate of conscious mental functioning. (This dividing-up of the brain into subsystems need not, as remarked earlier, correspond to anything that would seem intuitively at all natural; nor need the subsystem in question correspond to what would ordinarily be thought of as a *part* of the brain. The dividing-up would not, in general, be a *spatial*, or even a *spatio-temporal* division, so much as a partitioning of the *degrees of freedom* of the larger brain system—the distinct ways in which it can change state or store energy.)

Anyway, there is, I take it, such a brain subsystem. And from the point of view of consciousness, I contend, there is (at any given time, at least) a preferred set of compatible observables on that system. The conscious observer views his or her own brain through the eyes, so to speak, of this preferred set of observables, much as the observer, in relativity, views the world through the eyes of his own frame of reference. Indeed, just as, in relativity, the observer can, in a sense, be regarded as a concrete embodiment of a particular frame of reference, so, I suggest, may a conscious subject be thought of as, in some sense, the concrete embodiment of a set of compatible observables. Every quantum-mechanical observable has a so-called *spectrum of eigenvalues*, associated, respectively, with the eigenvectors comprising its eigenbasis; these are numbers corresponding to the possible results of measuring the observable in question. If we consider a *set* of observables, then their spectra can themselves be thought of as co-ordinate axes, jointly defining a further abstract space. And a value of each co-ordinate, corresponding to an eigenvalue of each observable in the set, will define a point or vector in this abstract space. When the set of observables is the set preferred by, or embodied in, consciousness, then this space may be equated with phenomenal or experiential space: points or vectors in the space correspond to distinct possible states of awareness. And the various *qualia* spaces of sense-perception—colour space, for example—are simply subspaces of this abstract space; specific *qualia*, as they figure in awareness, represent points or regions of such spaces encountered, so to speak, in the flesh. It is precisely here that the intrinsic character of the concrete reality that the abstract mathematical formalism of quantum mechanics purports to describe makes itself manifest.

But how does all this address the problem of how awareness is able to gloss over the complex microstructure which presumably underlies the phenomenal contents of any experience? Well quite simply, there are, in quantum mechanics, no observables, or sets thereof, which are *a priori* privileged. In particular, there is, in terms of quantum-mechanical observables, no rock-bottom level of structure to be discerned in the world. In quantum field theory, no sense can be attached, for example, to the notion of measuring the values of the field variables at a precise point—only their average values over some finite spatio-temporal region (which one can make as small as one wishes); indeed, no sense can be attached to their *possessing* a precise value at any precise point. (No more, in elementary quantum mechanics, can an electron be said to have, let alone be measured as having, a precisely defined position or momentum.) In quantum mechanics there is a sense in which all observables, and in particular observables corresponding to every level of structure, are to be regarded as equal in the sight of God, as are different frames of reference, relativistically conceived.[17] As I intimated earlier, quantum mechanics seems to be

[17] For the benefit of those familiar with quantum mechanics, let me say that I am, of course, glossing over the distinction between so-called *maximal* and *non-maximal* (or *degenerate*) observables, or sets thereof. (A maximal observable, or set of observables, is one corresponding to a measurement, or set of simultaneous

telling us that it is a classical prejudice to suppose that the world is not *intrinsically* structured at anything but the level of elementary particles, and their actions and interactions.

According to this approach, then, the apparent dissonance between brain activity, as seen through the eyes (and concepts) of the neurophysiologist, on the one hand, and the conscious subject, on the other, is to be attributed to three distinct considerations. First, this brain activity is revealed to the awareness of the corresponding conscious subject—as it is not to the probings of the neurophysiologist—*as it is in itself* (albeit only from a certain point of view). Second, introspective awareness is focused on a *subsystem* of the brain, selected according to principles that, from the standpoint of physiology, would seem very unnatural. And finally, the contents of consciousness correspond to eigenvalues of a set of *observables* which, again, are distinct from anything that the physiologist is likely to settle on: the dissonance between the subject's view, and that of the physiologist, might be conceived as analogous to that between, say, Schrödinger's wave mechanics and Heisenberg's matrix mechanics. Thinking in terms of coordinate systems for the Hilbert space of the relevant brain system, it is as though the co-ordinate system of the conscious subject were, so to speak, rotated with respect to that of the external observer.[18]

The state of a physical system—on the view that I am proposing —might be compared to a block of wood, distinct cross-sections

measurements, which yields a state of *maximum information* about the system in question—one that cannot be improved upon by the performance of further measurements.) In case someone thinks that maximal observables, or maximal sets of compatible observables, are privileged with respect to non-maximal ones, in a way that vitiates my argument, it should be pointed out that one could imagine the space of possible states of awareness of the conscious observer being generated, so to speak, in two stages. Any non-maximal set of compatible observables can, after all, be turned into a maximal set simply by adding observables to the original set. So suppose, to begin with, that there is (from the perspective of consciousness, though not of the world) a preferred maximal set of compatible observables (having the requisite non-maximal set as a subset). The spectra of eigenvalues of the observables in the set could then be thought of as co-ordinate axes, defining a state space, with respect to which the range of possible states of awareness could then be regarded as constituting a preferred subspace.

[18] Here I have been able to do no more than sketch the bare bones of the theory I favour. In *Mind, Brain and the Quantum*, I develop these ideas in far greater detail, and also, for the sake of those unversed in modern physics, provide an elementary account of quantum mechanics itself.

of which can reveal strikingly different sorts of patterns, depending on the angle at which it is sliced: concentric rings at one extreme, roughly parallel, gently undulating lines at the other. Though the analogy is very imperfect, one might think of the neurophysiologist, and the conscious subject in introspection, as likewise being confronted, so to speak, with different 'cross-sections' of what are in fact the same brain states. My claim is that, by appealing to the quantum-mechanical concept of an observable, we can render it intelligible, as with the grain of the wood, that a common underlying structure should manifest itself in superficially very different ways. On the side of introspection, moreover, such a conception removes the need to appeal to any inner representation, distinct from the state itself. For to be directly acquainted with a 'cross-section' of something is *a fortiori* to be directly acquainted with the thing itself, not merely some cognitive surrogate of it—in spite of the fact that what is thereby revealed to consciousness is revealed only under a certain aspect.

What, then, finally, is consciousness telling us about the nature of physical reality? Well, first (assuming materialism to be true), that there is more to matter than meets the physicist's eye. For there is nothing in the physicist's account of the world to explain why there should *exist* conscious points of view—why the world should contain such concrete embodiments of sets of quantum-mechanical observables. Thus we are in a position to know *a priori* that something like superstring theory, whatever its other merits, cannot literally be a theory of everything—since there is nothing in the theory that could, even in principle, explain how matter, suitably combined, is able to generate awareness. But on the positive side, it follows from what I have been saying that our states of awareness, corresponding as they do, on my account, to sequences of eigenvalues of brain observables, are providing us with the answers to specific questions concerning the intrinsic nature of a corner of the physical world—something that (as Russell rightly insisted) can never be revealed in ordinary measurement or observation. For our own awareness, so I have been urging, embodies a preferred set of observables, which in turn amounts to saying that its contents, at any given time, embody the answers to a set of questions about the state (the intrinsic state) of the underlying brain system. Sadly, however, we here find ourselves in a predicament akin to that of the characters in *The Hitch Hiker's Guide to the Galaxy*, on being told that the answer to life, the universe, and everything was 42. We know the *answers* to these questions, in a way that a scientist, merely by examining our brains from without, never could. But unfortunately, we have, as yet, no idea what the questions are!

# 13

# The Succinct Case for Idealism

## John Foster

### i. The Project

My aim is to establish the truth of phenomenalistic idealism, which takes the physical world to be something logically created by the organization of (i.e. the regularities in and lawlike constraints on) human sense-experience. This position stands in sharp contrast with physical realism, which takes the physical world to be logically independent of the human mind and metaphysically fundamental. Despite his reductive account of the physical world, the idealist is not, of course, committed to saying that there is *no* concrete reality external to, and independent of, the human mind. All he is committed to saying is that, if there is such a reality, it is not itself physical and only contributes to the existence of the physical world via its actual or potential influence on human experience. In fact, idealists normally do envisage some form of external reality to account for the experiential organization. Thus Berkeley, who espouses a form of phenomenalistic idealism in his *Principles*,[1] insists that human sense-experience and the laws which control it are the result of divine volition.

There is no denying that it is physical realism which expresses the view of 'common sense'—the view we all take for granted prior to philosophical reflection. But this is very largely because, prior to reflection, we have a naïve-realist view of sense-perception. Thus we assume our perceptual access to external objects to be direct in a very strong sense—a sense which represents these objects as featuring in the very content of perceptual experience. This view of perception is, it seems to me, clearly mistaken: philosophical reflection (e.g. on the phenomena of illusion and hallucination)

---

[1] At least this is how I interpret him. See my 'Berkeley on the Physical World', in J. A. Foster and H. M. Robinson, eds., *Essays on Berkeley* (Oxford, 1985).

reveals that, whatever its precise nature, perceptual contact with
an external item is always mediated by the occurrence of some
purely internal psychological state which is capable of occurring
without such contact being made.[2]

As well as eliminating much of its intuitive appeal, this result
may also put pressure on physical realism in a more direct way.
It is difficult to think of the external reality as constituting the
physical world—i.e. *our* physical world—if we do not have perceptual access to it. But, although naïve realism is false, it is not clear
how anything except a direct awareness would qualify as genuine
perception at all; after all, without direct awareness, the situation
is merely one of there being something in the mind which represents
or provides information about the external item. So it may be that
we have to construe the physical world as something internal to
the mind in order to render it perceptually accessible. In effect,
this is how Berkeley argued at the beginning of the *Principles*, when
he dismissed realism as involving a 'manifest contradiction'.[3]

I mention this point *en passant*. Whether or not such an anti-
realist argument can be successfully developed is something I shall
not explore further here. My own case against realism, and in
favour of idealism, follows a quite different course. Inevitably, in
the present context, the case will have to be set out much more
briefly, and in simpler terms, than the issues require. I have tried
to deal with the full complexities of the topic elsewhere.[4]

## ii. The Inscrutability of Physical Content

As well as precluding direct (and arguably *any* form of) perceptual
access to the physical world, realism also imposes a severe limit on

---

[2] For a full discussion of this point, see H. Robinson, 'The Argument for
Berkeleian Idealism', sect. 4, in Foster and Robinson, eds., *Essays on Berkeley*, and
my own *Ayer* (London, 1985), pt. 2, sect. 9.

[3] 'For what are the forementioned objects [houses, mountains, rivers, etc.] but
the things we perceive by sense, and what do we perceive besides our own ideas
or sensations; and is it not plainly repugnant that any one of these or any combination of them should exist unperceived?', *Principles of Human Knowledge*,
1. 4.

[4] In *The Case for Idealism* (London, 1982). The relation between the present
succinct version and the earlier full one is roughly as follows: sect. ii of this paper
corresponds to pt. 2 of the book; sect. iii corresponds to chs. 8–9; sect. iv to chs.
10–11; and sect. 5 to pt. 4. One crucial topic which I treat in detail in the book
(pt. 5), but do not discuss here at all, is the nature of time.

the scope of our *knowledge* of it. For, within the realist frame-work, we can at best acquire knowledge of the *structure and organization* of the physical world, not, at least at the fundamental level, of its *content*. Thus while, from our observations, and from the way these support certain kinds of explanatory theory, we may be able to establish the existence of an external space with a certain geometrical structure (one that is three-dimensional, continuous, and approximately Euclidean), we can never find out what, apart from this structure, the space is like in itself: we cannot discover the nature of the thing which has these geometrical properties and forms the medium for physical objects (or if we prefer to construe space not as a concrete thing, but as the abstract system of ways in which physical objects could be geometrically arranged, we cannot discover the nature of the distance-relations which form the building-blocks of these arrangements). Likewise, while, by the same empirical means, we may be able to establish the existence of external objects located in this space, and discover their shape and size, their spatial and spatio-temporal arrangement, their causal powers and sensitivities, and the various ways in which complex objects are composed of simpler ones, we can never discover the ultimate nature of their space-filling content. For we can never discover, beyond a knowledge of their spatio-temporal and causal properties, what the simplest objects (the elementary particles) are like in themselves. Of course, we ordinarily take our physical knowledge to be more than merely structural in this way. For, prior to reflection, we think of physical space and its occupants as being, in their intrinsic character, as our sense-experiences (especially our visual experiences) represent them. Thus we think of grass as genuinely pervaded by the intrinsic green which characterizes its standard visual appearance, and we think of the circular shape of a penny as being, in a way which transcends its formal geometrical description, distinctively like the circularity which can feature as a colour-boundary in the visual field. But while such ascriptions of sensible content to the physical world form part of our ordinary view of things, they do not, in the end, have any rational justification. We cannot directly compare our sensory representations with the external items to see if they match, since we only have access to these items through the representations. Nor can we employ an inference to the best explanation to justify the ascriptions, since it is only the theories about structure and organization which play an explanatory role. The only way we could legitimize the ascriptions would be by adopting a 'secondary-quality' account of the facts they purport to record, so that an object's possession of a sensible quality comes to be nothing more than its power to affect human sense-experience. But, in this framework, the ascriptions would cease to have any bearing on the issue of physical content, at least in its fundamental form.

One interesting and surprising consequence of this limitation on the scope of our physical knowledge is that we can envisage the possibility of the physical world's being, in substance and character, purely mental. For, being ignorant of its content, we are free to suppose that the relevant structure and organization are realized in a domain of minds and mental events. For example, we could suppose that physical space is a three-dimensional sense-field (existing in some non-human and non-embodied mind) and that the fundamental physical qualities distributed over its points and regions are *sense*-qualities. Alternatively, we could suppose that the elementary physical particles are minds (again, non-human and non-embodied), and that the spatial position of each particle at a time is fixed by some triple of quality-values which characterize its current psychological condition. In both cases, of course, there would have to be appropriate laws controlling events in the external mental reality (to form the relevant physical laws), and appropriate link-laws connecting these events with events in human minds (to form the relevant psychophysical laws). It must be stressed that mentalistic hypotheses of this sort constitute forms of physical realism, not forms of idealism. For although they offer mentalistic accounts of the physical world, they do so in a way which leaves it as something logically independent of human mentality and metaphysically fundamental. The fact that the envisaged world is composed of minds and mental events has no bearing on either its metaphysical status or its relation to us.

The idea that the physical world might turn out to be composed of psychological elements is a strange one, and might strike us as too bizarre to be taken seriously. But curiously, apart from the mentalistic hypotheses, we have no way of even forming a conception of what the inscrutable content might be. We cannot form such a conception in *physical* terms; for having evolved to serve the needs of empirical theorizing, our system of physical concepts is not equipped to provide a characterization of factors which are not amenable to empirical tests. Nor is there any third source of descriptive concepts—neither psychological nor physical—on which we can draw. However bizarre they may seem, the mentalistic accounts of what the physical world may be like are, within the framework of realism, the only ones available.

### iii. The Determinants of Physical Structure

Another way of responding to the epistemological situation would be to give up physical realism. For, without realism, we could say that what is empirically inscrutable is not the content of the *physical world*, but only that of the external reality (if there is one) which underlies it. In other words, by taking the physical world to be the logical creation of something else (whether something purely human-experiential or something partly external), we could ensure that it only embodies factors which are empirically accessible. For reasons which I shall now (over this and the next section) elaborate, I believe this to be the correct response. In elaborating these reasons, I shall focus on examples in which the external reality is assumed to be mental, since (for reasons already explained) these are the only ones available. And I shall focus in particular on cases in which the external item corresponding to physical space (and according to the realist identical with it) is a sense-field (or an aggregate of sense-fields), since this is the simplest way of envisaging something which is intuitively space-like in its character. I must stress, however, that all this is just for convenience of exposition and that the arguments themselves apply quite generally, whatever the external reality happens to be.

However inaccessible its content, we have so far not challenged the assumption that we can empirically discover the *structure and organization* of the external reality. But we can at least envisage the possibility that the real structure and organization differ from those which are empirically apparent at the human viewpoint. Thus suppose that the external reality consists of a three-dimensional sense-field, with a certain field–time distribution of qualities governed by certain distributional laws.[5] And let $R_1$ and

---

[5] We need not think of this sense-field as resembling anything which features in our own modes of sensory experience.

$R_2$ be two field-regions of exactly the same shape and size, $R_1$ containing (or containing those field-processes which underlie events in) Oxford, and $R_2$ containing (or containing those field-processes which underlie events in) Cambridge. We can then envisage the following possibility. $R_1$ is positioned within the sense-field where (or in the place which corresponds to where) we ordinarily take Cambridge to be, and $R_2$ is positioned within the sense-field where (or in the place which corresponds to where) we ordinarily take Oxford to be. The reason we do not notice this, and would never suspect it from the empirical evidence, is that everything in the external reality is organized, both internally and with respect to effects on human experience, exactly as if the positions of $R_1$ and $R_2$ were reversed, i.e. exactly as if they occurred in those field-positions where we ordinarily take their physical correlates to be. Thus, given any type of field-process which would normally continue in a straight line, if such a process comes (in the normal continuous way) to some point on the boundary of $R_1$, it instantaneously changes its location to the corresponding point on the boundary of $R_2$, and continues in the corresponding straight line from there. And conversely, if such a process comes (in the normal continuous way) to the boundary of $R_2$, it undergoes an exactly analogous shift to the boundary of $R_1$. (For an illustrative example, see Fig. 13.1.) Quite generally, by the standards of how, in the rest of the field, things behave and affect human experience, everything is organized, with respect to the boundaries of $R_1$ and $R_2$, as if $R_1$ had $R_2$'s location, and vice versa. We might put the situation succinctly thus: each of the two regions is *functionally* located where the other is *actually* (sensually) located. In speaking thus of the field's 'functional' geometry, we mean that (non-actual) geometry which its organization suggests—that geometry which the field would need to have, with its organization held constant, for the restoration of organizational (nomological) uniformity.

It is not difficult to find further examples to illustrate the same general point. Thus we could envisage a case in which the external item corresponding to physical space consisted of *two* sense-fields organized as if they were *one*. Or again, though the details of this would be technically complicated, we could envisage a case in which the external item corresponding to physical space was a *two*-dimensional sense-field organized as if it were *three*-dimensional. Nor are we restricted to examples in which the discrepancy between how things really are and how they empirically seem relates to

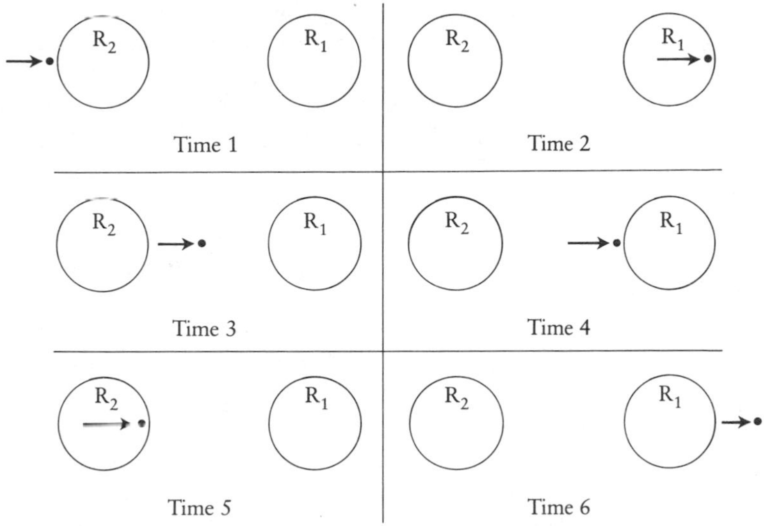

**Fig. 13.1.** The Oxford–Cambridge case: an illustrative example. *Suppose someone drives from Bath to Norwich, passing in turn through Oxford and Cambridge. Within the external sense-field, the path of the underlying process would be as here illustrated. Notice that whenever the process reaches a boundary of one of the regions, whether from the inside or the outside, there is an immediate jump to the corresponding point on the boundary of the other. As we shall see below, the crucial question is whether the path of the motorist in physical space is correspondingly disjointed*

*geometrical* structure. Thus, reverting to the case of a three-dimensional field, we could suppose that there are two sense-qualities $Q_1$ and $Q_2$ such that, in respect of some particular region, everything is organized as if $Q_1$ inside this region were the same as $Q_2$ outside it, and vice versa. Or again, we could suppose that, over the whole field, two sense-qualities exchange their current distributions and functional roles every hour, so that everything is organized as if each of the qualities in hours 1, 3, 5, 7, . . . was the same as the other quality in hours 2, 4, 6, 8, . . . These last two cases are ones in which the deviance of empirical appearance from external reality relates to qualitative rather than geometrical structure: it concerns the relations of sameness and difference between the forms of qualitative content distributed over the external space.

All these cases, of course, are, by ordinary canons of scientific reasoning, implausible: to postulate any of them would involve attributing a nomological irregularity or complexity to the external reality when the empirical evidence permits a more uniform or simpler interpretation. It is just for this reason that we can speak of the cases as exhibiting a discrepancy between how things externally are and how they empirically seem. And, in this sense, we may even be able to retain the assumption that the structure and organization of the external reality are empirically revealed.[6] All that matters for my purposes, however, is that, even if we are entitled to reject them on empirical grounds, such cases are logically possible and logically consistent with the empirical evidence.

Now the question I want to consider is this. In cases of the sort just envisaged, how are we to construe the situation of the physical world? When we hypothesize this kind of discrepancy between the structure of the external reality and its empirical projection on to the human viewpoint, how should we characterize things at the physical level? Let us start by focusing on the Oxford–Cambridge example, in which the functional positions of $R_1$ (the field-region corresponding to Oxford) and $R_2$ (the field-region corresponding to Cambridge) are the reverse of their actual (sensual) positions. There are three responses we could make to this case. The first would be to say that there is no physical world at all—that the organizational anomaly with respect to the two regions is simply inconsistent with the existence of a physical world. The second would be to accept the existence of a physical world and see its structure as coinciding with that of the external reality. This would involve saying that, contrary to our ordinary beliefs, and to what all the empirical evidence suggests, Oxford really is in Cambridgeshire (coinciding with the field-position of $R_1$), and Cambridge really is in Oxfordshire (coinciding with the field-position of $R_2$). The third response would be to accept the existence of a physical world, but say that its structure coincides with how things empirically seem at the human viewpoint. This would involve saying that, despite

---

[6] In fact I think we cannot. For although we have reason to reject the sorts of case just envisaged, and indeed to reject any case in which the external reality is organized in a way which runs counter to its own structure, I do not think that we have reason to reject the theistic account of the external reality proposed by Berkeley. The issues here, however, are ones which I have no time to discuss in the present paper.

the positions of $R_1$ and $R_2$ in the sense-field, Oxford and Cambridge are where we ordinarily take them to be. Now it seems to me that only the third of these responses has any plausibility. It is just obvious that the envisaged twist in the external organization would not suffice to eliminate the physical world altogether. But granted that we retain our belief in a physical world, we will surely want to model its topology on the functional rather than the actual topology of the sense-field. Thus we will surely want to say that Oxford not only meets all the empirical tests for being to the west of London, but that it actually is so, and that Cambridge not only meets all the empirical tests for being between London and Ely, but that this is its actual position in physical space. The point is that the physical world is, by definition, *our* world in some epistemologically crucial sense. Something can hardly qualify as the topological structure of *our* world, in *that* sense, if it is wholly and (by the laws of nature) necessarily concealed at the human viewpoint. However things may look to God, *our* world must be one to which *we* have empirical access.

Our response to all the other cases of this general sort will, it seems to me, be exactly the same. In each case, we will want to say that the existence of the physical world remains, but that its structure coincides with the structure which is empirically apparent, and reflects the underlying organization, rather than with that which characterizes the external reality. Thus, if we suppose the external reality to comprise two sense-fields which are organized as if they were one, we will conclude that there is only one physical space, reflecting the unitary character of the organization. Likewise, if we suppose that two external qualities exchange their current distributions and functional roles every hour, we will trace the space–time paths of the relevant physical qualities in a way which restores organizational uniformity, rather than in a way which matches the relations of qualitative sameness and difference in the external reality itself. And of course, our intuitions about such cases would be exactly the same without the supposition that the external reality involves a sense-field or anything else of a mentalistic type.

The upshot is that, whatever the nature of the external reality, we must take the structure of the physical world to be logically determined not by the external structure alone, but by this structure together with the way external things are nomologically organized

internally and in relation to human experience. This will be so
even in the case where, with no discrepancy between how things
externally are and how they empirically appear, the external and
physical structures coincide. For this coincidence will still logically
depend on the fact that the external laws are such as to 'endorse'
the external structure and make it empirically manifest at the
human viewpoint. Thus, with suitably different laws, we would
get a different physical structure—or with a sufficiently radical
nomological change, no physical structure (and therefore no physical
world) at all.

## iv. The Argument against Ontological Realism

Being logically determined by certain pre-physical facts about the
external reality, that is, by a combination of the external structure
and external organization, the structure of the physical world does
not qualify as metaphysically fundamental. Nor, in so far as a
crucial part of the external organization concerns the influence
of external events on human experience, is it logically independent
of the human mind. Already this sounds like an outright rejection
of physical realism, which takes the physical world to possess
such a status and independence. In fact, however, it would still
be possible, at this stage, for the realist to preserve an important
aspect of his position. For while conceding that the physical
*structure* is derivative and dependent, he could still insist that, at
an appropriately basic level of description, the physical *entities*
which feature in it, and which qualify as physical by so featuring,
are ingredients of the external reality and metaphysically fundamental. In other words, while conceding that realism fails in respect of physical facts and states of affairs, he could still maintain
that it succeeds in respect of the (basic) physical ontology.

  There are three ways in which this ontological realism could be
developed. First, the realist might recognize physical space—or, for
some exhaustive mode of division, its components—as metaphysically fundamental, but construe its physical occupants as the
logical creation of certain pre-occupant facts about it. Secondly,
and conversely, he might recognize physical occupants, or certain

categories of occupants, as metaphysically fundamental, but construe physical space as the logical creation of certain pre-spatial facts about them. Thirdly, he might assign a metaphysically fundamental status to both physical space and its occupants. Now it seems to me that the second of these approaches can be excluded at the outset. The approach requires us to think of the relevant space-occupying physical objects as only *contingently* located in physical space—as things which are logically capable of existing without spatial location. For it represents physical space as something which derives its very existence from the way in which these things are (in respect of their pre-spatial properties and relations) contingently organized. But it is surely clear that we cannot, in this way, think of the spatial location of physical objects as only contingent. For it is part of our basic conception of such objects that physical space is not just their container, but the very form of their existence. Thus our conception of a physical object is as something *existing in* space, something which exists *by and through* its spatial location, something for which spatial location constitutes (if one may put it thus) the *mode of being*. Moreover, and indeed in consequence, it is part of our conception of such objects that, in conjunction with time, the space which contains them forms the framework for their identity. Thus we think of a physical object as deriving its individuality-at-a-time from its spatial position, and as preserving its identity-through-time by following a spatio-temporally continuous path. In short, to suppose that a physical object has the logical capacity to exist without physical space is as absurd as supposing that an event has the logical capacity to exist without time. And here, of course, the point is not just that such an object needs spatial location to qualify as *physical*; it is that, being the (physical) sort of thing it is, the object needs spatial location to exist at all.

This leaves two approaches available to the ontological realist, in each of which he assigns a metaphysically fundamental status to physical space or its components. This assignment avoids the objection to the second approach: there is now no question of having to think of certain physical objects as only contingently located in space. None the less, it is vulnerable to a different, and rather more complex, objection, which I shall now elaborate.

Let us suppose, for the sake of argument, that the external reality (i.e. the external component of the metaphysically fundamental reality) consists of a three-dimensional sense-field (*F*), together with a field–time quality-distribution, distributional laws, and laws linking field-events with human-mental events. Call physical space *P*. The realist's claim, then, is that *P* is the same as *F*, or at least that, for some exhaustive division, the components of *P* are the same as the components of *F*. The point of giving the realist the choice of this second and weaker alternative is to leave room for cases in which the sensual and physical topologies do not coincide. For where this happens, there are bound to be regions in the one which do not correspond to regions in the other. For example, in the case of Oxford and Cambridge outlined earlier, the physical regions of Oxfordshire and Cambridgeshire will not correspond with *regions* (i.e. *uninterrupted* regions) in the field, since each county comprises two portions (namely, its main city and the surrounding area) whose field-correlates are not contiguous.

The first thing we need to recognize is that any genuine space possesses its (real) geometrical structure, or at least the topological aspects of this structure, *essentially*. Thus, given any space, the network of distance-relations between its points, or at least the network of topological relations, is essential to the identities of these points: they could not be the points they are while standing in different relations. In particular, then, we can apply this principle to the case of *physical* space in respect of its *physical* geometry.[7] Thus if we know that the *physical* Oxford-region is in Oxfordshire and that the physical Cambridge-region is in Cambridgeshire, it makes no sense to suppose that the positions of these regions (as portions of physical space) might have been reversed. Likewise, if we know that physical space is three-dimensional, it makes no sense to suppose that the very same set of physical points might have had a two-dimensional arrangement. The point of allowing for a case in which only the *topological* structure of a space is essential to it, is that it may be possible to

---

[7] For simplicity, I pretend that physical space can be detached from time. Strictly speaking, I should focus throughout on the geometry of P-*time*, or the geometries of the *momentary cross-sections* of P.

envisage a 'rubbery' space, in which points can preserve their identities through the kind of stretch-or-bend metrical alterations that rubber allows. What would remain invariant in such a space—both through time and across possible worlds—is topological arrangement: in other words, any (unbroken) line or (whole) region in the original condition of the space would remain a line or region after the permitted alterations.[8]

Now we have already established that the geometrical structure of physical space, and in particular its topological structure, depends not just on the *structure* of the external reality, but on its *structure and nomological organization*. Thus, in the case we are considering, if A and B are (actually) contiguous regions of F (the external sense-field), the nomological organization of F will determine whether A and B are also 'functionally contiguous', and hence determine whether the corresponding regions of P (the physical space) are actually contiguous. One way of expressing the point would be to say that, with its structure held constant, the nomological organization of the external reality, internally and in relation to human experience, determines its *physically relevant* geometry (topology). The description 'physically relevant' is designed to preserve neutrality between the realist's position, which takes physical space (or its components) to be metaphysically fundamental, and hence part of the external reality, and the non-realist's view, which rejects this.

The physically relevant geometry (topology) of F logically depends on its nomological organization. But this nomological organization, and in particular those aspects which contribute to the physical geometry, characterize F only *contingently*. We can envisage exactly the same sense-field existing with a relevantly different organization, yielding a different physical geometry or no physical geometry at all. For example, even if, as things are, the nomological organization endorses the field's actual topology, we can still envisage a possible situation in which, by the standards of uniformity, everything is organized as if two congruent regions were interchanged. It would just be a matter of envisaging appropriately different laws governing the field–time distribution

---

[8] In fact, for the purposes of my argument, I only need to assume that a space possesses *some* aspect of its geometrical structure essentially.

of sense-qualities and the effects of this distribution on human experience.

Putting the various points together, we can now provide a decisive argument against the realist claim. We know that the physically relevant geometry (topology) of F logically depends on its nomological organization. And we also know that F possesses this nomological organization (including those aspects relevant to the physical geometry) only contingently. From these premisses, it immediately follows that F possesses its physically relevant geometry (topology) only contingently. But we also know that, as a genuine space, P possesses its physical geometrical (topological) structure *essentially*. So, standing as they do in different modal relations to the physical (or physically relevant) geometry, P and F must be numerically distinct. Moreover, since the physical geometry (topology) which is essential to P is essential to the identities of its points, we can conclude, more strongly, that the points of P are numerically distinct from the points of F. And, points being the smallest components of a space, this means that there are no divisions of P and F relative to which the components of one can be identified with those of the other.

Now as formulated, this argument only explicitly deals with *one* hypothetical case, in which we take the external correlate of physical space to be a three-dimensional sense-field. But of course, exactly the same considerations would apply whatever the nature of the external correlate, and irrespective of whether it was intuitively space-like in its own character. So we can conclude, quite generally, that neither physical space nor its components are metaphysically fundamental: whatever the fundamental external reality, physical points and regions are not ingredients of it.

This means that no form of ontological realism is viable. Since the occupants of physical space are essentially space-occupying, we cannot assign a metaphysically fundamental status to them without assigning a similar status to the space itself. But we cannot assign such a status to physical space, since, in such a case, the dependence of its geometry on the underlying organization would not be reconcilable with the fact that it possessed this geometry, or at least its topological aspects, essentially. In short, once we have accepted that the physical geometry depends on the underlying organization, we cannot recognize any category of physical entities as metaphysically fundamental. All physical entities, along with the physical states of affairs in which they feature, will have to be seen as the logical creation of an underlying reality which is (in both its ontology and its states of affairs) wholly non-physical.

## v. From Non-Realism to Idealism

Physical realism is false: the physical world (assuming it exists) is the logical creation of a more fundamental reality which is wholly non-physical. But it does not immediately follow from this that idealism is true. The idealist claims that the physical world is entirely created by the organization of human experience: the external reality is relevant only in so far as it is responsible for this organization. So there is room for a middle position, between realism and idealism, which concedes that the physical world is metaphysically derivative, but insists that the external reality contributes to its creation *directly*, and not just by the way it affects human experience.

However, although there is room for this compromise position, it is hard to find any rationale for it. For on what principles would the external reality directly contribute, and why? We cannot insist on an external reality which is *isomorphic* with the physical reality it sustains; for we have already seen that such isomorphism is not necessary. Thus the structure of the physical world will deviate from the structure of the external reality if the latter (as it were) runs counter to the nomological organization. Nor can we insist on something *approaching* isomorphism; for there could be a *radical* discrepancy between the physical and external structures. Take, for example, the case in which a two-dimensional external sense-field gets a three-dimensional organization; or again, envisage a case in which something like the Oxford–Cambridge set-up is widespread. We cannot even insist that the external reality be as *rich* as the physical reality in its ontology. For there is surely no crucial difference between a case in which the external reality is organized as if its materials were differently structured and a case in which it is organized as if its materials were augmented. Thus we could presumably envisage a case in which the external correlate of physical space is a three-dimensional sense-field with an internal 'hole', but where everything is organized as if, by the standards of uniformity, the hole were filled in.

This last case is particularly interesting. For by envisaging a

series of such cases in which the size of the hole is steadily in-
creased—so that more and more of the physical world has no
ontological correlate in the external reality—we can gradually
approach the situation in which there is no external correlate at
all and the organization of human experience is doing all the
work. The anti-idealist is obliged to say that, at some stage in this
series, the ontological materials become too meagre for the
sustainment of a physical world. But it is difficult to see on what
rational basis the distinction between sufficient and insufficient
materials could be drawn. It is not just the problem of locating the
division in the series at a *precise point*: the theorist could perhaps
afford to say that, on this matter, our ordinary concept of a physical
world leaves us room for manœuvre—that it is irreducibly vague
in relation to the underlying quantitative factors on which its
application depends. The problem is rather that there seems to be
no rationale for imposing a minimum ontological requirement at
all. After all, the basic reason for allowing the structure of the
physical world to depend on the external organization, not just
on the external structure, was to ensure that (as our concept
of it surely requires) the physical world turns out to be, in an
epistemologically crucial sense, *our* world. But we can secure the
world as epistemologically *ours* by making its existence depend
solely on the organization of *our experience*—irrespective of the
external factors by which that organization is imposed. For, in
effect, we make sure that the world is epistemologically ours by
making sure that its structure matches what, if we were looking
for the best (i.e. the nomologically simplest and most uniform)
realist explanation of it, this experiential organization would lead
us to postulate.

In fact, once we have abandoned physical realism, the only
obstacle to the adoption of a full idealist position is that the latter
itself seems vulnerable to two crucial objections. I want to end,
therefore, by considering these objections and trying to answer
them. But to prepare the way, I need to say a little more about the
nature of the idealist view that I am advocating.

The idealist claims that the physical world is logically created by
the organization of human sense-experience. This might be taken
to imply the possibility of an analytical reduction of the physical
to the experiential—the possibility of analysing physical concepts
in experiential terms and translating statements about the physical

world into statements about experience.[9] If so, the idealist would be in trouble; for it is surely just obvious that such an analysis is not available. No doubt our ordinary physical assertions are, directly or indirectly, responses to our sensory experience; for it is only through such experience that we have any indication of the existence and character of the physical world. But it would surely be just absurd to suggest that such assertions are themselves experiential claims in linguistic disguise—that when we say such things as 'there are apples on the table', or 'the tree has been felled', what we really mean, set out more explicitly, is that our sense-experience is organized in a certain way. In fact, though, the idealist position I want to defend involves a claim of *metaphysical* rather than *analytical* reduction. Thus I am happy to concede that the physical realm is *conceptually* autonomous—that physical concepts cannot be analysed in non-physical terms and that what we say in the physical language cannot be said in any other way. What I want to insist is that physical facts (or states of affairs) are wholly *constituted by* human-experiential facts (or states of affairs)—by which I mean that each physical fact obtains *in virtue of* certain experiential facts, and that its obtaining is *nothing over and above* the obtaining of these facts.[10] In other words, I recognize two metaphysical levels of reality: a derivative level of physical facts, which are *sui generis* and not expressible in any but physical terms; and an underlying and more fundamental level of (non-physical) experiential facts, from which the physical world derives its existence.

As a *metaphysical* reductionist, the idealist need not be worried by the fact that physical concepts cannot be analysed in experiential terms, since this is something he accepts. However, he now seems to be vulnerable at two other points, and it is these that give rise to the two objections.

The first objection arises from the fact that, as well as resisting analysis in experiential terms, our ordinary physical concepts seem to be inherently realist, or at least anti-idealist. Thus our ordinary

---

[9] Or at least, the possibility of providing such a translation within the limits allowed by the possible vagueness or infinite complexity of physical concepts in relation to the experiential factors on which their application depends. I have discussed this point, though in connection with the analytical reduction of *psychological* concepts, in my book *The Immaterial Self* (London, 1991), ch. 2, sect. 3.

[10] For more on this notion of constitution, see ibid., ch. 5, sect. 3.

concept of (say) a table or a tree seems to be, by its very content, of something which exists outside and independently of the human mind; and the same, of course, is true of our concept of any other kind of physical object. So unless we revise such concepts, there seems to be no way of making sense of the claim that facts about physical objects are wholly constituted by facts about human experience. Moreover, it seems that any conceptual revision which was sufficiently drastic to avoid this problem would not leave us with concepts which were recognizably *physical* at all.

The answer to this is that the idealist can, in a sense, accommodate this realist, or quasi-realist, aspect of our ordinary physical concepts in his own system. This is because he can draw a distinction between two frameworks of assertion. Thus, on the one hand, there is the *mundane* framework, in which we make ordinary assertions about the physical world, but without claiming anything about their philosophical significance. It is in this framework that, in the course of everyday life, we might find ourselves saying such things as 'there are apples on the table' or 'the tree has been felled'. On the other hand, there is the *philosophical* framework, in which we try to set physical reality in its right philosophical perspective. This is the framework in which the realist and idealist advance their rival accounts. Now the claim that physical objects exist outside and independently of the human mind has quite different interpretations according to the framework in which it is made. Made within the philosophical framework, it is an explicitly anti-idealist claim, entailing the falsity of any position which takes physical facts to be wholly constituted by experiential facts. But made within the mundane framework, it is surely, even for an idealist, trivially true. For, in whatever sense the idealist counts it as true that there is a physical world, and accepts the truth of our ordinary beliefs about it, he must also accept it as true that the human mind causally interacts with this world at the point of the human brain—in the same sort of way that physical objects causally interact with one another. And in the sense in which he counts it as true that the mind and the physical world causally interact, he must also count it as true that the world is something external to human mentality and logically independent of it. But now the idealist can insist that it is only with respect to the *mundane* framework that our ordinary physical concepts represent the items to which they apply as external and human-mind independent. If we take these concepts to be inherently anti-idealist, it is simply because, failing to notice the distinction between the two frameworks, we mistake an uncontroversial claim about the relationship between mind and body at the level of everyday thought for one which advances a view about how things are in the final perspective.

The second objection arises from the fact that, without an *analytical* reduction, there seems to be no way of avoiding a collapse into physical nihilism, which rejects the existence of the physical world altogether. The idealist is claiming that the fundamental reality is wholly non-physical and that the physical world is logically created by the organization of human sense-experience. But it is quite unclear how this creation is supposed to work. Without a reductive analysis of physical concepts, there seems to be no prospect of a deductive route from the experiential facts to the physical, and without a deductive route, there would presumably be no way of establishing the existence of the physical world solely on the basis of the relevant experiential information. So how can the idealist see the experiential facts as genuinely sufficing for the physical? Surely the most he can say, given his view of the fundamental reality, is that the organization of our experience makes it very useful for us to believe in a physical world, but that, strictly speaking, such a belief is false. The organization systematically invites physical interpretation, but the interpretation is in fact mistaken.

To deal with this point, the idealist needs to draw a further distinction—this time between two quite different epistemic perspectives in which the philosophical issue of the physical world can be considered. On the one hand, there is what we might label the *external* perspective. In this, we start with a description of the metaphysically fundamental reality—and, in particular, of the experiential organization—and, without any prior commitment to the existence of a physical world, address ourselves to the question of whether such a reality (such an experiential organization) suffices to create one. On the other hand, there is what we might call the *internal* perspective. In this, we start with our ordinary physical beliefs, held in response to our empirical evidence, and address ourselves to the questions of whether the physical world (whose existence we are now taking for granted) is metaphysically fundamental, and if it is not, what ultimately underlies it. Now it is clear, I think, that, in the external perspective, we could not, without a phenomenalistic analysis of physical concepts, make sense of the claim that the experiential organization suffices for the existence of a physical world. For example, if we were told of a Berkeleian set-up in some *other* universe—a set-up in which the fundamental reality consists of just God and a group of finite minds, and in which God organizes their sense-experience in a way which systematically invites physical interpretation—we could not see this as creating a real physical world: we could only see it as making it seem to the minds in question that such a world exists and making it useful for them to believe that it does. But of course our *actual* perspective is not this, but the *internal* one. We do not start off with an account of the fundamental reality and have to work out from it what physical facts, if any, obtain. Rather, being the minds whose experiential organization invites physical interpretation, we start with the empirically founded assumption that there is a physical world, and only then pursue a philosophical investigation into the question of its relationship with the fundamental reality. In *this* epistemological framework, it seems to me that the idealist's claim is unproblematic. For al-though there is no way of establishing the existence of the physical world from a knowledge of the experiential organization, I can see no reason for our having to abandon our empirically based belief in its existence in the face of what philosophy reveals about its metaphysical status—the revelation that, if it exists, it is this or-ganization which ultimately creates it. Even though the conceptual autonomy of the physical realm precludes the establishing of physical facts on the basis of experiential, it seems to me that our physical beliefs are sufficiently flexible on the issue of what is metaphysically fundamental to allow us to discover, by philo-sophical argument, that it is the experiential facts that ultimately make them true.

We should also realize that the issue of whether we end up idealists or nihilists is not, philosophically, unimportant. At first sight, it might seem that it does not much matter whether we say that there is a physical world, but one which is logically created by the experiential organization, or say that there is no physical world, but the experiential organization makes it useful to suppose that there is. In fact, however, the nihilist view would undermine our epistemological situation altogether. For our knowledge of the experiential realm, and *a fortiori* our knowledge that it has the relevant (physical-world-suggesting) organization, depends very heavily on our physical information. This is obvious in the case of one person's knowledge of the experiences of others. But it is also true, in ways I have tried to elaborate elsewhere,[11] that a person's knowledge of his own earlier experiential biography is heavily dependent on his knowledge of his *physical* past. In the end, then, the choice is not between idealism and a nihilism which can preserve the cash value of the physical theory. It is between idealism and a nihilism which leaves us in an epistemic void. No doubt it is partly for this reason that our ordinary beliefs come to have the metaphysical flexibility which I attribute to them.

[11] e.g. in *Ayer*, pt. 2, sect. 12.

# BIBLIOGRAPHY

ACH, N., 1935, *Analyse des Willens*, Berlin.

ANTONY, L., 1989, 'Anomalous Monism and the Problem of Explanatory Force', *Philosophical Review*, 98. 153–87.

ARMSTRONG, D. M., 1961, *Perception and the Physical World*, Routledge, London.

—— 1968, *A Materialist Theory of the Mind*, Routledge, London.

—— 1978, *Universals and Scientific Realism*, CUP, Cambridge.

—— 1989, *Universals*, Westview, Boulder, Col.

AUSTIN, J. L., 1979, *Philosophical Papers*, ed. J. O. Urmson and G. J. Warnock, OUP, Oxford.

BAKER, L. R., 1987, *Saving Belief: A Critique of Physicalism*, Princeton University Press, Princeton, Ill.

BEALER, G., 1979, 'Theories of Properties, Relations and Propositions', *Journal of Philosophy*, 76. 634–48.

—— 1982, *Quality and Concept*, OUP, Oxford.

—— 1984, 'Mind and Anti-Mind: Why Thinking has No Functional Definition', *Midwest Studies in Philosophy*, 9. 283–328.

—— 1986, 'The Logical Status of Mind', *Midwest Studies in Philosophy*, 10. 231–74.

—— 1991, 'Three "Arguments for Dualism"', forthcoming.

BENACERRAF, P., 1965, 'What Numbers Could not Be', *Philosophical Review*, 74. 47–73.

—— 1973, 'Mathematical Truth', *Journal of Philosophy*, 70. 661–79.

—— and PUTNAM, H., eds., 1983, *Philosophy of Mathematics: Selected Readings*, 2nd edn., CUP, Cambridge.

BIGELOW, J., and PARGETTER, R., 1989, 'A Theory of Structural Universals', *Australasian Journal of Philosophy*, 67.

BLACKBURN, S. W., 1973, *Reason and Prediction*, CUP, Cambridge.

BLOCK, N., 1978, 'Troubles with Functionalism', in *Perception and Cognition: Issues in the Foundations of Psychology*, Minnesota Studies in the Philosophy of Science, 9, ed. C. W. Savage, University of Minnesota Press, Minneapolis, 261–325; repr. in Block, ed., *Readings*, 268–305.

—— 1983, 'Mental Pictures and Cognitive Science', *Philosophical Review*, 93. 499–542; repr. in W. G. Lycan, ed., *Mind and Cognition: A Reader*, Blackwell, Oxford, 1990. 577–607.

—— ed., 1980, *Readings in Philosophy of Psychology*, 1, Methuen, London.

BOYD, R., 1980, 'Materialism Without Reductionism: What Physicalism Does not Entail', in Block, ed., *Readings*, 67–106.

BRANDT, R., and KIM, J., 1967, 'The Logic of the Identity Theory', *Journal of Philosophy*, 64. 515–37.

BRENTANO, F., 1874, *Psychologie vom Empirischen Standpunkt*, Dunker and Humbolt, Leipzig.

CAMPBELL, K., 1971, *Body and Mind*, Macmillan, London.

—— 1983, 'Abstract Particulars and the Philosophy of Mind', *Australasian Journal of Philosophy*, 61. 129–41.

—— 1990, *Abstract Particulars*, Blackwell, Oxford.

CARTWRIGHT, N., 1983, *How the Laws of Physics Lie*, OUP, Oxford.

CAUSEY, R. L., 1972, 'Attribute Identities in Micro-Reduction', *Journal of Philosophy*, 69. 407–22.

CHISHOLM, R., 1957, *Perceiving: A Philosophical Study*, Cornell University Press, Ithaca.

—— 1960, *Realism and the Background of Phenomenology*, Free Press, New York.

—— 1967, 'Intentionality', in P. Edwards, ed., *The Encyclopedia of Philosophy*, Macmillan, New York, 201–4.

—— 1989, 'The Nature of the Psychological', in his *On Metaphysics*, University of Minnesota Press, Minneapolis.

CHURCHLAND, P. M., 1981, 'Eliminative Materialism and Propositional Attitudes', *Journal of Philosophy*, 78. 67–90; repr. in Churchland, *A Neurocomputational Perspective*, 1–22.

——1984, *Matter and Consciousness*, MIT Press, Cambridge, Mass.

—— 1985, 'Reduction, Qualia, and the Direct Introspection of Brain States', *Journal of Philosophy*, 82. 8–28; repr. in Churchland, *A Neurocomputational Perspective*, 47–66.

—— 1989, *A Neurocomputational Perspective*, MIT Press, Cambridge, Mass.

—— 1989, 'Knowing Qualia: A Reply to Jackson', in Churchland, *A Neurocomputational Perspective*, 67–76.

—— and CHURCHLAND, P. S., 1981, 'Functionalism, Qualia and Intentionality', *Philosophical Topics*, 1; repr. in Churchland, *A Neurocomputational Perspective*, 23–46.

CHURCHLAND, P. S., 1988, *Neurophilosophy*, MIT Press, Cambridge, Mass.

CORNMAN, J., 1971, *Materialism and Sensations*, Yale University Press, New Haven, Conn.

CRAIG, E., 1975, 'The Problem of Necessary Truth', in S. Blackburn, ed., *Meaning, Reference and Necessity*, CUP, Cambridge, 1–31.

CUDWORTH, R., 1678, *The True Intellectual System of the Universe*, Richard Royston, London.

CUMMINS, R., 1989, *Meaning and Mental Representation*, MIT Press, Cambridge, Mass.

DAVIDSON, D., 1970, 'Mental Events', in L. Foster and J. W. Swanson, eds., *Experience and Theory*, University of Massachusetts Press, Amherst, Mass., 79–101; repr. in Block, ed., *Readings*, 107–19, and Davidson, *Essays on Actions and Events*.

—— 1980, *Essays on Actions and Events*, OUP, Oxford.

—— 1984, *Inquiries into Truth and Interpretation*, OUP, Oxford.

—— 1984, 'First Person Authority', *Dialectica*, 38. 2–3. 101–11.

DENNETT, D. C., 1969, *Content and Consciousness*, Routledge, London.

—— 1978, *Brainstorms*, Harvester, Hassocks.

—— 1978, 'Skinner Skinned', in Dennett, *Brainstorms*, 53–70.

—— 1981, 'Three Kinds of Intentional Psychology', in R. Healey, ed., *Reduction, Time and Reality*, CUP, Cambridge; repr. in Dennett, *The Intentional Stance*, 43–68.

—— 1984, *Elbow Room*, OUP, Oxford.

—— 1987, *The Intentional Stance*, MIT Press, Cambridge, Mass.

DRETSKE, F. I., 1981, *Knowledge and the Flow of Information*, Blackwell, Oxford.

—— 1983, 'Precis of Knowledge and the Flow of Information' (with peer review), *Behavioral and Brain Sciences*, 6. 55–90.

—— 1988, *Explaining Behavior*, MIT Press, Cambridge, Mass.

FIELD, H., 1972, 'Tarski's Theory of Truth', *Journal of Philosophy*, 69. 347–75.

—— 1980, *Science Without Numbers*, Blackwell, Oxford.

—— 1982, 'Realism and Anti-Realism about Mathematics', *Philosophical Topics*, 13. 45–69.

—— 1984, 'Is Mathematical Knowledge Just Logical Knowledge?', *Philosophical Review*, 93. 509–52.

—— 1985, 'On Conservativeness and Completeness', *Journal of Philosophy*, 81. 239–60.

—— 1986, 'The Deflationary Concept of Truth', in G. Macdonald and C. Wright, eds., *Fact, Science and Morality*, Blackwell, Oxford, 55–117.

—— 1988 'Realism, Mathematics and Modality', *Philosophical Topics*, 19. 57–107.

—— 1989, *Realism, Mathematics and Modality*, Blackwell, Oxford.

FODOR, J., 1975, *The Language of Thought*, Thomas Y. Crowell, New York.

—— 1987, *Psychosemantics*, MIT Press, Cambridge, Mass.

FORREST, P., 1985, 'Backwards Causation in Defence of Freewill', *Mind*, 94. 210–17.

—— 1988, *Quantum Metaphysics*, Blackwell, Oxford.

—— 1988, 'Supervenience: The Grand-Property Hypothesis', *Australasian Journal of Philosophy*, 66. 1–12.

—— 1991, 'Aesthetic Understanding', *Philosophy and Phenomenological Research*, 51. 3 (Sept.), 525–40.

FOSTER, J. A., 1982, *The Case for Idealism*, Routledge, London.

—— 1985, 'Berkeley on the Physical World', in Foster and Robinson, *Essays on Berkeley*, 83–108.

—— 1985, *Ayer*, Routledge, London.

—— 1991, *The Immaterial Self*, Routledge, London.

—— and ROBINSON, H. M., 1985, *Essays on Berkeley*, OUP, Oxford.

FRANKFURT, H., 1971, 'Freedom of the Will and the Concept of a Person', *Journal of Philosophy*, 68. 5–20.

GILLETT, G. R., 1986, 'Multiple Personality and the Concept of a Person', *New Ideas in Psychology*, 4. 178–84.

—— 1986, 'Disembodied Persons', *Philosophy*, 61. 377–86.

—— 1987, 'The Generality Constraint and Conscious Thought', *Analysis*, 47. 20–4.

—— 1988, 'Learning to Perceive', *Philosophy and Phenomenological Research*, 48. 601–18.

—— 1989, 'Representations and Cognitive Science', *Inquiry*, 32. 261–76.

—— 1992, *Representation, Meaning and Thought*, Oxford.

GÖDEL, K., 1944, 'Russell's Mathematical Logic', in Benacerraf and Putnam, eds., *Philosophy of Mathematics*, 447–69.

—— 1947, 'What is Cantor's Continuum Problem?', in Benacerraf and Putnam, eds., *Philosophy of Mathematics*, 470–85.

GOODMAN, N. and QUINE, W. V. O., 1947, 'Steps towards a Constructive Nominalism', *Journal of Symbolic Logic*, 12. 105–22.

GRANDY, R. E., 1980, 'Ramsey, Reliability and Knowledge', in D. H. Mellor, ed., *Prospects for Pragmatism*, CUP, Cambridge, 197–209.

GREEN, M. B., 1986 (Sept.), 'Superstrings', *Scientific American*, 255. 44–56.

GRICE, H. P., 1958, 'Meaning', *Philosophical Review*, 66. 377–88.

GRÜNBAUM, A., 1973, *Philosophical Problems of Space and Time*, Boston Studies in the Philosophy of Science, 12, Reidel, Dordrecht.

GUYER, P., 1987, *Kant and the Claims of Knowledge*, CUP, Cambridge.

HALE, BOB, 1987, *Abstract Objects*, Blackwell, Oxford.

—— 1990, 'Nominalism', in A. D. Irvine, ed., *Physicalism in Mathematics*, Kluwer, Dordrecht, 1990.

HAMPSHIRE, S., 1979, 'Some Difficulties in Knowing', in T. Honderich and M. Burnyeat, eds., *Philosophy as it is*, Penguin, Harmondsworth.

HARE, R. M., 1952, *The Language of Morals*, OUP, Oxford.

—— 1984, 'Supervenience', *Proceedings of the Aristotelian Society*, Suppl. vol. 58. 1–16.

HAUGELAND, J., 1982, 'Weak Supervenience', *American Philosophical Quarterly*, 19. 93–103.

HODES, H., 1984, 'Logicism and the Ontological Commitments of Arithmetic', *Journal of Philosophy*, 81. 123–49.

HOOKER, C., 1981, 'Towards a General Theory of Reduction, 2. Identity in Reduction', *Dialogue*, 20.

HORGAN, T., and GRAHAM, G., 1988, 'How to be Realistic about Folk Psychology', *Philosophical Psychology*, 1. 69–81.

—— —— 1991, 'In Defense of Southern Fundamentalism', *Philosophical Studies*, 62. 107–34.

—— and WOODWARD, J., 1985, 'Folk Psychology is Here to Stay', *Philosophical Review*, 94. 197–226.

HORNSBY, J., 1980–1, 'Which Physical Events are Mental Events?', *Proceedings of the Aristotelian Society*, 81. 73–92.

——1984, 'On Functionalism, and on Jackson, Pargetter and Prior on Functionalism', *Philosophical Studies*, 46. 75–95.

HUSSERL, E., 1900–1, *Logische Untersuchungen*, Max Niemayer, Halle: tr. J. N. Findlay, Humanities Press, New York, 1970.

IRVINE, A. D., ed., 1990, *Physicalism in Mathematics*, Kluwer, Dordrecht.

JACKSON, F., 1982, 'Epiphenomenal Qualia', *Philosophical Quarterly*, 32. 127–36.

—— 1986, 'What Mary Didn't Know', *Journal of Philosophy*, 83. 291–5.

KANT, I., 1902–, *Kant's gesammelte Schriften*, ed. by the Königlich Preussische Akademie der Wissenschaften and its successors, Berlin.

—— 1929, *Critique of Practical Reason*, 6th edn., tr. T. K. Abbott, Longmans, London.

—— 1929, *The Critique of Pure Reason*, tr. N. Kemp Smith, Macmillan, London.

—— 1953, *The Moral Law*, 3rd edn., tr. H. J. Paton, Hutchinson, London.

—— 1974, *Logic*, tr. by R. Hartman and W. Schwarz, Bobbs-Merrill, Indianapolis.

KIM, J., 1987, ' "Strong" and "Global" Supervenience Revisited', *Philosophy and Phenomenological Research*, 48. 315–26.

KRIPKE, S., 1976, *Wittgenstein and Rule-Following*, OUP, Oxford.

—— 1980, *Naming and Necessity*, Blackwell, Oxford.

LEVIN, J., 1986, 'Could Love be a Heatwave? Physicalism and the Subjective Character of Experience', *Philosophical Studies*, 49. 245–61; repr. in W. G. Lycan, ed., *Mind and Cognition: A Reader*, Blackwell, Oxford, 1990, 478–90.

LEWES, G. H., 1874, *Problems of Life and Mind*, 2, London.

LEWIS, D., 1972, 'Psychophysical and Theoretical Identifications', *Australasian Journal of Philosophy*, 50. 249–58.

—— 1973, *Counterfactuals*, Blackwell, Oxford.

—— 1980, 'Mad Pain and Martian Pain', in Block, ed., *Readings*, 216–22.

LEWIS, D., 1983, 'New Work for a Theory of Universals', *Australasian Journal of Philosophy*, 61. 343–7.

LLOYD, A. C., 'The Self in Berkeley's Philosophy', in Foster and Robinson, *Essays on Berkeley*, 187–209.

LLOYD MORGAN, C., 1923, *Emergent Evolution*, Williams and Northgate, London.

LOCKWOOD, M., 1989, *Mind, Brain and the Quantum: The Compound 'I'*, Blackwell, Oxford.

LUCAS, J. R., 1961, 'Minds, Machines and Gödel', *Philosophy*, 36. 112–27.

LYCAN, W. G., ed., 1990, *Mind and Cognition: A Reader*, Blackwell, Oxford.

MCGINN, C., 1983, *The Subjective View*, OUP, Oxford.

—— 1989, 'Can We Solve the Mind–Body Problem?', *Mind*, 98. 349–66.

MACKIE, J. L., 1977, *Ethics: Inventing Right and Wrong*, Penguin, Harmondsworth.

MADDY, P., 1980, 'Perception and Mathematical Intuition', *Philosophical Review*, 89. 163–96.

—— 1981, 'Sets and Numbers', *Nous*, 15. 495–511.

—— 1990, 'Physicalistic Platonism', in Irvine, *Physicalism in Mathematics*.

MAXWELL, G., 1978, 'Rigid Designators and Mind–Brain Identity', *Perception and Cognition*, Minnesota Studies in the Philosophy of Science, 9, ed. C. W. Savage, University of Minnesota Press, Minneapolis, 365–403.

MELLOR, D. H., 1973, 'Materialism and Phenomenal Qualities', pt. 2, *Proceedings of the Aristotelian Society*, supp. vol. 47. 107–19.

—— and CRANE, T., 1990, 'There is no Question of Physicalism', *Mind*, 99. 185–206.

MICHOTTE, A. and PRÜM, E., 1910, 'Étude expérimentale sur le choix volontaire', *Archives de psychologie*, 10. 113–20.

MILL, J. S., 1872, *A System of Logic*, 9th edn., Longman, London.

MILLIKAN, R. G., 1984, *Language, Thought and Other Biological Categories*, MIT Press, Cambridge, Mass.

—— 1989, 'Biosemantics', *Journal of Philosophy*, 86. 281–97.

MOORE, A., 1990, *The Infinite*, Routledge, London.

MOORE, G. E., 1922, *Philosophical Studies*, Routledge, London.

NAGEL, T., 1965, 'Physicalism', *Philosophical Review*, 74. 339–56.

—— 1974, 'What is it Like to be a Bat?', *Philosophical Review*, 83. 435–50; repr. in Nagel, *Mortal Questions*, 165–80.

—— 1979, *Mortal Questions*, CUP, Cambridge.

—— 1986, *The View From Nowhere*, OUP, Oxford.

NATHAN, N., 1986, 'Simple Colours', *Philosophy*, 61. 345–53.

—— 1991, *Will and World*, OUP, Oxford.

NOONAN, H., 1987, 'Supervenience', *Philosophical Quarterly*, 37. 78–85.

NOZICK, R., 1981, *Philosophical Explanations*, Harvard University Press, Cambridge, Mass.

NEMIROW, L., 1990, 'Physicalism and the Cognitive Role of Acquaintance', in Lycan, *Mind and Cognition*, 490–9.

NEURATH, O., 1972, 'Physicalism', in R. Cohen and M. Neurath, eds., *Philosophical Papers, 1913–45*, Reidel, Dordrecht.

O'SHAUGHNESSY, B., 1980, *The Will*, CUP, Cambridge.

OWENS, J., 1986, 'The Failure of Lewis's Functionalism', in L. Stevenson, R. Squires, and J. Haldane, eds., *Mind, Causation and Action*, Blackwell, Oxford, 49–53.

PEACOCKE, C., 1986, *Thoughts: An Essay on Content*, Blackwell, Oxford.

PENROSE, ROGER, 1990, *The Emperor's New Mind*, OUP, Oxford.

PETRIE, B., 1987, 'Global Supervenience and Reduction', *Philosophy and Phenomenological Research*, 48. 119–30.

PITCHER, G., 1971, *A Theory of Perception*, Princeton University Press, Princeton, Ill.

POLLOCK, J. L., 1974, *Knowledge and Justification*, Princeton University Press, Princeton, Ill.

POST, J. F., 1984, 'Comment on Teller', *Southern Journal of Philosophy*, 23, suppl. 1984.

PUTNAM, H., 1970, 'On Properties', in Putnam, *Mathematics, Matter and Method*, CUP, Cambridge, 305.

—— 1978, *Meaning and the Moral Sciences*, Routledge, London.

—— 1978, 'Reference and Understanding', in *Meaning and the Moral Sciences*.

—— 1987, *The Many Faces of Realism*, Open Court, La Salle, Ill.

—— 1988, *Representation and Reality*, Cambridge, Mass.

PYLYSHYN, Z., and DEMOPOULOS, W., eds., *Meaning and Cognitive Structure: Issues in the Computational Theory of Mind*, Norwood, NJ.

QUINE, W. V. O., 1951, 'Two Dogmas of Empiricism', *Philosophical Review*, 60. 20–43; repr. in Quine, *From a Logical Point of View*, Harvard University Press, Cambridge, Mass., 1953, 20–46.

—— 1960, *Word and Object*, MIT Press, Cambridge, Mass.

—— 1970, *Philosophy of Logic*, Prentice Hall, England Cliffs, NJ.

—— 1975, 'On Empirically Equivalent Systems of the World', *Erkenntnis*, 9. 313–28.

—— 1977, 'Facts of the Matter' in R. W. Shahan, ed., *American Philosophy from Edwards to Quine*, University of Oklahoma Press, Norman, 1977, 176–96.

—— 1981, 'Goodman's Ways of Worldmaking', *Theories and Things*, Harvard University Press, Cambridge, Mass.

ROBINSON, H. M., 1982, *Matter and Sense*, CUP, Cambridge.

—— 1983, 'Aristotelian Dualism', *Oxford Studies in Ancient Philosophy*, 1. 1–25.

—— 1985, 'The General Form of the Argument for Berkeleian Idealism', in Foster and Robinson, *Essays on Berkeley*, 163–86.

—— 1988, 'Un dilemme pour le physicalisme', *Hermes*, 3. 128–50.

—— 1990, 'The Objects Of Perceptual Experience', *Proceedings of the Aristotelian Society*, suppl. vol. 64. 151–66.

—— 1991, 'The Flight from Mind', in R. Tallis and H. Robinson, eds., *The Pursuit of Mind*, Carcanet, Manchester, 1991, 9–25.

—— 1993, forthcoming, 'Physicalism, Externalism and Perceptual Representation', in Edmond Wright, ed., *New Representationalisms*, Avebury Press, Avebury.

RUSSELL, B., 1927, *The Analysis of Matter*, Kegan Paul, London.

—— 1948, *Human Knowledge: Its Scope and Limits*, Unwin, London.

SAGAN, C., *Contact: A Novel* (New York, 1985).

SARTRE, J.-P., 1943, *Being and Nothingness*, tr. H. E. Barnes, Methuen, London.

SCHEFFLER, I., 1976, *Science and Subjectivity*, Bobbs-Merrill, Indianapolis.

SCHIFFER, S., 1981, 'Truth and the Theory of Content; in H. Parret and J. Bouveresse, eds., *Meaning and Understanding*, Gruyter, Berlin.

SCHILLP, P. A., ed., 1942, *The Philosophy of G. E. Moore*, Northwestern University Press, Evanston, Ill.

SEAGER, W. E., 1988, 'Weak Supervenience and Materialism', *Philosophy and Phenomenological Research*, 48. 697–709.

SEARLE, J., 1980, 'Minds, Brains and Programs', *Behavioral and Brain Sciences*, 3. 417–58.

—— 1980, 'Analytic Philosophy and Mental Phenomena', in *Midwest Studies in Philosophy*, 5, ed. P. A. French, T. E. Uehling, T. K. Wettstein, 405–23.

—— 1983, *Intentionality*, CUP, Cambridge.

—— 1991, 'Is the Brain a Digital Computer?' *American Philosophical Association Proceedings*, 64. 21–37.

SELLARS, W., 1965, 'The Identity Approach to the Mind–Body Problem', *Review of Metaphysics*, 18. 430–51.

—— 1970–1, 'Science, Sense Impressions, and Sensa: a Reply to Cornman', *Review of Metaphysics*, 24. 391–447.

—— and CHISHOLM, R., 1958, 'Intentionality and the Mental', in H. Feigl *et al.*, eds., *Concepts Theories and the Mind–Body Problem*, University of Minnesota Press, Minneapolis, 507–39.

SHOPE, R. K., 1983, *The Analysis of Knowing*, Princeton University Press, Princeton, Ill.

SIMONS, P., 1987, *Parts*, OUP, Oxford.

SMART, J. J. C., 1959, 'Sensations and Brain Processes', *Philosophical Review*, 68. 141–56.

SMITH, A. D., 1990, 'Of Primary and Secondary Qualities', *Philosophical Review*, 99.

SMITH, B., and MULLIGAN, K., 1982, 'Pieces of a Theory', in B. Smith, ed., *Parts and Moments,* Munich and Vienna, 15–109.

SPECTOR, M., 1978, *Concepts of Reduction in Physical Science,* Temple University Press, Philadelphia.

SPERRY, P. W., 1969, 'A Modified Concept of Consciousness', *Psychological Review*, 76. 532–6.

STICH, S., 1983, *From Folk Psychology to Cognitive Science: The Case against Belief,* MIT Press, Cambridge, Mass.

STRAWSON, G., 1989, 'Consciousness, Free Will, and the Unimportance of Determinism', *Inquiry*, 32. 3–27.

STRAWSON, P. F., 1976, *The Bounds of Sense,* Methuen, London.

SWINBURNE, R. G., 1986, *The Evolution of the Soul,* OUP, Oxford.

TALLIS, R., and ROBINSON, H., 1991, eds., *The Pursuit of Mind,* Carcanet, Manchester.

—— 1991, *The Explicit Animal,* Macmillan, London.

TARSKI, A., 1956, 'The Concept of Truth in Formalized Languages', in *Logic, Semantics, Metamathematics,* OUP, Oxford.

TYE, M., 1983, 'Functionalism and Type Physicalism', *Philosophical Studies*, 44. 161–74.

—— 1986, 'The Subjective Qualities of Experience', *Mind*, 95. 1–17.

—— 1989, *The Metaphysics of Mind,* CUP, Cambridge.

URMSON, J. O., 1953, 'Some Questions Concerning Validity', *Revue internationale de philosophie*, 217–29; also in A. G. N. Flew, ed., *Essays in Conceptual Analysis,* Macmillan, London, 1963.

VENDLER, Z., 1984, *The Matter of Minds,* OUP, Oxford.

WAGNER, S., 1987, 'The Rationalist Conception of Logic', *Notre Dame Journal of Formal Logic*, 28. 3–35.

—— 1992, 'Logicism', in M. Detlefsen, ed., *Proof and Knowledge in Mathematics,* Routledge, London.

—— 1992, 'Why Realism Can't be Naturalized', in S. J. Wagner and R. Warner, eds., *Naturalism: A Critical Approach* (Notre Dame, Ind., 1992).

WALKER, R. C. S., 1978, *Kant,* Routledge, London.

—— 1988, 'The Rational Imperative: Kant against Hume', *Proceedings of the British Academy*, 74. 113–33.

—— 1989, *The Coherence Theory of Truth,* Routledge, London.

—— 1989, 'Transcendental Arguments and Scepticism', in. E. Shaper and W. Vossenkuhl, eds., *Reading Kant,* Blackwell, Oxford, 55–76.

—— 1990, 'Kant's Conception of Empirical Law', *Proceedings of the Aristotelian Society*, suppl. vol. 65.

324 *Bibliography*

WARNER, R., 1986, 'A Challenge to Physicalism', *Australasian Journal of Philosophy*, 64. 249–65.
—— 1989 (Jan.), 'Why is Logic A Priori?', *The Monist*, 72, 1. 40–50.
WELLS, H. M., 1927, 'The Phenomenology of Acts of Choice', *British Journal of Psychology*, monograph suppl. 4. 1–155.
WILKES, K. V., 1978, *Physicalism*, Routledge, London.
WILLIAMS, D. C., 1966, 'The Elements of Being', in *The Principles of Empirical Realism*, Springfield, Ill., 74–109.
—— 1986, 'Universals and Existents', *Australasian Journal of Philosophy*, 64. 1–14.
WILLIAMS, M., 1977, *Groundless Belief*, Yale University Press, New Haven, Conn.
WINCH, P., 1958, *The Idea of a Social Science*, Routledge, London.
WOLFF, R. P. 1973, *The Autonomy of Reason*, Harper and Row, New York.
WRIGHT, C., 1983, *Frege's Conception of Numbers as Objects*, Aberdeen University Press, Aberdeen.
—— 1988, 'Why Numbers Can Believably Be', *Revue internationale de philosophie*, 42. 425–73.
YOLTON, J., 1983, *Thinking Matter*, Blackwell, Oxford.

# INDEX